MACMILLAN **EXAMS**

Ready for
FCE

coursebook

Roy Norris

Updated for
the revised
FCE exam

Contents map

iii

Introduction

Welcome to *Ready for FCE*, a course which is designed to help you prepare for the Cambridge First Certificate in English examination.

This book contains a wide range of activities aimed at improving your English and developing the language and skills which you will need to pass the examination. As well as providing relevant practice in reading, writing, listening and speaking, each unit of *Ready for FCE* includes one or more Language focus sections, which revise the main grammar areas, together with Vocabulary slots which will help you to increase your word store.

A significant feature of the Use of English syllabus in the book is the systematic approach to Word formation. At regular intervals you will find special sections which focus on the most important aspects of word building, ensuring that you are properly prepared for this part of the examination.

At the end of every unit there is a two-page Review section, which enables you to revise and practise the new language you have encountered in the unit.

Throughout the book you will find the following boxes, which are designed to help you when performing the different tasks:
• **What to expect in the exam**: these contain useful information on what you should be prepared to see, hear or do in a particular task in the examination.
• **How to go about it**: these give advice and guidelines on how to deal with different task types and specific questions.
• **Don't forget**!: these provide a reminder of important points to bear in mind when answering a particular question.

Further information and advice is included in the five supplementary 'Ready for ...' units, one for each of the five papers in the examination. These are situated after every third unit in the book and can be used at appropriate moments during the course.

At the end of the book you will find detailed explanations of the grammar areas seen in the units in the Grammar reference, together with a topic-based Wordlist.

Overview of the examination

The Cambridge First Certificate in English examination consists of five papers, each of which carries 20% of the total marks. A low mark in one paper does not necessarily mean a candidate will fail the examination; it is the overall mark which counts. A, B and C are pass grades; D and E are fail grades.

Paper 1: Reading   1 hour

There are three parts to this paper, with a total of 30 questions. Each question in Parts 1 and 2 carries 2 marks; each question in Part 3 carries 1 mark. Texts are taken from a variety of sources including newspaper and magazine articles, fiction, advertisements and brochures. For more information and advice on appropriate reading strategies for each part, see the Ready for Reading unit on pages 38 to 41, as well as the relevant sections in the main units of the book.

Part	Task Type	Number of questions	Task Format
1	Multiple choice	8	A text followed by multiple-choice questions with four options A, B, C or D.
2	Gapped text	7	A text from which sentences have been removed. Candidates replace each of these in the appropriate part of the text.
3	Multiple matching	15	A text preceded by multiple matching questions which require candidates to find specific information in a text or texts.

Paper 2: Writing   1 hour 20 minutes

There are two parts to this paper, each of which carries the same number of marks. Part 1 is compulsory, so must be answered by all candidates, whereas in Part 2 candidates choose one from four tasks. Candidates are required to write between 120 and 150 words for Part 1, and between 120 and 180 for Part 2. For more information and advice on the questions in this paper, see the Ready for Writing unit on pages 118 to 121, as well as the relevant sections in the main units of the book.

Part	Task Type	Number of Tasks	Task Format
1	Letter or email	1 (compulsory)	Candidates write a letter or an email in response to a given situation. Prompts are provided in the form of written input material such as a letter, an advertisement and/or notes.
2		4 (candidates choose one)	A situation-based writing task with a clear context, purpose for writing and target reader. Candidates write one of the following: article, essay, letter, report, review, short story
			The last question has two options, each based on one of the two set reading texts. Candidates write either an article, an essay, a letter, a report or a review.

Paper 3: Use of English   45 minutes

This paper consists of four parts with a total of 42 questions, which test grammar and vocabulary. Each question in Part 4 carries up to 2 marks; questions in all other parts each carry 1 mark. For more information on this paper, see the Ready for Use of English unit on pages 78 to 81, as well as the relevant sections in the main units of the book.

Part	Task Type	Number of Questions	Task Format
1	Multiple-choice cloze (Emphasis on vocabulary)	12	A text with 12 gaps; there is a choice of 4 answers for each gap.
2	Open cloze (Grammar and vocabulary)	12	A text with 12 gaps, each of which must be completed with one word.
3	Word formation (Vocabulary)	10	A text containing 10 gaps. The task is to complete each gap with the correct form of a given word.
4	Key word transformations (Grammar and vocabulary)	8	Gapped sentences which must be completed using a given word.

Paper 4: Listening   about 40 minutes

This paper consists of four parts with a total of 30 questions, each of which carries one mark. Each part contains one or more recorded texts, which are heard twice. Candidates are tested on their ability to understand, for example, opinions, gist, the main points or specific information. For more information on this paper, see the Ready for Listening unit on pages 158 to 161, as well as the relevant sections in the main units of the book.

Part	Task Type	Number of Questions	Task Format
1	Multiple choice	8	Short unrelated extracts of approximately 30 seconds each with one or more speakers. Multiple-choice questions have 3 options, A, B or C.
2	Sentence completion	10	One or more speakers talking for approximately 3 minutes. Candidates write a word or short phrase to complete sentences.
3	Multiple matching	5	Five short monologues, each lasting approximately 30 seconds. The extracts are all related to a common theme. Candidates match extracts with prompts.
4	Multiple choice	7	One or more speakers talking for approximately 3 minutes. Multiple-choice questions have 3 options, A, B or C.

Paper 5: Speaking   14 minutes

There are four parts to this paper. There are usually two candidates and two examiners. Candidates are given marks for range and correct use of grammar and vocabulary, pronunciation, communication and successful completion of tasks. For more information on this paper, see the Ready for Speaking unit on pages 196 to 199, as well as the relevant sections in the main units of the book.

Part	Task Type	Time	Task Format
1	Interview	3 minutes	Candidates give personal information in response to questions from the interviewer.
2	Talking about photographs	4 minutes	Each candidate talks about two pictures for about 1 minute, and comments briefly on the other candidate's pictures.
3	Collaborative Task	3 minutes	Candidates are given visual material and then speak to each other about it in order to complete a task.
4	Further discussion	4 minutes	The interviewer leads a discussion which is related to the topic of Part 3.

Roy Norris

Vocabulary 1: Clothes

1 Find the following items of clothing and accessories in the pictures above. Which item is not there? What other items can you see?

waistcoat	jumper	dungarees	tracksuit bottoms
bracelet	trainers	blazer	dinner jacket
scarf	cardigan	bow tie	high-heeled shoes

2 The following adjectives can be used to describe clothes. Which of them can you match to the pictures above?

tight-fitting	formal	tasteful	trendy
baggy	colourful	unfashionable	shabby
casual	plain	smart	waterproof

3 In exercises A and B, put the correct form of the appropriate verb in each space.

A *fit   suit   match   go with*

Personally, I don't think those shoes **(1)** _____ that dress. I mean red and blue just don't **(2)** _____ , do they? And as for those earrings, well they really don't **(3)** _____ her – someone with short hair should not be wearing long ones like that. He looks alright though, except perhaps for those trousers. Do you think they **(4)** _____ him properly? They look a little tight on him to me.

B *wear   put on   get dressed*

As it was Sunday I got up and had breakfast in my dressing gown. I didn't **(1)** _____ until well after 11 o'clock. I **(2)** _____ a long-sleeved jumper at first, but immediately changed my mind. It was far too hot outside and I spent the whole day **(3)** _____ just a short-sleeved cotton shirt and shorts.

4   Using the vocabulary from exercises 1, 2 and 3, describe what the people are wearing in the photographs on page 2.

 5   Describe the clothes that you most like wearing. Use the vocabulary from exercises 1, 2 and 3 and the Wordlist on page 202 to help you. Say why you like them, when you wear them and when you wouldn't wear them.

Reading:
FCE Part 2

Gapped text

1   You are going to read a written account by a woman whose job it once was to 'care for and protect' teenage models, such as those in the photographs.

   What do you imagine the lifestyle of teenage fashion models is like?
How do you think they spend a typical week?
What do they need protection from?

2   Read the article on the next page quite quickly. Do you think the writer would recommend this lifestyle to teenagers?

3   Read the following instructions for this Part 3 Reading task.

Seven sentences have been removed from the article. Choose from the sentences **A–H** the one which fits each gap **(1–7)**. There is one extra sentence which you do not need to use.

How to go about it

- Check that the whole sentence fits in with the meaning of the text before and after the gap.
- To help you do this, parts of the text are written in **bold**. These show connections between the language in the text and the language in the missing sentences.
- In addition, connections between pronouns and other words are shown in *italics*.
- Now look at gap number **1** and answer the following questions.

a What pronouns could be used in the missing sentence to refer to *'our girls'*?
b Which sentence **(A–H)** contains one of these pronouns *and* mentions *'talking'* and *'getting a job'*?
c When you think you have found the sentence, read the whole paragraph again to check that it fits.
- Now complete the rest of the gaps with an appropriate sentence.

Handle with care

After recent accounts of drug-taking amongst teenage models in the care of their model agencies, the catwalk world has once again come under public scrutiny. Jess Hallett used to be a booker, taking bookings for models, organizing their itineraries and generally running their lives. She talks about the lengths she went to in order to protect her girls.

While bad behaviour in the modelling world evidently exists, there are many in the fashion industry who work very hard to try and make sure it doesn't. I spent almost ten years as a booker, and became emotionally involved with almost every girl in my care. Bookers care for and protect these young models to such a point that they are often too tired at the end of the day even to go home.

We did all kinds of things for **our girls**. [1 ⬚] Sometimes **we had to talk to them** and cheer them up **even when they did get the job they wanted**; such as the cover of Italian 'Vogue' or the Chanel show in Paris. They were terrified they were going to do it badly and the booker would reassure them and tell them they looked fantastic.

The trend of using girls as young as 14 or 15 means a lot of responsibility. **The consequences of not taking good care of them** are too huge for any agency to consider. [2 ⬚] Backstage at any show in New York, Paris or Milan, you see bookers from all over the world, there to support their girls and make sure that another agency doesn't try to attract them with a better contract.

[3 ⬚] I'll never forget the time when Charles de Gaulle airport was closed down because of a strike and **Kate Moss had to get to Paris** for a very important job. The Channel Tunnel hadn't been built then, so I flew with her to Brussels **with the idea of getting the train** from there. [4 ⬚] **The whole journey took 12 hours**, but with a studio full of people waiting for her at the other end, we had no choice.

One danger we had to protect models from was **their parents**. [5 ⬚] It was quite clear that **she** was humiliated by **his behaviour** and wasn't at all interested in being a model.

There were **some parents** who would let their daughter go **alone** to fashion shoots if it meant fame and fortune. [6 ⬚] At the model agency where I worked, parents were usually encouraged to get involved in their daughters' careers and travelled with them whenever they could.

The fact is that **the majority of girls** love the lifestyle. [7 ⬚] The Russian model Lida Egorova told me recently how happy she was, working with creative and talented people. She was wealthy and living in Paris; and the night before she had met Madonna at a party. What more could any girl want?

A *One father* insisted that *his daughter* was better-looking than anyone in 'Vogue' and **complained about me** to my boss because I wouldn't employ *her*.

B **If you don't look after *them* properly**, then someone else will.

C *Others* never allowed them to go anywhere **unaccompanied**.

D Whether it was because *they* were having a hard time at school, had split up with their boyfriend, or **hadn't got a job** *they* **really wanted, their booker was the one** *they* **talked to**.

E And considering how many of *them* there are nowadays, **you don't hear many complaints**.

F However, it seemed that the rest of Europe had the **same idea**, so we had to persuade a taxi driver to take us **all the way to Paris**.

G *She* said *she* was **having a wonderful time** and couldn't imagine doing any other job.

H **Models tend to travel a lot** and whenever necessary a booker will accompany them on a trip.

When you have finished, check that the sentence which you have not used does not fit into any of the gaps.

Reacting to the text ◯

Jess Hallett finishes with the words: 'What more could any girl want?' Do you agree with this assumption?

Do you think that children who are encouraged to step into adult roles, such as catwalk modelling, are being exploited?

Do you think it is right that models should be so highly paid?

Language focus 1: Habitual behaviour

A General tendencies

1 Which of the alternatives in this sentence is not possible?
Models <u>tend to</u>/<u>use to</u>/<u>usually</u> travel a lot.

 Look in the Grammar reference on page 206 to see how *tend to* is used.

2 Make three general statements about the habits of the following groups of people in your country using *tend to*.

- pop stars
- teenagers
- old people
- teachers
- people in big cities

Example:
Pop stars in my country tend to arrive late for concerts and interviews. It's very irritating, especially as you have to pay so much to go and see them perform.

B Frequency adverbs

1 Look at the following extracts from the text.

*They are **often** too tired at the end of the day even to go home.*
***Sometimes** we had to talk to them and cheer them up even when they did get the job they wanted.*
*I'll **never** forget the time when Charles de Gaulle airport was closed down…*
*Parents were **usually** encouraged to get involved in their daughters' careers…*
*Others **never** allowed them to go anywhere unaccompanied.*

2 What is the normal position in the sentence for frequency adverbs with the following?

a main verbs   **b** the verb *to be*   **c** auxiliary verbs

Practice

1 For sentences **1–6**, decide if the position of the adverb is possible. If it is not possible, correct the sentence.

1 I hardly ever get clothes for my birthday or for Christmas.
2 I have sometimes breakfast in my pyjamas.
3 Always I fold my clothes up before I go to bed.
4 Someone in my family is always borrowing my clothes – it's so irritating!
5 When I go shopping for clothes, I rarely can find jeans which fit me perfectly.
6 Occasionally I wash my own clothes, but normally my mum or dad does it.

 Check your ideas on page 206 of the Grammar reference.

2 ◯ Say whether or not the sentences in exercise 1 are true for you. Use frequency adverbs and *tend to*.

Example:
Well, unfortunately number 1 is not true for me. My aunt often buys me clothes but they're usually not very tasteful or fashionable, so I don't tend to wear them often.

C *Used to* and *would*

1 *Used to* and *would* can be used to talk about past habits. Look at these sentences from the reading text.
   a *The booker **would** reassure them and tell them they looked fantastic.*
   b *There were some parents who **would** let their daughter go alone to fashion shoots.*
   c *Jess Hallett **used to** be a booker.*

2 In sentences **a** and **b** *used to* is also possible. In sentence **c** *would* is not possible. Why is this?

 Check your ideas on page 206 of the Grammar reference.

Practice

1 In the following paragraph, decide whether the underlined verbs can be used with:
   a both *used to* and *would*
   b only *used to*
   c neither *used to* nor *would*

From a very early age I often **(1)** <u>looked</u> at models in catalogues and **(2)** <u>said</u>: 'I'd like to do that.' I **(3)** <u>was</u> a very small child so one day my mum **(4)** <u>gave</u> me one of her tops to wear as a dress and on sunny days I **(5)** <u>walked</u> up and down the garden path as if I was modelling it on the catwalk. I **(6)** <u>loved</u> that top and I really **(7)** <u>believed</u> that one day I'd be a model. I **(8)** <u>found</u> it recently when I was cleaning the house and I **(9)** <u>smiled</u> to myself.

2 Write six sentences comparing your life now with your life five years ago. Write about things which have changed.

Example:
I didn't use to have a job, but now I work on Saturdays so I have more money.

Vocabulary 2: Get

A Expressions with *get*

The following sentences all contain phrasal verbs or expressions with *get*. Decide which answer **A**, **B**, **C** or **D** best fits each gap and underline it. There is an example at the beginning **(0)**.

0 That jumper looks so old and dirty. When are you going to get _____ of it?

   A away   **B** throw   **C** waste   **D** <u>rid</u>

1 Here's my telephone number. If you have any problems, just get in _____ with me.

   A talk   **B** speak   **C** touch   **D** tact

2 I heard she was a lovely woman. Unfortunately, I never got the _____ to meet her.

   A occasion   **B** opportunities   **C** possibilities   **D** chance

3 I asked him how much he got _____ but he refused to tell me.

   A paid   **B** earned   **C** money   **D** salary

4 Come on, hurry up and get _____ ! Your bus leaves in five minutes.

   A ready   **B** ordered   **C** fit   **D** prepare

5 His parents are worried about his behaviour. He's always getting into _____ at school.

   A problems   **B** trouble   **C** difficulty   **D** punishment

6 His girlfriend left him in March and he still hasn't got _____ it.

   A by   **B** over   **C** off   **D** past

7 I can't speak French very well, but I always manage to get _____ with a dictionary and a few gestures.

   A by   **B** over   **C** across   **D** through

8 He wanted to get to the town centre but he got _____ the wrong bus and ended up at the station.

   A in   **B** out of   **C** on   **D** off

B Meanings of *get*

1 *Get* can have many different meanings. Look at the uses of *get* **(1–8)** and match each one with an appropriate equivalent **(a–h)**. The first one has been done for you.

1 *get* better	**a** receive
2 *get* the bus	**b** ask
3 *get* to the station	**c** become
4 *get* a headache	**d** become ill with
5 *get* somebody to do something	**e** catch
6 *get* something for Christmas	**f** arrive at/reach
7 *get* a newspaper	**g** go out
8 *get* out of the house	**h** buy

2 Look back at the text on teenage models and find examples of *get*. Decide on the meaning in each case.

3 Discuss the following questions.
- How long does it take you to *get* to work/school?
- When did you last *get* away for the weekend?
- What presents did you *get* for your last birthday?
- Do you often *get* angry?
- Where do you usually *get* your clothes?

Listening:
FCE Part 3

Multiple matching 1.1–1.5

You will hear five people talking about occasions when a person's clothes and appearance caused surprise or concern. Match the speaker to the correct occasion in the list **A–F**. Use the letters only once. There is one extra letter which you do not need to use.

Before you do the task…

What to expect in the exam

- You will have 30 seconds to read the descriptions. Use this time to try to predict some of the ideas and language you might hear (see below).
- You are not expected to understand everything you hear.

- Some of the extracts may contain distractors (key words or expressions which could cause you to make the wrong decision).
- Pay close attention the second time you hear the recording. You may discover that you need to change your answers.

Prediction

| guest |
| spectator |
| audience |
| competitor |
| witness |
| star |
| candidate |
| host |
| invigilator |
| opponent |

1 Match each of the people in the box to the appropriate occasion **A–F** in the listening activity below. More than one word may be used for each occasion and some words may be used twice.

eg A wedding: *guest, witness*

What other people might you also find in each of the situations?

eg *At a wedding the people who get married are the bride and groom.*

2 Where does each occasion take place?

eg *A wedding usually takes place in a church or a registry office.*

3 What clothes would you wear on the occasions **A–F** mentioned in the listening task below?

eg *If I was going to a wedding I would buy an expensive dress. I would probably wear high-heeled shoes.*

Now you are ready to do the task.

A a wedding	Speaker 1	☐
B a birthday party	Speaker 2	☐
C a job interview	Speaker 3	☐
D a sporting event	Speaker 4	☐
E a film premiere	Speaker 5	☐
F an examination		

Have you ever been in a situation where someone's appearance caused surprise?

Language focus 2: *Be used to, get used to* and *used to*

1 Look at the following sentences from the listening. In which of them does *used to*

a mean 'accustomed to'?
b refer to a past state which has now finished?

1 *Her unconventional, yet practical clothing shocked spectators, who **were used to** seeing women play in the long, heavy dresses which were typical of that period.*
2 *And he **used to** live in France, which means he probably wouldn't mind changing countries if we needed him to.*
3 *...he will have to **get used to** wearing something a little more formal.*

2 What is the difference in meaning between *be used to* and *get used to*?

3 What form of the verb is used after *be used to* and *get used to*?

G Check your answers on page 206 of the Grammar reference.

Practice

1 🔘 Talk about all the things you have to *get used to* in the following situations.

- you get your first job
- you become famous
- you go on a diet
- you get married
- you have children
- you retire

Example:
In a new job, you might have to get used to working together with other people.

2 a If you went to live in Britain, what aspects of life there would you find it difficult to *get used to*?

b Read the following text about Juan, who moved from Spain to live in England. Ignore the gaps for the moment. How many of the things which you spoke about in **a** are mentioned?

Now that Juan has been living in England for five years he **(0)** *is used to doing* (do) things differently, but it hasn't always been the case. When he first moved there he couldn't **(1)** _____ (have) lunch at 1pm, so he often **(2)** _____ (cook) for himself in his flat and eat at 3pm, as his family does in Spain. Even now I don't think he **(3)** _____ (eat) English food, because when he comes home to Madrid, he buys Spanish 'delicacies' to take back with him.
I remember how he **(4)** _____ (write) to me and complain about the shop closing times. It took him a long time to **(5)** _____ the fact that you can't buy anything after about five o'clock. Most shops in Spain close at eight in the evening.
He bought an English car a year ago, so he should **(6)** _____ (drive) on the left by now. I wonder if he'll ever be able to **(7)** _____ (drive) on the right again when, or if, he comes back to live in Spain!

c Read the text again and complete each of the gaps using the correct form of *used to, be used to* or *get used to*. If a verb is given in brackets, you should write the appropriate form. There is an example at the beginning **(0)**.

d 🔘 What do you think a British person coming to your country might find it difficult to *get used to*?

Speaking:
FCE Part 2

Talking about photos 🔘

Look at the four photographs on page 9. They show people who have different lifestyles. Before you do the speaking task, read the How to go about it box below.

How to go about it

Student A
- In Part 2 of the speaking exam you are not asked to describe the photographs in detail, but to compare them. When doing this, comment on the similarities and differences:
  Similarities: 'Both pictures show ...'
  Differences: 'In the first picture ... whereas in the second one ...'
- When talking about what kind of lives you think the people lead, comment on some of the following:
  daily routine   working hours   leisure time
  eating habits   health   travel
  family life   type of home   clothes

- Useful language for speculating:
  I get the impression *it's a stressful life.*
  I expect / imagine *he travels a lot.*
  He probably *spends a lot of time working.*
  Perhaps *she doesn't have her own home.*
  She might / may *have a wide circle of friends.*
- Give reasons for your opinions.

Student B
When you say which person you would prefer to change with, don't forget to give your reasons.

Student A: Compare photographs **1** and **2** and say what kind of lives you think these people lead.

Student B: When your partner has finished, say which person you would prefer to change places with for a month if you had to choose.

> What kind of lives do the people lead?

Now change roles. Follow the instructions above using photographs **3** and **4**.

What to expect in the exam

- The second part of Student A's task, which begins 'and say', is reproduced as a question above the photographs.

<table>
<tr><td>Writing:</td></tr>
</table>

Informal letters

1 Read the following letter, which you have received from your English penfriend, Mark. What two things does he ask you to tell him?
Would *you* accept Mark's invitation? Why/Why not?

Dear _____ ,

a) <u>Many thanks for your last letter.</u> The new house sounds brilliant — how are you settling in? b) <u>I'm sorry I haven't written sooner,</u> but I've been really busy helping my parents out on the farm.

It's great fun, though I still haven't got used to getting up at six every morning to milk the cows! We often have the radio on while we're doing it, so it's not too bad. Then, once we've had breakfast, we tend to spend the rest of the day outside, either in the fields or looking after the sheep.

c) <u>That reminds me,</u> do you remember Lady, our oldest sheepdog? Well, she's just had puppies! If you're free in the summer, you could come and see them all and help with the harvest as well. d) <u>Let me know</u> if you can make it — we'd love to see you again.

Anyway, e) <u>I must go,</u> as it's getting late and tomorrow we've got another early start. f) <u>Can't wait to hear from you.</u>

g) <u>Best wishes</u>
Mark

2 What is the purpose of each of the four paragraphs?
Example:
Paragraph 1: *To say thank you for the letter and to apologize for not writing before.*

3 Match each underlined expression **a–g** from Mark's letter with an appropriate alternative from **1–10**. Which three phrases cannot be used and why are they inappropriate?
Example: 1 e)

1 I'd better close now
2 Thanks a lot for the letter
3 Yours sincerely
4 By the way
5 All the best

6 I would be most grateful if you could inform me
7 I look forward to your prompt reply
8 Please write and tell me
9 I'm sorry it's taken me so long to write to you
10 I'm looking forward to hearing from you

Notice the use of contractions in Mark's letter: *I'm, it's* and *haven't*. These are typical of informal writing.

4 Find and circle the following linking words in Mark's letter. Then use an appropriate linker from the box to complete the gaps in sentences **1–6**. Each linker can be used more than once.

but	while	so	and	as well	as

1 You'll never guess what happened to me _____ I was shopping in the centre of town the other day!
2 I'm writing to ask you to do me a favour _____ I've got myself into trouble.

3 We're having a party next Saturday _____ we were wondering if you'd like to come. Bring a friend _____ .

4 I'd love to accept your invitation, _____ I'm afraid I'm going to be busy.

5 I haven't got any plans _____ I'll certainly be able to go.

6 I'm very sorry, _____ I'm afraid I lost your camera _____ I was in the disco on Friday.

5 Match each of the following six reasons for writing with an appropriate sentence **1–6** from exercise **4**.

inviting	accepting an invitation
giving news	asking for help
apologizing	refusing an invitation

6 Read the following instructions.

Six months ago you moved to a new house in another part of your country. Write a reply to Mark's letter giving news about how you are settling in to your new surroundings and what a typical day is like. You should also say whether or not you can accept his invitation to go and stay on his farm in the summer.

Write your **letter**. You should write **120–180** words.

Before you write your letter…

Planning

Look at the following paragraph plan. In each paragraph decide which points would be relevant in your letter. Tick (✓) those which are relevant and put a cross (✗) next to those which are not. The first one has been done for you.

Paragraph 1	• Thank Mark for his letter. ✓ • Make a friendly comment about his life on the farm. • Tell him you have moved. • Give a detailed description of the house.
Paragraph 2	• Mention what you have/haven't got used to. • Say whether you have made any friends. • Give details of their names, ages and jobs. • Say two or three things about your daily routine. • Mention how long it takes to get to school/work. • Describe your school/workplace in detail.
Paragraph 3	• Refuse the invitation but don't say why. • Accept or refuse the invitation and give a reason.
Paragraph 4	• Talk about what you did last Christmas. • Explain why you have to finish the letter. • Refer to a possible future meeting/letter.

Not all of the points that you ticked have to be included in the letter and you may also add relevant points of your own.

Don't forget!

- Organize your letter into paragraphs using the plan above.
- The language of your letter should be informal. Use some of the informal language and linkers that you have just studied.
- Your answer must be relevant to the question.
- Write between 120 and 180 words.

11

1 Review

Transformations

For questions **1–9**, complete the second sentence so that it has a similar meaning to the first sentence, using the word given. **Do not change the word given**. You must use between two and five words, including the word given. Here is an example **(0)**.

0 How long was your journey from London to Manchester?
take
How long _did it take you to_ get from London to Manchester?

1 Rick is making a slow recovery from his illness.
getting
Rick _____ his illness.

2 Why don't you throw away that old blouse?
rid
How about _____ that old blouse?

3 We usually buy our food from the local market.
tend
We _____ our food from the local market.

4 He never asks when he borrows my things!
always
He is _____ asking!

5 When I was younger we often used to go on holiday abroad.
would
When I was younger _____ on holiday abroad.

6 I'm sure I won't have any problems sharing a flat after a couple of weeks.
get
I'm sure I'll _____ a flat after a couple of weeks.

7 I still find it difficult to work with a computer.
used
I still haven't _____ with a computer.

8 I can't wait to see you again.
forward
I'm really _____ you again.

9 I ought to phone my dad to tell him I've arrived safely.
better
I _____ my dad to tell him I've arrived safely.

Vocabulary

A Clothes

For questions **1–6,** decide which of the three words is not normally used with the word in capitals at the end of the line. The first one has been done for you.

1 evening	<u>afternoon</u>	fancy	DRESS
2 colourful	smart	baggy	BOW-TIE
3 waterproof	expensive	tasteful	NECKLACE
4 shabby	plain	tight-fitting	SCARF
5 high-heeled	long-sleeved	trendy	SHOES
6 dinner	casual	waist	JACKET

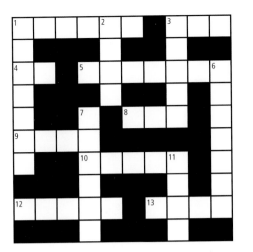

B Expressions crossword

Expressions for use in informal letters

Across

1 Many _____ for your letter.
5 I'm looking _____ to hearing from you.
8 By the _____, how did the exam go?
9 Write back soon.

_____ ,
Susie

12 I'm sorry it's _____ me so long to write to you.

Down

2 Let me _____ if you can make it.
7 Anyway, I'd _____ close now.
11 Can't wait to _____ from you.

Expressions with *get*

Across

3 Chewing gum is forbidden in class – get _____ of it now!
4 If you don't get _____ the train now, it'll leave without you!
10 They said they'd get in _____ with me, but so far they haven't written or phoned.
13 How much do you get _____ a week in your job?

Down

1 He's always getting into _____ with the police.
3 Turn off your PlayStation now and get _____ for school.
6 I had a shower, got _____ and then went out for a walk.

C People

Each of the words for people **1–6** has a relationship of some kind with one of the words **a–f**. Match the words and then use them to complete the sentences below. You may need to use plural forms.

1 invigilator	**a** groom
2 host	**b** spectator
3 bride	**c** patient
4 competitor	**d** audience
5 performer	**e** candidate
6 doctor	**f** guest

1 The youngest _____ in the stadium surprised the _____ by winning the 400 metres in record time.

2 The only person I recognized at the party was the _____ ; I didn't know any of the other _____ .

3 The _____ and _____ looked very happy as they walked back down the aisle after the ceremony.

4 Many members of the _____ left the theatre before the end of the play, disappointed at the acting of some of the _____ .

5 After a thorough examination the _____ could find nothing wrong with his _____ .

6 One of the _____ was caught cheating in the exam by the _____ .

2 High energy

Vocabulary 1: Music

1 Would you go to see any of these musicians or singers perform?
What would be the ingredients of the ideal concert for you?
Who would you see? Where would the concert be? What would you wear?

2 **a** How many of the musical instruments in the photographs can you name?

b All the words in each of the groups below can be used in combination with one of the words in the box. Write an appropriate word from the box in each of the gaps. There is an example at the beginning **(0)**.

play (v)
~~rock~~
lead (adj)
on
in
instrument
live (adj)
a song
musician

0 _rock_	band singer star	**3**	talented rock session	**6**	album performance music
1 _____	vocalist singer guitarist	**4** _____	tour stage the radio	**7** _____	the charts concert tune
2 sing perform mime _____		**5** _____	a track a tune a record	**8** musical wind stringed _____	

3 Study the word combinations in exercise 2 for two minutes. Then look at the words in the box and cover the exercise. How many word combinations can you remember?

4 Imagine that you are the organizing committee for a charity and you want to make a CD to raise money. Try to agree what the title of the CD will be, which musicians you will include and which tracks would be best. Where would you advertise it?

14

Listening 1:
FCE Part 2

Sentence completion ◉▶ 1.6

1 Do you enjoy going to discos?
What type of music do you prefer to dance to?
How important is the DJ?

2 You will hear a radio interview with Brad Andrews, a club DJ. For questions **1–10**, complete the sentences which summarize what he says.

Before you do the task…

What to expect in the exam

- You don't normally need to write more than three words for each answer.
- You hear the answers in the same order as the questions.
- The words you **read** in the question may not be the same as the words you *hear* in the recording, eg Question 1:
  You *read*: DJ-ing isn't the same as it was in…
  You *hear*: 'DJ-ing has changed an awful lot since…'
- However, the word or words you need to write are actually spoken on the cassette.
- You will hear the recording twice.
- You have 45 seconds to read the questions before you listen. Use this time to try to predict the type of information you might hear.

Example:
Question 1: *We might hear the name of a town or country. The present and past tenses in the question make me think it might be comparing DJ-ing now with DJ-ing in the past, so perhaps it's a year.*

3 Look at the other questions and try to predict the information you might hear for each one. Then listen to the recording and complete the sentences.

1 DJ-ing isn't the same as it was in _____ .
2 DJs often use _____ turntables at the same time.
3 Many DJs are also _____ .
4 Their job consists mainly of _____ .
5 They can earn as much as _____ pounds for a performance.
6 Fans can see their favourite DJs perform every _____ .
7 For Brad, performing a gig is like taking people _____ .
8 To prepare himself mentally, Brad practises _____ before a gig.
9 In the future DJs may use _____ instead of vinyl records.
10 DJs are employed by famous groups to help them attract _____ .

Is DJ-ing something you would like to try?
What do you think are the positive and negative aspects of the job?

Language focus 1: Indirect ways of asking questions

1 Questions can be asked in a more indirect way by introducing them with certain expressions, as in these two examples from the listening.

Would you mind telling us how much you earn for a single gig?

Could you tell us what the future of dance music is?

Asking questions in this way can make them sound more polite.

2 a How are indirect questions formed?

Think about:
- word order
- auxiliary verbs

b What happens when there is no question word such as *when, how, what, where* etc?

Rewrite the following question to make it indirect.
Does a gig require much preparation?
I'd like to know _____ ?

 Check your ideas on page 206 of the Grammar reference.

Practice

Rewrite the following questions to make them indirect. Choose an appropriate phrase from the box to begin each question.

> I'd be interested to know… Could you explain…
> Would you mind telling us… We'd like to know…
> I was wondering if you could tell me… Could you tell us…

1 Why is dance music so popular?
_____

2 What does a clubber have to pay to see you perform?
_____

3 When did you do your first gig?
_____

4 Do you plan to work with any famous groups?
_____

5 What do you like most about DJ-ing?
_____

6 How did you become a DJ?
_____

7 Has anything ever gone wrong at a gig?
_____

Writing 1:
FCE Part 1

Letters: Asking for information

1 Read the following Writing Part 1 instructions.

You are interested in going to England to study music in the summer and you have seen this advertisement in a magazine. Using the notes you have made, write to Charlesworth House asking for more information.

Write a **letter** of between **120 and 150** words in an appropriate style. Do not write any postal addresses.

2   Would it be more appropriate to write the letter using formal or informal language? Read the example letter below and for questions **1–8**, underline the most appropriate word or phrase. There is an example at the beginning **(0)**.

Dear Sir/Madam,

(0) I'm writing about/<u>I am writing in response to</u> your advertisement, which appeared in last week's edition of 'International Musician'. I am interested in having violin lessons at your school in the summer and I **(1) would like/want** further information about your courses.

Firstly, **(2) you could give me a few/I would be grateful for** details about the classes. **(3) I would/I'd** be interested to know how many hours of lessons there are each day and whether tuition is individual or in groups.

I also have **(4) a couple of questions/some queries** regarding costs. In particular, I would like to know the price of a one-month course from July 16th to August 15th. Could you also **(5) let me know/indicate** whether the cost of excursions is included?

If you have a brochure with photographs of the school, **(6) send me/I would be pleased to receive** a copy. Thank you in advance for your assistance. **(7) I look/I'm looking** forward to **(8) getting your answer/receiving your reply**.

Yours faithfully,
Marianna Ilyina

3   **a** You will lose marks if you do not answer the question fully. Does this example answer cover all the notes in the question?

b Candidates who write good answers build on the information given and add relevant points of their own. Find examples of this in the model.

c Avoid copying phrases or sentences from the input material. Find examples of how the writer of the model has rephrased language from the notes in the question.

4   Now do the following Writing Part 1 task.

You and two of your friends would like to go to a rock music festival in July and you have seen this advertisement in a magazine. Using the notes you have made, write a letter to Melody Tours and ask for more information.

Spend a weekend of summer fun at

THE BENNINGTON ROCK FESTIVAL

at Bennington Park, near Oxford. Friday 15th – Sunday 17th July

Bands include The Sheets, Garage Door, Flaming Spears, Mouthpiece and many more.

'Melody Tours' will organize everything for you.

Our package includes:
- Entrance tickets for all three days
- Transport to and from London's Heathrow airport
- Accommodation for two nights
- Half board

Total cost: £230

times?

cheaper for just two days?

Arrive Heathrow late Fri night

Last flight back on Sunday: 9.15pm

Room for three if possible

Write a **letter** of between **120 and 150** words in an appropriate style. Do not write any postal addresses.

Don't forget!

- Write in a formal style and try to use indirect rather than direct questions.
- Cover all the notes in the question.
- Good answers build on the information given in the notes and other materials.
- You should not copy phrases or sentences from the question.
- Write between 120 and 150 words.

1

2

3

4

1 The pictures above all show extreme or dangerous sports.

Student A: Compare two of the sports and say which of them you think is more enjoyable.

Student B: Compare the remaining two sports and say which sport you think is more difficult to learn.

2   Read the magazine article about extreme sports on page 19 quite quickly and match each paragraph to a picture. Have you changed your ideas about each sport?

3   You are going to read the article again. For questions **1–15**, choose from the sports **(A–D)**. The sports may be chosen more than once. When more than one answer is required, these may be given in any order.

How to go about it

- Read all the questions to see the kind of information you are looking for.
- Read text A, then look again at the questions, answering any that you can. To help you, parts of text A have been underlined. Match these parts to the appropriate questions.
- Do the same for the other three texts. Underline the relevant parts of the texts as you answer the questions.
- If there are any questions you have not answered, scan the texts again, looking for the specific information you need.

A Street luge   **C** Base-jumping
B Ice-climbing   **D** Zorbing

Which text(s) mention(s) the following?

You need to be both physically and psychologically prepared.	1
It was not at first intended as a land-based sport.	2
The equipment is usually specially made to suit the participant.	3
Slow speeds represent a risk.	4
You do not need to have any special abilities.	5
The sport goes by other names as well.	6
It can be practised in an artificially created environment.	7
Participants are protected from serious injury.	8 9
It demands previous experience in a related sport.	10
The equipment required depends on the conditions.	11
It has caused deaths.	12
There is a less secure variation on the basic sport.	13
Your feet play an important role in reducing speed.	14
Participants often break the law.	15

Going to extremes

Alex Benton takes a look at four extreme sports which are guaranteed to add a bit of spice to life – for those intrepid enough to want to try them.

A Street luge

Also known as road luge or land luge, street luge was born in California in the 1970s, when skateboarders found they could go faster by lying flat on their backs. In this position pilots can reach up to 130 kilometres per hour, but the sport is equally thrilling at much lower speeds. And it's surprisingly safe, too. Being so low to the ground means there's far less distance to fall, and even if you do, your crash helmet and full protective leathers prevent any real harm coming to you. Street luges are around two metres long and most are custom-built by the pilots themselves, although some commercial models are now available. You can steer them round bends by shifting your bodyweight to one side, and the only way to slow down or stop is by slamming down the thick heavy rubber soles of your boots onto the ground – not exactly a state-of-the-art braking system, but very effective nonetheless!

B Ice-climbing

As the name suggests, practitioners of this sport clamber up ice formations, usually with an ice axe in each hand and in the case of steeper slopes, crampons – metal spikes which grip the ice – on the bottom of their boots. The type of ice you climb also determines the tools you take with you. Water ice, such as that found in frozen waterfalls, is formed from water and is colder and more brittle than alpine ice, the frozen snow that forms glaciers. Whatever the conditions, the sport requires you to be mentally tough and have the agility and upper-body strength of a monkey. But you don't always need to go to the great outdoors to do your ice-climbing. Just as there are indoor climbing walls for rock climbers, you can also find specially built ice walls which recreate the basic conditions but take the unpleasant chill factor out of the experience.

C Base-jumping

BASE is an acronym for Building, Antenna, Span (a bridge, arch or dome) and Earth (a mountain or cliff), and was coined in 1978, when parachutists first began jumping systematically from fixed objects, either man-made structures or natural formations. Since then, the sport has claimed over 100 lives, the details of which are all rather morbidly recorded on the Internet. Indeed, so dangerous is it that before making your first jump, experts recommend you should do around 250 skydives in order to get fully used to the feeling of freefalling. But even this does not prepare you for the dangers involved in falling at such a relatively low velocity, and so close both to the fixed objects and to the ground. Be warned too that jumping from buildings is usually illegal, since gaining access to the top of them usually involves some form of unlawful entry.

D Zorbing

Developed in New Zealand in the 1990s, originally as a means of crossing water, this sport involves rolling downhill in a large PVC ball, an activity which requires no more skill than that of a hamster running inside its wheel. The three-metre zorb has two skins, with the area between them inflated to provide effective cushioning and so prevent zorbonauts from hurting themselves as they hurtle along at speeds of up to 50 kilometres per hour. Zorbers are also harnessed inside the ball to stop them moving around, although in 'Hydrozorbing' you can do away with the straps and slide around in a bucket or two of water. This version can be enjoyed alone, or you can share the experience with up to two other people inside the same zorb. But don't be surprised if you get the odd bump or bruise!

Reacting to the text

Which of these extreme sports would you most and least like to do? Give reasons for your answers.
Have you ever tried any unusual sports?

Language focus 2: Gerunds and infinitives A

1 Look at the following sentences from the reading text. Do you remember which sport each one refers to?

   a *This sport involves **rolling** downhill in a large PVC ball.*

   b ***Gaining** access to the top of them usually involves some form of unlawful entry.*

   c *Before **making** your first jump experts recommend you should do around 250 skydives.*

2 The words written in **bold** in exercise 1 are all gerunds. Match each of these gerunds with the appropriate explanation for its use, 1–3.

   1 as the subject of a clause or sentence
   2 after prepositions
   3 after certain verbs

3 Look at the following sentences from the text. What verb form follows each of the verbs in **bold**?

   a *But you don't always **need** to go to the great outdoors to do your ice-climbing.*

   b *[The acronym] was coined in 1978, when parachutists first **began** jumping systematically from fixed objects.*

   c *Your crash helmet and full protective leathers **prevent** any real harm coming to you.*

4 Certain verbs are usually followed by either the gerund or the infinitive. Which of the verbs in **bold** in exercise 3 can be used with either the gerund or infinitive without a change in meaning?

Practice

1 Complete each of the following sentences using the gerund or the infinitive of the verbs in brackets. One verb will be in the gerund and the other in the infinitive.

   1 When I *suggested* _____ (go) skiing she was extremely enthusiastic and we *arranged* _____ (meet) at seven o'clock on Saturday morning.

   2 I *can't help* _____ (smile) when I see my dad playing tennis. He's had hundreds of lessons but he still hasn't *learnt* _____ (hit) the ball properly.

   3 Playing with golfers better than myself has certainly *helped* _____ (improve) my game. Now I'm even *considering* _____ (take) golf up professionally.

   4 One of my cousins has *promised* _____ (take) me windsurfing with him as soon as I've *finished* _____ (study).

   5 At first my parents *refused* _____ (let) me go to karate lessons, but I *kept* _____ (ask) and eventually they agreed.

   Ⓖ Check your answers on page 206 of the Grammar reference.

2 The verbs in the box can be used to talk about our likes and dislikes. They are all usually followed by the gerund. Write each verb in an appropriate place on the line below according to the strength of its meaning.

really enjoy	don't mind	quite like
detest	can't stand	don't like
love	absolutely adore	hate

STRONG DISLIKE   STRONG LIKE
├───────────────────────────────────┤
detest   *absolutely adore*

3 Certain adjectives followed by a preposition and the gerund can also be used to talk about what does and doesn't interest you. Study the following table and complete each space with a preposition from the box. The first one has been done for you.

at	in	~~on~~	about	with	of

	adjective + preposition	noun or gerund
I'm (really)	keen _on_	sport/cinema etc
I'm not (really)	interested _____	listening to… etc
I've never been	fond _____	watching…
I've always been	good/bad _____	playing…
I get (really)	bored _____	doing…
I never get	excited _____	going…

4 Write eight sentences about your likes and dislikes using the language you have just studied.

Examples:

Preposition + gerund: I never get excited about going to the cinema.

Verb + gerund: I quite like listening to jazz.

Gerund as subject: Collecting postcards is one of my favourite pastimes.

5 ◯ Compare your sentences with your partner's. Ask questions about each other's likes and dislikes.

Example:

A: I've always been keen on going to the cinema.
B: How often do you go?
A: I tend to go once every two weeks or so.
B: And what are your favourite films?
A: Well, I really enjoy watching science fiction, but I don't like films with a lot of violence. I get bored very easily if there are lots of deaths.

You may be asked to talk about your interests in Part 1 of the Speaking Test. Make sure you develop your answers, explaining and justifying your opinions.

Multiple choice 1.7

1 How popular is snowboarding in your country? Have you ever done it?
What are the potential dangers of snowboarding?
What are sponsors? How do you think they might help snowboarders?

2 Read the following Listening Part 4 instructions.

You will hear an interview about snowboarding. For questions **1–7**, choose the best answer **A**, **B** or **C**.

What to expect in the exam

● Look at question 1 below and the following extract from the tapescript. The underlined words all appear in the possible answers **A**, **B** and **C**, but only one of these answers fits the question. The other words are distractors. Decide which is the correct answer and say why the others are incorrect.

Tapescript:
I first did it when I was on holiday with my parents. When I was younger I used to go skiing <u>every year</u> with them and then <u>one year</u> I tried snowboarding and I haven't skied since then. That was <u>five years</u> ago.

1 How long has Liz been snowboarding?
  A one year
  B five years
  C every year since she was a child

2 According to Liz, if you want to be a snowboarder
  A you have to be naturally sporty.
  B you need to be born with good co-ordination and balance.
  C you don't need long to acquire the skills.

3 What injuries has Liz suffered?
  A She broke her back.
  B She broke an arm.
  C She fell badly on her back.

4 What does Liz say about the ratio of male to female snowboarders?
  A There are nearly the same number of girls as boys.
  B You almost never see girls who snowboard.
  C There are a lot more girls than boys.

5 What does Liz say about money?
  A Girls don't get paid as much as boys.
  B Her sponsors don't give her any money.
  C She doesn't have to pay for her equipment.

6 What does she recommend to girls who want to snowboard?
  A They should have lessons on an artificial slope.
  B They should buy lots of warm clothing.
  C They should go to a place where it snows.

7 Why does Liz do modelling work?
  A She earns money to finance her snowboarding.
  B It will improve her job prospects.
  C She has always wanted to be a model.

Don't forget!

● Pay close attention the second time you hear the recording. You may discover that you need to change your answers.

Is there any sport which you would like to take up?
What qualities or strengths would you need to have?
Are there any dangers involved?

Word formation: Affixes

1 **1–7** show different suffixes which can be used to form the words for people. Add an appropriate suffix from the box to the root words **8–14** to form the words for the corresponding people. You may need to make changes to the root word.

	Root word		Person		Root word		Person
-er	1 snowboard	→	snowboard**er**		8 instruct	→	_____
-ist	2 spectate	→	spectat**or**		9 economic	→	_____
-eer	3 parachute	→	parachut**ist**		10 mountain	→	_____
-or	4 participate	→	particip**ant**		11 electric	→	_____
-ant	5 engine	→	engin**eer**		12 entertain	→	_____
-ee	6 employ	→	employ**er**/employ**ee**		13 assist	→	_____
-ian	7 politics	→	politic**ian**		14 interview	→	_____

2 The prefixes in the box can be added to some nouns, verbs and adjectives to make them negative. In **1–7** below, the same prefix can be used with all three adjectives to make them negative. Choose the appropriate prefix for each group and write the negative forms. The first one has been done for you.

	Adjectives	Negative
dis-	1 lucky/pleasant/reliable	*unlucky/unpleasant/unreliable*
un-	2 experienced/competent/tolerant	_____
in-	3 legal/logical/legible	_____
ir-	4 moral/mature/modest	_____
il-	5 practical/patient/perfect	_____
im-	6 regular/responsible/relevant	_____
	7 honest/obedient/satisfied	_____

Note that *in-* is not normally used with words beginning with *l*, *m*, *p* or *r*. What happens instead?

3 What meaning do the affixes in bold have in the following words?

undercook	**over**eat	**pre**historic	**post**graduate	**hyper**market
microelectronics	**mis**spell	**re**write	**ex**-wife	manager**ess**

Language focus 3: Gerunds and infinitives B

1 Look at the following extracts from the listening and answer the questions below.

1 Liz: *I came first in the Big Air event and won some money.*

Interviewer: *Let's hope you can go on winning!*

2 Liz: *... and any part-time modelling work now could be useful for the future.*

Interviewer: *You mean, you might go on to become a full-time model?*

In which sentence does *go on* mean
a continue to do the same activity?
b change to a different activity?

...ing is also affected when using either the gerund or the ...with the following verbs:

forget   stop   regret   mean   try

...nce in meaning is between the two ...e following pairs of sentences.

1 a I remember studying this piece of grammar last year.
b I must remember to study my notes on gerunds and infinitives tonight.

2 a We regret to announce that all trains to York will experience delays of up to two hours.
b I regret catching the train to York. I got to the meeting two hours late.

3 a I stopped to buy a newspaper on my way home from the office.
b I've stopped buying newspapers. You can't believe a word you read in them.

4 a I tried having tennis lessons, but they didn't make much difference to my game.
b I tried to have tennis lessons, but none of the teachers was available in the evening.

5 a I'm glad I took the exam. It meant doing a lot more studying, but it was worth it in the end.
b I meant to do some studying last night, but Tom called and we spent an hour on the phone.

Vocabulary 2: Sports

1   Can you name all the sports in the pictures? Write the name of each sport next to the verb which it is used with. The first one has been done for you.

do   _athletics_

go   _____

play _____

2   Where do each of the sports in exercise 1 take place? Use the words in the box.

| court   slopes   track   gym   pitch   pool |

Example: *You do athletics on an indoor or an outdoor track.*

3   What are the people who do each sport called?

Example: *A person who does athletics is called an athlete.*

4   In **1–4** write each word in **bold** on the appropriate line.

1 to take place or **to take part**

_____ (= to participate) in a competition/sporting event

_____ (= to happen) on a court/in a gym

2 to win or **to beat**

_____ a competition/a sporting event/a game/a medal

_____ an opponent/another team

3 to play or **to practise**

_____ a sport

_____ serving the ball/a particular shot (in order to improve)

4 the audience or **the spectators**

_____ at a football match/a sporting event/an athletics meeting

_____ in a cinema/in a theatre/at a concert

Writing 2:
FCE Part 2

Articles

1   Read the following Writing Part 2 instructions.

You have just seen the following advertisement.

Write your **article** for International Sports Weekly magazine. You should write **120–180** words.

> ### INTERNATIONAL SPORTS WEEKLY
>
> ➤ What is your favourite sport?
> ➤ Why do you like it?
> ➤ What advice would you give to someone who wants to take it up?
>
> We are looking for short articles answering these questions and we will publish some of the best articles next month.

How to go about it

- Before you write your article, read the model and analysis on page 200.
- To help you plan your article, answer the following questions and make notes.

Paragraph 1:

What is your favourite sport?

What is special about it?

Paragraph 2:

Why do you like it?

What are the benefits of doing it?

Paragraph 3:

What advice can you give to people who want to take it up?

Are any special qualities, equipment or clothes needed?

Paragraph 4:

What final encouragement can you give?

- Give your article a title and include some of the features of style from page 200.

Word formation

1 In **1–6** below, one of the four words is not normally used. Underline the word.

1 undercook	undercharge	underestimate	undersleep
2 overgrown	overweight	overlittle	overcrowded
3 overeat	oversing	oversleep	overwork
4 misbehave	misunderstand	misspell	missucceed
5 dislove	dishonesty	disappearance	disobedience
6 manageress	doctoress	actress	waitress

2 For questions **1–6**, complete each of the gaps with the correct form of one of the words from exercise 1.

1 These jeans should have cost £30, but the assistant made a mistake and _____ _____ me. I only paid £20 for them.

2 The house has been abandoned for years. That's why the garden is looking so _____ _____ .

3 I'm sorry I'm late. My alarm didn't go off, so I _____ .

4 You've _____ my surname. There are two 't's in Hutton, not one.

5 Police are investigating the _____ of confidential documents from the Prime Minister's office.

6 Shall I ask the _____ for the bill?

3 Now write five sentences of your own using some of the other words from exercise 1. Leave a space in each sentence where the word should be and ask another student to complete them.

Use of English:
FCE Part 3

Word formation

Read the following text about the sport of free-diving. Use the word given in capitals at the end of some of the lines to form a word that fits in the gap **in the same line**. There is an example at the beginning **(0)**.

Former swimming **(0)** _instructor_ Tanya Streeter, 26, has achieved what many	INSTRUCT
thought was **(1)** _____ and dived to 370 feet below the sea on a single	POSSIBLE
lungful of air. **(2)** _____ in free-diving take a deep breath before	COMPETE
(3) _____ into the depths of the ocean. Rigorous training has helped	APPEAR
Tanya to go deeper than male **(4)** _____ and break one of the most	DIVE
difficult diving records.	
Free-diving is a dangerous sport. Deaths are frequent and it is not	
(5) _____ to pass out or have a nose bleed on the descent. Tanya, who	COMMON
can hold her breath for five minutes **(6)** _____ , says that many men tried	WATER
to **(7)** _____ her from attempting to break the record. 'They all said	COURAGE
it was **(8)** _____ that a woman could reach such depths without breathing	LIKELY
equipment. They **(9)** _____ my abilities and I proved them wrong.' In 1988	JUDGE
the French film **(10)** _____ Luc Besson made a film about free-diving,	DIRECT
Le Grand Bleu, which became the biggest box-office hit in France of all time.	

How long can you hold your breath for?
How far can you swim underwater?

Gerunds and infinitives

1 Complete each of the gap below with the correct form of the verb in brackets.

1 I've been meaning _____ (write) to you for ages but I just haven't had the time.
2 If we go skiing tomorrow, it'll mean _____ (get) up early. The slopes get crowded very quickly.
3 I wish you'd stop _____ (tap) your foot!
4 These long car journeys make me really hungry. Can we stop _____ (have) lunch soon?
5 When I tell you to be quiet, why must you always go on _____ (talk)?
6 After looking at verbs which take the gerund, we went on _____ (study) those which are followed by the infinitive.
7 I tried hard _____ (open) the window, but I couldn't move it. It was stuck.
8 These plants look as if they need a lot more light. Try _____ (put) them a little closer to the window.

2 In each of the groups below, one of the verbs is grammatically different from the other three. Decide whether the verbs take the gerund, the infinitive or both, in order to discover which verb is the odd one out. The first one has been done for you.

Example: admit *takes the gerund, whereas the others take the infinitive*

0 expect	**2** remember	**4** keen on
hope	begin	interested in
<u>admit</u>	forget	tend to
agree	regret	fond of
1 promise	**3** want	**5** can't afford
offer	would like	can't imagine
refuse	feel like	can't help
finish	decide	can't stand

3 Now look at the verb lists on pages 206 and 207 of the Grammar reference and make two groups of your own like those in exercise 2. Then give them to another student, who will try to find the odd one out.

Vocabulary: Music

Complete each of the gaps below with an appropriate word combination from page 14 of this unit. You may need to use nouns in the plural. There is an example at the beginning **(0)**.

0 I never buy *live albums* . You don't get the same quality of sound as you do with a studio recording.
1 Ricky Martin's latest album sounds great. I heard a couple of tracks _____ _____ last night.
2 I spend all my time in piano lessons practising the scales. I still haven't learnt to _____ .
3 Her last record only got as far as number ten _____ .
4 When groups make a record they often have to employ _____ to play some of the instruments.
5 That guitar sounds awful! Are you sure it's _____ ?
6 I hate it when they _____ on the TV. It's so obvious they aren't really singing.
7 The band is going _____ again next year. They'll be playing in nine European countries in three months.
8 Next on Capital Radio we're going to _____ from the latest 'Sidewinder' album. It's called *Ready for love* – I hope you like it.

3 A change for the better?

Vocabulary: Machines and devices

Here are three words which are often used to talk about everyday inventions.

a domestic appliance:

A machine, usually an electrical one, which is used in the house to do a job such as cooking or cleaning.
Examples: a vacuum cleaner, a cooker, a dishwasher

a device:

A word for a useful machine or instrument.
Example: We've just bought a useful little device for peeling oranges.

a gadget:

Another word for a useful machine or instrument. (It can sometimes be used to suggest that a device or appliance is unnecessary.)
Example: Our kitchen is so full of gadgets you can hardly move.

1 Make a list of appliances, devices and gadgets that you have at home.

How useful is each one? Use the following adjectives, giving reasons for your ideas.

| handy | labour-saving | useless | clever | unusual | complicated | simple |

Which of the objects would you find it difficult to live without?

2 Look at the pictures at the side of the reading text.

Do they show 'appliances', 'devices' or 'gadgets'?
Which adjectives would you use to describe these objects?

Reading:
FCE Part 1

Multiple choice

1 The following text was written by Bill Bryson, an American who writes about his fellow Americans, mainly for a British audience. Read through the text quickly and choose the best answer **A**, **B**, **C** or **D**, to the following question.

1 What is the author's opinion of everyday inventions?
   A On the whole they make life easier.
   B Some people do not know how to use them very well.
   C They cause more problems than they solve.
   D He likes them now more than he used to.

2 Now read the text by Bill Bryson again and for questions **2–8** on pages 27 and 28, choose the best answer **A**, **B**, **C** or **D**.

How to go about it

- Find the part of the text which relates to the particular questions you are answering. As in the exam, the questions follow the same order as the text.
- Eliminate the answers which are obviously wrong, then check the answer or answers which you have not eliminated.
- If you still cannot decide, make an intelligent guess. Do not leave questions unanswered.

26

The Convenience Society, or con for short

The other day I took my younger children to a Burger King for lunch and there was a line of about a dozen cars at the drive-through window. Now, a drive-through window is not a window you drive through, but a window you drive up to and collect your food from, having placed your order over a speakerphone along the way; the idea is to provide quick takeaway
5 food for those in a hurry.

We parked, went in, ordered and ate and came out again, all in about ten minutes. As we departed, I noticed that a white pickup truck that had been last in the queue when we arrived was still four or five cars back from collecting its food. It would have been much quicker if the driver had parked like us and gone in and got his food himself, but he would never have thought
10 that way because the drive-through window is supposed to be speedier and more convenient.

Americans have become so attached to the idea of convenience that they will put up with almost any inconvenience to achieve it. The things that are supposed to speed up and simplify our lives more often than not have the opposite effect and I started wondering why this should be.

15 Americans have always looked for ways to increase comfort. It is an interesting fact that nearly all the everyday inventions that take the difficulties out of life – escalators, automatic doors, passenger lifts, refrigerators, washing machines, frozen food, fast food – were invented in America, or at least first widely used here. Americans grew so used to seeing a constant stream of labour-saving devices, in fact, that by the sixties they had come to expect machines to do
20 almost everything for them.

The moment I first realized that this was not necessarily a good idea was at Christmas of 1961 or '62, when my father was given an electric carving knife. It was an early model and not as light as the ones you can buy today. Perhaps my memory is playing tricks on me, but I have a clear impression of him putting on goggles and heavy rubber gloves before plugging it in. What
25 is certainly true is that when he sank it into the turkey it sent pieces flying everywhere and then the blade hit the plate with a shower of blue sparks and the whole thing flew out of his hands and shot across the table and out of the room, like a creature from a *Gremlins* movie.

My father was always buying gadgets that proved to be disastrous – clothes steamers that failed to take the wrinkles out of suits but caused wallpaper to fall off the walls in whole sheets,
30 or an electric pencil sharpener that could consume an entire pencil (including the tips of your fingers if you weren't quick) in less than a second.

But all of this was nothing compared with the situation today. Americans are now surrounded with items that do things for them to an almost absurd degree – automatic cat-food dispensers, refrigerators that make their own ice cubes, automatic car windows, disposable
35 toothbrushes that come with their own ration of toothpaste. People are so addicted to convenience that they have become trapped in a vicious circle: the more labour-saving devices they buy, the harder they need to work; the harder they work, the more labour-saving appliances they feel they need.

When we moved into our house in New Hampshire it was full of gadgets installed by earlier
40 owners, all of them designed to make life a little easier. Most, however, were completely useless. One of our rooms, for instance, came equipped with automatic curtains. You flicked a switch on the wall and four pairs of curtains effortlessly opened or closed. That, at least, was the idea. In practice what happened was that one opened, one closed, one opened and closed repeatedly and one did nothing at all for five minutes and then started to produce smoke. We didn't go anywhere
45 near them after the first week.

Automatic curtains, electric cat-food dispensers and clothes steamers only *seem* to make life easier. In fact, all they do is add expense and complication to your existence.

2 What point is the author making with the story of his experience at Burger King?

A Fast food restaurants are not very fast.

B Some aspects of modern life are not always as convenient as they are intended to be.

C The driver of the pickup truck had parked in the wrong place.

D The queues at the drive-through windows are usually very long.

3 What does the author tell us about everyday inventions in America?

    A They were all invented there.

    B They make life less exciting.

    C People assumed they would make life more comfortable.

    D There aren't as many now as there used to be.

4 What does the author mean by 'Perhaps my memory is playing tricks on me' (line 23)?

    A He is sometimes very forgetful.

    B He cannot remember all the details.

    C What he says might not be completely true.

    D He remembers having fun.

5 What does 'the whole thing' in line 26 refer to?

    A the turkey

    B the plate

    C the rubber gloves

    D the carving knife

6 What does the author say about labour-saving devices today?

    A People cannot stop buying them.

    B People try to do ridiculous things with them.

    C They are better than the ones in the sixties.

    D They help people to do more work.

7 What does 'them' in line 40 refer to?

    A earlier owners

    B the gadgets

    C houses in New Hampshire

    D the writer's family

8 What are we told about the automatic curtains?

    A They had been brought from a previous house.

    B Some of them worked as they were supposed to.

    C The room where they were fitted was never used.

    D The author and his family decided not to use them.

What to expect in the exam

In Part 2 of the Reading paper, the eight multiple-choice questions may test some or all of the following:

- a detailed understanding of the text: **see questions 3,6** and **8 above** (the most common type of question).
- a general understanding of the text: **see question 1** (this type of question comes last in the exam).
- an understanding of the writer's purpose: **see question 2.**
- an understanding of reference words in context: **see questions 5** and **7** (these are often pronouns such as 'it' or 'they').
- the ability to decide meaning from context: **see question 4.**

Reacting to the text

Do you agree with Bill Bryson when he says that 'the things that are supposed to speed up our lives more often than not have the opposite effect'?

Have you ever had a device or appliance which created problems for you?

Are there any devices or appliances you think should or will be invented in the future?

Language focus 1: Comparisons

Complete the following sentences from the text. If a word is given in brackets, write the correct form of that word.

1 It would have been much _____ (quick) if the driver had parked like us.

2 The drive-through window is supposed to be _____ (speedy) and _____ _____ (convenient).

3 The things which are supposed to simplify our lives _____ often _____ not have the opposite effect.

4 The electric carving knife was an early model and not _____ light _____ the ones you can buy today.

5 The electric pencil sharpener could consume an entire pencil in _____ _____ a second.

6 But all of this was nothing compared _____ the situation today.

7 The _____ labour-saving devices they buy, the _____ (hard) they need to work.

8 The gadgets were designed to make life a little _____ (easy).

Now check your answers in the reading text.

A Comparative and superlative adjectives

1 What are the comparative and superlative forms of the adjectives *quick, speedy* and *convenient* in sentences **1** and **2** above?

2 What are the comparative and superlative forms of the following adjectives?

| clean | hot | strange | clever |
| good | bad | far |

3 In sentences **1** and **8** above, Bill Bryson uses *much* to talk about a big difference (*much quicker*) and *a little* to talk about a small one (*a little easier*). Are the following used for big or small differences?

a bit   far   significantly   a lot   slightly

B Other comparative expressions

1 To talk about people or things that are the same in some way we can use *as* + adjective or adverb + *as*.

*They're **just as silly as** each other.*

In negative sentences, which talk about differences, *so* can be used instead of the first *as*.

*She's **not so fit as** she used to be.*

2 *The... , the...*
The structure *the* + comparative is used to talk about things which occur together.

***The more** labour-saving devices they buy, **the harder** they need to work.*

 Read more about comparisons on pages 207 and 208 of the Grammar reference.

Practice

1 Match each sentence **1–6** with a sentence **a–f** which expresses a similar idea. The first one has been done for you.

1 She's far lazier than anyone else.   *c*
2 She works a lot less than she ought to.   ___
3 She's not quite as lazy as she used to be.   ___
4 She doesn't have as many problems as she used to.   ___
5 She's the least successful student in the class.   ___
6 The more she works, the more success she has.   ___

a She doesn't work nearly as much as she should.
b She has fewer difficulties than before.
c Everyone works much harder than her.
d She's more successful when she works harder.
e She's slightly more hardworking than before.
f No one does as badly as she does.

2 Using some of the comparative structures you have just studied, write eight sentences about yourself. Compare yourself with a friend or friends, a member of your family and/or yourself as you used to be.

3 Match each line of dialogue **1–6** with an appropriate response **a–f**. The first one has been done as an example.

1 That's the third time this week. It really needs repairing.   *d*
2 When would you like to discuss this?   ___
3 Where have you been? It's 10 o'clock!   ___
4 It doesn't hurt, but I'll make an appointment.   ___
5 It was overbooked? What happened then?   ___
6 Can I bring a friend?   ___

a Better late than never.
b It's better to be safe than sorry.
c The sooner the better.
d No sooner said than done.
e The more the merrier.
f Things went from bad to worse.

4 Complete the second sentence so that it has a similar meaning to the first sentence, using the word in **bold**.

1 The film wasn't nearly as good as I thought it would be. **far**
The film _____ I thought it would be.

2 She's happier than she used to be. **sad**
She isn't _____ was before.

3 I've never had such a boring time on holiday! **enjoyable**
This is _____ holiday I've ever had!

4 If you work harder now, you won't have to do so much later. **the**
The harder _____ you'll have to do later.

5 Kate has slightly more experience than the others. **quite**
The others don't have _____ Kate.

Word formation: Suffixes *-ful* and *-less*

Some adjectives can be formed by adding the suffixes *-ful* or *-less* to nouns or verbs.

USE *We've just bought a **useful** device for peeling oranges.*
*Most of the gadgets were completely **useless**.*

Sometimes only one of the suffixes may be used:

SLEEP *I've had a few **sleepless** nights, worrying about it.*
*I'm going to bed: I feel a little **sleepy**. (**not** sleepful)*

GRATITUDE *I'd be very **grateful** if you could help me.*
*She didn't even say 'thank you'! How **ungrateful**. (**not** grateless)*

1 Which of the suffixes *-ful* and *-less* can be used to form adjectives from the words in the box? If either of them cannot be used, is there an alternative?

success	skill	home	cheer	delight	thought
harm	pain	end	power	care	price

*Example: success → successful → unsuccessful (**not** successless)*

2 Look at the following adjectives formed from the word *taste*.

TASTE → *tasty, tasteful, tasteless*

In what way are *tasty* and *tasteful* different?
a a tastefully decorated room/a tasteless pink shirt
b very tasty food/a tasteless soup

Put the correct form of *help* in the sentences below. You may need to use an adjective or an adverb, in the positive or the negative.

1 I'm so pleased I spoke to him. He made several very _____ suggestions.
2 Her arms tied behind her back, she watched _____ as the thieves got away with all her priceless paintings.
3 The hotel was comfortable but the staff were so _____ . We won't be going back there again.

3 For questions **1–10** use the word given in capitals at the end of each line to form a word that fits in the space in the same line. You may need to form a noun, an adjective or an adverb.

1 The Prime Minister handled the situation extremely _____ and managed to avoid a scandal. **SKILL**
2 Before Hillary and Tensing reached the peak in 1953 there had been several _____ attempts to conquer Everest. **SUCCESS**
3 Road accidents are very often caused by drivers' _____ at the wheel. **CARE**
4 Thank you so much! That's very _____ of you. **THOUGHT**
5 Until my eldest brother went to university his life had been rather dull and _____ . **EVENT**
6 The school banned cigarettes from the premises and warned pupils of the _____ effects of smoking. **HARM**
7 Despite her initial concerns, she was reassured that the operation would be _____ . **PAIN**
8 One of her most positive and attractive qualities is her almost constant _____ . **CHEER**
9 He'll never change his mind. It's absolutely _____ trying to argue with him. **POINT**
10 The Government announced plans yesterday to tackle the problem of _____ . **HOME**

Multiple matching 👁 1.8–1.12

1 Read the following Listening Part 3 instructions.

You will hear five people talking about solar-powered gadgets, some of which are shown above. Match the speaker to the correct description in the list **A–F**. There is one extra letter which you do not need to use.

2 Before you do the listening task, look at the solar-powered gadgets **A–F** below and discuss the following questions.

What are the advantages and disadvantages of each of the solar-powered gadgets compared with the more conventional models?
Where might you expect to use each of them?

A a torch	Speaker 1 ☐
B a radio	Speaker 2 ☐
C a digital video camera	Speaker 3 ☐
D path lights	Speaker 4 ☐
E an oven	Speaker 5 ☐
F a refrigerator	

Noticing language

1 Look at the following sentences from the listening. Can you suggest alternative words or expressions in English for the underlined parts? How would you express them in your own language?

1 *They come on <u>as soon as</u> it gets dark.* (Speaker 1)
2 *It'll charge itself in a couple of hours – <u>as long as</u> it's sunny, of course!* (Speaker 2)
3 *<u>As well as</u> a handle to wind it up, it comes equipped with a solar panel.* (Speaker 4)
4 *Cost an arm and a leg, mind you, but <u>as far as I'm concerned</u> it was worth every penny.* (Speaker 5)

2 Complete the following sentences using words from the box.

far long much many soon well

1 You can go out, as _____ as you do your homework first.
2 As _____ as he got home he got changed and went back out again.
3 There are plenty of biscuits. Eat as _____ as you want.
4 As _____ as being an excellent sportswoman, she's a brilliant scientist.
5 'Are Claire and Mario still going out with each other?'
  'As _____ as I know they are, yes.'
6 That exam was really difficult. I did as _____ as I could and left the rest blank.

Speaking 1:
FCE Part 3

Collaborative task

Your class has been doing a project on developments over the last 100 years and you have been asked to write an article. Talk with your partner about some of the changes that have taken place in each of the areas shown in the photos and then decide which theme you will write your article on.

> ● What changes have taken place in each of the areas?
> ● Which theme will you write your article on?

Education

Communication

Travel and transport

Free time

How to go about it

What to say
● The instructions tell you to talk about *each* of the areas. Don't just talk about your favourite!
● The pictures are there to help you, but you can also think of other ideas related to each theme.
    Example: Education:
    Discipline, number of children attending school and university, school leaving age, equipment etc.
● You could discuss whether you think each of the changes has been for the better or for the worse. In some cases you may feel there haven't been any changes!

How to say it
● In the Speaking Test the examiners will give you marks for using a range of structures. Answer the following questions:
    a Which language area can you use to talk about regular past actions or situations?
    b Which language area is useful for expressing present habitual behaviour?
    c Why is the present perfect used in the following sentence?
    There <u>have been</u> a lot of changes in education over the last 100 years.
    d Which language areas can you use to talk about the differences between the past and the present?

Speaking 2:
FCE Part 4

Further discussion

In Part 4 of the Speaking Test the examiner will ask you questions which are related to the topic in Part 3.

How to go about it

- Answer the questions fully, giving reasons for your opinions.
- You can also talk to your partner, as well as the examiner, during this part.

- Try to keep the conversation going as much as possible. You can ask your partner questions to achieve this:
  What do you think about that?
  Do you agree with me on that?

Discuss the following questions, which are related to Part 3 on page 32, and try to keep the conversation going as much as possible.

- What other changes have there been in the last 100 years?
- Do you think the quality of life in general is better now than it used to be?
- Can computers ever replace teachers?
- Do you agree that there are too many cars?
- In what ways has life changed for you in the last few years?
- What do you think will be the biggest changes in the next 100 years?

Language focus 2: Articles

1 Read the text entitled 'The home computer', ignoring the spaces for the moment, and answer the following questions.

What is the attitude of these people to the educational value of computers?

a parents
b the government
c some educationalists

What are *your* views?

2 Now read the text again and complete each of the gaps with *a*, *an* or *the*, or leave it blank. There is an example at the beginning (0).

3 Read the main rules for the use of articles on page 208 of the Grammar reference. Then use them to give reasons for each of the answers in exercise 2.

Example: 0 *a singular noun is being mentioned for the first time*

The home computer

Many parents believe that having (0) __*a*__ home computer is an investment in (1) _____ future of their children and they often pay more than (2) _____ thousand pounds for a product they do not fully understand.

According to (3) _____ recent survey, over two thirds of parents firmly believe in (4) _____ educational importance of (5) _____ personal computers. But as the pressure on parents to buy (6) _____ extremely sophisticated and expensive equipment increases, (7) _____ concern is growing in (8) _____ Britain over the real educational value of (9) _____ computer.

(10) _____ concern comes as schools are being encouraged by private industry to invest in (11) _____ latest technology. (12) _____ Government also intends to make (13) _____ access to computers easier in schools as (14) _____ best way to win what it calls the 'Knowledge Race' against other nations.

However, according to some educationalists, parents who think of (15) _____ computer as some form of home tutor could be heading for (16) _____ trouble. Dr George Hadley, who is (17) _____ lecturer in educational computing at (18) _____ Oxford University, stresses that (19) _____ educational software can never completely replace (20) _____ teachers.

Listening 2:
FCE Part 4

Multiple Choice 1.13

1 Look at the photographs, newspaper headlines and dictionary definition.
What different uses for robots can you think of?

Hospital takes delivery of robot

Company reveals robot with 'sense of smell and taste'

robot / ˈrəʊbɒt / noun [C]:
a a machine that can do work by itself, often work that humans do
b a machine that looks and talks like a human, and can do many of the things humans do

Robot dog – the perfect companion

2 You will hear an interview with a robot scientist.
For questions **1–7**, choose the best answer (**A, B** or **C**).

1 What does Keith say about his company's latest project?
  A He does not want to talk about it.
  B He is not allowed to talk about it.
  C He does not know much about it.

2 How does Keith describe his work?
  A monotonous
  B tiring
  C varied

3 One reason for equipping robots with emotions is
  A to provide them with motivation.
  B to help them understand their owners.
  C to make them feel useful.

4 What does Keith say about robots in films?
  A They are not always shown in a positive light.
  B They often have a good sense of humour.
  C They are not particularly well designed.

5 Keith expresses concern that robots might cause us
  A to do less physical exercise.
  B to become less intelligent.
  C to think less for ourselves.

6 Keith says that progress in the robotics industry
  A has been as fast as that of computers.
  B has been slower than predicted.
  C has been constant over the last century.

7 What does Keith say about humanoid robots?
  A They are unable to perform many tasks.
  B Many people consider them to be a toy.
  C People are getting used to seeing them.

Don't forget!
- You will hear distractors. Listen carefully to the recording both times.

 Do you think that robots will one day be as common in homes as computers? Why/ Why not?

Writing:
FCE Part 2

Essays

1 Read the following Writing Part 2 instructions.

Your class has been discussing the role of technology in today's society. For homework your teacher has asked you to write an essay, giving your opinions on the following statement.

The mobile phone has made a positive contribution to our lives today.

Write your **essay**. You should write **120–180** words.

Mobile phones are no longer a luxury item and they clearly have many advantages for those who use them. However, there are also some drawbacks.

On the positive side, they enable us to communicate with other people wherever they may be and at any time of the day. Teenagers who need help can contact their parents immediately and emergency services can be called to the scene of an accident without delay. Another advantage is that many models now have more than one function and can be used as cameras, MP3 players or even computers.

On the negative side, the mobile phone is thought to be a serious threat to health, particularly in the case of children. Moreover, drivers who use one at the wheel constitute a danger to others and fatal accidents have occurred. Finally, what for many people is a useful device, for others is a nuisance and they object to the constant ringing tones in public places.

In conclusion, mobile phones have certainly improved many people's lives, but we need to be careful about when and where we use them.

2 Read the model answer to the instructions above. What is the *purpose* of each of the four paragraphs?

Example: Paragraph 1 – *a general introduction*

3 **a** The underlined words and expressions in the model can be grouped in the following way:

Expressing contrasts	Adding information	Concluding
On the positive side	Another advantage is	In conclusion
On the negative side	Moreover	
	Finally	

b Add the following alternative linking devices to the appropriate group in exercise **a**.

In addition (to this)	On the one hand	What is more
On the other hand	Besides this	Furthermore
Some people feel that	On balance	Others argue that
Another disadvantage is	To sum up	

The following linkers can also be used to organize ideas.

First of all.../ To begin with...   Secondly...   Finally...

4 Examiners look for evidence of a good range of structures and vocabulary. Which words has the writer of the model answer used to avoid repeating 'mobile phones'?

5 Read the following Writing Part 2 instructions and the advice in the How to go about it box.

Your class has been discussing the role of technology in today's society. For homework your teacher has asked you to write an essay, giving your opinions on the following statement:

The computer has greatly improved our lives today.

How to go about it

- Read the question carefully. Irrelevant answers lose marks.
- List the positive and negative aspects of computers.
- Select some points from the list for the body of your composition. Note down any supporting reasons and examples.
- Organize your ideas and opinions using:
  a some of the linking devices you saw above
  b paragraphs: 4 is the usual number (introduction, points for the statement, points against the statement, conclusion)

- Check your work for grammar, vocabulary, spelling and punctuation errors. In addition, answer the following questions:
  Have you written a relevant answer to the question?
  Is the style appropriate?
  Is your work the correct length?
  Have you organized your ideas into logical paragraphs?
  Is there a good range of language or are words and expressions repeated?

Now you are ready to write your **essay** in **120–180** words.

③ Review

Vocabulary: Word partnerships

1 Write a noun in each of the gaps below to complete the word partnerships. Try to do the exercise without looking at the nouns, which are given in the box below.

1 takeaway _____
2 an electric carving _____
3 a microwave _____
4 a washing _____
5 an electric pencil _____
6 a clothes _____
7 a remote _____
8 a labour-saving _____
9 a domestic _____
10 a disposable _____

device	machine	appliance	knife	control
oven	food	toothbrush	sharpener	steamer

2 Write down:

a three more adjectives to go with the noun *device*.
b three more adjectives to go with the noun *food*.
c three more nouns for objects which are *disposable*.
d three more devices or appliances which are not mentioned in exercise 1.

Comparisons

1 Match each sentence beginning **1–8** with a suitable ending **a–h**. The first one has been done for you.

① They can stay⎯⎯⎯ **a** as soon as we heard.
2 I did it   **b** as soon as you can.
3 We came   **c** as long as she pays.
4 Let me know   **d** as long as they like.
5 She isn't here   **e** as well as I could.
6 She can come   **f** as well as a handbag.
7 A purse   **g** as far as the coast.
8 You can see   **h** as far as I know.

2 Write a four-line dialogue. The first or last line of the dialogue must be one of the sentences from exercise 1.

3 Complete the following sentences in an appropriate way.

1 The more I study, _____ .
2 The older I get, _____ .
3 The less chocolate he eats, _____ .
4 The more quickly I do my homework, _____ .
5 The more it rains, _____ .
6 The hotter it gets, _____ .

4 Write two sentences making comparisons for each of the following. Try to use a variety of structures.

two actresses	two films	two countries	two types of pet
two sports	two (pop) groups or singers		

Articles

1 Read the following text quite quickly. To what extent do you share the writer's views?

1 I am͡ₐ self-confessed technophobe. I have come to hate technology and the way it
2 dominates every aspect of ~~the~~ life. One of the worst offenders is the computer,
3 which for many has become the most important object both in home and the
4 workplace, where they spend the more time staring at a screen than interacting
5 with the people around them. Computers have killed an art of conversation.
6 Sure, they can be used to write the emails and 'chat' to friends – or even to total
7 strangers – but isn't it ironic that the more we communicate, less communicative
8 we seem to become? Equally irritating is mobile phone, or 'cell phone', as it is
9 also known, perhaps because the people who use one should be put in the
10 prison cell for doing so. They shout into them on train or send pointless text
11 messages to one another. I once sat in a bar and watched young couple text each
12 other from opposite sides of the same table. But it's not just young who are
13 addicted to these toys: the high percentage of over-60s have joined in the 'fun'.
14 Indeed, the older you are, the louder you have to shout into the your phone – or
15 so it seems, anyway. But maybe I'm a one with the problem, maybe I should
16 just get myself a laptop and a mobile, go away to mountains and then contact my
   friends and family from there. I might get to talk to them more that way.

2 Each numbered line in the text has one mistake in the use of articles. You may have to **add, change** or **delete** an article. The first two have been done for you.

Word formation

Read the following text about the benefits of email. Use the word given in capitals at the end of some of the lines to form a word that fits in the gap in the same line. There is an example at the beginning (**0**).

Don't forget!

- You may need to write a word in a negative form or in the plural. The meaning of the text before and after the spaces will help you make the correct decisions.
- Read the whole text through once before writing your answers. Approximately how old do you think the writer is?

An email fan

I think the computer is such a **(0)** ___useful___ invention. Take email, for	**USE**
example. It's such an easy and **(1)**_____ way to write letters. When	**PAIN**
I was younger, I rarely ever put pen to paper, not even to say 'thank you'	
for presents sent by **(2)**_____ relatives. They must have thought I	**THOUGHT**
was so **(3)**_____. Now, though, you can't keep me away from the	**GRATITUDE**
keyboard. I can **(4)**_____ spend hours typing away on my computer,	**CHEER**
all types of messages to all types of people.	
One of the worst **(5)**_____ for me of writing by hand was always the	**ADVANTAGE**
(6)_____ of knowing that people would be able to see and criticize my	**EMBARRASS**
untidy handwriting and **(7)**_____ spelling. Now, of course, thanks to the	**CARE**
spellcheck, I can edit what I've written quickly and **(8)**_____ before I	**EFFORT**
send it off. I just can't get over how **(9)**_____ fast everything is.	**WONDER**
Teenagers nowadays take all this for granted, but when I was their age, none	
of this existed. Young people don't realize how **(10)** _____ they are.	**FORTUNE**

Introduction

In Paper 1 you have one hour to answer questions on three texts. Understanding of each of the three texts is tested in a different way with a different type of task each time.

Part 1: Multiple choice

1 Part 1 consists of a text followed by eight multiple-choice questions. Sometimes, the last question tests your general understanding of the text. Read through the article on page 39 and choose the best answer, **A, B, C** or **D,** for question 8.

2 In all parts of the reading paper there will inevitably be words you do not know the meaning of. On many occasions it is not essential for you to understand these words in order to complete the task, and you can ignore them. If necessary, though, you may be able to use the context in which the word appears to help you work out the meaning.

Find the words below in the text, and then use the context and the clues below to work out the approximate meaning of each one. The number in brackets refers to the line in which the word appears.

(1)	pump (verb)	*What does your heart do all the time you are alive?*
(7)	intake (noun)	*This word is composed of two parts: what are they?* *What does the rest of the paragraph talk about in relation to water?*
(12)	raging (adjective)	*What type of thirst do you develop in high temperatures if you wait for a long time before you have a drink?*
(13)	swig (noun)	*Look at the advice given in the first half of this sentence. What type of action, therefore, is 'to take a swig' of water?*
(15)	palatable (adjective)	*What do you improve by adding fruit juice to water?*

3 Use context to work out the meanings of the words in italics in the second column. These words will help when you answer questions **4, 5** & **7**.

4 Now for questions **1–8**, choose the answer which you think fits best according to the answer.

A walk in the midday sun
When the heat is on, walkers need to be on their guard.

Hot weather makes your heart pump harder, and if you're not very fit, you start to understand why the majority of mountain rescue statistics are made up from summer walkers suffering heart attacks. Heat exhaustion is quite easy to get when
5 you're making a great physical effort. It happens where your body can't produce enough sweat to keep you cool.

The answer is to keep up your water intake. It's a good idea to drink a pint of water for every 10 degrees Fahrenheit every 24 hours. So, if the temperature is in the 70s, and you are
10 doing a five-hour walk, you'll need a minimum of around one and a half pints of water. It's vital that you don't wait until you develop a raging thirst before you stop for a drink – keep taking regular swigs from your water bottle.

Many walkers flavour their water with fruit juice, which makes
15 it a lot more palatable. You could even use one of the isotonic drinks made for athletes, which replace the body's salts lost through sweating. Powders such as Dioralyte, which you may have in the house as a treatment for diarrhoea, will do the job just as well, as its main aim is also effective rehydration.

20 Given that evaporation is your body's cooling mechanism, you can help things along with an external application of water. Soaking your hat with water is a great way to cool the head, though if the sun is beating down, **it** will probably dry off almost immediately. Better still then if you can plunge into a
25 river or the sea fully-clothed. And if that's not possible, then at least take off your boots and socks and paddle in a cool stream.

Walking in the heat increases the rate at which your feet *swell*, which can lead to them feeling tight in your boots. Cool water from a stream reduces any swelling and helps general
30 foot comfort. At the same time, you can check out your feet for signs of *blisters*. Extra sweating makes the skin softer and increases the chance of blisters forming, in the same way as when water *leaks* into your boots and gets to your feet.

As for what clothing you wear, this should be lightweight and
35 reasonably loose-fitting. Tight clothing will feel uncomfortable and may even lead to the formation of an irritating *rash* known as 'prickly heat' on your skin. The answer, if this does develop, is to try and stay cool as much as possible. Do this by either keeping in the shade, or washing the affected area
40 with cold water, but without soap. But prevention is by far the best approach, so keep your clothing light.

It's understandable to want to remove any extraneous clothing when it's extremely hot, but it doesn't really make much sense to take off T-shirts. The sun's rays can be quite strong,
45 and shoulders are always very sensitive to sunburn. This is the worst place to be red and sore when you are wearing a heavy rucksack on your back. Wearing shorts can also create problems for walkers, as the backs of the legs can catch the sun very easily.

50 In fact, those days when an apparently harmless *breeze* is blowing can be the most *deceptive*. It might not feel so hot, so you probably won't notice the damage being done so soon. As on every other day then, a good strong sun cream should therefore be applied to any skin which is exposed. Make the most of the
55 summer, but treat the sun with the respect it deserves.

1 The writer says that hot weather
A is the main cause of heart attacks.
B requires walkers to have frequent drinks.
C is the worst type of weather for mountain walking.
D ensures that mountain walkers stay fit.

2 What does the writer say about 'Dioralyte'?
A It helps to reduce sweating.
B It prevents the loss of body salts.
C It will prevent you getting diarrhoea.
D It works in the same way as an isotonic drink.

3 'it' in line 23 refers to
A the sun.
B your hat.
C the head.
D water.

4 According to the text, when might your feet suffer?
A when they cool down
B if you are wearing tightly-fitting boots
C when they are wet
D if you have to walk through water

5 According to the writer, it is better to wear loose-fitting clothing because
A it keeps you cool.
B it is very light.
C it is less likely to create problems for your skin.
D it lasts longer than tight-fitting clothing.

6 What does the writer mean by 'extraneous' clothing in line 42?
A clothing which is no longer needed to keep you warm
B clothing which most people would consider unusual in hot weather
C clothing which is too tight
D clothing which is too heavy to wear

7 According to the writer, when are walkers particularly at risk from the effects of the sun?
A when they are unaware of the heat
B if their sun cream is not strong enough
C when there is a strong wind
D if they have suffered an injury

8 Who has the text been written for?
A people who go walking in the mountains
B walkers who are unfit
C people who go walking in hot weather
D people who only go walking in summer

Part 2: Gapped text

1   Part 2 consists of a text from which paragraphs or sentences have been removed and placed in a different order after the text. You have to decide which part of the text the paragraphs or sentences have been removed from. This part of the Reading Paper tests your understanding of the way texts are structured, so look carefully at the language both before and after each gap.

2   Read the headline for the following newspaper article and predict what the text is about. Then read through the text (ignoring the questions in blue) and check your predictions.

3   Students who do well in Part 2 also try to predict the general content of each gap before making their choices.

Use the questions after each gap as well as the underlined language to help you predict the sentences which have been removed from the gaps. Write your predictions for each gap on a separate piece of paper. No help is given for gaps 5 and 6.

Internet ends 38-year search

A woman who spent 38 years searching for her brother traced him during a free 90-minute lesson on how to use the Internet. [1] *The next sentence begins 'After that'. What moment or incident do you think is mentioned in this gap? The next sentence talks about both 'he' and 'she'. Look through the rest of the text and find the full names of these two people: these names will probably be mentioned in this gap.*

After that he moved repeatedly round the world, while she married and settled in the North East. [2] *Look ahead to the next sentence. Who will be the subject in this gap; the woman or her brother? What did she do in this gap to make her become desperate?*

In desperation she called into a branch of Age Concern near her home in Gateshead and asked for help on their computer.

[3] *The previous sentence to this gap tells us she looked for her brother on a computer. Now look at the next sentence. Which part of the world did she start looking in? Was she immediately successful?*

It was only when the search was extended to include the rest of the United States that Eileen finally located a P. Rider living in Largo, Florida. [4] *What did Eileen do in this gap? The next sentence will help you. What does the word 'Finally' tell us?*

Finally, a woman, who turned out to be her brother Percival's wife, picked up the phone in Florida. [5] The following week Mrs Stevens flew to Florida, to be reunited with her brother and meet her sister-in-law for the first time. [6] But thankfully we are back in touch again, thanks to a simple computer lesson.'

4   Turn to page 200 and read the sentences which were removed. Try to match each of the sentences to your own. There is one extra sentence which you do not need to use. Always check that the extra sentence which you have not used does not fit anywhere in the text.

Part 3: Multiple matching

1   Part 3 consists of either one continuous text divided into sections, or a number of smaller texts. Fifteen questions are placed before the text or texts. You have seen an example of a Part 3 task in Unit 2. For this part of the reading paper you are asked to find specific information in the text or texts.

2   Read the following Part 3 instructions.

Read this article about different study websites. For questions **1–15**, choose from the websites (**A–F**). The websites may be chosen more than once. When more than one answer is required, these may be given in any order.

What to expect in the exam

Questions in Part 3 carry one mark. In Parts 1 & 2 they carry two marks.

How to go about it

- Read through the situations **1–15** first, to see the kind of information you need.
- Read each of the texts, looking for information which is relevant to each situation.
  The situations for text A have been given. For each of these situations, underline and label the relevant section of the text, as in the example for number 4. Then do the same for texts B–F.
- If there are any situations you have not matched, scan the texts again looking for the information you need.

Which of the websites would you consult in the following situations?

You want to check the exact meaning of the verb 'to swell'.   `1` ☐ `2` ☐

You are curious to see what problems other students have had.   `3` ☐

You need some advice on how to prepare for your exams.   `4` `A` `5` ☐

You are going to Australia to study English and you need to know the exchange rate for the Australian dollar.   `6` ☐

You want to receive some personal attention from someone.   `7` ☐ `8` ☐ `9` ☐

You are 16 and your cousin is 13: you both need information about chemistry which is appropriate to your level.   `10` `A` `11` ☐

You want to consult a site which is not too serious.   `12` ☐

You do not want to waste time looking at sites which turn out to be irrelevant to you.   `13` `A`

For geography homework you have been told to find out the capitals of all the countries in south-east Asia.   `14` ☐

You are interested to see what the person answering your questions looks like.   `15` ☐

Exploring the Web: Education

Emma Houghton looks at several useful websites for students who need information fast. The sites offer links to other websites, search engines and the increasingly popular ask-the-expert sites.

A Topmarks   **www.topmarks.co.uk**

An excellent UK site offering links to sites across all subjects, including astronomy, classics, design technology, economics, personal and social education, physical education and religious studies. You can select under subject and age group, and each link has a five-line description so you know exactly where you are going. <u>There is a particularly good section on exam help, with lots of links to help revise different subjects</u>, while the parents' area has a number of useful articles. ④

B Homework Elephant   **www.homeworkelephant.co.uk**

A UK service with 700 links to some of the best educational sites on the Web, as well as other resources like dictionaries and search engines. You'll also find revision tips for each subject, and a section pointing towards relevant online experts, who may be able to give you more individual help. If you're still stuck, consult the Agony Elephant, which will point you in the right direction. Not to be missed.

C StudyWeb   **www.studyweb.com**

Over 118,000 links across subjects as diverse as agriculture, philosophy, architecture, criminology and medicine, as well as all the usual curriculum subjects. Each link has a US school grade to indicate its approximate age level, while the Study Buddy offers a wide range of online useful extras, including a calculator and currency converter.

D Kid Info School Subjects   **www.kidinfo.com**

An easy-to-use site offering links across the full range of subjects, as well as calendars, dictionaries, quotations, atlases, encyclopedias and museums.

E Pitsco's Ask an Expert   **www.askanexpert.com**

Can connect you to hundreds of real live experts, from astronomers to zoologists and plenty in between. You can browse via category or keyword search to find the most likely candidate, then visit their website to see if your answer is already there; if not, stick it in an email, press send, and wait for your reply. In the Arts/Humanities section, for example, there is a fine art expert, an artist, a classical musician, a composer and even a piano teacher.

F Ask Dr Universe   **www.wsu.edu/DrUniverse/**

A good-looking and appealingly light-hearted site which lets you pose questions to researchers at Washington State University, then follow them up by email if you want to explore further. You can also look up archives of former questions, which are usually accompanied by photos of the answering academic.

4 A good story

Vocabulary 1: Films

1   Look at these film posters. Do you know any of these films? What type of film is each one? Choose from the words in the box.

> thriller   horror film   comedy   romance   historical drama
> science fiction film   action film   western

2   For exercises **A** and **B**, decide which word best fits each space.

A   *terrible   terrific   terrifying*

1 It was a _____ performance, for which he deserves to win an Oscar.
2 Absolutely _____ ! I 've never been so frightened in all my life.
3 This was probably the worst film I've seen all year. The plot was non-existent and
  the acting was _____ .

B   *review   criticism   critic*

It seems that every **(1)** _____ I read of this film gives a different opinion. For example, the **(2)** _____ who writes for *The Times* is very enthusiastic about it and has nothing but praise for George Lucas. The same director, however, comes under strong **(3)** _____ in the magazine *Premiere*.

3 Read the following review of 'The Matrix', which appeared in a student magazine. Does this type of film appeal to you?

THE MATRIX

'The Matrix' is one of the most entertaining science fiction films I have seen. It combines frenetic action with terrific <u>special effects</u>, and <u>stars</u> Keanu Reeves as Neo, and Laurence Fishburne in the <u>role</u> of Morpheus.

The film is <u>set</u> in the future, in a world controlled by machines. In order to hide this reality from humans, the machines have constructed the Matrix, a vast virtual reality system resembling Earth at the end of the twentieth century. The <u>plot</u>, which focuses on a revolt led by Morpheus against the Matrix, is complicated and at times confusing. However, the <u>cast</u> is very strong and the film features a surprisingly competent <u>performance</u> from Keanu Reeves.

As for the visual elements, the special effects are stunning, with the <u>main characters</u> walking on walls and avoiding machine gun bullets. The action <u>scenes</u>, which include a wide variety of kung fu techniques, are convincingly choreographed.

I would recommend the film to anyone who likes science fiction. If you ignore the complexities of the plot and just enjoy the action, you will not feel disappointed.

4 Complete each gap **1–8** using the underlined words from the review of 'The Matrix'. Do not change the words in any way. There is an example at the beginning (0).

0 Some of the ___*scenes*___ in *Casablanca* are memorable, particularly when Humphrey Bogart and Ingrid Bergman say goodbye at the end of the film.
1 *The Remains of the Day* is _____ in England in the 1930s.
2 The film has an international _____ , with French, Polish and Italian actors.
3 One of my least favourite films is *Notting Hill*, which _____ Julia Roberts as a world-famous film actress.
4 I found Hugh Grant irritating in the _____ of a nervous bookseller who has an unlikely romance with the film star.
5 This was not Kevin Costner's most convincing acting _____ .
6 The _____ is straightforward and easy to follow.
7 The _____ were well portrayed by Antonio Banderas and Anthony Hopkins, but some of the supporting roles were rather disappointing.
8 SFX is the abbreviation for _____ .

5 Talk about the following using some of the vocabulary in exercises 1–4.
- a film you didn't enjoy
- your favourite film
- the most frightening film you have ever seen
- the most exciting film you have ever seen

Language focus 1: *So* and *such*

Look at these two sentences.

*I was **so** impressed with the soundtrack of the film that I went out and bought the CD the next day.*
*She has **such** a wonderful voice that it seems a shame to dub her films into English.*

Why are *so* and *such* used in each of these sentences? What types of words follow *so* and *such*?

Check your ideas in the Grammar reference on page 209.

Practice
For Questions 1–4 complete the second sentence so that it has a similar meaning to the first sentence, using the word given. **Do not change the word given.** You must use between **two** and **five** words, including the word given.

1 We decided to see the film because it got such good reviews.
that
The reviews for the film _____ we decided to see it.
2 The weather was so bad that we decided to come home.
such
It _____ that we decided to come home.
3 I got so bored during the film I fell asleep.
such
It _____ film I fell asleep.
4 The party was so crowded we could hardly move.
so
There _____ people at the party we could hardly move.

Word formation: Adjectives ending in *-ing* and *-ed*

To describe how we feel about something or someone we can use past participles as adjectives.

*I got really **frightened** when I saw the main character being killed.*

To describe the thing or person that produces the feeling we can use present participles as adjectives.

*It was an extremely **frightening** scene.*

Adverbs can be formed from present participle adjectives.

*Not **surprisingly**, we were disappointed that we couldn't get tickets to see the film.*

1 Look back at the review of 'The Matrix' and find examples of adjectives and adverbs formed with *-ing* and *-ed*. Note that not all the words ending in *-ing* and *-ed* in the text are adjectives.

2 Put the past participle of each of the following regular verbs in the appropriate group, according to how the *-ed* ending is pronounced.

annoy	frustrate	tire	disappoint	disgust	astonish	
amuse	fascinate	bore	impress	frighten	relax	terrify

/d/	/t/	/id/
surprised	*embarrassed*	*excited*

3 The present participle (*-ing*) form of the verbs in exercise 1 can all be used as adjectives, except in the case of one of the verbs. Which one is it and how is the adjective formed?

4 Complete each gap with the present or past participle form of an appropriate verb from exercise 2. You may need to use an adverb.

1 Teachers need long holidays. They do a very _____ job.
2 I'm sorry, but I'm just not _____ . I don't find it at all funny.
3 I wish you'd stop whistling. It's extremely _____ !
4 My mark in the exam was _____ low. I thought I had done much better.
5 I find the whole subject of genetic engineering extremely _____ . I really would like to read more about it.
6 I'm not eating that – it smells _____ ! What is it?
7 _____ , she was still alive after spending 20 days buried under a building which had collapsed in the earthquake.

Writing 1:
FCE Part 2

Reviews

Your teacher has asked you to write about a film you have seen recently on DVD for the school's English magazine. Write a review for the magazine, giving your opinions on the film and saying whether you would recommend it.

How to go about it

Here is a paragraph plan for your review. However, the paragraph summaries are not in the correct order. Look again at the review of 'The Matrix' and put them in order.

   a A brief summary of the plot and comments on the acting, with opinions.
   b Recommendations with reasons.
   c A general opinion of the film, together with some factual details *eg type of film, actors/actresses, director.*
   d Other aspects of the film together with opinions.

● Decide on the film you are going to review and make notes for each of your four paragraphs, using the above plan as a guide.

● Include relevant film vocabulary as well as some participle adjectives to express your opinion.

● Work with a partner and tell each other about your films, following the notes you have made. Have you each included a balance of information and opinions?

Now you are ready to write your **review** in **120–180** words.

Talking about photos

Student A   The following two photographs show different types of entertainment. Compare these photographs and say why people enjoy activities like these.

Student B   When Student A has finished, say whether you enjoy these forms of entertainment.

Don't forget!

Student A
- Compare the photos. Do not describe them in detail.

Student B
- Your comment should be brief but you do have time to give reasons for your feelings or opinions.

> Why do people enjoy activities like these?

Now change roles.

Student A   The following two photographs show different types of cinemas. Compare these photographs and say what the advantages and disadvantages are of watching films in cinemas like these.

Student B   When student A has finished, say in which of the places you would prefer to see a film.

> What are the advantages and disadvantages of watching films in cinemas like these?

Preparing for listening: Focus on distractors

1 Match each sentence beginning **1–5** with an appropriate ending **a–e**.

① My brother was so scared he couldn't watch the film

2 **Although** most critics agreed that the film was her best ever

3 **Although** snow is now unlikely

4 My daughter wanted me to help her with her homework

5 **Whereas** in most of his other films he plays the 'baddie'

a we can expect a certain amount of rain later on.

b in this one he's definitely the good guy.

c **whereas** I didn't find it at all frightening.

d I was rather disappointed by her performance.

e **but** I told her to ask her mother.

2 Now decide on the correct alternative in each of the following interpretations of the sentences in exercise 1. Give reasons for your answers.

The speaker in sentence…

1 **A** was frightened by the film.   **B** was not frightened by the film.

2 **A** loved the actress's performance.   **B** was not enthusiastic about the actress's performance

3 **A** says it will probably rain.   **B** says it will probably snow.

4 **A** helped his daughter.   **B** didn't help his daughter.

5 **A** says the actor is the villain.   **B** says the actor is the hero in the film.

The incorrect answers in exercise 2 are typical of the distractors you might find in a Part 1 Listening task. The ideas in them are similar to the information in exercise 1 but not the same. Note the use of contrast linkers, written in **bold**.

Listening:

FCE Part 1

Multiple choice ◉ 1.14–1.21

You will hear people talking in eight different situations. For questions **1–8**, choose the best answer, **A**, **B** or **C**.

Don't forget!

In this Part 1 exercise you will hear distractors of the type you met in the Preparing for listening section.

1 Listen to this woman talking about an actor. What is her opinion of him?

   A He is handsome.

   B He is fashionable.

   C He is rude.

2 You overhear this conversation between two friends. What type of film are they going to see?

   A an historical drama

   B a romance

   C a thriller

3 You hear a conversation in a video hire shop. How long has the customer had the video for?

   A one day

   B two days

   C three days

4 You hear an actress talking about her performance in a play. How does she feel?

   A tired

   B disappointed

   C excited

5 You overhear this man talking on the telephone. Who is he talking to?

   A an old school friend

   B a work colleague

   C a relative

6 You hear a young woman talking to her friend about a film. Why didn't she like it?

   A It was too slow.

   B There was too much violence.

   C It was very predictable.

7 You hear a woman telephoning a bookshop. What is she doing?

   A making a complaint

   B making a suggestion

   C apologizing

8 You hear this young man talking on the phone. What does he have in common with his girlfriend?

   A They were born under the same star sign.

   B They share the same taste in music.

   C They have the same sense of humour.

Vocabulary 2: *Take*

A Phrasal verbs with *take*

Like *get*, which you saw in Unit 1, *take* can be used in many different phrasal verbs and expressions.

1 What is the meaning of this phrasal verb from the listening?

*I **took** [the video] **out** on Saturday.*

2 Read the following short story and give it a title.

I a) take after my father in many ways, particularly in my love of good food and a tendency to eat more than I need to. However, several years ago the situation had reached crisis point – my clothes no longer fitted me – so I decided to b) take up some form of sport. Karate seemed like a good idea, so I signed up for a course at the local sports centre.

I c) took to it immediately and by the end of the first class I was hooked. Over the next four years I progressed through the different levels until two years ago I achieved my ambition and qualified as an instructor. And now the same sports centre where I started all those years ago has just d) taken me on as a full-time karate teacher. What's more, they

needed someone to e) take over from the man who was my very first teacher and who has left to set up his own gym. I am certainly very grateful to him!
Now, what with training, competitions and the classes themselves, karate has become my life and f) takes up all my time. I still manage to go out for a good meal now and again though!

3 Match each of the underlined phrasal verbs in exercise 2 to one of the meanings in the box below. Use the context of the story to help you.

| employ | start doing | resemble | occupy | start to like | replace |

B Expressions with *take*

1 Complete each gap **1–8** with an appropriate form of the verb *take*.

A 1 My dad used to _____ me to school, but now I have to get the bus.
   2 A pair of shoes should last longer than two months. If I were you, I _____ them back to the shop.

B 3 I lost money on that business deal! Of course I regret _____ his advice!
   4 She criticizes everybody else and refuses _____ any of the blame herself.

C 5 If you _____ more interest in the children, they'd probably respond better!
   6 The stray cat was looking a lot healthier. It was clear that someone _____ pity on it and given it something to eat.

D 7 Street luge _____ a great deal of courage. You wouldn't catch me doing it!
   8 Come on! I can't understand why you _____ so long to do this exercise.

2 In each of the sentences in exercise 1, identify the expression with *take* and underline it.
Example: *Who is taking care of the children tonight while you're at the party?*

3 The expressions in exercise 1 are organized into four groups, **A**, **B**, **C** and **D**. Match each of the following general meanings for *take* to an appropriate group.

   1 to express what is needed or required
   2 to talk about the movement of something or someone from one place to another
   3 to talk about the way people feel or react to others
   4 to accept

4 Which group in exercise 1 do the following expressions belong to?

to take pride in something   *to be taken to hospital*
to take a joke   *to take the infinitive*

5 Now write a short story of your own using at least three expressions and three phrasal verbs with *take*.

Review

Transformations

For questions **1–10** complete the second sentence so that it has a similar meaning to the first sentence, using the word given. **Do not change the word given**. You must use between two and five words, including the word given.

1 When the meeting was over, they went out for a drink.
had
As _____ finished, they went out for a drink.

2 When we eventually arrived at the party, all the food had been eaten.
got
By _____ the party, all the food had been eaten.

3 Immediately after he went, we started to relax.
once
We started to relax _____ gone.

4 He put everything back in its place before he left.
until
He didn't _____ everything back in its place.

5 I liked him the first time I met him.
took
I _____ the first time I saw him.

6 They decided against employing him because of his age.
take
They decided _____ because of his age.

7 She is proud of her achievements.
pride
She _____ her achievements.

8 She isn't very interested in my work.
in
She doesn't _____ my work.

9 His exam mark was such a disappointment.
so
He _____ with his exam mark.

10 I was so tired after that walk.
such
It _____ walk.

Correcting mistakes

In each short text **1–5**, there are two words which should not be there. Find these words and cross them out. The first one has been done for you.

1 At first we weren't sure whether we could afford to go on holiday, but in the end we ~~had~~ felt we ought to spend at least ~~during~~ a week on the coast.

2 I was extremely impressed with the special effects and some part of the action scenes. As for as the acting, though, I felt many amateurs could have done better.

3 After that the invigilators had taken in our answers to the reading exam, they handed out of Paper 2, the Writing test.

4 When he had came home from work he was made himself a cup of tea and read the newspaper. It had been an exhausting day.

5 I'm so pleased we took to your advice and went to the new Indian restaurant that's just opened. The service was marvellous and it was such a good food.

Review

Transformations

For questions **1–10** complete the second sentence so that it has a similar meaning to the first sentence, using the word given. **Do not change the word given**. You must use between two and five words, including the word given.

1 When the meeting was over, they went out for a drink.
   had
   As _____ finished, they went out for a drink.

2 When we eventually arrived at the party, all the food had been eaten.
   got
   By _____ the party, all the food had been eaten.

3 Immediately after he went, we started to relax.
   once
   We started to relax _____ gone.

4 He put everything back in its place before he left.
   until
   He didn't _____ everything back in its place.

5 I liked him the first time I met him.
   took
   I _____ the first time I saw him.

6 They decided against employing him because of his age.
   take
   They decided _____ because of his age.

7 She is proud of her achievements.
   pride
   She _____ her achievements.

8 She isn't very interested in my work.
   in
   She doesn't _____ my work.

9 His exam mark was such a disappointment.
   so
   He _____ with his exam mark.

10 I was so tired after that walk.
   such
   It _____ walk.

Correcting mistakes

In each short text **1–5**, there are two words which should not be there. Find these words and cross them out. The first one has been done for you.

1 At first we weren't sure whether we could afford to go on holiday, but in the end we ~~had~~ felt we ought to spend at least ~~during~~ a week on the coast.

2 I was extremely impressed with the special effects and some part of the action scenes. As for as the acting, though, I felt many amateurs could have done better.

3 After that the invigilators had taken in our answers to the reading exam, they handed out of Paper 2, the Writing test.

4 When he had came home from work he was made himself a cup of tea and read the newspaper. It had been an exhausting day.

5 I'm so pleased we took to your advice and went to the new Indian restaurant that's just opened. The service was marvellous and it was such a good food.

What to expect in the exam

- You may be asked to begin or end with the words in the question.
- Don't forget to read the question carefully!

A

It was such a relief to see my glasses again. I lost them when I was at the fairground on one of the rides.

We went there because it was my birthday and I wanted to celebrate it at the fairground. I went there with my friends. We went on all the rides except the ghost train. It's not very frightening. We were walking home when I noticed I didn't have my glasses. 'Where are my glasses?' I asked. 'I don't know,' said my friend. 'Perhaps you lost them on one of the rides.' So we went back and I asked at all the rides we had been on. They didn't have them at the rollercoaster, they didn't have them at the dodgems and what's more no one knew where they were. At last I found them. They were on the ground near the big wheel. What a relief!

B

My sister and I had just been to the cinema and when we came out we were thrilled to see it was snowing. The ground was covered in a sparkling white blanket of snow and although it was getting late, we couldn't resist having a quick snowball fight.

However, by the time we arrived at the bus stop, we had missed the last bus. Unfortunately, we couldn't afford to get a taxi back to our village and our parents had gone away for the weekend, so we had no choice but to set off on foot in the snow.

After we had been walking for nearly an hour we were both freezing cold and exhausted. It was snowing so heavily that we could hardly make out where we were going and we had both fallen over several times in the deep snow.

Just as our situation was becoming desperate, a car pulled up beside us and my mother wound down the window. 'Would you like a lift?' she asked. My parents had had to come home because of the poor weather conditions. It was such a relief to see them again.

4   Your teacher has asked you to write a story for the school's English magazine. It must end with the following words:

I had never been so surprised in all my life.

How to go about it

- First think of a general outline for your story. Choose two of the categories below and think of possible story lines for each one. Remember, your story has to *end* with a surprise.

   a discovering the truth about someone
   b meeting someone you hadn't seen for a long time
   c finding something you thought you had lost forever
   d achieving something you had thought impossible
   e an unexpected birthday surprise

   Example: applied for a job – went for an interview – car broke down – hitchhiked – wet, cold – got a lift – arrived at interview – interviewer was person who gave lift

- Make a plan, organizing your ideas into logical paragraphs.

   Opening: Set the scene.
   Main events: One or two paragraphs on what happened. Remember the word limit is 180 words, so do not write about too many events.
   Ending: The surprise. Don't forget to end with the exact words in the question.

- Make sure your story has well organized paragraphs, a variety of past tenses, a wide range of vocabulary and appropriate linking words.
- Remember to write between 120 and 180 words.

Now you are ready to write your **story** in **120–180** words.

Practice

1 For each of the sentences **1–6** decide which of the three alternative time expressions fits the gap. Pay attention to both grammar and meaning.

1 He wasn't allowed to go home _____ he'd apologized to the teacher.

   A until   **B** afterwards   **C** as soon as

2 _____ she was coming home, she fell over and hurt herself.

   A After   **B** During   **C** As

3 It can get very hot here _____ the summer.

   A while   **B** during   **C** when

4 First of all he won the 100 metres freestyle competition. _____ he went on to break the record for backstroke and crawl at the same distance.

   A After   **B** After it   **C** Afterwards

5 She got so tired of waiting for him that _____ she just went home.

   A at the end   **B** in the end   **C** at last

6 _____ she'd gone, he started to cry.

   A Eventually   **B** Until   **C** As soon as

2 Read the following texts in which two people tell the story of an embarrassing moment. In each of the spaces write the appropriate past form of the verb in brackets. There is an example at the beginning **(0)**.

Bus blush

Something very embarrassing **(0)** _happened_ (happen) to me while I **(1)** _____ (travel) home from school on the bus one day. We **(2)** _____ (have) a laugh at the back of the bus when I **(3)** _____ (see) a friend from school. She **(4)** _____ (sit) at the front, so I **(5)** _____ (run) up and **(6)** _____ (sit) down behind her, pulling her ponytail and shouting, 'Hi there, Rebecca!' I felt so stupid when a man I **(7)** _____ (never/see) before turned round! 'Actually, my name's Andrew,' he **(8)** _____ (smile). I **(9)** _____ (not/stop) blushing until I **(10)** _____ (get) home.

Mobile control

I **(11)** _____ (go on) at my parents for months to let me have a mobile phone and they eventually **(12)** _____ (agree) to buy me one. Keen to show it off, I **(13)** _____ (take) it with me when I **(14)** _____ (go) out with my friends one night. By 10pm no one **(15)** _____ (phone) me, so I thought I'd impress everyone by making a call. As soon as I **(16)** _____ (get) my phone out of the bag, I realized I **(17)** _____ (take) the TV remote control with me instead. As if that wasn't bad enough, when I finally **(18)** _____ (arrive) home my dad **(19)** _____ (keep) going on about the fact that he **(20)** _____ (have) to watch the same TV channel all night!

Writing 2:
FCE Part 2

Short stories

1 Read the following Writing Part 2 instructions.

You have decided to enter a short-story competition. The rules say that the story must end with the following words:

It was such a relief to see them again.

Write your **story** in **120–180** words.

2 Read the two sample answers on page 51 and decide which is the better entry.

3 The box below shows the criteria which an examiner would use when marking these competition entries. Decide how well each story satisfies the criteria by answering the questions in each category. Give examples from the stories to support your opinions.

Content:	Have the instructions in the question been followed?
Range:	Have a variety of past tenses been used? Is there a wide range of vocabulary?
Organization and cohesion:	Are the ideas and events organized logically? Are linking devices used well?
Style and format:	Is the story written using suitably neutral language? (neither too formal nor too informal)
Target reader:	Would the reader be sufficiently interested to want to read to the end? Would it have a chance of winning the competition?

3 Seven sentences have been removed from the text. Choose from the sentences **A–H** the one which fits each gap **(1–7)**. There is one extra sentence which you do not need to use.

Don't forget!

- Look carefully at the meaning and the language of the text both *before* and *after* the gap. For number 1 in the first paragraph, note the following: *Before the gap* we are told about a problem: the heating does not work and the candidates are cold.

After the gap we learn that the situation has not improved. The contrast linker *However* suggests that the missing sentence might mention requests, promises or even attempts to have the heating fixed.

A The girl was wearing loose fitting trousers and had pulled one of the trouser legs up as far as the knee.

B He counted the number of separate window panes (85), worked out the most popular colour for coats (blue) and calculated the ratio of females to males in the room (5:2).

C There were lists of names to make, seating plans to draw and identity papers to check.

D This brief delay gave her hope that he might turn a blind eye and forget he had seen anything.

E She had obviously not heard him approaching.

F They had only been writing for some 20 minutes when he received the first complaint.

G For a brief moment they stared at each other in disbelief, neither one of them quite sure what to do next.

H The cold was terrible and the caretaker of the building had assured him that a heating engineer was trying to solve the problem.

Reacting to the text ⬤

Does this method of cheating surprise you?
What do you think happened to the girl next?

Language focus 2: Past tenses

1 Look at the following sentences from the text about cheating and name the underlined past tenses. Choose from:
past simple   past continuous
past perfect simple   past perfect continuous

1 *He was invigilating the exam in the Casa de Cristal.*
2 *It was a cold December day and the heating had broken down.*
3 *He was walking back up the exam room in his soft shoes when he caught her.*
4 *Suddenly she felt his presence behind her and she pulled the trouser leg down to her ankle and looked round.*
5 *They had only been writing for some 20 minutes when he received the first complaint.*

2 In which sentence in exercise 1 is the past tense or combination of tenses used to describe:
a a series of actions following each other in chronological order?
b an event which occurred before the other past actions in the narrative?
c the duration of an action until a specific point in the past?

d a situation which occurred over a period of time and which forms the background to the other past actions in the narrative?
e an action which was in progress when another action occurred?

3 Name the tenses in the following pairs of sentences and explain the difference in meaning between each pair.
1 a When he was taking the exam, he felt ill.
  b When he had taken the exam, he felt ill.
2 a I was listening to the radio when I heard about it.
  b I listened to the radio when I heard about it.
3 a I lived in Oxford for six years.
  b I had been living in Oxford for six years.

4 In which of the sentences in exercise 3 can *while* be used in place of *when*?
In which sentences can *as soon as* be used in place of *when*?
Do these words change the meaning of the sentences in any way?

🄖 Look at pages 208 and 209 of the Grammar reference for more information about past tenses and time linkers.

Reading 2:
FCE Part 2

Gapped text

1 Look at this photo of an examination centre.

How many invigilators can you see?
What different duties does an invigilator have to perform on the day of an exam?
What do you think the job is like?

2 Now read the extract and compare your ideas in exercise 1 with the text.
What exam are they sitting for?

He was invigilating the exam in the *Casa de Cristal*, a huge glass-fronted building on the edge of the city used twice-yearly as an examination centre. It was a cold December day and the heating had broken down.

With their coats and scarves pulled tightly round them, the four hundred or so candidates struggled to forget the temperature and focus their attention instead on the four examination papers which would take them most of the day to complete. **1** However, no obvious improvement was ever made.

The job of invigilator was not one he particularly enjoyed, but it earned him some much-needed cash before the approaching Christmas holidays. As well as patrolling a small part of the large examination room, answering questions and discouraging cheats, he had to carry out a number of administrative duties. **2** And then, of course, there were the question papers to hand out and answers to take in. It was all rather dull, but it made a change from the rigours of teaching.

To relieve the boredom he set himself several simple arithmetical tasks to perform. **3** This helped to pass the time and made the whole thing more bearable. Now and again he would walk up and down the aisles, giving out rough paper, reminding candidates to use pens rather than pencils and picking up items which had been dropped on the floor.

He was walking back up the exam room in his soft shoes when he caught her. **4** The candidates were now on the third paper, which tested English grammar and vocabulary, and as he neared her desk from behind, he could hardly believe what he saw. He had heard of some ingenious methods of cheating but nothing like this.

5 She was now looking down at the back of her exposed leg, which was covered with several columns of phrasal verbs and their translations, copied out onto her skin in fine blue ink. Suddenly, she felt his presence behind her and she pulled the trouser leg down to her ankle and looked round.

6 Then she blushed, acutely embarrassed but also uncomfortably aware of the possible consequences of having been found out and she looked away to contemplate her fate.

None of the other candidates seemed to have noticed what was happening, which gave him time to decide how best to deal with the situation. **7** But this was not a course of action he had considered and as he asked her to accompany him to the front, he noticed the tears forming in her eyes.

Vocabulary 2: *Take*

A Phrasal verbs with *take*

Like *get*, which you saw in Unit 1, *take* can be used in many different phrasal verbs and expressions.

1 What is the meaning of this phrasal verb from the listening?

*I **took** [the video] **out** on Saturday.*

2 Read the following short story and give it a title.

I **a)** take after my father in many ways, particularly in my love of good food and a tendency to eat more than I need to. However, several years ago the situation had reached crisis point – my clothes no longer fitted me – so I decided to **b)** take up some form of sport. Karate seemed like a good idea, so I signed up for a course at the local sports centre.

I **c)** took to it immediately and by the end of the first class I was hooked. Over the next four years I progressed through the different levels until two years ago I achieved my ambition and qualified as an instructor. And now the same sports centre where I started all those years ago has just **d)** taken me on as a full-time karate teacher. What's more, they

needed someone to **e)** take over from the man who was my very first teacher and who has left to set up his own gym. I am certainly very grateful to him! Now, what with training, competitions and the classes themselves, karate has become my life and **f)** takes up all my time. I still manage to go out for a good meal now and again though!

3 Match each of the underlined phrasal verbs in exercise 2 to one of the meanings in the box below. Use the context of the story to help you.

employ   start doing   resemble   occupy   start to like   replace

B Expressions with *take*

1 Complete each gap **1–8** with an appropriate form of the verb *take*.

A 1 My dad used to _____ me to school, but now I have to get the bus.
2 A pair of shoes should last longer than two months. If I were you, I _____ them back to the shop.

B 3 I lost money on that business deal! Of course I regret _____ his advice!
4 She criticizes everybody else and refuses _____ any of the blame herself.

C 5 If you _____ more interest in the children, they'd probably respond better!
6 The stray cat was looking a lot healthier. It was clear that someone _____ pity on it and given it something to eat.

D 7 Street luge _____ a great deal of courage. You wouldn't catch me doing it!
8 Come on! I can't understand why you _____ so long to do this exercise.

2 In each of the sentences in exercise 1, identify the expression with *take* and underline it.
Example: *Who is <u>taking care of the children</u> tonight while you're at the party?*

3 The expressions in exercise 1 are organized into four groups, **A**, **B**, **C** and **D**. Match each of the following general meanings for *take* to an appropriate group.
1 to express what is needed or required
2 to talk about the movement of something or someone from one place to another
3 to talk about the way people feel or react to others
4 to accept

4 Which group in exercise 1 do the following expressions belong to?
to take pride in something   *to be taken to hospital*
to take a joke   *to take the infinitive*

5 Now write a short story of your own using at least three expressions and three phrasal verbs with *take*.

Vocabulary: Cinema

1   In the word square below there are ten words related to acting and cinema. The words are written from left to right, top to bottom or diagonally. Find the words and write them in the spaces on the right.

R	T	U	S	C	E	N	E	N	B
A	O	P	H	O	R	R	O	R	C
C	C	L	O	M	D	E	R	E	H
T	A	R	E	N	C	R	A	H	A
R	W	E	I	A	U	B	N	A	R
E	A	V	M	T	C	L	T	G	A
S	T	I	E	X	I	S	O	H	C
S	N	E	Y	F	A	C	R	F	T
A	C	W	M	C	P	L	O	T	E
S	B	T	H	R	I	L	L	E	R

_____   _____

_____   _____

_____   _____

_____   _____

_____   _____

_____   _____

_____   _____

_____   _____

_____   _____

_____   _____

2   Now write ten more words related to the cinema. The words can be nouns or verbs.

Word formation

1   Read the following text about special effects, ignoring the gaps for the moment. How many of the films mentioned have you seen?

George Lucas's *Star Wars* transformed 20th-century entertainment and raised audience expectations to **(0)** ___*alarming*___ heights for film producers. Since *Star Wars* was made in 1977 special effects have become **(1)** _____ important in selling a film. The script of *Jurassic Park*, for example, was rather **(2)** _____ but the film was a box office success because the dinosaurs were so **(3)** _____ realistic. However, special effects do not always guarantee success. **(4)** _____ , when *Lost World* came out the technology was far superior, but people had become **(5)** _____ of dinosaurs and were simply not **(6)** _____ enough to want to go and see them any more. The film was not nearly as successful as its predecessor.

But who is not **(7)** _____ when they see Jar Jar Binks in *The Phantom Menace*, the first ever 3D interactive digital character seen on film? Computer generated actors, or 'synthespians' are certainly the way ahead, but you may be **(8)** _____ to discover that the most expensive special effect was filmed in 1956. The parting of the Red Sea in Cecil B DeMille's *The Ten Commandments* cost an **(9)** _____ £2 million! But what does the future hold? It is **(10)** _____ to think that with CGI (computer generated imagery) filmmakers may be able to recreate deceased movie stars, such as James Dean or Marilyn Monroe.

ALARM
INCREASE
DISAPPOINT
AMAZE
INTEREST
TIRE
MOTIVATE

IMPRESS

SURPRISE

ASTONISH
FASCINATE

2   Read the text again and use the word given in capitals at the end of some of the lines to form a word that fits in the gap **in the same line**. There is an example at the beginning **(0)**.

⑤ Doing your duty

Speaking 1:
FCE Part 2

Talking about photos

Compare these photos and say which
learning environment you prefer and why.

Reading:
FCE Part 3

Multiple matching

1 In the UK children can be educated by teachers at school or by their parents at home.
What do you think are the advantages and disadvantages of education at home?

2 Read through the article on home education quite quickly. Are any of your ideas from
exercise 1 mentioned in the text?

3 Read the text again. For questions **1–15**, choose from the paragraphs (**A–D**). The
paragraphs may be chosen more than once. When more than one answer is required,
these may be given in any order.

Don't forget!

- Read all the questions.
- Read paragraph A and answer any
  questions you can.
- Do the same for the other three
  paragraphs.
- Scan the texts again to find information
  which matches any unanswered questions.

Which paragraphs mention the following?

common causes of dissatisfaction with the school system	1	
official requirements which do not apply to home education	2	
asking for assistance if necessary	3	
an increase in the range of families whose children are taught at home	4	
being forced to do something unnecessarily	5	
checking that the law is being respected	6	
the practical application of knowledge	7	
somebody's normal activity being prevented by illness	8	9
a situation in which legal action could be taken	10	
optional study outside normal timetable hours	11	
somebody not being able to achieve their full potential	12	13
realizing that something was wrong at school	14	
alerting parents to the nature of the job	15	

Home is where the school is

A   At 8am, when other children have to catch trains or buses to school, 14-year-old Rhiannon Cassell walks into the family living room in Huntly, Aberdeenshire, and checks on the day's assignments with her teacher – her father Matthew. Then Rhiannon, like her older sisters Tess, 16, and Abigail, 15, heads back to her own room, while their father works with the two youngest children, James, ten, and Alicia, eight, who need more individual attention. Rhiannon spends an hour and a half studying science (today's subject: static electricity), then switches to maths. If she is having difficulties, she seeks her father's help. 'He doesn't do the work for us, just helps us reason it out.' After lunch Rhiannon is back at work for a practical follow-up on the morning's science lesson: an experiment with balloons and dust. She then reads her current literary classic *Little Women* until 2.30pm. Although, that's the official end of the school day, Rhiannon may carry on with a subject she enjoys or is having problems with.

B   Matthew Cassell, 37, has been supervising his children's education since he retired on health grounds 4 years ago. He is not anti-school or critical of teachers. 'It's just that I can give the children more time than they'd get in a large class.' Regular tests and careful record keeping ensure Matthew keeps a check on their progress. The Cassells are in good company. Once only possible for the wealthy, home schooling is increasingly popular among parents fed up with bullying, narrow curriculums, rigid timetables, or the lack of proper religious teaching. Matthew's daughter, Rhiannon, echoes another common reason for parents opting for home education: 'At school I always felt they were holding me back. Now I can learn at my own pace.'

C   Alarm bells rang for Beverley Young after her four-year-old daughter Cassandra's teacher suggested the girl's numerical skills were weak because she had failed a simple sorting activity. Beverley asked Cassie why she had not put coloured balls in the correct holes. 'But, Mummy, I'm a big girl,' she replied. 'We do that sort of thing with my baby brother.'

Cassie was also much better than her classmates at reading but the teacher still made her sound out the individual letters of words. Although she rapidly became bored with everything, the school would not let her go up to a higher class. Then Cassie contracted an infectious skin disease and had to stay at home for a fortnight, with a package of homework to keep her going. 'She completed it in an hour,' recalls Beverley. Soon afterwards, she and her husband removed Cassie from school, and Beverley began supervising her work at home. Now ten, Cassie reads voraciously over a wide range of subjects. She and her brother Alexander, seven, don't follow a fixed timetable and there's no bell to bring studies to an abrupt end. Cassie approves of this flexible regime. 'If it's a nice day I can go for a bike ride with my dad,' she says.

D   As well as being more fun, home education can be positively beneficial. 'On average, home-schoolers are two years ahead of their schooled counterparts,' says Roland Meighan, professor of special education at Nottingham University. A parent need not be a qualified teacher to be a home educator and children do not have to follow the national curriculum or sit formal tests. It is perfectly legal to keep a child away from school, as long as he or she is being educated. Parents do not even need to tell the local authority, although it is necessary for the head teacher to be informed if a child is withdrawn from a state school. In that case, responsibility for ensuring that alternative arrangements are satisfactory does lie with local authorities, which can take parents to court if children's needs are not being met. Laurence Purcell, head of school services for Kensington and Chelsea, claims there is no official hostility to the idea. 'We don't wish to discourage parents,' he says. 'But we do warn them of the heavy workload they are taking on.' At first his inspectors visit parents once a term, and then once a year if everything is fine.

Reacting to the text ⬤
Do you think that home schooling is a good idea?
Would it have worked for you?
Can parents be good teachers?

Don't forget!
● Justify your opinions, saying why you think the way you do.

Vocabulary 1: Recording prepositions

1 Did you notice that the article was full of prepositions? To help learn prepositions these can be recorded in different categories in your notebook. Look for the following prepositions in the reading text. There is an example for each category.

Adjective + preposition	to be good/better __at__ (reading) to be/become bored _____ (everything) to be fed up _____ (bullying)
Verb + preposition	to check __on__ (the day's assignments) to approve _____ (this flexible regime) to switch _____ (maths)
Noun + preposition	a reason __for__ (opting for home education) to have responsibility _____ (ensuring that) to have problems _____ (a subject)
Preposition + noun	__in__ good company _____ average (to learn) _____ your own pace

2 Can you find any more prepositions in the text for each category?

3 Can you remember how the prepositions were used in the text?

Example:
'I think it was Cassie who was better than her classmates at reading.'
'Yes, and because of that she became bored with school.'

Language focus: Obligation, necessity and permission

1 Look at these sentences and answer the questions **1–4** below.

a *At 8am, when other children <u>have to catch</u> trains or buses to school...*
b *Cassie... <u>had to stay</u> at home for a fortnight.*
c *Children <u>do not have to follow</u> the national curriculum.*
d *Parents <u>do not need to tell</u> the local authority.*
e *A parent <u>need not be</u> a qualified teacher.*
f *Rhiannon <u>is not</u> simply <u>allowed to do</u> just what she wants.*
g *She <u>can listen</u> to music but she <u>can't watch</u> television.*
h *She <u>mustn't distract</u> her sisters when they're working.*

1 Which underlined forms talk about what is permitted?
2 Which forms talk about what isn't permitted?
3 Which ones express necessity and/or obligation?
4 Which express a lack of necessity and/or obligation?

2 Who might say the following sentences?

a *You must hand in your homework tomorrow.*
b *We have to hand in our homework tomorrow.*

Why is *must* used in the first sentence and *have to* in the second?

3 🔍 *G* In the following sentences the forms which express obligation, necessity and permission are all incorrect. Correct the mistakes and then check your answers in the Grammar reference on pages 209 and 210.

1 I have not to tidy my room up today; I did it yesterday.
2 Do you must make such a noise? I'm trying to concentrate!
3 Last week I must went to the hairdresser. Mum said my hair was far too long.
4 Did you be allowed to watch that film on telly last night?
5 They've changed my hours! Now I must start work at 7.30 instead of 8.30!
6 At my school we mustn't wear a tie if we don't want to.
7 You need prepare your bags tonight if your train leaves at 6.30 in the morning.
8 You really should to go and see that film.

4 *Make* (obligation) and *let* (permission)

Note that both of these verbs in the active are followed by the infinitive without *to*.

a Rewrite the following two sentences from the text in the passive.

1 The teacher still made her sound out the individual letters.
She was still _____ out the individual letters.

2 The school would not let her go up to a higher class.
She was not _____ go up to a higher class.

b Complete the following sentences using the correct form of *make*, *let* or *allow*.

1 I wanted to watch the film last night but I wasn't _____ to.

2 I'd love to come but I don't think my boss will _____ me have the day off work.

3 I hate cabbage but my mum _____ me eat it.

5 a Rhiannon is talking about being taught at home by her father. Complete the gaps with a verb from the box.

| must | mustn't | have to | don't have to | need to |

The best thing about home-schooling is that I **(1)** _____ get up very early to go to school. OK, I **(2)** _____ start studying at eight o'clock but my school day's over at 2.30. I can carry on working in the afternoon, but I **(3)** _____ if I don't want to. Well, that's not quite true actually. If my dad feels I **(4)** _____ spend more time on a certain subject, he says, 'Well, I think you'd better carry on, don't you?' He's good like that, my dad; not strict. You know, he doesn't get all bossy and say 'You **(5)** _____ do some extra work this afternoon.' He just tries to persuade us. There is one thing I **(6)** _____ do, though and that's chat to my sisters when we're supposed to be working. Tess, Abigail and I all **(7)** _____ work alone in our own rooms at certain times of the day. James and Alicia, on the other hand, both **(8)** _____ spend more time working together with my dad, because they're a lot younger.

I think you'd better carry on...

b *Be supposed to* and *had better* both appear in the passage. Which one means 'should do because of a rule or because it is expected' and which means 'should do because it is a good idea'?

6 Complete the second sentence so it has a similar meaning to the first sentence, using the word given. **Do not change the word given.** You must use between two and five words, including the word given.

1 When I was young I wasn't allowed to watch much TV.
let
When I was young my parents _____ _____ much TV.

2 She had to wash up before she could go out.
made
She _____ wash up before she could go out.

3 I'm never allowed to do what I want.
can
I _____ what I want.

4 Why can't we go to the party?
allowed
Why _____ go to the party?

5 In my opinion parents ought not to smack their children.
should
I don't think _____ their children.

6 There's no need for you to hand the report in until next week.
need
You _____ in the report until next week.

7 I think you should tell your parents exactly what happened.
better
I think you _____ your parents exactly what happened.

8 Do you know what the homework is?
supposed
Do you know what we _____ for homework?

7 ⬭ Talk about the things you *have to*, *should* or *ought to* do and those things you *don't have to* or *aren't allowed to* do at:

- home
- school/college/work
- the weekend

Example: home:
I ought to tidy my room more often, but I never seem to find the time. I don't have to clean it, though. My mother does that for me.

Word formation: Nouns and adjectives

The adjectives of the nouns *tolerance* and *patience* are *tolerant* and *patient* and the verb form of *tolerant* is to *tolerate*.

1 Put the verb forms in the box below into the table according to whether they follow the pattern of *tolerance* (*-ance* and *-ant* endings) or *patience* (*-ence* and *-ent* endings). Write both the noun and adjective formed from each verb. One of them has been done for you as an example.

confide	ignore	obey	differ
signify	depend	*appear	*please

Verb	Noun	Adjective
tolerate	toler**ance**	toler**ant**
–	pati**ence**	pati**ent**
confide	*confidence*	*confident*

*These words do not follow exactly the same pattern as either *tolerant* or *patient*.

2 Where this is possible use the prefixes *un-*, *in-*, *im-*, or *dis-* to form the opposite of the adjectives you formed in exercise 1.

Example: *in*tolerant

How are the adverbs of each word formed?

Use of English 1: **Word formation**
FCE Part 3

For questions **1–10**, read the text below. Use the word given in capitals at the end of some of the lines to form a word that fits in the gap **in the same line**. There is an example at the beginning **(0)**.

A changed person

I don't see my teenage godson as **(0)** _frequently_ as I did in the past and	FREQUENT
when I visited him and his family today I was **(1)** _____ surprised.	PLEASE
He's changed **(2)** _____ since the last time I saw him. Whereas he	SIGNIFY
used to be such a horrible **(3)** _____ little boy, now he is extremely	OBEY
well-behaved and a **(4)** _____ to be with. He seems to attach more	PLEASE
(5) _____ now to what others might be thinking of him and he	IMPORTANT
takes more care over his **(6)** _____ . He has developed greater	APPEAR
(7) _____ in himself and his own judgement and he puts up stiff	CONFIDE
(8) _____ to his parents' advice and decisions if he feels they are	RESIST
wrong. **(9)** _____ he is beginning to take an interest in girls and his	APPEAR
mum tells me he's got a girlfriend. These, it seems, are his first steps towards	
(10) _____ and it won't be very many years before he leaves home.	DEPEND

Listening 1:   True/False   1.22

1   Which of the following jobs or duties do you have to do?
    How do you feel about doing them?

2   Richard and Louise are discussing how *they* feel about doing these jobs and which
    three they both think are the worst. Listen to their conversation and decide whether
    the following statements are true or false. Write **T** for True or **F** for False.

Richard does most of the washing up in his family.   _____
Richard's father makes him clean his shoes.   _____
Louise doesn't mind shopping for food.   _____
Richard's grandparents are all still alive.   _____
Louise prefers to wait for her grandparents to visit her.   _____
Louise has to take her dog for a walk every day.   _____
Louise's father cleans the car himself.   _____

   Which three do *you* think are the worst?
    Are there any other things you have to do but don't like doing?

Speaking 2:   Collaborative task
FCE Part 3

When a mixed group of teenagers and adults was asked what they thought were the
qualities of a good parent they came up with the following list. Talk to each other
about how necessary it is for a parent to have each of these qualities, and then decide
which three are the most important.

> ● How necessary is it for a parent to have these qualities?
> ● Which three qualities are the most important?

a sense of humour   *an interest in pop music*   **good fashion sense**

fairness   *strictness*   **patience**   **tolerance**   **energy**   *the ability to listen*

How to go about it

● You have about three minutes to talk,
  so don't make your decision too soon.
● Ask your partner one or two
  questions to give him or her the
  opportunity to speak.
● You can disagree with your partner.

Useful language
Listen to Richard and Louise's
conversation again and tick the
expressions you hear. You can then use
some of the phrases in your discussion.

Starting the conversation
Which one shall we start with?
Let's see. Where shall we begin?
Let's talk about... first.
I think we should start with...

Moving to a new point
Which one now?
Shall we move on?
So, that could be one of our three.
Let's have a look at the next one.

Finishing the discussion
So, what have we decided?
Which ones do we agree on then?
We'll have to agree to disagree.
We both seem to agree on...

Vocabulary 2: The world of work

1 a The following verbs can all be used before the countable noun *job*.

get   look for   apply for   ~~be out of~~   go for an interview for

Put the verbs in the boxes below depending on the order they normally occur in. The first one has been done for you.

b The following verbs all indicate ways of ending a job. Put each one into an appropriate gap below.

sacked   made redundant   resigned

1 Because of the economic crisis 50 workers were _____ in order to ensure the survival of the company.
2 She had become increasingly bored in her job, so she _____ from the company in order to take up a more challenging post.
3 He was _____ for stealing and he's finding it difficult to get another job.

2 a Which of the verbs below is not normally used before the countable noun *career*?

to change   to give up your   to devote yourself to your   to study a   to start a

b Which of the nouns below is not normally used after the verb *to earn*?

a high salary   a weekly wage   a good living   a competition   a lot of money

3 What is the difference in meaning between the following?

to work shifts   to work long hours   to work overtime
to work part-time   to work full-time   to work flexitime

4 Can you identify the jobs in the photographs?

5 Describe the jobs in the pictures in exercise 4, but without saying the name of the job. Your partner has to decide which one you are describing. Use the vocabulary below to help you.

A Skills
telephone   computer   artistic   organizational   language

B Adjectives for personal qualities
patient   confident   intelligent   brave   well-educated   talented
strong   creative   hard-working   polite   cheerful   fit

C Adjectives for jobs
well-paid   responsible   satisfying   challenging
badly-paid   tiring   unpleasant   monotonous

Listening 2:
FCE Part 2

Sentence completion 1.23

You will hear a radio interview with Allan Nicholls, station officer at Hove Fire Station. For questions **1–10** on page 61, complete the sentences.

Don't forget!

Underline the correct alternative in each of the following sentences.

- You *need to/don't need to* write more than three words for each answer.
- You *should/shouldn't* write a word or phrase that you actually hear.
- You *need/don't need* to rephrase.
- Minor spelling errors *can/can't* be made, but the words you write *need/don't need* to be recognizable to the examiner, so you *should/shouldn't* check your spelling.
- You *can/can't* expect to hear the answers in the same order as the questions.

Before you listen to the recording, read through all the questions and try to predict the type of information you will hear for each one.

Potential recruits are not required to have any [____1____].

They do not have to satisfy any [____2____] requirements.

However, there are tests to measure the strength of their [____3____].

Hove Fire Station currently employs [____4____] women.

After working a series of day and night shifts firefighters have [____5____].

At the Watch Parade they have to [____6____].

Then they carry out a thorough inspection of the [____7____] as well as the equipment.

Most call-outs occur during [____8____].

Firefighters can spend [____9____] clearing up after a fire.

Being a firefighter is a [____10____] job.

Use of English 2: Multiple-choice cloze
FCE Part 1

For questions **1–12**, read the text below and underline which answer (**A, B, C** or **D**) best fits each gap. There is an example at the beginning (**0**).

Before you do the task, make sure you read the whole text through first. As you read, answer the following question:

How does Roger Press feel about his decision to change career?

A more commercial tune

Roger Press, 40, has **(0)** _____ his career. After spending five years **(1)** _____ a concert pianist he has gone into business, recently **(2)** _____ up his own company.

'After leaving university I decided to **(3)** ____ myself to a career in music. I loved performing but it was very hard **(4)** ____ . I played at concerts in Europe and America, made recordings and got good **(5)** ____. But after a while I felt I had gone as **(6)** ____ as I could. Unless you're one of the world's top pianists, it's difficult to earn a good **(7)** ____ and I wasn't one of the greatest.

When I **(8)** ____ up my performing career, people around me were more sad and disappointed than I was. But I felt free and **(9)** ____ I knew I was getting serious about life. After getting a **(10)** ____ in business administration I joined the recording company EMI and started their classical video division, producing programmes about famous artists. A year ago I left EMI and formed a new company, New Media Systems, which **(11)** ____ in multimedia programmes.

Now that I run my own business I am in control of my life and I can feel proud of my achievements. Although the stress is high and I work **(12)** ____ hours, the stress involved in piano playing was much worse. It took physical, emotional and mental skills. I prefer the pressures I live with now.'

0 A moved	**B** changed	**C** adjusted	**D** stopped
1 A like	**B** working	**C** how	**D** as
2 A giving	**B** setting	**C** forming	**D** bringing
3 A devote	**B** take	**C** assign	**D** employ
4 A job	**B** effort	**C** work	**D** career
5 A reviews	**B** critics	**C** reports	**D** praise
6 A soon	**B** often	**C** far	**D** much
7 A life	**B** living	**C** money	**D** payment
8 A took	**B** brought	**C** gave	**D** put
9 A lastly	**B** at last	**C** at the end	**D** lately
10 A qualification	**B** title	**C** graduate	**D** grade
11 A specializes	**B** focuses	**C** concentrates	**D** dedicates
12 A overtime	**B** large	**C** long	**D** bonus

Letters: An application

1 Read the following Writing Part 2 instructions.

You have seen the following advertisement in an international newspaper.

Write a **letter of application**, giving your reasons for applying and saying why you think you would be suitable for the job.

2 Read this model letter of application for the job. Do you think the applicant would be suitable? Give reasons for your answer.

We are looking for

CAMP HELPERS

to work in the UK on one of our International Summer Camps

Applicants should be hard-working, energetic and able to organize activities for young children in the following areas:

▲ workshops
▲ sports
▲ outdoor pursuits
▲ indoor and outdoor games

Minimum age: 18
Some knowledge of English essential
Previous experience preferred

Write in English stating relevant skills and experience to:
Camp GB, Wargrave, Wokingham RG11 9PA

Camp GB,
Wargrave,
Wokingham
RG11 9PA

Dear Sir or Madam,

I would like to apply for the job of Camp Helper as advertised in this month's issue of Recruitment International.

I like working with children very much and I would enjoy the challenge of organizing activities for them on one of your camps. Moreover, I have just finished school and in October I will be starting a degree course in English. I am therefore very keen to improve my language skills in an English-speaking country before I go to university.

My interests include basketball, tennis and orienteering and I can also play the guitar. For the past seven years I have attended summer camps in my country with the scouts and last year I helped to run a number of events, including an orienteering competition and a kite-making workshop.

I feel I have the necessary patience and energy to make a positive and enthusiastic contribution to your camps and I hope you will consider my application favourably.

I am available for interview at any time and look forward to hearing from you soon.

Yours faithfully
Costas Stergis

3   Read the letter again and find the sentence or sentences which cover each of the following points.

a   reasons for writing the letter   *I would like to apply for the job of Camp Helper*

b   reasons for applying for the job   _____

c   suitability for the job   _____

d   experience   _____

e   language skills   _____

f   other relevant skills/interests   _____

g   age   _____

h   closing comments   _____

4   Read the following Writing Part 2 question. You have just read this job advertisement.

Coastal Campsites require

- Reception Assistants
- Bar and Restaurant Staff
- Shop Staff
- Gardeners
- Swimming Pool Attendants

to work in the UK on our busy, five-star campsites this summer.

Applicants must have a reasonable command of English and be willing to work hard.

- Relevant skills and experience an advantage
- Good pay and conditions
- Free board and accommodation

Apply in writing to:
Coastal Campsites, 79 North Road, Brighton BN1 6TF

Write a **letter** in **120–180** words to Coastal Campsites applying for one of the jobs. Say why you would be suitable for the job and ask for more details about the working hours and the length of contract. Do not write any postal addresses.

5   Look at pages 200 and 201. You will find one student's answer to question 4, together with further work on using formal expressions in letters of application.

6   Now write your own letter, applying for one of the other jobs available at Coastal Campsites. Say why you would be suitable for the job and ask for more details about the pay and the accommodation.

Don't forget!

- Write in a formal style using some of the expressions in the model letter and in exercise 2 on page 201.
- Do not use contractions.
- Try to use indirect rather than direct questions in formal letters.
- Organize your letter into logical paragraphs.

Open cloze: Prepositions

For questions **1–12** read the text below and think of the word which best fits each gap. Use only **one** word in each gap. In this exercise, each missing word is a preposition. There is an example at the beginning **(0)**.

Don't forget!

- Always read the text through once before you start to fill the gaps in order to gain an overall understanding of the passage. For this text, answer the following two questions:

How does talking to babies and young children benefit them?
What is one of the main obstacles to a child's progress, according to the text?

Gift of the gab

Chatting to babies in a particular way boosts their intelligence and gives them a head start **(0)** _in_ life, a new study has found. Speech and language therapist Dr Sally Ward selected 140 nine-month-old children from Manchester. She then gave 70 of the parents detailed advice **(1)** _____ the best way to communicate **(2)** _____ their child and left the other 70 without guidance. The 'communicating' parents were told to spend at least 30 minutes every day talking to their child, **(3)** _____ any background noise, about subjects which their infant might take an interest **(4)** _____. More than six years later, and after regular checks had been kept **(5)** _____ their progress, the children had IQ tests. Those in the talking group were, **(6)** _____ average, a year and three months ahead **(7)** _____ the other group. Nine children had IQs in the gifted category, whereas none in the non-talking group was as bright.

In a separate study at the American Academy of Paediatrics, experts have warned **(8)** _____ the dangers of children under the age of two watching television. Research has shown that exposure to television is responsible **(9)** _____ anything from delayed speech to Attention Deficit Hyperactivity Disorder. The problem **(10)** _____ television is that it confuses infants, who block out the background noise coming from it. They consequently learn to ignore all noise, and this includes speech. Paediatric and language specialists also disapprove **(11)** _____ radio, which has much the same effect **(12)** _____ a child's language development.

Word formation

Write down as many forms as possible of the words below.

Example: depend (v) *dependent (adj), independent (adj), independently (adv), dependence (n), independence (n), dependant (n), dependable (adj), dependably (adv), dependability (n)*

1 differ   (v) _____
2 appear   (v) _____
3 frequent (adj) _____
4 please   (v) _____
5 tolerate (v) _____

Vocabulary: The world of work

Use the clues to help you complete the grid. When you have all the answers you will find an extra item of vocabulary for number 12 down. Write your own clue for number 12 down in the gap provided.

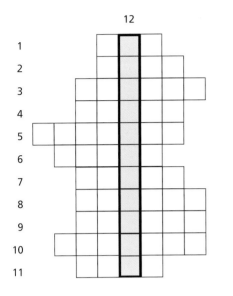

1 It's a good job but I don't _____ paid very much.
2 We had to _____ him. He was stealing money from the cash till.
3 After 20 years as a teacher she decided to change _____ and become a social worker.
4 You don't have to have a _____ of humour to work here but it certainly helps.
5 I didn't like working for someone else, so I decided to set up my own _____ .
6 This job sounds good. Why don't you _____ for it? You've got nothing to lose.
7 Don't phone her during the day. She's working the night _____ at the hospital so she'll be asleep.
8 He gave up his job in order to _____ himself to his painting.
9 To get to the top in this profession you need to have good organizational _____ .
10 There's a lot of stress involved in _____ your own business.
11 The people who work for me get a weekly _____ of £315.
12 _____

Modal verbs

For questions **1–8** decide which answer **A**, **B** or **C** best fits each space.

1 You _____ take an umbrella; it's not going to rain.
   A mustn't   **B** can't   **C** needn't

2 I think we _____ to phone Marta and ask her if she wants to come.
   A should   **B** ought   **C** can

3 The best thing about my job is that I _____ to get up early. I don't start until 10 am.
   A needn't   **B** don't have   **C** am not supposed

4 A 'Non-uniform Day' is a day when we're _____ to wear 'normal clothes' to school if we want.
   A let   **B** made   **C** allowed

5 We'd _____ make too much noise; we might wake the baby up.
   A better not   **B** shouldn't   **C** ought not to

6 Where have you been? You were _____ to be here half an hour ago!
   A allowed   **B** supposed   **C** had

7 The rules are very clear. You know you _____ wear jewellery to school.
   A mustn't   **B** don't have to   **C** don't need to

8 I _____ to stay at my friend's house last night.
   A may   **B** could   **C** was allowed

6 Relative relationships

Reading:
FCE Part 3

Multiple matching

You are going to read an article about family mealtimes. For questions **1–15**, choose from the people (**A–E**). The people may be chosen more than once. When more than one answer is required, these may be given in any order.

How to go about it

- Look at the title and introductory sentence and try to predict what the text will say. Read the text quite quickly and check your predictions.

- The key words in question 1 have been underlined. Underline the key words in the other questions.

- Now read the text again and try to find the answers, thinking about the key words in the questions. Underline the part of the text which you think gives the answer. This has been done for you for the part of the text which relates to question 1.

A The writer **B** Gerry **C** Andrew **D** James **E** Ben

Which of the people A–E

sees the <u>positive side of arguments</u> at the meal table?	1	
is influenced by past experiences?	2	
doesn't let his children watch television at mealtimes?	3	
doesn't mind what his children talk about?	4	
says his family argues at mealtimes?	5	6
doesn't see as much of his children as he used to?	7	
rarely eats with his children?	8	
says his family eat all together only on certain days?	9	10
sees family meals as preparation for eating in other situations?	11	
organizes his working day to be with his family for meals?	12	
has children who complain about what they have to eat?	13	14
would prefer not to be doing things in a hurry so often?	15	

Family Feuds
— or just lunch?

If you find family meals tense and unpleasant, you're not alone. Alan Jefferson explains.

The nation's eating habits have changed and many families no longer eat together on a regular basis. To be honest, this doesn't strike me as particularly surprising. Lunchtime last Sunday in my own home consisted of my two-year-old son happily throwing his food on the floor whilst – yet again – his older brother and sister protested loudly about the vegetables they were being made to eat.

Despite the noise and chaos, though, we still prefer to have meals as a family. On weekdays that's difficult as there are too many things going on and there just isn't enough time for me and my wife to sit with the children at breakfast. Only our youngest is with his mother for lunch and the children's supper is too early for me to participate. But we do our best at weekends.

If, as some research shows, parents now talk to their children for an average of just 12 minutes a day, then our decision to eat together as much as possible is more than justified. Whilst the quality of the kitchen table chat is not particularly high – a mixture of bad jokes, song lyrics and gossip – we are at least communicating, which is the main thing, so it doesn't matter to me what the topic of conversation is.

Of course, family meals can be tense and we don't always see eye to eye. But for me, arguing together is an essential part of family life and all part of learning to get on with each other.

Gerry, a 35-year-old father of two young girls, would not agree. He had enough of stressful family meals as a child and now sees them as both impractical and undesirable.

'I hardly ever get home early enough to eat with my kids, but I don't particularly mind that. It has a lot to do with my own childhood memories. Mealtimes were very formal occasions, and they provided my parents with the opportunity to interrogate me about everything I'd done that day. I used to feel very uncomfortable. Later, during my teenage years, the meal table became the scene of terrible rows. Of course, I'd like to spend less time rushing around and more time with my family, but I don't miss family meals at all.'

Andrew finds family meals difficult, but necessary. 'We're always having rows, particularly when the kids start moaning about what's on their plate,' he says. 'Trying to keep everyone happy isn't easy, especially with three children under nine who all have different tastes and a teenage stepdaughter who would much rather be eating her dinner on the sofa in front of the TV. But eating with others is an important social skill. I want my children to get used to doing it in the home so that they will know how to eat in public.'

James, the father of two teenage boys, says: 'The older my kids become, the less contact I have with them and the more important family meals become. They're often the only opportunity we get to talk.'

As a travelling sales representative, James is responsible for his own time management and he tries to organize his appointments in such a way that he can return to his Liverpool home in time for dinner with his family at 7.00 pm. 'I've made it a priority,' he says, 'because I feel that mealtimes are an important point of family contact.'

So have **Ben** and Angela, who manage to get their four children aged 5 to 16 around the table for weekend family meals. 'We try to keep everyone at the table for at least half an hour on Saturdays and Sundays. We have a telly in the kitchen but the kids aren't allowed to have it on when we are eating there – that would make the whole thing rather pointless,' says Ben.

He recalls a recent trip to the States, where his American friends had the television on all day. 'Different members of the family would wander in at different times, grab something from the fridge and eat alone, always in front of the TV. I think it's a shame that Britain is becoming much more like that now.'

Reacting to the text ⬤

How often do you eat with all your family?
Do you have the television on when you eat?
Are mealtimes in your country becoming more like those described in the last paragraph?
Which way of eating do you prefer? Why?

Language focus 1: *Too* and *enough*

1 Look at these sentences from the reading text.

*On weekdays... there are **too** many things going on and there just isn't **enough** time for me and my wife to sit with the children at breakfast.*
*...the children's supper is **too** early for me to participate. I hardly ever get home early **enough** to eat with my kids.*

2 Choose the correct alternative in each of these sentences.
  a *Too* is followed by **nouns/adjectives and adverbs**.
  b *Too much* or *too many* is followed by **nouns/adjectives and adverbs**.
  c *Enough* is used **before/after** nouns.
  d *Enough* is used **before/after** adjectives and adverbs.

3 Look at the sentences in exercise 1. What do you notice about the structure of the sentence after *too* and *enough*?

G For a summary of the rules for using *too* and *enough* read the Grammar reference on page 210.

Practice

1 Write six sentences of your own using the phrases in the box below.

Example: enough time – *I didn't have enough time to do all my homework last night.*

enough money	too difficult	strong enough
too much noise	old enough	too many people

2 Complete the second sentence so that it has a similar meaning to the first sentence, using the word given. **Do not change the word given.** You must use between two and five words, including the word given.

1 I couldn't hear what they were saying because they were speaking so quietly.
  too
  They were speaking _____ hear what they were saying.

2 He couldn't see over the wall because he was so small.
  enough
  He was _____ see over the wall.

3 We'll need more eggs if we want to make an omelette.
  enough
  There _____ make an omelette.

4 I can't drink this tea because it's too sweet.
  sugar
  There _____ in this tea for me to drink it.

5 I didn't go into the bar because it was too crowded.
  too
  I didn't go into the bar because _____
  _____ people.

Vocabulary 1: Phrasal verbs

A Romance

1 The following sentences tell the unhappy love story of a young couple. Match a sentence beginning **1–6** with an ending **a–f**. The first one has been done for you.

① It would be our first 'anniversary' today. We started **going**
2 It was her smile which first attracted me and I **fell**
3 We were in a disco. Someone told me she had just **split**
4 We shared the same sense of humour and we **got**
5 Unfortunately, we had an argument last week and we **fell**
6 I think about her a lot, so I suppose I haven't **got**

  a up with her boyfriend, so I asked her to dance.
  b on with each other really well, always laughing and joking together.
  c out with each other exactly one year ago.
  d over her yet. I miss her very much.
  e for her immediately. It was love at first sight.
  f out with each other. We haven't spoken since.

2 Write the infinitive of each of the phrasal verbs from exercise 1 next to its meaning.

  1 to argue and stop being friendly with someone _____
  2 to end a relationship with someone _____
  3 to have a romantic relationship with someone _____
  4 to have a good relationship with someone _____
  5 to fall in love with someone _____
  6 to recover after the end of a relationship with someone _____

B Family

1 Work out the meaning of the phrasal verbs in **bold** in the following sentences. Use the context of the sentence to help you.

1 Her parents died when she was very young, so her grandparents **brought** her **up** as if she was their own daughter.
2 I was born in England but I **grew up** in France; I lived in Paris until I was 18.
3 My brother was very naughty as a child. He **got up to** all sorts of things he knew he shouldn't, just to annoy my parents.
4 His mother **told** him **off** for breaking the plate and he started crying. He didn't like it when she was angry.
5 My father is an important figure to me. I have always **looked up to** him because of his patience and calmness.
6 They felt they had been badly **let down**. They had given their son so much freedom and he had 'thanked' them by becoming a thief.

2 What is the infinitive form of each of the phrasal verbs in exercise 1?

3 Write six sentences, each containing one of the phrasal verbs from Vocabulary 1. Leave a space instead of writing the phrasal verb and ask your partner to complete the sentences with the correct phrasal verb.

Speaking 1:
FCE Part 3

Collaborative task

Below are some pictures of different types of relationships. Talk with your partner about the positive and negative aspects of each relationship and then decide which two are the most important to you.

1 Write down at least three of the phrasal verbs from the Vocabulary exercises which you think might be useful.
2 Now add three expressions from the Useful language section on page 59 of Unit 5.
3 Try to use all of this language in your conversation.

> * What are the positive and negative aspects of each relationship?
> * Which two are the most important to you?

Marriage

Parents and children

Team games

Bosses and employees

People and animals

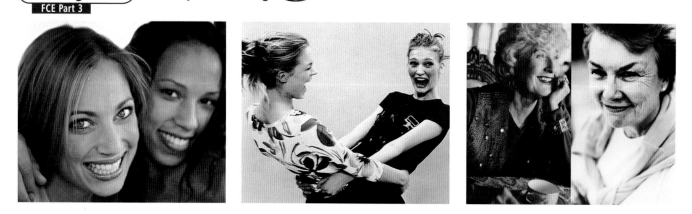

Listening 1: | Multiple matching ◉ 1.24–1.28

Listening 1: **Multiple matching** ◉ 1.24–1.28

⬤ **1** Look at these photographs of sisters.

Which photograph shows twins?
What type of relationship do you think the sisters have with each other?

2 You will hear five of the people in the photos talking about their sisters. For questions **1–5**, choose from the list **A–F** what each speaker says about her relationship with her sister. Use the letters only once. There is one extra letter you do not need to use.

> ## How to go about it
>
> - The key words in the questions have been underlined. However, if you hear one of these words or phrases do not assume that the question which contains those words is the answer.
> - Listen carefully both times before making your final decision.

A Her sister <u>teased</u> her.   Speaker 1 ☐

B They <u>don't get on</u> with each other.   Speaker 2 ☐

C They <u>compete</u> with each other.   Speaker 3 ☐

D They have always led very <u>different lives</u>.   Speaker 4 ☐

E She <u>admires</u> her sister's <u>strength of character</u>.   Speaker 5 ☐

F She <u>protected</u> her sister.

3 Can you match any of the speakers to the women in the photographs?

Speaking 2: | **Interview** ⬤

In Speaking Part 1 you may be asked to talk about your family. Talk to your partner, answering the following questions.

> ## Don't forget!
>
> Say as much as possible about each question. One word answers are not enough!

- Do you have a large family?
- How many brothers and sisters have you got?
- If you don't have any brothers or sisters, what are the advantages of being an only child?
- Do you have many cousins? Do you get on well with them?
- Describe the relationship you have with one of your family members.
- Do you take after your mother or your father? In what ways?
- Do you see your grandparents very often?

Language focus 2: Defining relative clauses

Defining relative clauses contain information which is essential for our understanding of the whole sentence.

1 Look at the following extracts from the listening exercise and answer the questions.

I moved into a flat with a boy who played drums in a punk band.
I wore clothes that got all the neighbours talking.

The underlined words are relative pronouns. What alternative pronouns can be used?

Can the relative pronoun be omitted from these two sentences? Why/Why not?

2 *She'd come home with blackberries she'd picked and tales of wild rabbits she'd seen.*

Two relative pronouns have been omitted from this sentence. Where could they be inserted and which ones could be used? Why is it possible to leave them out in this case?

3 *The woman to whom I spoke had no idea what was going on.*
The woman who I spoke to had no idea what was going on.

Which of these sentences is more formal?

Can the relative pronoun be omitted in either of them?

4 Complete these sentences using *when, where, why* or *whose*.
 a What's the name of the place _____ we had that accident last year?

b The reason _____ people from Mediterranean countries live so long is because they eat so well.
c I'll always remember the day _____ I got my first job.
d That's the woman _____ husband you spoke to on the phone.

Check your answers and read more about defining relative clauses on pages 210 and 211 of the Grammar reference.

Practice

Complete each of the gaps below with an appropriate relative pronoun or relative adverb. Decide in which sentences there is more than one possibility and whether the word can be left out.

1 I'd like to go back to the restaurant _____ we celebrated your birthday last year.
2 Have you been to the new cyber café _____ has just opened in the town centre?
3 Ironic, really. The person _____ car they stole had just finished a three-year prison sentence for car theft.
4 Have you finished the book _____ I lent you?
5 I wish I could remember the name of the man _____ sold me this computer.
6 The only thing _____ worries me is the cost. Will we be able to afford it?
7 Here's that phone number _____ you wanted.
8 I was born in 1969. That was the year _____ the first man landed on the Moon.

Reading

Read the following text about a type of club and answer the following questions. Who goes to these clubs and what do they do there? What are the benefits according to **a** Ben Sassen, aged 17? **b** his father?

Rock of ages

It may sound surprising, given that you'd imagine the average child wouldn't be seen dead near his or her parents on a disco floor, but there is an amazing new trend towards families going clubbing together. Child-friendly venues are appearing everywhere, the main difference being that they are predominantly alcohol- and smoke-free zones and parents and their children actually get up on the dance floor together to have a bop.

The Whirl-Y-Gig club, which held its first family club nights over 15 years ago, is currently one of the most popular places for different generations to let their hair down together. It plays credible music, there's a cool atmosphere and children under 12 are allowed in free. Ben Sassen, 17, first started going there with his father, Michael, 36, when he was just six years old. His parents were separated and he was then living with his mother, so it was a good opportunity for father and son to have some fun together.

'Occasionally I was embarrassed that my father was there,' says Ben. 'But usually friends thought it was great because of the relationship I had with him. It's one thing to get on well with your parents, but another to have something specific in common, that you can sit down and talk to them about.'

For Michael, who dances with every bit as much energy and enthusiasm as his teenage son, the experience brought back memories of his own youth. 'It was certainly an interesting experience watching someone go through the same stages as I did growing up and to have a unique insight into what he was doing and thinking about.'

 Would you consider going to a club like the Whirl-Y-Gig? Why/Why not? Is there a big generation gap between children and parents in your country?

Vocabulary 2: *Have*

A Expressions with *have*

1 In the text on page 71 the expression 'to have a bop' is an informal way of saying 'to have a dance' or 'to dance'. Look at the text and find four more expressions with *have*.

to have _____   to have _____
to have _____   to have _____

2 Talk to your partner about the following:

- something that you have difficulty doing
- someone who has had a strong influence on you
- somewhere you go to have a good time
- something you would like to have more time to do
- something you would like to have the power to change
- something you have in common with a brother, sister or friend

3 What does 'it' refer to in each of the following sentences? Match each item in the box to an appropriate sentence **1–6**. There may be more than one possible answer.

a headache   hair   a scarf   a tooth   something private   a book

1 Can I have it back next week, please?
2 You had it on this morning when we left the house.
3 I'm afraid you'll have to have it taken out.
4 That's nice; where did you have it done?
5 It's got nothing to do with you – mind your own business!
6 I see, and how long have you had it?

Can you think of any other possible meanings for *it* in each of the sentences?

4 With your partner make up a short dialogue which includes one of the sentences from exercise 3. Compare your dialogue with those of other students in the class.

B Causative *have*

1 In **1** and **2** below, explain the difference in meaning between the two sentences.

1 a She wants to dye her hair red.
   b She wants to have her hair dyed red.
2 a He took a photo of his daughter.
   b He had a photo taken of his daughter.

1 b and **2 b** contain the causative use of *have*. Complete the following sentence:

To use this structure we need the appropriate form of the verb *to* _____ + the object + the _____ of the main verb.

G Read more about causative *have* on page 210 of the Grammar reference.

2 In questions **1–6**, write a suitable form of *have* in the first gap and the correct form of the verb in brackets in the second. The first one has been done for you.

1 Do you think it would be interesting *to have* your head completely *shaved* (shave)?
2 Do you like _____ your photo _____ (take)?
3 Would you like _____ any part of your body _____ (pierce)?
4 When was the last time you _____ a tooth _____ (fill)?
5 When are you next _____ your hair _____ (cut)?
6 Do you know anyone who _____ their house _____ (break) into?

3 Ask and answer questions **1–6** in exercise 2.
Example:
A: Do you think it would be interesting to have your head completely shaved?
B: Well, I think it would be OK in summer, but not very practical in winter. I suppose one important advantage is that you wouldn't have to dry your hair after a shower.

Language focus 3: Non-defining relative clauses

1 Look at the following two sentences from the reading text.

a *The Whirl-Y-Gig club, which held its first family club nights over 15 years ago, is currently one of the most popular places for different generations to let their hair down together.*

b *For Michael, who dances with every bit as much energy and enthusiasm as his teenage son, the experience brought back memories of his own youth.*

Each of these sentences contains two separate ideas.

a **Main idea:** The Whirl-Y-Gig club is currently one of the most popular places for different generations to let their hair down together.

Second idea: The Whirl-Y-Gig club held its first family club nights over 15 years ago.

b **Main idea:** For Michael the experience brought back memories of his own youth.

Second idea: Michael dances with every bit as much energy and enthusiasm as his teenage son.

The information contained in the second idea is not essential to our understanding of the meaning of the main idea. A relative clause which contains non-essential information is called a *non*-defining relative clause.

2 Underline the correct alternative in the following rules for non-defining relative clauses.
a *who* or *which* **can/cannot** be replaced by *that*
b the relative pronoun **can/cannot** be omitted
c commas **are/are not** used

Practice

For **1–5** below, link the ideas contained in the two sentences to form one sentence. Use an appropriate relative pronoun (*who, which, whose*) or relative adverb (*when, where*) and make any other necessary changes. Don't forget to add commas.

Example:

Main idea: Michael has always enjoyed the mixed-generation nights.

Second idea: Michael first took Ben to the club when he was six.

Michael, who first took Ben to the club when he was six, has always enjoyed the mixed-generation nights.

1 **Main idea:** We spent the weekend in York.
Second idea: My mother was born in York.

2 **Main idea:** My best friend has just got married.
Second idea: My best friend always said she wanted to stay single.

3 **Main idea:** My oldest sister lives in Thessaloniki.
Second idea: My oldest sister's husband is Greek.

4 **Main idea:** We're having our holiday in September.
Second idea: Everywhere is a lot less crowded in September.

5 **Main idea:** His daughter borrowed the car.
Second idea: He wasn't very happy about the fact that his daughter borrowed the car.

Open cloze: Relative clauses

For questions **1–8** read the text below, which is the continuation of the text on mixed-generation clubs. Complete each of the gaps with either a relative pronoun (*who, which, that, whose*) or a relative adverb (*when, where*). If there is more than one possibility, or the word can be left out, you should also indicate this. There is an example at the beginning **(0)**.

Unfortunately, those clubs (0) *which/that* depend on serving alcohol to make a profit are less keen on the idea of allowing youngsters in. But places such as Whirl-Y-Gig, (1) _____ opens from 9pm–2am, aim to prove them wrong. The Barefoot Boogie, in Highgate, north west London is another venue (2) _____ hosts regular mixed-generation nights. Elizabeth Payne, (3) _____ runs the twice-monthly club, says it's a unique evening for everyone. 'It is one of the only places (4) _____ I can go to with my three children, (5) _____ ages range from two to fourteen, confident that we'll all have a good time,' she says. Places (6) _____ parents can take their children and know they'll be safe are useful for those days (7) _____ you have trouble getting a babysitter. But do not mistake it for a crèche. Payne had to circulate a memo (8) _____ explained to parents that they should only go if their children also wanted a night out.

Vocabulary 3: Describing people

A Personality

1 The following adjectives can all be used to describe a person's character. Which of them are positive and which are negative? Make two groups in your notebook.

sociable	mean	tolerant	patient	sensitive
polite	sincere	selfish	decisive	lazy
reliable	cheerful	practical	mature	
bad-tempered	adventurous	moody	sensible	

2 Arrange the adjectives in exercise 1 into the columns below according to the prefix which is used to form the negative. If none of the prefixes is used for a particular word, write a new word which expresses the opposite idea.

un-	in-	im-	different word
unsociable			mean – generous

 3 Think of two people you know, for example a relative and a friend, and describe what these people are like, using the adjectives you have just studied to help you.

B Appearance

1 One adjective in each group is not normally used before the noun in capital letters. Underline the adjective which does not fit.

1 flowing   untidy   bald   shoulder-length   straight   spiky   HAIR
2 dark   hazel   sparkling   almond-shaped   piercing   pierced   EYES
3 wrinkled   freckled   thinning   round   tanned   expressive   FACE
4 smooth   pale   dark   healthy   well-built   spotty   COMPLEXION

Which of these features can you see in the photographs above?

2 What is the difference between the words in each of the following groups?

a fat   plump   overweight
b thin   slim   skinny

3 Work in pairs. Take it in turns to compare two people in the photographs above and say which of the two people you would prefer to meet and why. As well as describing physical appearance and clothes, you should also talk about personality.

Writing:
FCE Part 2

Descriptions

1 Read the following Writing Part 2 instructions.

Your teacher has asked you to write about someone you met for the first time in unusual circumstances. Explain what happened and describe the person. Write your **story** in **120–180** words.

2 👁 **1.29**

You will hear three teenagers discussing the Writing Part 2 question above and deciding what they are going to write about. For questions **1–7**, decide whether the idea was stated (✓) or not stated (✗).

1 Marion had nearly reached her destination. _____
2 Eilean didn't know how to mend the car. _____
3 Steven and Marcia met in the theatre. _____
4 Steven didn't do what he was supposed to. _____
5 Marion and Eilean still write to each other. _____
6 Karen invented her story. _____
7 Karen was comfortable during the rescue. _____

3 Read the following model answer to the Writing Part 2 question in exercise 1. Who wrote it: Marion, Steven or Karen? The person who wrote it decided to make some changes to the original story. What factual differences do you notice between the story in the recording and the one in the model?

Last summer while my parents and I were driving to the coast to spend our holliday with some relatives our car broke down. After we had been on the road for nearly three hours steam began to pour from the engine and we had to stop. My parents, who know nothing about mecanics, were extremly relieved when another driver pulled over and offered to help.

When his daughter Eilean stepped out of the passenger seat to stretch her legs I couldn't help noticeing how incredibly tall she was. I wondered how she had managed to fit into the car. But perhaps her most striking feature was her spiky green hair, wich seemed to grow out of her head like grass. That and her colourfull 'hippy' clothes were as bright and cheerfull as she was and we spent the whole time chating and laughing as if we had known each other for years.

We've kept in touch and she always says, rather misteriously, that Destiny brought us together. I must admit, I never thought I'd make a friend on the hard shoulder of a moterway.

4 The model answer contains ten spelling mistakes. Read the story again and try to find and correct the ten mistakes.

5 Organization
- The story in the model contains three paragraphs. What is the purpose of each of the paragraphs?
- What proportion of the answer
  a explains what happened?
  b describes the person?

Narrative elements
- As we saw in Unit 4, in addition to well organized paragraphs a good narrative should contain the following elements:
  a a variety of past tenses
  b a wide range of vocabulary
  c appropriate linking words (including relative clauses)
  Find examples of each of these in the model story.

Descriptive elements
- When we describe someone we can talk about their physical appearance, personality, clothes, actions (what they do or say) and their interests. Which of these appear in the model?

Now you are ready to write your story.

Don't forget!
- Plan your answer first.
- Check you have answered both parts of the question.
- Check your work for spelling and grammatical mistakes when you have finished writing.

6 Review

Relative clauses

Decide whether the relative clause in each of the following sentences is defining or non-defining. If the relative clause is non-defining, add commas in the appropriate place(s). If it is defining, say whether the relative pronoun or adverb can be omitted or not. There are two examples at the beginning (**0** and **00**).

0 My father who works in a chocolate factory never eats sweet things.
Non-defining – add commas after father *and* factory.

00 There'll be a prize for the student who tells the most jokes in 5 minutes.
Defining – the relative pronoun who *cannot be omitted.*

1 Jennifer Aniston who is perhaps best known for her role as Rachel in 'Friends' has also appeared in several major films.

2 What's the name of the village where you got married?

3 He hasn't given me back the book that I lent him.

4 She told me that Vasilis had failed his driving test which didn't surprise me at all.

5 That song always reminds me of the time when I was working in Brazil.

6 He's the only person in this class whose first name begins with 'Z'.

7 Emma received a phone call from the Managing Director who had been impressed by her sales performance.

8 Few written records have survived so it is a period of history about which we know very little.

Vocabulary

A Phrasal verbs

Complete the gaps in sentences **1–8** below with the correct form of an appropriate phrasal verb. Use the verbs and particles from the boxes.

fall	bring	get	look
let	tell	fall	get

out	over	for	off
on	up	down	up

1 When I kept getting into trouble at school, my parents understandably felt I had _____ them _____ .

2 He was _____ _____ for hitting his sister and made to apologize to her.

3 I was _____ _____ by my parents to believe that honesty is the best policy.

4 I was extremely disappointed when I found out that my uncle had spent three years in prison: I had always _____ _____ to him and considered him a role model.

5 I don't _____ _____ very well with my mother-in-law. I don't think she's forgiven me for taking her son away from her.

6 It was love at first sight. I _____ _____ him immediately.

7 They're always _____ _____ over the silliest of things. They'll be talking to each other again tomorrow, you'll see.

8 He wasn't ready for a new relationship as he still hadn't _____ _____ his divorce.

B Describing people

Complete the crossword using the following clues.

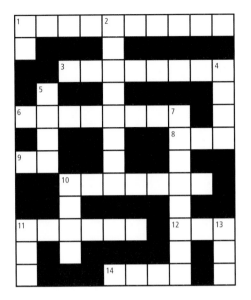

Across

1 Someone who doesn't like meeting and spending time with other people is _____ .
3 Hazel eyes are _____ brown in colour.
6 'Thank you for your donation to our charity. It was extremely _____ of you.'
8 'He's going to have his left _____ pierced.'
9 negative prefix for *decisive*
10 'She's so _____: she only ever thinks about herself.'
11 unattractively thin
12 'Unfortunately, he's in a _____ mood today.'
14 Unlike Mediterraneans, people in northern Europe tend to have a rather _____ complexion.

Down

1 negative prefix for *adventurous*
2 'She's such a _____ child: always so happy and positive.'
4 'She looks much nicer with shoulder-length _____ .'
5 opposite of 6 across
7 'Please try to be _____ about this. Think with your head rather than with your heart.'
10 attractively thin
11 'He was too _____ to ask her to go out with him, so he got his friend to do it for him.'
13 negative prefix for *honest*

Use of English:
FCE Part 4

Transformations

For questions **1–7** complete the second sentence so that it has a similar meaning to the first sentence, using the word given. **Do not change the word given.** You must use between two and five words, including the word given.

1 He doesn't find it hard to make new friends.
   difficulty
   He has _____ new friends.

2 My relationship with Jerry is none of your business.
   nothing
   My relationship with Jerry _____ you.

3 His guitar playing style was strongly influenced by Eric Clapton.
   a
   Eric Clapton had _____ his guitar playing style.

4 I don't think I'm strong enough to lift it.
   the
   I don't think I _____ to lift it.

5 We're getting a friend to repair the roof.
   having
   We _____ by a friend.

6 They took his tonsils out when he was 11.
   taken
   He _____ when he was 11.

7 We don't want a complete stranger to do it.
   have
   We don't want _____ a complete stranger.

Introduction

In Paper 3, the Use of English Paper, you are given 45 minutes to complete four different tasks. In this unit we will look specifically at three of the tasks:

Part 1   Multiple-choice cloze
Part 2   Open cloze
Part 3   Word formation

Information on the content of **Part 4 (Key word transformations)** appears at frequent intervals throughout this book.

What do you know about the Use of English Paper?

Look at the following statements and decide which are true and which are false. If you think a statement is false, give reasons for your answer.

1 All four parts of the Use of English paper are in the form of a text.   _____
2 You should read texts through at least once before you attempt the task.   _____
3 One mark is given for each correct answer in the Use of English paper.   _____
4 Parts 1, 2 & 3 each contain twelve gaps.   _____
5 All four parts of the paper contain an example.   _____
6 You should not write the answer for the examples on your answer sheet in the exam.   _____
7 In **Part 1** (Multiple-choice cloze) if you are not sure of the answer it is better to leave a blank.   _____
8 In **Part 2** (Open cloze) you sometimes have to write two words.   _____
9 In **Part 3** (Word Formation) an answer is given no marks at all if the word is misspelt.   _____
10 In **Part 4** (Transformations) the key word must not be changed in any way.   _____

Part 1: Multiple-choice cloze

What to expect in the exam

- Part 1 of the Use of English Paper focuses mainly on vocabulary. The following examples show some of the different features of the language which are tested in the Multiple-choice cloze.

  Look carefully at the words in italics and underline the answer A, B, C or D which best fits each space.

1 **Knowing the meaning of a word.**
  If you need anything during the exam, you should ask one of the ____.
  A invigilators   B surveyors
  C observers   D superintendents

2 **Knowing the grammar of a word.**
  His doctor ____ him to eat less and do more exercise.
  A said   B suggested
  C advised   D insisted

3 **Knowing which words go together.**
  a The match was postponed because of the ____ rain.
  A strong   B hard
  C forceful   D heavy

  b Could you ____ in touch with John and arrange a time to meet?
  A put   B find
  C get   D go

4 **Phrasal verbs**
  He was offered the job, but he turned it _____ because of the low salary.
  A up   B down
  C off   D on

5 **Linking words**
  We'll let you buy a motorbike _____ you ride it carefully.
  A as if   B whenever
  C although   D as long as

"Taglines" ©2004 Amy Francisconi
Limited Edition Bookplate #13 www.bookcrossing.com/artists/francisconi

I'm a *very special* book. You see, I'm traveling around the world making new friends. I hope I've made another one in you. If so, please go to www.bookcrossing.com, where you can make a brief journal entry with my BCID number (below). You will see where I've been, and my old friends will be happy to know I'm safe here in your hands. Then help keep my dream alive - *READ & RELEASE* me!

BCID:

First Registered By:

When & Where:

bookcrossing.com™
the karma of literature • free and anonymous

© 2001-2005 **book**crossing.com

1 Look at the title of the text below. What do you think you will read about?
Now read the text through quickly, ignoring the gaps, and check your predictions.

2 Read the text again and for questions **1–12**, decide which answer (**A**, **B**, **C** or **D**) best fits each gap and underline it. There is an example at the beginning (**0**).

Bookcrossing

If you (**0**) _____ to be walking in your local park tomorrow and you find an abandoned book with a label inside (**1**) _____ 'Read and Release me', don't just treat it as a (**2**) _____. You've probably come (**3**) _____ an example of 'bookcrossing', a book-sharing movement started in 2001 by American software developer Ron Hornbaker, whose stated aim is to 'make the (**4**) _____ world a library'.

Bookcrossers 'release' books either by (**5**) _____ them on to friends, or else by leaving them in public places for others to pick up, or 'catch', and then read, before they in (**6**) _____ release them back 'into the wild'. (**7**) _____ a book has been 'caught', the person finding it is (**8**) _____ to record the event by logging on to the bookcrossing website and entering the book's ID number written on the label. That (**9**) _____, both the original owner and subsequent readers of the book can keep track of its progress.

Over half a million people worldwide participate in bookcrossing, 'releasing' books in a (**10**) _____ range of locations including cafés, airports, bus stations, telephone boxes and (**11**) _____ underwater in public fountains. Often a book is left in a place which is relevant to its (**12**) _____ or content: Agatha Christie's *Murder on the Orient Express* on a train, for example, or an archeology book in a museum.

0 **A** <u>happen</u>	**B** occur	**C** pass	**D** arise
1 **A** telling	**B** saying	**C** talking	**D** answering
2 **A** joke	**B** fun	**C** humour	**D** comedy
3 **A** away	**B** across	**C** aside	**D** along
4 **A** full	**B** absolute	**C** overall	**D** whole
5 **A** letting	**B** giving	**C** leaving	**D** passing
6 **A** turn	**B** result	**C** order	**D** part
7 **A** Soon	**B** Since	**C** Once	**D** While
8 **A** animated	**B** suggested	**C** encouraged	**D** promoted
9 **A** time	**B** place	**C** manner	**D** way
10 **A** deep	**B** wide	**C** high	**D** long
11 **A** still	**B** even	**C** yet	**D** already
12 **A** heading	**B** headline	**C** title	**D** calling

Part 2: Open cloze

1 What type of person do you think lives behind each of these doors?

2 Read the following text, which is about a door which was used in a film. Which of the doors in the photos is most similar to the one mentioned in the text?

Selling a door

It looks like **(1) an** ordinary, somewhat battered blue front door, but **(2) it** came to symbolize the negative side of celebrity for its owner.

The door is, in fact, famous **(3) for** its starring role in the British film, *Notting Hill*. But **(4) the** owner of the house, Caroline Freud, got so tired of crowds of tourists having **(5) their** photograph taken in front of it that she sold it - the door, that is.

Usually it is the actors **(6) who** are remembered for their roles in a hit film, but the door was **(7) so** important that it was actually written into the script. At the beginning of the film, William Thacker, played by Hugh Grant, says: 'So this is where I spend my days and years ... in a house with a blue door **(8) that** my wife and I bought together before she left me for a man who looked like Harrison Ford ...'

The house and the door, previously belonged to Richard Curtis, who wrote the film, and **(9) his** wife, Emma Freud. Shortly after the film came out they sold it for £1.2 million and moved **(10) to** a quieter location. It **(11) was** bought by Caroline Freud, who quickly discovered that living behind **(12) such** a famous door brought problems.

What to expect in the exam

- In Part 2 of the Use of English paper there is a text with 12 gaps to be filled. This task focuses mainly on grammar. The following are some of the typical types of words which are omitted. Look at the words in **bold** in the text above and write each one with its number next to the corresponding type. The first two have been done for you.

Type of word	Example and number
Articles	*(1) an*
Prepositions	
Auxiliary verbs	
Personal Pronouns	*(2) it*
Possessive Adjectives	
Relative Pronouns	
Intensifiers (so / such)	

3 Read the continuation of the text below and think of the word which best fits each gap. Use only **one** word in each space. There is an example at the beginning **(0).**

More famous doors

Jenny Cooper, a locations adviser for **(0)** _the_ London Film Commission, said many people **(1)** _____ allowed their homes to be used as film sets found tourists turning up on the doorstep for months afterwards. Public attention, it seems, is an inevitable consequence of owning a house **(2)** _____ has featured in a film.

A celebrity sale, however, **(3)** _____ not always add to the value of a house. Freddie Mercury's old house in Kensington is very private, but **(4)** _____ became a place of pilgrimage to **(5)** _____ fans. **(6)** _____ whole of his garden wall was covered in graffiti and this detracted from its value. The wall has **(7)** _____ cleaned, but messages from adoring fans are still written **(8)** _____ the pavement.

The front door of the Apple Studios was covered in graffiti by the Beatles; when it **(9)** _____ sold it made £20,700, almost five times its estimate. And the plain white door from John Lennon's mansion in Surrey, was sold by Christie's **(10)** _____ £2,300 in 1994. There is **(11)** _____ a passionate market for memorabilia that if you have something that immediately brings a film to mind, then it will sell well.

Indeed, the *Notting Hill* door fetched £6,000 at auction. As **(12)** _____ the film fans, they will now have to use their detective skills to find the wooden star of the film. The famous blue door has been replaced by a plain black one.

Part 3: Word formation

1   For questions **1–8** use the word given in capitals at the end of each line to form a word that fits in the gap in the same line. Use the words in **bold** to help you decide on the correct form of your answer. There is an example at the beginning (**0**).

0 The ___length___ of the Channel tunnel is roughly fifty kilometres.	**LONG**
1 His third book is a **lively and** _____ account of family life.	**HUMOUR**
2 The company took on **two thousand new** _____ last year.	**EMPLOY**
3 Rising prices have forced consumers **to** _____ their belts.	**TIGHT**
4 It is **becoming** _____ **difficult** for young people to find work.	**INCREASE**
5 Unfortunately, the train was **both noisy and very** _____.	**COMFORT**
6 Desert animals cope with **the** _____ in a number of ways.	**HOT**
7 Cook the mixture on a low heat **in a medium-sized** _____.	**SAUCE**
8 This _____ **achievement** won her a place in the **record books**.	**ORDINARY**

2   Describe each answer in exercise **1** using the words in the box below.

noun	adjective	adverb	verb
negative	plural	compound	spelling change

Example
   (0): 'Length' is a noun. A spelling change is required to form it: the 'o' in 'long' becomes an 'e' in 'length'.

3   Look at the title of the paragraph below. What do you think the text will say?
   Read through the text quite quickly, ignoring the gaps, and check your predictions.

4   Now read the text again and for questions **1–10**, use the word given in capitals at the end of some of the lines to form a word that fits in the gap in the same line. There is an example at the beginning (**0**).

Careers information: circus performers

Here is some brief **(0)** _information_ for anyone thinking of following a career in the circus. There is, of course, a wide range of jobs available: trapeze artists, acrobats, clowns, **(1)** _____ , fire-eaters and tight-rope walkers are all to be found in the big top.

INFORM

MAGIC

A few circuses train their own performers, but usually they are more **(2)** _____ in someone who can already demonstrate a circus-related **(3)** _____ or skill. Circus schools are the best way of obtaining the necessary training, and can be either connected to a large circus or else totally **(4)** _____.
Good circus performers are talented, **(5)** _____ and enthusiastic. They need to be **(6)** _____ fit and possess the necessary mental **(7)** _____ to cope with the intense training and obvious demands of the job. They are also flexible and able to adapt **(8)** _____ to new situations, particularly as circuses are frequently on the move.

INTEREST
ABLE

DEPEND
ENERGY
PHYSICAL
STRONG
EASY

Additionally, for many jobs within the circus, good concentration is essential. Fire-eaters and acrobats can't afford to be **(9)** _____ as mistakes can have **(10)** _____ consequences.

CARE
DISASTER

Vocabulary 1: Shopping

1 Complete each of the gaps below with a word from the box.

foodstuffs	own-brand	cashier	value	brands
trolley	out-of-town	receipt	convenience	checkout
corner	range	till	aisles	

I prefer a trip to a large **(1)** _____ supermarket to shopping in the local
(2) _____ shop because there's so much more variety. You can choose between
all the usual well-known **(3)** _____ , or if you prefer, there are the store's
cheaper **(4)** _____ products. As well as tinned and frozen **(5)** _____ food,
there's a wide **(6)** _____ of fresh fruit and vegetables, meat, fish and other
(7) _____ . The household goods are particularly good **(8)** _____ for
money, compared to other shops.
Once I've walked down all the **(9)** _____ , filling my **(10)** _____ with
enough food to last a month, I head for the **(11)** _____ . I try not to look when
the amount I've spent is displayed on the **(12)** _____ and I try not to listen as
the **(13)** _____ reads it out. I hand over my credit card and hurriedly put the
(14) _____ in my purse, preferring not to look at it until I get home.

2 What are the advantages of shopping in smaller local shops?
Do you plan carefully what you are going to buy? Do you ever buy things on impulse?
What shops have you been in during the last fortnight? What did you buy?

Speaking: Supermarket psychology

Did you know that supermarket chains tend to design their stores in the same way?
For example, supermarkets sell a lot of milk, so they usually put it at the back of the
store, leading customers to walk past, and hopefully buy, lots of other products.

In which area of the supermarket do you think they put the following products? Give
reasons for your answers.

Products
confectionery
(chocolates and sweets)
bread
alcoholic drinks
fruit and vegetables
fresh meat

Areas of the supermarket
at the back of the shop
in the middle of the shop
at the checkouts
near the entrance
near the exit

Sentence completion 1.30

You will hear part of a radio programme in which the head of a supermarket chain explains how supermarkets are planned. For questions **1–10** below, complete the sentences.

Don't forget!

- In the exam you have 45 seconds to read the questions. Use this time to try to predict the type of information you might hear.

The location of the entrance is intended to encourage customers to visit [____1____] as possible.

Fruit & vegetables are situated near the entrance so that customers feel they are entering [____2____].

On sale next to the fruit and vegetables are products aimed at keeping [____3____] interested.

The [____4____] counter is usually to be found at the back of the store.

Pre-packed meat prevents customers relating the product to [____5____].

Usually only [____6____] are sold in the frozen food section.

Sales of goods at the end-of-aisle areas are often [____7____] than at other locations.

The [____8____] section is situated in the far corner of the supermarket.

By the time customers reach the alcholic drinks, they will be used to the [____9____].

On sale at the checkouts are products which encourage customers to [____10____].

How do your ideas in the speaking task compare with those of Matthew Brereton? Think of a supermarket you know. Is it designed the way he describes?

Gapped text

You are going to read a newspaper article about shopaholics. Seven sentences have been removed from the article. Choose from the sentences **A–H** the one which fits each gap **(1–7)**. There is one extra sentence which you do not need to use.

Before you do the task, read the text and the paragraphs on page 84 through quickly and answer the following questions.

What type of people are shopaholics?
What do they buy?
What effect does it have on them?

I JUST HAD TO HAVE THEM!

SHOPAHOLIC PILLS

shopping: a curable disease?

An American psychiatrist has launched trials of a drug to help people who cannot stop spending. Professor Lorrin Koran of Stanford University in California believes he has found a cure for shopaholics.

The news will come as a great relief to millions of people suffering from compulsive shopping disorder, a condition which is thought to afflict up to one in 30 American women. **1 [____]** Koran, however, describes it as a 'hidden epidemic' comparable to compulsive gambling, kleptomania and pyromania.

Since the announcement of his test programme, Koran's office has been inundated with hundreds of calls from shopping addicts keen to become his guinea pigs. **2 [____]** But just what type of people suffer from it? According to Koran's research, the majority of shopaholics are women.

3 [____] However, an increasing number of men are also becoming addicted to shopping. They usually collect power tools and car accessories. One man could not stop buying spanners, even though he already had 4,000, while another had bought over 200 different seat covers for his car.

Lorrin Koran's clinic is ideally located in Silicon Valley, the high-tech region near San Francisco that has seen some of the fastest wealth creation in America's history. **4 [____]** Whereas the former get pleasure from shopping and only occasionally splash out on something expensive, typical shopaholics go on a binge at least once a week. They experience urges to buy items that are not needed and then feel sadness and remorse. With good reason: they often get into financial difficulties.

'The thrill they have is in the *purchase* and not in the possession,' said Koran, who identifies low self-esteem as a common factor. 'They are filling their life with things because they feel empty inside.'

5 [____] As she made her way through an expensive shopping centre in Stanford last week, she confessed that she recently spent $35,000 on fashion accessories, getting herself $22,000 into debt. Saleswomen at her favourite boutiques assume she is a rich businesswoman rather than a design assistant at a furniture store.

'I've been doing it since I was 12 when my father would give me his credit card,' she said. She has tried giving up her own cards and leaving her handbag at home, but has never managed to stop shopping. **6 [____]** 'It is ruining my life,' she said.

In the 12-week trial, Laura and 23 others will be treated with a drug which restores levels of serotonin. Serotonin carries messages between nerve cells in the brain and deficiencies are thought to lead to compulsive behaviour. **7 [____]** Lee Smith, a retail consultant, claims that people have always used shopping as a way of cheering themselves up.

A Her addiction was the main cause of her split with a boyfriend of nine years.

B The considerable interest in the supposed cure comes as no surprise to Koran, who has been aware of the extent of the problem for many years.

C Design assistant Laura Olsen, who is the exception to this rule, says she has absolutely no regrets.

D Koran believes that a clear distinction must be made between recreational shoppers and those who cross the line to addiction.

E Until now, few psychiatrists have regarded the problem as worthy of serious medical attention.

F However, not everyone agrees that compulsive shopping is a disease which needs treating.

G Most buy items that improve their appearance such as clothes, shoes, make-up and jewellery.

H For Laura, 44, who has a liking for designer clothes, Koran's trial is a lifeline.

Reacting to the text ⬤

Do you ever buy things to cheer yourself up? If so, give some examples.
If you were a shopaholic, what would you buy?

Language focus 1: The present perfect

A The present perfect simple

The present perfect links past events and situations with the present. The present perfect simple is used:

1 to give news of recent past events with some relevance to the present.
*An American psychiatrist **has launched** trials of a drug to help people who cannot stop spending.* (The trials are taking place now.)

2 to describe something that started in the past and continues until the present.
*Koran **has been** aware of the extent of the problem for many years.* (He is still aware now.)

3 to describe events which occurred at some time between the past and the present (exactly when they happened is not important).
*She **has tried** giving up her own cards and leaving her handbag at home, but she **has never managed** to stop shopping.* (She is still a shopaholic now.)

4 to talk about something which occurred in the past, but in an unfinished time period (ie which includes the present).
*His office **has received** 180 calls from shopaholics so far this week.* (And there may be more in the rest of the week.)

Practice

1 Which of the four descriptions above can be used to explain the use of the present perfect in these sentences?

a I've known Keith since we started school together.
b I've had several jobs but never liked any of them.
c Fishing is so frustrating. I haven't caught anything all day!
d I've been shopping this afternoon.
e I've lost my pen. Can you help me look for it?
f I've already seen that film twice.

2 Look back at the reading text and underline more examples of the present perfect simple. In each case, say why the present perfect is used.

3 a Decide which of the time expressions in the box you would use with the present perfect and which with the past simple. Make two groups of expressions in your notebook.

yet	last summer	in September
so far today	in the last few days	since I got up
two weeks ago	before I came here	for the last two years
over the last week	on my 10th birthday	when I was younger
already	this month	

b Choose four expressions from each group in exercise **3a** and write sentences about yourself, using the appropriate tense.

Example: So far today I've eaten two bars of chocolate.

B The present perfect continuous

The present perfect continuous can be used:

1 to emphasize the duration of a situation or activity.
*I've **been waiting** here for ages.*

2 to suggest that a situation or activity is temporary.
*I'm decorating my room so **I've been sleeping** on the sofa.*

3 to suggest that a situation or activity is incomplete.
*I've **been painting** the kitchen. I hope to finish it soon.*

4 to focus on the repetition of a situation or activity.
*I've **been** trying to phone Tim all day, but there's no reply.*

Like the present perfect simple, the continuous form can be used to talk about the effects in the present of a past event.

Continuous: *I think she's been crying. Her eyes are very red.* (activity)

Simple: *You've cut yourself. There's blood on your shirt.* (single action)

However, it is not normally used to talk about the number of things that have been completed.

Continuous: *I've been writing letters this morning.* (focus on the activity)

Simple: *I've written five letters this morning.* (focus on the finished result)

Practice

1 For questions **1–4** explain the difference in meaning between sentences **a** and **b** and why the present perfect simple or continuous is used in each case.
1 a I've been reading a new novel. I can't put it down.
  b I've read a new novel. I really enjoyed it.
2 a He's been staying with his aunt, but he's hoping to buy a place of his own.
  b She's lived in the same house since she was born.
3 a We've been going to the local shop to do our shopping.
  b I'm afraid they're not here. They've gone shopping.
4 a I've been baking all day. I'm exhausted.
  b I've baked a couple of cakes. Would you like to try one?

2 Complete the gaps in this telephone conversation with the past simple, the present perfect simple or the present perfect continuous form of the verbs in brackets.

Dave: Hi Andy, it's Dave. I **(1)** _____ (just/hear) that you and Sandra are getting married next May. How long **(2)** _____ (you/be) engaged?

Andy: About six months. I **(3)** _____ (propose) to her when we were in Fiji. We **(4)** _____ (keep) it secret for a month or so after that, just until we **(5)** _____ (be) sure of the date for the wedding.

Dave: So **(6)** _____ you _____ (make) all the arrangements yet?

Andy: Yes, more or less. Of course, since we got engaged we **(7)** _____ (save) up for a flat as well. We **(8)** _____ (both/work) overtime to earn a bit extra. We **(9)** _____ (already/save) enough to pay a deposit. Anyway, how about you? What **(10)** _____ you _____ (do)?

Vocabulary 2: *Come*

A *to come as*

Look at the following two sentences from the reading text.
*The considerable interest in the supposed cure **comes as no surprise to** Koran.*
*The news will **come as a great relief to** millions of people.*

Notice the adjective + noun collocation *great relief*. Other possible adjectives which collocate with *relief* are *tremendous* and *enormous*. In the following sentences, three of the alternatives **A**, **B**, **C** and **D** fit each gap. Which one does not?

1 The news of their engagement *came as a* _____ *surprise*.

   A big   **B** great   **C** complete   **D** pleased

2 *It came as a* _____ *shock* to discover that our house had been broken into.

   A great   **B** terrible   **C** permanent   **D** dreadful

B *to come to*

1 Complete each of the gaps **1–6** with one of the words from the box. The first one has been done for you.

> harm   ~~power~~   nothing   end   decision   conclusion

1 It was a sad day for this country when they *came to* _*power*_ .
2 If you do exactly as we ask, your son won't *come to any* _____ .
3 We'll go on strike unless you *come to a/an* _____ soon.
4 We hid under the seats just as the film was *coming to a/an* _____ .
5 When he told me he wasn't going, I *came to the* _____ that he wasn't interested in me.
6 I spent ages planning it and then, because of one silly mistake, it all *came to* _____ .

2 For each of the sentences in exercise 1, discuss with your partner who you think is speaking and why they are saying it.
***Example: 1** It might be someone complaining about the government. He or she probably voted for a different party in the elections.*

C **Phrasal verbs with** *come*

1 Work out the meaning of the phrasal verbs in **bold** in the following sentences. Use the context of the sentence to help you.

1 We were walking in the woods when we **came across** an old abandoned cottage.
2 My parents are out tonight. Would you like to **come round** and watch TV with me?
3 Do you remember the meaning of 'binge'? It **came up** in the last lesson.
4 I don't feel very well. I think I'm **coming down with** flu.
5 That's *my* suggestion. If you **come up with** a better idea, let me know.

2 Which of the phrasal verbs in exercise 1 can be used with each of the following?

   a mysterious illness   my old school reports   in the exam
   to my flat   a solution to the problem

3 Write five sentences of your own. Each sentence should include a phrasal verb from exercise 1 and one of the phrases from exercise 2.

Language focus 2: Contrasting ideas

Rewrite the following sentence in three different ways using *although*, *however* and *despite* instead of *but*. In each case the grammar of the sentence will be different and for one of the words you will need two sentences.

*The weather was bad **but** she enjoyed the trip.*

Check your answers on pages 211 and 212 of the Grammar reference.

Practice

For **1–6**, complete each gap with a word from the box.

although	but	whereas
however	in spite	despite

1 _____ it's quite expensive, we tend to go to the supermarket for fresh fish.
2 He didn't get the job, _____ of the fact that he was the most highly qualified candidate.
3 He went to work this morning _____ not feeling well.
4 They said that they'd sent the parcel on February 1st. _____ , I didn't receive it until the 28th.
5 Esme left the house at ten this morning _____ she didn't say where she was going.
6 In Italy people often live in flats, _____ in Britain people tend to live in houses.

Listening 2: FCE Part 4   Multiple choice 👁 1.31

1 What are the advantages and disadvantages of living in the country and living in a city?

2 You will hear part of a radio programme in which two people, Rebecca and Greg, are interviewed about their life in the countryside. For questions **1–7**, choose the best answer (**A**, **B** or **C**).

1 Rebecca moved out of the city to escape
  A the traffic.
  B the noise.
  C the pollution.

2 What gives Greg less cause for concern now that he lives in the countryside?
  A his neighbours' opinions
  B the amount of violent crime
  C his children's safety

3 Rebecca is unhappy about the fact that
  A she does not live close to local amenities.
  B the neighbours enter her house uninvited.
  C she is unable to drive.

4 What does Greg say about buses where he lives?
  A They are too infrequent.
  B They are unreliable.
  C There is no service.

5 How does Greg react to Rebecca's concerns that her children may grow bored?
  A He sympathizes with teenagers who live in the country.
  B He advises her to move back to the city when they are older.
  C He criticizes parents who do not do enough for their children.

6 What does Greg say about the future?
  A He will probably move back to the city.
  B He says that the future is uncertain.
  C He would like to work in an office.

7 What inconvenience does Rebecca mention in relation to her return to work?
  A Her children will have to change schools.
  B She will spend very little time at home.
  C Her journey to work will be time-consuming.

Language focus 3: Expressing preferences

The following sentences from the listening show three different ways of expressing preferences.

a *prefer* + gerund + *to* + gerund

Now **we prefer** living with less noise (to living in a noisy city).

b *would prefer* + infinitive with *to* + *rather than* + infinitive without *to*

I'd prefer to stay in the village and work at home **rather than do** a nine-to-five job in an office.

c *would rather* + infinitive without *to* + *than* + infinitive without *to*

I'd rather drive to work everyday **than give up** my life in the country.

Practice

For questions **1–4**, complete the second sentence so that it has a similar meaning to the first sentence. Use up to five words including the word in **bold**.

1 I think we'd prefer to watch rather than take part. **rather**

I think we'd _rather watch than take_ part.

2 My sister thinks it's better to buy books than borrow them. **to**

My sister prefers _buy to borrow_ them.

3 I'd rather phone him than send an e-mail. **rather**

I'd prefer _rather phone him_ send an e-mail.

4 I'd prefer to stay in tonight. **not**

I'd rather _not stay in_ tonight.

Vocabulary 3: Towns and villages

1 Match the words **1–8** with the words **a–f** to form places you might find in a town. You may use some of the words more than once.

1 shopping
2 pedestrian
3 housing
4 industrial
5 residential
6 office
7 building
8 apartment

a area 2 4 5 6
b block 6 8
c site 4
d estate 3 4 5 6
e precinct 2 1
f centre 1

Example:

shopping centre and *shopping precinct*

Can you think of an example for each of these in the area where you live?
Are they *on the outskirts* of your town or village or *in the centre*?

2 The following adjectives can all be used to describe a town or a village. Which of them are positive and which are negative? Make two groups in your notebooks.

lively	pleasant	run-down	picturesque	shabby
dull	quaint	depressing	prosperous	bustling

Which adjectives would you use to describe the area where you live?

Speaking 1:
FCE Part 1

Interview

In Part 1 of the Speaking Test, you may be asked to talk about where you live. Ask and answer the following questions with your partner.

- Whereabouts in (*name of town or area*) do you live?
- How long have you lived there?
- What are the amenities like? (eg shops, sports facilities, cinemas, libraries)
- Is everything within easy walking distance?
- What are the good points about living there?
- Is there anything you don't like about it?
- What changes have there been in your local area in recent years?
- Have they been changes for the better or for the worse?

Speaking 2:
FCE Part 2

Talking about photos

Look at these two photos. They show different places where people live.

Student A: Compare the photographs and say what you think it would be like to live in these places.

Student B: When your partner has finished, say which of the two places you think would be safer.

> #### How to go about it
>
> When you are comparing life in the two types of places, you could consider the following aspects:
>
> *contact with other people*
> *comfort   noise   space*
> *surroundings   leisure time*
> *convenience   expense*

Now change roles.

Student A: Compare the photographs on page 87 and say which area you think would be more expensive to live in.

Student B: When your partner has finished, say which of the two places you would prefer to live in.

Writing:
FCE Part 1

Emails

1 Read the following instructions. Which property would you prefer to rent? Why?

This is part of an email you have just received from a friend.

> As we'll both be studying English in York next year, why don't we
> share a house or a flat together? Do you have any ideas about where
> we could live? The language school's in the city centre, I think.

You have seen the advertisements below and decide to write to your friend about them. Read the advertisements and the notes you have made. Then, using **all** your notes, write an email to your friend. Say which property you would prefer to rent and why.

cheap

Properties to rent in York

House in Fulford Road

Monthly rental: **£540**

Two-bedroomed house situated in a quiet residential area overlooking the picturesque river Ouse and within walking distance of the city centre.

good, because …   *3 kilometres!*

above a pub

Flat in Market Street

Monthly rental: **£625**

Modern two-bedroomed flat in excellent condition situated in the heart of historic York, with shops and all amenities nearby.

… very near the school too

2 Read the sample answer. Does the writer choose the same property as you? Does she write in an appropriate style?

To: A Martin

Subject: Renting in York

Hi Ana

I think it's a great idea to rent somewhere together. I've found two places that might be alright.

One is a house in a quiet neighbourhood by the river, which is an advantage, because I have trouble sleeping if there's too much noise. The advert says you can walk to the centre, though I looked on the map and it's about 3 kilometres away.

The other place is a modern flat. It's more central and really close to everything, including the school, so we wouldn't have to get up early for class. The problem is that it's above a pub and that could be a bit noisy for me.

All in all, I think I'd rather live in the house — it's quieter and £75 cheaper than the flat, and the walk to school would be good for us!

Let me know what you think.

All the best

Sara

What to expect in the exam

- In Part 1 of the Writing Paper you will have to write either a letter or an email. The requirements for emails are similar to those of letters. Answers must be grammatically correct with accurate spelling and punctuation and in a style which is relevant to the target reader and the situation. The abbreviated language of text messages is not appropriate.

3 What is the purpose of each of the four main paragraphs in Sara's email?

  Example: Paragraph 1: *A general response to Ana's suggestion and a brief introduction to the two properties.*

4 Find examples of the following:

  a the way in which she rephrases language from the input material.
      Example: Input material: *share a house or a flat together*
               Sara's email: *rent somewhere together*

  b the way she builds on the information given, adding relevant points of her own.
      Example: *because I have trouble sleeping if there's too much noise*

5 Find examples in the email of the following features of informal writing:

  a Informal vocabulary   *Example: Hi*
  b Contractions   *Example: it's*
  c Informal punctuation *Example: dash in the final paragraph*

6 Read the following Part 1 instructions.

  This is part of an email you have just received from a friend who, like you, is studying in the south of England.

  > Do you fancy going somewhere this weekend? Maybe we could go on one of those shopping trips – the kind of thing coach companies organise. They usually offer something quite cheap.

  You have obtained information on the trips below and decide to write to your friend about them. Read the information and the notes you have made. Then, using all your notes, write an email to your friend. Say which trip you would prefer to go on and why.

BRIGHTON MARINA COACHES

Shopping trip to France: — *interesting, because ....*
Boulogne and hypermarket
for just £21 return via Eurotunnel

After two hours in the popular 'Eco' — *can buy things like ...*
hypermarket we move on to the
delightful town of Boulogne, with its
pleasant shopping streets
and charming
restaurants.

Depart: 6.00 am — *very early!*
Return: 11.00 pm

BRIGHTON MARINA COACHES

Take advantage of our special Economy Shopper Fare.

£7.00 for the return journey from Brighton to London's Oxford Street*. — *excellent clothes shops*

Departing
Leaves Brighton   **Arrives London**
8.00   **11.00**

Returning   — *three hours!!*
Leaves London   **Arrives Brighton**
18.00   **21.00**

*All journeys include a 45-minute wait at London Gatwick Airport.

Write an email of between **120 and 150** words. You must use grammatically correct sentences with accurate spelling and punctuation in a style appropriate for the situation.

Don't forget!

- Organize your email into paragraphs.
- Write in a more informal style.
- Avoid copying words and phrases from the input material.
- Add relevant points of your own, but keep within the word limit.
- Begin and end your email in a suitable way *eg Hi Mike, Dear Sue, All the best, Best wishes, Take care, Bye for now.*

Vocabulary: Shopping

1 Complete each of the phrases with an appropriate word from the box. The first one has been done for you.

meat	range	convenience	~~walking~~	brand
out-of-town	own-brand	goods	value	corner

1 easy _____walking_____ distance
2 wide _____ of products
3 good _____ for money
4 local _____ shop
5 fresh _____ counter
6 large _____ supermarket
7 frozen _____ food
8 cheap _____ goods
9 well-known _____ of washing powder
10 household _____ section

2 Write five sentences, each including one of the phrases in exercise 1.

Example:
There is a very good shopping centre within easy walking distance of our house.

Use of English:
FCE Part 2

Open cloze

For questions **1–12**, read the text below and think of the word which best fits each gap. Use only **one** word in each gap. There is an example at the beginning (**0**).

Don't forget!

● Read the whole text through first.
● The Open cloze focuses <u>mainly</u> on grammar.

Microflats

In Britain today, many urban centres (0) _are_ suffering from a chronic lack (1) _____ affordable housing. For many first-time buyers, (2) _____ only solution to this problem is the microflat, a recent trend in apartments which in some cases measure little more (3) _____ 15 square metres. With just enough room (4) _____ enable the occupier to sleep, eat and wash, microflats represent the ultimate in small-scale city living.

(5) _____ of the best publicised designs of microflat was that of young architects Stuart Piercy and Richard Conner, who (6) _____ up with their idea when they realised they couldn't afford to buy a place to live in the capital, (7) _____ the fact that they were earning reasonable salaries. Their 30-square-metre prototype (8) _____ first exhibited in the shop window of Selfridges department store in London in January 2002.

Teacher Sally Wright, who has been living in her London microflat (9) _____ nearly two years now, sees her home as a short-term option. 'Naturally, I would (10) _____ live in a bigger flat, but I had no choice. It came (11) _____ quite a shock when I moved down to London and saw how expensive everything was. I rapidly came (12) _____ the conclusion that I'd have to think small for a while.'

Transformations

A The present perfect

1 Match each sentence **1–3** with two of the sentences **a–f** which both express a similar idea.

1 I haven't done this before.

a It's five years since I started doing this.
b It's five years since I last did this.

2 I haven't done this for five years.

c I've never done this.
d The last time I did this was five years ago.

3 I've been doing this for five years.

e It's the first time I've done this.
f I began doing this five years ago.

2 Complete the second sentence so that it has a similar meaning to the first sentence, using the word given. **Do not change the word given.** You must use between two and five words, including the word given.

1 I haven't spoken to her since she had her baby.
last
The _____ her was before she had her baby.

2 I haven't eaten Greek food before.
time
This is the _____ Greek food.

3 My nephew began to play tennis in 1999.
since
My nephew _____ 1999.

4 He hasn't seen his sister for many years.
ages
It's _____ his sister.

5 The last time I went swimming was three months ago.
for
I _____ three months.

6 I've never seen a supermarket as big as this before.
supermarket
This is the _____ seen.

B Language of contrast

Complete the second sentence so that it has a similar meaning to the first sentence, using the word given. **Do not change the word given.** You must use between two and five words, including the word given.

1 Although he can speak Russian fluently, he still has problems with listening.
able
Despite _being able to speak fluent_ Russian, he still has problems with listening.

2 Although there has been an improvement in his behaviour, his teacher is still concerned.
the
Despite _the fact that his behaviour_ has improved, his teacher is still concerned.

3 In spite of a good performance, she didn't win the match.
lost
Although _she performed well she lost_ the match.

4 Although the price of the car had increased, we decided to buy it.
increase
We decided to buy the car, _despite the increase_ in the cost.

⑧ Time travel

1 Space hotels such as the one in the picture may soon become a reality.

What do you think it would be like to stay in one of these?
How would you spend your time? What might be some of the drawbacks of being a guest? Would there be any dangers?

2 Now read this text about holidays in space, ignoring the gaps. How many of the things you spoke about in exercise 1 are mentioned in the text?

Wish you were here?

*B*een to Benidorm, Bali and the Greek Isles? Tired of all the typical tourist resorts? Why not treat yourself to a holiday in space?

In just a few years from now your local travel agent may well try to tempt you in this way into taking a short break in a futuristic space hotel, with the chance to look down on all the sights of our planet from over 60 miles up.

1 [   ] Now, at the start of the new millennium, it is beginning to become a reality. With the first short commercial passenger flights into space already fully booked, private companies are now turning their attention to holidaymakers wanting to spend longer periods of time outside the Earth's atmosphere. Tourists will soon be preparing to stay for several days in an orbiting space hotel, such as the one designed by American construction company, Gerard and Burns.

The hotel will rotate as it orbits the Earth every 90 minutes, resulting in weightlessness at its centre and 20 per cent of normal gravity in all other areas. **2** [   ]

Mark Levy of Gerard and Burns says: 'We are currently working out what experiences we can provide for the 200 guests which the hotel will accommodate – a 30-minute space walk, for example, or maybe one day an optional trip orbiting the Moon.' **3** [   ]

Before that can happen engineers have to develop safe and low-cost spacecraft to transport us there. NASA has already invested a billion dollars in a project to build a reusable space vehicle. **4** [   ]
One such company, Dream Ships of California, is about to start building its Cosmos Freeway hypersonic aircraft, which will be capable of travelling at Mach 10 at a height of 65 miles and able to fly from New York to London in 20 minutes.

Don't forget!

- Before reading sentences A–H, try to predict the general content of each gap. After the first gap, *Now, at the start of the new millennium …* probably contrasts with some time in the past mentioned in the missing sentence. Similarly, *…it is beginning to become a reality* suggests that the missing sentence talks about space hotels as previously being no more than a vision or fantasy.
- When making your choices, look for connections between the language in the missing sentences and the language in the text, both before *and* after the gap.

3 Read the following instructions for this Part 3 Reading task.

Seven sentences have been removed from the article. Choose from the sentences **A–H** the one which fits each gap (**1–7**). There is one extra sentence which you do not need to use.

A He also foresees games played in weightless conditions including 'zero-gravity basketball' and 'air tennis'.

B And everyone will notice the effects of space adaptation syndrome, which affects one's sense of direction and causes bodily fluids to move towards the head.

C Not so long ago the idea of space travel for all was just a dream.

D So book your tickets now.

E This lack of space is not the only discomfort the first guests will have to put up with.

F And more than a dozen small private companies in the US and Europe are racing to do the same.

G It will probably take some two years to assemble and fit out the hotel, which is expected to travel about 200 miles above the planet.

H But there are one or two potential problems which might make people think twice before heading for space.

Reacting to the text

Would you like to spend a few nights in a space hotel, or have the potential problems put you off?
What other unusual types of holiday do you think will exist in the future?

Vocabulary 1: Phrasal verbs

Each of the following sentences from the reading text contains a phrasal verb. Match each phrasal verb in **bold** to a word or expression in the box with a similar meaning.

> go towards   compensate for
> tolerate   think about and plan
> provide with everything that will be needed

1 We are currently **working out** what experiences we can provide for the 200 guests.
2 The view will definitely **make up for** the drawbacks.
3 But for those who are prepared to **put up with** the lack of comfort in space, the view will definitely make up for the drawbacks.
4 It will probably take some two years to assemble and **fit out** the hotel.
5 But there are one or two potential problems which might make people think twice before **heading for** space.

5 [H] Thousands of small objects orbiting the Earth – parts of old satellites and other space debris travelling at several thousand miles per hour – could do serious damage to spacecraft.

Even if they do manage to get there safely, many of the passengers are likely to suffer space sickness: feel dizzy, sweat and maybe vomit. **6** [B]

But for those who are prepared to put up with the lack of comfort in space, the view will definitely make up for the drawbacks. 'From nowhere else can you appreciate the full size and wonder of the Earth,' says Mark Levy. 'It's a chance not to be missed.'
7 [D] The holiday of a lifetime awaits you.

Language focus: The future

A Making predictions

The following sentences from the reading text all represent opinions, predictions or expectations about the future. Decide which of the words and expressions in **bold** express:

a certainty   **b** probability   **c** possibility

1 The view **will definitely** make up for the drawbacks.
2 Many of the passengers **are likely to** suffer space sickness.
3 It **will probably** take some two years to assemble and fit out the hotel.
4 Your local travel agent **may well** try to tempt you in this way.
5 But there are one or two potential problems which **might** make people think twice before heading for space.
6 Small objects orbiting the Earth… **could** do serious damage to spacecraft.

What is the negative form of each of the phrases in bold?
Example: *will definitely – definitely won't/will not*

Practice

Look at the following predictions for the year 2015. Make your own predictions by completing each gap below with either the positive or the negative form of one of the words or expressions in section A.

1 Robot pets _____ take over from animals in the home.
2 The car _____ cease to be the main means of transport.
3 Children _____ receive most of their education at home.
4 Human cloning _____ be legal in most countries.
5 Scientists _____ have found a cure for cancer and AIDS.

B Other futures

Match each of the future forms **1–9** with an explanation **a–i**.

1 Dream Ships of California is about to start building a hyper-sonic aircraft.
2 This time tomorrow I'll be flying over France on my way to Italy.
3 When you come to visit us, I will have finished all my exams.
4 The train leaves at seven o'clock tomorrow evening.
5 That suitcase looks very heavy. Here, I'll carry it for you.
6 I'm meeting Susana at eight o'clock.
7 I'm going to try and book a flight to the Moon.
8 Considering his lack of effort, I'd say he's going to fail.
9 The hotel will rotate as it orbits the Earth every 90 minutes.

a something which is on the point of happening
b a prediction based on present evidence
c timetabled or scheduled events
d actions or events in progress at a certain time in the future
e actions or events which will be completed by a certain time in the future
f an intention or plan
g future fact
h an arrangement
i an offer to help; a decision made at the moment of speaking

Check your ideas in Parts A and B of the Grammar reference on page 212.

C Time linkers

Complete each of the following gaps with a word or expression from the box. There may be more than one possible answer.

as soon as   by the time   when   before   until

1 I'd like you to make a brief plan of your composition _____ _____ you start writing it.
2 What an awful traffic jam! _____ we get to the airport, the plane will have left.
3 Don't open your Christmas presents yet. Let's wait _____ your father gets up.
4 I'll phone you _____ I know the date of our wedding.

Which tense is used after these time linkers to talk about the future?

Practice

1 In sections A and B below choose the most likely alternative. For sections C and D complete the gaps with an appropriate future form of the verbs in brackets.

A

I've just heard on the radio weather forecast that it
(1) *is raining/is going to rain* tomorrow. That's a real shame because **(2)** *we're going/we'll go* to the countryside for a picnic and **(3)** *we'll have to/we're having to* eat in the car if the weather's bad.

B

Lola's plane **(4)** *is about to take off/takes off* at six tomorrow morning, so **(5)** *I'll get up/I get up* at four and give her a lift to the airport. While you're still in bed, **(6)** *we'll be driving/we're driving* along the motorway!

C

I should be able to leave work a little early tomorrow. I
(7) _____ (see) a client at four, but I don't think our meeting **(8)** _____ (last) very long. We **(9)** _____ (only/sign) a few papers so I expect we **(10)** _____ (finish) by half past four.

D

Kath: What time **(11)** _____ (we/meet) tomorrow to go to the cinema?

Pascal: Well, the doors **(12)** _____ (not/open) until four, but we could have a coffee beforehand.

Kath: That's a really good idea. In that case, I **(13)** _____ (get) the three o'clock bus and I **(14)** _____ (probably/see) you there at about 3.30. OK?

2 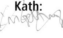 Discuss these questions with your partner.

What will you be doing this time tomorrow?
What plans have you made for next weekend?
Are you planning to buy anything special in the near future?
How will your life have changed in ten years' time?

Vocabulary 2: Travel

1 Complete each of the gaps **1–6** with a word from the box.

journey	travel	flight	voyage	cruise	trip

1 Our _____ was delayed because of bad weather, so we had to spend the night at the airport.
2 The *journey* from London to Brighton takes under an hour by train.
3 I'm afraid Ms Curtis is away on a business *trip* . She'll be back on Tuesday.
4 My interests include music, *travel* and good food.
5 About 1,500 people died when the Titanic sank on its first *voyage* in 1912.
6 I wouldn't recommend going on a Caribbean *6* . You're on the ship for most of the holiday, so you don't see much of the different islands.

2 If you go sightseeing in a city, what types of places do you visit?
Where would you go to get the best view of your town or city?
Which are the most popular tourist resorts in your country?

3 For questions **1–8**, decide which is the correct alternative. Pay close attention to the words before and after each pair of words before making your decision.

Last year we went on (1) *holiday/holidays* to Scotland and booked two weeks on a (2) *camping/campsite*, where we (3) *stayed/lived* in a caravan. Unfortunately, we couldn't really (4) *enjoy/relax* because it was very noisy and it rained nearly every day. We all laughed, though, when my dad fell over in a puddle, but he didn't think it was very (5) *funny/fun*. One day we went on a half-day (6) *excursion/tour* to a castle, but it was (7) *full/crowded* with noisy tourists so we were almost glad to get back to the caravan. Dad's promised that this year he'll take us all on a (8) *pack/package* holiday in the Mediterranean to make up for last year's disaster.

Speaking 1:
FCE Part 1

Interview

In Part 1 of the Speaking Test the examiner might ask you about your holidays.

Student A: Imagine you are the examiner. Ask your partner the following questions.
Student B: You are the exam candidate. Answer the questions as fully as possible.

- Where do you usually spend your holidays?
- What types of things do you like doing on your holiday?
- Do you know where you're going next summer?
- What's the best holiday you've ever had? And the worst?
- Would you prefer to go on holiday with your family or your friends? Why?
- Is there anywhere you would particularly like to visit? Why?
- Would you like to go on a cruise? Why/Why not?
- When you go on holiday do you usually buy souvenirs for yourself?

Now change roles and follow the same instructions again.

Speaking 2:
FCE Part 2

Talking about photos

Before you do the following Speaking Part 2 task, study the Useful language section below.

The two photographs on this page show people enjoying their holiday in different places.

Student A: Compare these photographs and say what type of people go on these holidays and what they do there.

Student B: When your partner has finished, say in which of the places you would prefer to spend a holiday.

Now change roles and repeat the instructions for the photos on pages 100 and 101.

> • **What type of people go on these holidays and what do they do there?**

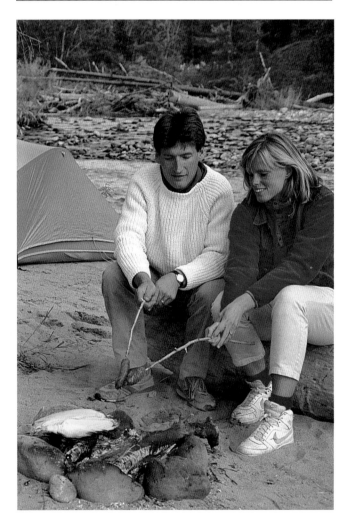

Useful language

Student A

Try to use a variety of expressions to impress the examiners. Here are some alternatives to *perhaps, maybe* and *I think.*

Speculating about the places and the people

looks + adjective	*This place looks popular/ crowded/isolated/exotic.*
looks like + noun	*It looks like the type of place where wealthy/adventurous/ young/independent people go.*
looks as if + verb phrase	*This resort looks as if it's very popular with tourists/ couples/families/walkers.*

Speculating about what people do there

I suppose...   I imagine...   I expect...

*They **could** be looking for something different.*
*They **might** want to breathe fresh air.*
*They **may** go there to relax.*

Student B

*I'd **prefer to** spend a holiday here **rather than** in this place.*
*I'd **rather** go to a campsite **than** stay in a hotel.*

Remember to give your reasons.

Listening:
FCE Part 1

Multiple choice 1.32–1.39

You will hear people talking in eight different situations. For questions **1–8**, choose the best answer, **A**, **B** or **C**.

Before you do the task…

How to go about it

- In questions 1, 2 and 3 you will hear the type of distractors which you encountered in the Part 1 listening exercise in Unit 4.
- In question 4 you are asked to identify the place which the man is describing: *a cathedral, an art museum or a castle*. What are the similarities and differences between the three alternatives?

- In question 5 you have to identify the man who is talking: *the boy's father, a chemist or a doctor*. Think about how each of the three people might speak to the teenage boy.
- Remember to listen carefully the second time to check your answers.

Now you are ready to do the task.

1 You overhear this man talking about his hotel.
How does he feel about his room?
A impressed
B disappointed
C angry

2 Listen to this woman in an interview.
What job has she applied for?
A a tour operator
B a travel agent
C a restaurant manager

3 You hear a woman talking to a tour guide.
What is the woman's problem?
A She doesn't have her passport.
B She has left her money in the hotel.
C She thinks she has been robbed.

4 You overhear a man talking about a place he tried to visit on holiday.
What place is he describing?
A a cathedral
B an art museum
C a castle

5 Listen to this conversation between a man and a teenage boy.
Who is the man?
A the boy's father
B a chemist
C a doctor

6 You hear a local resident talking about tourists in her town.
What is she complaining about?
A They have no money to spend.
B There are too many of them.
C They make too much noise.

7 You hear this boy talking to his mother.
Why is he disappointed?
A He thinks his parents' idea is boring.
B His parents had promised to do something else.
C He's tired of doing the same things.

8 You hear a man telephoning a railway station.
What does he want to do?
A cancel his ticket
B change the date of his ticket
C change the destination of his ticket

Reading 2: Multiple choice
FCE Part 1

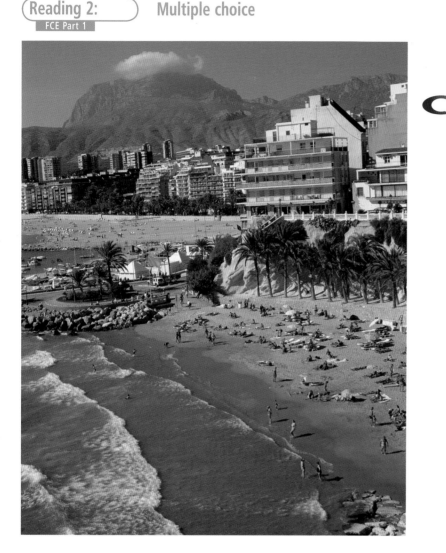

1 Look at this photograph together with the photograph on the opposite page.

What effects, both positive and negative, do you think tourism might have on places like these and the people who live there? What are the benefits to tourists of going to places like these? Are there any negative effects?

2 You are going to read a newspaper article about the effects of tourism. For questions 1–5, choose the correct answer **A**, **B**, **C** or **D**.

How to go about it

- Before you begin to answer the multiple-choice questions in Part 1 of the Reading Paper, read the text through fairly quickly to form a general impression.
- Read the following text in no more than three minutes and compare the writer's views with your ideas in exercise 1. Does he give any arguments which you did not mention?

TRAVEL NARROWS THE MIND

Is your journey really necessary?
John Rentoul makes the case against travel and tourism.

I do not understand the modern fashion for long-distance travel. Of course, there was once an evolutionary advantage to it all; people moved around in the search for food and better living conditions. But now we do so without a purpose.
5 We travel thousands of miles to get to the other side of the world, and then two weeks later we come back again. What for? To see the sights… and make a mess of them? To get to know other cultures? You must be joking.

The instinct to explore has been exhausted. Humans have
10 been everywhere, done everything. They have climbed to the top of Everest so often the summit resembles a rubbish dump. Driven by their genes to invent ever more absurd frontiers to cross, the sort of people who might once have trekked across the Rocky Mountains are now chartering jets
15 so they can freefall parachute over Antarctica.

This restlessness and our ever increasing desire to travel long distances is disastrous for the environment. Air travel burns up unimaginable quantities of fuel and is the most energy-hungry thing that people can do. It is a scandal that aviation fuel for
20 international flights is not taxed. If the governments of the world could agree to do something about it, they would have a permanent source of income – and put the brakes on the fastest-growing source of global warming gases.

As for the idea that travel broadens the mind, widens people's
25 horizons and promotes international understanding, this is just nonsense. You can only really learn anything about foreign countries by living and working in them and I applaud those who do it. It is tourism I object to, and especially the desire to go to the remotest, wildest and often poorest places in
30 the world and build four-star hotels in them. It does not do the local people much good: the hotels are all owned by foreign companies and only 30 percent of the profits stay in the country. Instead, it encourages the demand for Coca-Cola and McDonalds and accelerates the homogenization of world

1 What does the author say about the fashion for long-distance travel?

   A It enables us to understand other cultures.

   B There is no longer any point to it.

   C It helps us to relax.

   D It takes up a lot of time.

2 Why do people do things such as freefall parachuting in Antarctica, according to the author?

   A They are trying to solve personal problems.

   B They feel the need for greater challenges.

   C It is safer than climbing mountains.

   D They want to go trekking in isolated places.

3 Why, according to the author, should aviation fuel be taxed?

   A It would ultimately help reduce pollution.

   B It would enable governments to buy more fuel.

   C It would help governments stay in power.

   D Other types of fuel are taxed.

4 What does the author mean when he says that tourism 'accelerates the homogenization of world culture' (line 34)?

   A Everyone is eating fast food.

   B People are rapidly becoming the same wherever you go.

   C People in remote places are becoming poorer.

   D The pace of life is speeding up.

5 What does the author feel about road travel?

   A Distances are too long.

   B Motorways are safe.

   C Other countries are safer than the United Kingdom.

   D Driving can be dangerous.

Don't forget!

- Apart from the general understanding questions, which usually come last, the multiple-choice questions follow the same order as the text.
- If you have problems choosing the best answer, eliminate those answers which are obviously wrong, then check the answer or answers which you have not eliminated. If you're still not sure, make an intelligent guess. Do not leave a question unanswered.

Reacting to the text

Do you agree with the writer's opinions?
Give reasons for your answer.
What effect does tourism have on your own country?

35 culture. Go abroad and do exactly what you do at home.

But it is not just travel to remote places which is unwise. Even in the United Kingdom, there is no way I would travel
40 long distances by car. As with air travel, statistics may tell us that motorways are not dangerous, but no one can tell me that it is safe for people to be hurtling along within feet of each other at more than 70
45 miles per hour. If you have to travel long distances, the only civilized way is by train.

Next summer, as you hold on to your seat nervously during take-off, and prepare yourself for a week or two of
50 jet lag and sunburn, think of me, enjoying uninterrupted sleep on the overnight train to Glasgow.

Word formation: -en suffix

*...travel **broadens** the mind, **widens** people's horizons...*

1 Some verbs, such as *broaden* and *widen*, are formed by adding the suffix *-en* to the adjective (*broad*, *wide*). To form the verb you may need to add the suffix to the noun. Complete the table with the corresponding nouns and verbs.

Adjective	Noun	Verb
broad	*breadth*	*broaden*
wide	*width*	*widen*
deep		
high		
long		
short		
strong		
weak		
deaf		

2 Complete the gaps with one of the words from the table in exercise 1. You may need to change the form of the word.

1 It fits you very well, sir. The sleeves on the jacket are a little short, but we can certainly _____ them.
2 His life is not in danger now, but naturally the illness has _____ him considerably.
3 I'm pleased to see they're finally _____ the road. The extra lane will make a lot of difference.
4 Can you help me move the sofa? It's not very heavy, so it won't take much _____ to lift it.
5 She lives next to the airport and the noise of the planes is _____ .
6 On a recent expedition to Everest, Burns reached a _____ of 7,900 metres before turning back because of worsening weather conditions.

Writing:
FCE Part 2

Essays

1 Read the following Writing Part 2 instructions.

You have been doing a project on travel and tourism. Your teacher has asked you to write an essay giving your opinions on the following statement.

Travel broadens the mind and widens our horizons.

Write your **essay**. You should write between **120 and 180** words.

2 The writer of the article 'Travel narrows the mind' did not agree with this statement. However, there are two sides to any argument. Read this example essay. How does the writer feel about travel?

Travel abroad is no longer a luxury and nowadays most people in my country have had at least one foreign holiday. Personally, I think this has benefited our society in a number of ways.

Firstly, it enables us to observe and value other cultures and to understand that ours is not the only way of life. Consequently, this helps combat ignorance and narrow-mindedness, which so often lead to racial prejudice and even violence. Secondly, foreign tourists can learn from and 'borrow' those aspects of other cultures which are better than in their own country. It seems to me that the improvement in my country's eating habits owes a great deal to foreign travel.

Another benefit is that more people can now see the world's most spectacular natural sights and visit its most important historic monuments. As a result, we discover our planet and become more knowledgeable in a way which is simply not possible with the Internet or television.

To conclude, I strongly believe that if we travel with an open mind, our horizons will be widened even further.

3   In Unit 3 you saw an essay which looked at both sides of the argument. You can also answer this type of question by considering only one point of view, giving reasons to support your opinion. How many reasons does the writer give to support his/her opinion in the model above? What is the purpose of the first and last paragraphs?

4   Underline any linking devices which the writer uses. The first one has been done for you. Under each of the following headings write down those linkers which are used to:

1 Introduce the writer's opinion *Personally, I think*	3 Show the result or consequence of something
2 Indicate the order of points	4 Bring the essay to an end

Can you add any more linking devices to each of these categories?

5   Look at the following Writing Part 2 instructions.

Your class has been doing a project on travel and transport. Your teacher has asked you to write an essay with the following title.
The best way to travel in a town or city you know well.
Write your **essay**. You should write between **120 and 180** words.

6   Decide which town or city you would like to write about and which means of transport. Note down all the positive features of this type of transport in the town or city you have chosen, together with examples of the benefits to travellers.

Example: Positive feature   Benefits
(underground)   *comfortable*   →   *can read or sleep; arrive at*
                                                       destination free of stress
(car)   *good car parks*   →   *no time wasted looking for parking spaces*

7   You now need to organize your ideas into paragraphs.

Paragraph 1:   Your introductory paragraph should contain one or two sentences introducing your choice and making a general statement saying why you think it is the most suitable.

Paragraphs 2 and 3:   Select three or four of the best arguments from exercise 6 and decide on the order you will write them in your essay.

Paragraph 4:   You will only need to write one or two concluding sentences in your final paragraph. Restate your opinion and leave the reader in no doubt that yours is the best choice.

Don't forget!
- Write in a formal or semi-formal style.
- Use appropriate linking devices (see exercise 4 above and page 35 of Unit 3).
- Write between 120 and 180 words.
- Check your work when you have finished.

Now you are ready to write your essay.

Use of English:
FCE Part 4

Transformations: Future forms

1. In the box below match each sentence **1–6** with a sentence **a–f** which expresses a similar idea. The first one has been done for you.

① She isn't going to go out.
2 She's likely to go out.
3 She's about to go out.
4 She might not go out.
5 She's unlikely to go out.
6 She'll have gone out.

a She'll probably go out.
b She may not go out.
ⓒ She isn't planning to go out.
d She won't be at home.
e She probably won't go out.
f She's on the point of going out.

2. Complete the second sentence so that it has a similar meaning to the first sentence, using the word given. **Do not change the word given**. You must use between two and five words, including the word given.

1 Where are you going to spend your holidays this year?
   planning
   Where _____ your holidays this year?

2 He was about to say something when the phone rang.
   point
   He was _____ something when the phone rang.

3 Unemployment will probably rise in the next few months.
   likely
   Unemployment _____ in the next few months.

4 She's unlikely to change her mind about the job.
   probably
   She _____ change her mind about the job.

5 The plants will probably all be dead by the time we get home.
   have
   The plants _____ by the time we get home.

Use of English:
FCE Part 3

Word formation

Use the word given in capitals at the end of some of the lines to form a word that fits in the gap **in the same line**. There is an example at the beginning **(0)**.

A disastrous holiday

Last year I won a **(0)** _competition_ in a newspaper and the prize was a holiday for two in a	COMPETE
well-known Mediterranean resort. It turned out to be an extremely **(1)** _____ experience	PLEASE
and one which my husband and I would not like to repeat.	
Our room overlooked the road, which was unfortunately being **(2)** _____ at that time,	WIDE
and the noise from the machinery was **(3)** _____ . For some strange reason the road	DEAF
works went on twenty-four hours a day and as a result we suffered several **(4)** _____	SLEEP
nights. **(5)** _____ to put up with the constant noise, we decided to complain to the	ABLE
manager. We **(6)** _____ expressed our dissatisfaction with the room and asked if we	POLITE
could possibly change. However, our request was not **(7)** _____ as the hotel was fully	SUCCEED
booked and there were no spare rooms.	
The situation **(8)** _____ when my husband suffered food poisoning as a result of	WORSE
eating some local seafood. By that stage we'd had enough and decided to **(9)** _____ our	SHORT
stay and catch the first available flight home. They say that travel **(10)** _____ the mind	BROAD
but we shall happily narrow our horizons this year and enjoy a week in our own back garden.	

Use of English: FCE Part 1

Multiple-choice cloze

For questions **1–12**, read the text below and decide which answer (**A, B, C** or **D**) best fits each gap. There is an example at the beginning (**0**).

Marrakech

Where can you go in January for almost guaranteed (0) ____ – without travelling for most of the day to get there? The answer is Marrakech in Morocco, a four-hour (1) ____ from Britain, where the average temperature is a pleasant 66°F.

Marrakech is a city of (2) ____ beauty, with its pink buildings and green palm trees contrasting with the snow-covered (3) ____ of the Atlas Mountains in the distance. For tourists, there's the added attraction of excellent food at reasonable prices, and high quality accommodation, such as Hotel La Momounia, (4) ____ as one of the top hotels in the world.

(5) ____ Marrakech is one of Morocco's busiest and most modern cities, the influence of the Middle Ages is still very evident. (6) ____ can admire the battlements, towers and mosques, which were built (7) ____ centuries ago. And forget about shopping malls – for perfumes, fabrics, antiques, spices and crafts, (8) ____ the 'souks', open-air marketplaces where you'll almost (9) _____ find something to take back home.

For those who want to (10) ____ sport Marrakech has plenty to offer. (11) ____ to golf and tennis, there is also skiing on the slopes of the High Atlas Mountains, where the (12) ____ of the surrounding area are quite spectacular. Alternatively, you could just relax by a heated swimming pool and dream of your next visit.

0	**A** sunset	**B** suntan	**C** sunshine	**D** sunshade
1	**A** travel	**B** trip	**C** flight	**D** voyage
2	**A** big	**B** great	**C** large	**D** high
3	**A** peaks	**B** hills	**C** heads	**D** surfaces
4	**A** thought	**B** regarded	**C** believed	**D** guessed
5	**A** Because	**B** However	**C** Despite	**D** Although
6	**A** Spectators	**B** Viewers	**C** Sightseers	**D** Onlookers
7	**A** several	**B** plenty	**C** other	**D** all
8	**A** work out	**B** put up with	**C** head for	**D** make up for
9	**A** likely	**B** certainly	**C** probably	**D** possibly
10	**A** do	**B** exercise	**C** take off	**D** go in
11	**A** As well	**B** Apart	**C** In addition	**D** Moreover
12	**A** visions	**B** views	**C** aspects	**D** appearances

Writing: FCE Part 2

Articles

You see this announcement in an international magazine.

HOLIDAY COMPETITION

Write an article about a holiday destination you know well, giving details of what tourists can see and do there. The top ten articles will be included in the next edition of our magazine.

How to go about it

Use the Multiple-choice cloze text on Marrakech above as a model.
How many paragraphs are there?
What type of information does each one contain?
What tense is used throughout the article?
Are there any expressions which you could use in your own article?

Write your **article** for the competition. You should write **120–180** words.

9 Fact or fiction?

Reading 1:
FCE Part 1

Multiple choice

1 Do you believe that alien life forms exist? If so, what appearance might they have? What scientific explanations are often given for UFOs?

2 You are going to read an article about UFOs. Read through the text quickly and for question 1 choose the best answer **A**, **B**, **C** or **D**.

1 Which of the following sentences best sums up the writer's views?

A Aliens have visited our planet.

B All UFO sightings can be explained scientifically.

C Alien life forms may exist.

D Most UFOs are practical jokes.

UFOs – have we been visited?

Is there a scientific explanation for UFOs or do alien life forms really exist? Kevin McCullough investigates two cases of UFO sightings.

On a cold, dark winter's evening in 1988, Jon Hickes and Richard Williams were driving to a friend's house near Canterbury when they saw a bright red object glowing above the
5 fields about 500 metres in front of them. As they drove nearer to investigate they were amazed to find a large area of molten metal, bubbling on the ground like a pool of volcanic lava. When firemen arrived shortly
10 after, it took them over an hour to cool down the boiling mass and make it safe.

Samples of the solidified metal were taken to the nearby University of Kent where they were found to contain iron and small
15 amounts of tin and chromium. James Radcliffe, a specialist at the university, concluded that material such as this could not have come from a meteor, and military experts, for their part, were quick to point
20 out that **it** could not have fallen from any aeroplane or spacecraft; space debris does not hit the earth's surface in a liquid state.

Of course, there were suggestions that the whole thing might have been a hoax, but a
25 practical joke on this scale would have been very difficult to set up. The only factory in the area capable of producing molten metal had recently closed down, and besides, arranging for large quantities of the metal
30 to be dropped from the sky would not be very easy. Clearly, this was not a simple open-and-shut matter.

Unexplained aerial phenomena of this nature have been observed and noted down
35 for centuries, but the modern preoccupation with UFOs began in 1947, when there was an unusually large number of reported sightings. In the last 50 years there have been over 10,000 such reports in Britain
40 alone. Most of these can be attributed to man-made objects such as aircraft and satellites, or astronomical phenomena such as shooting stars. Just over five per cent of cases, however, remain unexplained,
45 leading many UFO experts to the conclusion that aliens have indeed visited our planet.

In another case in the 1980s Les and Linda Burnham were cycling together along a country road near Rye in Sussex when a
50 sudden, blinding light almost caused them to fall off their bicycles. As the couple stopped to cover their eyes, they felt intense heat and heard a deafening roar like the sound of a high-speed train. A
55 minute or so later they were able to look up again, and were greeted with the sight of a huge, diamond-shaped metal object floating above the treetops, spitting flames and emitting a loud, high-pitched noise.
60 They watched in shocked silence as the gigantic structure climbed high into the air and disappeared at great speed out to sea. Then, they claimed, five or six jet aircraft appeared from nowhere and raced off after
65 the mysterious object.

As they cycled the short distance home, Les and Linda suffered headaches and sickness, and during the next few days experienced diarrhoea and minor skin burns. As a result
70 of illness and depression Linda was unable to go to work for nearly six weeks.

Underneath where the object had been floating, an area of woodland had burnt down, electricity cables had snapped and the
75 road surface had melted. Whatever caused it, the heat must have been incredibly intense to do all that. As for the jet aircraft, military bases denied all knowledge of them and to this day their origin, like that of the
80 diamond-shaped object, remains a mystery.

Secret military activities or rare atmospheric phenomena may account for some of the unexplained sightings but the origins of others could lie elsewhere. And until the
85 opposite is proved, that 'elsewhere' might include visits from extraterrestrial beings.

3 Now read the text again and for questions **2–8**, choose the correct answer.

2 What are we told about the object which Jon Hickes and Richard Williams witnessed?

A It was very hot.

B It came up through the ground.

C They watched it change from solid to liquid.

D It was 500 metres wide.

3 'it' in line 20 refers to

A a meteor.

B a spacecraft.

C the metal.

D the university.

4 What does the writer mean when he says, 'this was not a simple open-and-shut matter' (line 32)?

A It was a complicated hoax.

B The factory was no longer open.

C The sighting is still being investigated.

D There was no obvious explanation for the incident.

5 Records of mysterious happenings in the sky were first made

A 50 years ago.

B in 1947.

C hundreds of years ago.

D in the nineteen eighties.

6 The object which Les and Linda saw

A was travelling at the same speed as a train.

B made two different sounds.

C was made of metal and diamonds.

D was on fire.

7 As a result of their experience Les and Linda

A began to feel unwell soon afterwards.

B were ill for several weeks.

C were badly burnt.

D started feeling sick when they got home.

8 According to Les and Linda, the jet aircraft they saw

A were involved in secret military activity.

B followed the strange object.

C probably came from a nearby military base.

D were the same shape as the unidentified object.

Reacting to the text

Do you know any other stories of mysteries which have never been solved? What theories have been put forward to explain what happened?

Language focus 1: Modal verbs of speculation

Look at these extracts from the text and answer the questions.

a *James Radcliffe...concluded that material such as this* **could not have come** *from a meteor.*

b *Of course, there were suggestions that the whole thing* **might have been** *a hoax.*

c *Whatever caused it, the heat* **must have been** *incredibly intense to do all that.*

1 Which of the forms in **bold** express
   a certainty about what did or didn't happen?
   b a possible explanation for what happened?
2 Which verb form is used after each of the modal verbs?
3 Which of the following modal verbs can be used in place of *might* in sentence **b** without changing the meaning?
   could   should   may   can
4 Is it possible to use *must* in place of *could* in sentence **a**?

🔍 Check your ideas on page 213 of the Grammar reference and read more about modal verbs of speculation.

Practice

1 Can you explain what happened in the following situations? Write two or three sentences for each using modal verbs.

Example: 1
He might have been working in the garden.
He could have fallen over while playing football.
He may not have had a wash for several days.

1 His face and hands are very dirty.
2 Angela's crying. *She must have been lost her dog*
3 The kitchen window is broken. *The children must have been*
4 There's a red mark on Derek's shirt collar. *could have meeting a pri*
5 Jonathan was late for school. *might have been going to the doc*
6 Nobody in the class did their homework last night. *might*

2 Match each of the sentences **1–6** with a suitable continuation **a–f**.

1 Don't make too much noise.   *b*
2 What do you mean, you don't know what to do?   *D*
3 Would you lend me yours?   *E*
4 I've tried calling several times but there's never any answer.   *A*
5 You should ask her.   *E*
6 I want everyone to search the area.   *C*

a She might not be living there any more.
b He might still be asleep.
c He can't have got very far.
d You can't have been paying attention.
e I must have left mine at home.
f You never know; she might be interested.

3 Look at sentences **a–f** in exercise 2 again and for each one decide whether the speaker is talking about the past or present. What form of the verb is used after the modal verb in each case?

4 ⬤ Use modal verbs to speculate about possible contexts for each of the sentence combinations in exercise 2.

Example: 1 *'This could be a mother speaking to her children. They might be playing in the house and their father may be ill in bed.'*

Listening:
FCE Part 4

Multiple choice ⬤ 1.40

⬤ 1 Do ghosts really look like this?
   What are the typical characteristics of ghosts?
   Where are they normally seen? What do they do?
   Have you or anyone you know ever seen a ghost?

2 You will hear a radio interview with the Chairman of the Ghost Club, Alastair Agnew. For questions **1–7**, choose the best answer (**A**, **B** or **C**).

   1 Alastair confirms that ghosts are
      A transparent.
      B dressed in white.
      C capable of passing through solid objects.

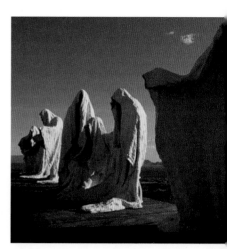

2 He adds that often when ghosts are sighted

    A they are only partially visible.

    B their legs are bent at the knees.

    C they are floating above the ground.

3 What do we learn about the sounds associated with ghosts?

    A People react in different ways to the sounds.

    B Footsteps are by far the most frequent sound.

    C A variety of sounds have been reported.

4 What does the 'stone-tape theory' say?

    A Most ghostly sounds can be attributed to cassette recordings.

    B Sounds can be stored then later emitted by walls.

    C Ghosts can most easily be recorded in stone buildings.

5 What is Alastair's opinion of the theory?

    A It does not explain ghostly smells.

    B It was not proposed by experts.

    C There may be some truth in it.

6 Ghosts often haunt buildings

    A near former execution sites.

    B which are empty or abandoned.

    C belonging to car crash victims.

7 What does Alastair say about our ability to see ghosts?

    A We are not as well-equipped as domestic animals.

    B Everybody stands some chance of seeing one.

    C Some people refuse to acknowledge they can see them.

Language focus 2: Question tags

1 The following two sentences from the listening both end with a question tag. Look at the words in **bold**. How are questions tags formed?

That's *a fair enough description of a ghost,* **isn't it**?

And as Chairman of the Ghost Club **you would not** *agree with that explanation,* **would you**?

2 Listen to the two examples from the recording again. In which of the sentences in 1 is the interviewer:

a asking a real question because she is *unsure* if her statement is true or not?

b expecting agreement to her statement, which she feels *sure* is true?

How can you tell the difference?

 Read more about question tags on page 213 of the Grammar reference.

3 Add an appropriate question tag to each of the following statements.

  1 You don't believe him, _____DO YOU_____?

  2 You won't let me down, _____WILL YOU_____?

  3 You went away for the weekend, _____DIDN'T YOU_____?

  4 He's not playing very well, _____IS HE_____?

  5 He's already passed First Certificate, _____? HASN'T HE

  6 I'm right about that, _____aren't I_____? AM I NOT

  7 You can play chess, _____CANNOT YOU_____?

  8 Let's phone Paul, _____? SHALL WE

1.41 Now listen and check your answers.

4 Listen to the sentences in exercise 3 again and next to each question tag draw an arrow to show if the intonation is rising or falling at the end.

5 Practise saying the sentences with the same intonation as the speakers in the recording.

6 Write down four statements about your partner that you are *sure* are true and four that you are *unsure* about, adding a question tag to each one.

Examples: *You don't like heavy metal music, do you?*
You went abroad for your holiday last year, didn't you?

7 Ask and answer each other's questions, using appropriate intonation.

Example
A *You don't like heavy metal music, do you?*
B *No, I don't. You're right. And you went abroad for your holiday last year, didn't you?*
A *No, I didn't, actually. I went abroad the year before last. Last summer we stayed in our house in the countryside.*

Vocabulary: *Give*

A Phrasal verbs with *give*

1 Look at these sentences from the listening. Match each of the phrasal verbs in **bold** with its definition **a–c**.

> **1** …ghosts look solid, just like real people. The only thing that **gives** them **away** is the fact that, as you rightly say, they can walk through walls.
> **2** So a building that was once used as a church, for example, may **give off** the smell of incense.
> **3** We'll be **giving out** their address at the end of the programme.

a to produce and send into the air
b to show someone's true nature or identity
c to announce or broadcast information

2 Work out the meaning of the phrasal verbs in **bold** in the following sentences. Use the context of the sentence to help you.

> **1** She's such a gossip – you can't tell her anything! She loves **giving away** other people's secrets.
> **2** I'm so unfit! I really ought to **give up** smoking.
> **3** I'm going to **give out** the test papers now but you mustn't begin until I tell you.
> **4** I'd like you to **give in** your homework at the end of the lesson. I'll mark it tonight and **give** it **back** to you tomorrow.
> **5** Although my parents were against the idea at first, I went on about the all-night party so much that eventually they **gave in** and agreed to let me go.

B Expressions with *give*

1 In sections **A** and **B** below match a sentence beginning on the left with a suitable ending on the right.

A

1 Convinced it was a ghost, she **gave a piercing**…
2 When he heard the good news he **gave a broad**…
3 She said goodbye, **gave** him **a tender**…
4 Hearing his ex-girlfriend's name, he **gave a deep**…
5 As she spoke, her son **gave** her **a blank**…

a **sigh** and dreamt of getting back together with her.
b **look** as if he hadn't understood a word.
c **smile**, showing all his teeth.
d **scream** and ran out of the building.
e **kiss** on the cheek and walked out of his life for ever.

B

1 It's been great to see you again. **Give my best**…
2 After the accident I had to **give full**…
3 Your gifts of toys will **give great**…
4 She was **given a nasty**…
5 Sharon Stone **gives an impressive**…
6 The President **gave a lengthy**…

a **shock** when she discovered her purse was missing.
b **performance** in this, her latest film.
c **speech** on the challenges facing the country.
d **details** of what had happened to the police.
e **regards** to your family.
f **pleasure** to the many children in the orphanage.

2 The expressions in exercise 1A all refer to *physical actions* of some kind. Match each of the following general meanings to each expression in 1B.

a to cause someone to experience an emotional feeling
b to perform or present something in public
c to communicate information, opinions or greetings

3 The *verb + adjective + noun* combinations in sections 1A and B are fairly *strong* collocations. When you hear the first two words of the combination, you can predict quite accurately what the next word will be. For example, if someone begins, *he gave a broad...* there is a very strong chance that the next word will be *smile*.

Cover up the sentence endings in the right hand column of exercises 1A and B and see how many of the *nouns* you can remember for the corresponding *verb + adjective* combinations on the left.

4 **a** Describe situations in which you might:

- give a broad smile
- give a piercing scream
- give a deep sigh
- give a nervous laugh
- give someone a blank look

b Think of a time when someone or something:

- gave you a nasty shock
- gave you a pleasant surprise
- gave you great pleasure
- gave an impressive performance
- gave a lengthy (and boring!) speech

Example:
You might give a broad smile when you find out you've passed an exam, or you ask someone to go out with you and they say 'yes'.

Use of English:
FCE Part 2

Open cloze

For questions **1–12**, read the text below and think of a word which best fits each space. Use only **one** word in each space. There is an example at the beginning **(0)**.

How to go about it

- Look at the title and try to predict what you are going to read about. The title of this text is 'How to tell a ghost story'. What do you think are the essential ingredients of a good ghost story?
- Read the text through first, ignoring the spaces, for a general understanding. Compare what it says with your own ideas.
- Now start completing the spaces. Look at the whole sentence and not just the words before and after the space. You may also need to look at the previous or next sentence to make your decision.

- What are some of the typical types of words which are omitted in the Open cloze? See page 80.
- Make sure there is only **one** word in each of the spaces.
- Don't leave any spaces unfilled. If you're not sure, work out the part of speech required and make an 'intelligent guess'.
- The answers are never contractions (eg *can't, she's*) or hyphenated words (eg *three-hour, open-air*).
- Remember that you may need a word with a negative meaning (eg *not, without, unless*).

How to tell a ghost story

A classic ghost story must contain **(0)** _the_ figure of somebody who is known to have **(1)** _been_ alive, who is known to have died and **(2)** _whose_ form is seen after their death. You could have a ghostly animal, a ghostly dog for example, **(3)** _____ you can't have vampires, bats or monsters - they belong in horror. In a ghost story you're trying to chill people, to make them look **(4)** _over_ their shoulder and frighten them, whereas in horror you're aiming to terrify people and **(5)** _make_ them scream.

Atmosphere is the key. **(6)** _without_ it you won't chill anyone. You need a sense of a haunted place, often a house, preferably isolated or **(7)** _in_ some way unnerving, although not always; there have been a **(8)** _lot_ of good ghost stories set in London in broad daylight, and the unexpected appearance of a ghost there can work well.

Stories of knights in armour walking down stairs or ladies in white floating through walls are fine, but your ghost needs to have some **(9)** _sort_ of reason or moral purpose for them to return and for you to see them.

The closer your ghost resembles a person, **(10)** _the_ more chilling it becomes. Come back to the ordinary now and again in your story, otherwise it ceases to **(11)** _be_ frightening. You need a balance between the everyday and the abnormal; something happens and then everything is normal for a while. In the back of **(12)** _their_ minds people will be wondering when it will happen again.

Gapped text

1 These photos were taken on the night of Hallowe'en.

What do you know about this festival? Can you answer the following questions?
When is Hallowe'en?
What does the word 'Hallowe'en' mean?
Why is Hallowe'en celebrated?
Why do people dress up as witches and ghosts?
What is 'trick or treat'?
Why are pumpkins made into lanterns?
Look on page 201 to find the answers.

2 You are going to read an article about Hallowe'en. Seven sentences have been removed from the article. Choose from the sentences **A–H** the one which fits each gap (**1–7**). There is one extra sentence which you do not need to use.

How to go about it

- For this text, the grammatical links are particularly important. To help you, key reference words in sentences **A–H** (*this*, *them*, *he*, *it* and *they*) – are shown in **bold italics**, together with other relevant words.

- Use these words to find links with language and information *before the gaps*. Be sure to check that your answers fit in with the meaning of what comes *after the gaps* as well. Remember, one of these sentences is not required.

THE TROUBLE WITH HALLOWE'EN

One of my greatest disappointments as a child was not having been born in America. I knew from my library that they had a great deal of fun over there. They had Disneyland on their doorstep, and perhaps more importantly, they celebrated Hallowe'en.

Exactly what Hallowe'en meant, the books never really explained: I knew its origins were Irish, but little more. **1** [ ] Besides, any festival that involved ghosts, skeletons, dressing up, doing clever things with exotic vegetables (I had never seen a pumpkin) and annoying grumpy old neighbours just had to be fun.

Twenty years on we now have EuroDisney on our own doorstep, and Hallowe'en is almost as important in Britain as New Year's Eve or Christmas Day. **2** [ ] However, I have recently had cause to wonder whether Hallowe'en is such a good thing after all and now I view the whole thing with deep suspicion.

This change of attitude occurred last October, when I spent my first Hallowe'en with my girlfriend's son, James. **3** [ ] The pumpkin was overpriced, but I had never made a death's head mask before and I found it very satisfying cutting out the teeth shapes in its mouth. So satisfying, indeed, that I didn't want to stop. This led to a disagreement between James and myself as to how much of the pumpkin each of us should be allowed to carve. The disagreement turned into a heated argument and James left the scene in a raging temper.

Worse was to follow. While I made pumpkin soup in the kitchen I heard shrieks of protest from the sitting-room. James wanted to go trick-or-treating. **4** [ ] Feeling a bit of a killjoy after the pumpkin incident, I decided to act as mediator. Yes, he could go, I decreed, provided he went with a group of friends. Now it was his mother's turn to get upset. It just wasn't safe for the boy to go knocking on strange people's doors on a dark, foggy October night.

5 [ ] But by then, there had been another row. 'No way!' I shouted. 'No way am I going to let you cut holes in a perfectly good sheet just to make a ghost costume which will only be used for 10 minutes!' Only after being assured that it was partly made of polyester did I give in.

It all seemed worthwhile when James returned from his expedition clutching an impressive quantity of sweets and fruit. At least he would spend his pocket money on something other than chocolate for the next few weekends. James had other ideas. **6** [ ] And so began another argument which might have gone on until bedtime if we had not been rescued by the arrival of numerous other trick-or-treaters.

However, our supply of tangerines had run out. There was only one thing for it: we would have to dip into James's sweet collection. Needless to say, it ended in tears. **7** [ ] Guy Fawkes Night seems a safer, less controversial alternative.

A His mother thought *he was too young*.

B Understandably, perhaps, *it is celebrated* by fewer people than before.

C *They have* of course *dried up* now, but they left their mark and a feeling that Hallowe'en may be more trouble than it is worth.

D At first *it all seemed quite enjoyable*.

E *This problem* was resolved when a neighbouring parent agreed to escort the trick-or-treat party on their rounds.

F However, *this element of mystery* added to the excitement.

G He intended to *eat them* all immediately.

H Considering my love of America and its traditions as a child, I suppose I should see *this development* as a cause for rejoicing.

Reacting to the text

Do you sympathize with the writer that 'Hallowe'en may be more trouble than it's worth'? Why/Why not?
Many people in Britain, including the police, do not like Hallowe'en.
What reasons do you think they give? What do *you* think?

Word formation: Adjectives

1 The following adjectives in **bold** are all taken from the text on Hallowe'en.
For each adjective write the form which is indicated in brackets at the end of the line. The first one has been done for you.

1 a dark, **foggy** October night   _fog_____ (noun)
2 the arrival of **numerous** other trick-or-treaters   _____ (noun)
3 a safer, less **controversial** alternative   _____ (noun)
4 an **impressive** quantity of sweets and fruit   _____ (verb)

2 All four words in each of the groups below require the same suffix to form adjectives.
Choose the correct suffix *-y*, *-ous*, *-al* or *-ive* and then decide what, if any, further changes are necessary.

Example:

anger *(angry)*   hunger *(hungry)*   thirst *(thirsty)*   guilt *(guilty)*

suffix: -y   changes: angery, hungery

1 ambition	religion	infection	caution
2 occupation	profession	emotion	sensation
3 cloud	wind	rain	ice
4 decide	include	explode	offend
5 biology	geography	economy	history
6 danger	disaster	humour	poison
7 compare	imagine	compete	sense
8 anxiety	variety	curiosity	generosity
9 benefit	influence	residence	finance
10 health	wealth	fun	luck

Speaking 1:
FCE Part 3

Collaborative task

Imagine that you have been asked to organize an event in your neighbourhood to celebrate an important festival or occasion in your country. Talk to your partner about each of the suggestions below and say how they might appeal to different people and then choose two that you think would be most popular.

Firework display

Mini funfair

Open-air concert

Parade

Disco

Fancy dress competition

How to go about it

For each different activity consider the following:

Who? eg *families, young children*
Why? *don't forget to give reasons for your opinions*
Where? eg *in the park, in the square*
When? eg *all day, in the evening*
What? eg *What type of concert might appeal to most people?*

Before you do the task complete the following exercises.

Useful language

1 Correct use of question tags would certainly impress examiners in the Speaking Test. Add an appropriate question tag to each of the following useful phrases.

1 That could be a little dangerous,
_____ ?

2 It won't appeal to all age groups,
_____ ?

3 Everyone likes that type of thing,
_____ ?

4 Elderly people wouldn't like that,
_____ ?

5 It would add colour to the event,
_____ ?

6 Let's talk about this one now,
_____ ?

2 This speaking task provides you with the opportunity to use a range of adjectives. Which of the following are positive and which are negative?

colourful	impressive	enjoyable
dull	exciting	inexpensive
costly	entertaining	impractical
spectacular	uninspiring	lively
thrilling	cheerful	bright

Speaking 2:
FCE Part 4

Further discussion

Thinking about the Part 3 task on page 114, discuss these Speaking Part 4 questions.

- What other activities do you think might be popular in a celebration like this?
- How important are festivals in your country?
- What problems might there be during public events like these?
- What is the best organized event you have ever been to?
- How do you normally celebrate special occasions?

Writing:
FCE Part 2

Informal letters

1 Read the following Writing Part 2 instructions.

You attended an event last weekend to celebrate a traditional festival in your country. Write a letter to your English-speaking penfriend, describing the event. Briefly explain the origins of the festival to your penfriend, then describe what happened and say whether you enjoyed yourself.

Write your **letter** in **120–180** words. Do not write any postal addresses.

2 Underline key words in the question and say why you think the words you have underlined are important.

Example: *'last weekend' is important. It would clearly be wrong to write in your letter that the event occurred last Tuesday.*

3 Now read the following model letter and answer the questions below.

Dear Maria Luisa,
  Sorry it's taken me so long to write, but as you know I've been decorating the house. In fact, I finished last Saturday, so I celebrated by going to a Bonfire Night party here in the village. Every November 5th we commemorate the Gunpowder Plot of 1605, when Guy Fawkes and a group of Catholic conspirators tried unsuccessfully to blow up Parliament with gunpowder.
  There's always a bonfire and the one they had built on the village green was enormous. It gave off an impressive amount of heat, which is very welcome on these chilly November nights. As you can imagine, the effigy of Guy Fawkes, which is burnt on top of the fire, disappeared in a matter of minutes.
  Unfortunately, the firework display was disappointing, but I imagine it must be very costly to put one on. Anyway, the organizers made up for it by providing some excellent food. The baked potatoes and sausage rolls were delicious and the mulled wine certainly kept everyone smiling!
  Well, that's all from me. Let me know what you've been doing recently.
  All the best
  Andy

4 Has the writer answered all the parts of the question? In which paragraphs does Andy:
a explain the origins of the festival?
b describe what happened?
c say whether he enjoyed himself?

5 Find examples in the model of the following features. Explain the meaning of the phrasal verbs and the adjectives.

Phrasal verbs: eg *blow up* – to destroy with an explosion
Adjectives: eg *enormous* – very big
Linking words: eg *but, in fact*
Relative clauses: eg *It gave off an impressive amount of heat, which is very welcome...*
Useful expressions for informal letters: *Sorry it's taken me so long to write*

Now you are ready to write your own letter.

⑨ Review

Word formation

1 The adjective *healthy* is formed by adding *-y* to the noun *health*. Which of the following words are formed in the same way?

thirsty	guilty	lively	happy	mystery	stormy	sleepy
silly	hilly	party	nasty	cloudy	lengthy	injury

2 Write the adjective formed from the following nouns.

Noun	**Adjective**
1 finance	*financial*
2 commerce	_____
3 psychology	_____
4 politics	_____
5 anxiety	_____
6 variety	_____
7 influence	_____
8 residence	_____
9 mystery	_____
10 advantage	_____

3 Write five sentences using five of the adjectives you formed in exercise 2.

Example: *Since my brother lost his job he's been having serious financial problems.*

4 To form the adjectives for the following verbs, the suffix *-ive* is used. What other spelling changes are required?

compare	defend	compete	describe	receive	represent	produce

(**Use of English:**)
FCE Part 3 **Word formation**

Read the following story of an unsolved mystery. Use the word given in capitals at the end of some of the lines to form a word that fits in the gap **in the same line**. There is an example at the beginning **(0)**.

A strange journey

It was a warm, **(0)** <u>sunny</u> October morning in 1593 and in front of the palace in Mexico City   **SUN**
there were the usual bustling crowds of people moving **(1)** _____ across the plaza.   **NOISE**
One soldier stood out from the rest. Unlike the **(2)** _____ grey uniform of the other   **TRADITION**
palace guards his was a bright **(3)** _____ one and he carried a different kind of gun.   **COLOUR**
(4) _____ , the strange soldier said his orders that day were to guard the governor's   **SURPRISE**
palace in Manila, in the Philippines. '**(5)** _____ I am not in Manila,' he said, 'but   **EVIDENCE**
this is a palace so I am doing my duty.' By now, officers were **(6)** _____ of the   **SUSPICION**
man and his **(7)** _____ tale of overnight transportation thousands of miles   **AMAZE**
from Manila to Mexico City. And when he told them that the governor of Manila had
been killed the night before he was **(8)** _____ .   **PRISON**
(9) _____ afterwards a ship arrived from the Philippines. It brought news that the   **SHORT**
governor had been murdered – on the night before the soldier had appeared. The soldier
was released and sent back to Manila. Over 400 years later his **(10)** _____ journey   **MYSTERY**
through space and time remains unexplained.

Use of English:
FCE Part 4

Transformations

For questions **1–8**, complete the second sentence so that it has a similar meaning to the first sentence, using the word given. **Do not change the word given.** You must use between two and five words, including the word given.

1 The goalkeeper was injured, so maybe he isn't playing today.
might
The goalkeeper was injured, so he _____ today.

2 I expect you were pleased to get home after such a terrible holiday.
must
You _____ get home after such a terrible holiday.

3 I'm sure he didn't phone, because I was at home all day.
have
He _____ , because I was at home all day.

4 It's possible that someone stole your purse when we were in the restaurant.
might
Someone _____ when we were in the restaurant.

5 Tim hasn't had a single cigarette today so perhaps he has stopped smoking completely.
may
Tim hasn't had a single cigarette today so he _____ up smoking completely.

6 You can keep a secret, can't you?
give
You wouldn't _____ you?

7 If you don't let me have your essay tomorrow, there'll be trouble!
better
You _____ in your essay tomorrow or there'll be trouble!

8 When she spoke to him, he laughed nervously.
a
He _____ when she spoke to him.

Writing:
FCE Part 2

Short stories

Your teacher has asked you to write a short story for the school's English language magazine. It must begin with the following words:

I heard a noise and went downstairs to investigate.

Write your **story** in **120–180** words.

Don't forget!

- Plan your story before you start writing. Think of a general outline of what is going to happen.
- You may choose to write a ghost story. To help you with ideas, use the information from the listening activity on ghosts and the Open cloze text on page 111 on how to tell ghost stories.
- Look at the Wordlist on page 204.
- Look again at pages 50 and 51 to remind yourself of the ingredients of a good narrative.
- Consider using one or two expressions with *give*.

Introduction

In Paper 2 you have to complete two different writing tasks in 1 hour 20 minutes; the compulsory Part 1 task and then another from a choice of four in Part 2.

Part 1

For Part 1 questions, you have to write between **120** and **150** words.
You will have to write either   **a** a formal letter or email
            or   **b** an informal letter or email

Guidance is given in the form of written input material, such as a letter, a note or an advertisement. The context of the input material and the target reader will help you decide whether you should write in a more formal or informal style.

In your letter or email, you will be asked to do something specific, such as giving or requesting information, persuading somebody to do something, describing something, apologizing, giving an opinion or making a recommendation.

Part 2

For Part 2 questions, you have to write between **120** and **180** words.
You will have a choice of four questions. A formal or informal letter is one possible task type. You can also expect to find the following:

c an article
d an essay
e a report
f a review
g a short story
h a description (often as part of another task type such as a short story or a letter)
i background reading text: there are always two options for this question, one for each book. Articles, essays, letters, reports and reviews are all possible tasks.

Extracts

Decide which writing task **a–i** each extract (**1–9**) is taken from.

1 Anyway, I hope that answers all your questions. Remember we can always put you up for the night if you want – just let us know when you're thinking of coming.
2 Some people feel that the practice of cloning animals is unethical and should therefore be banned. However, others argue that it has many important advantages.
3 Have you ever wondered what it would be like to be an animal in a cage? I have, and it's made me realize just how cruel zoos are.
4 I would be grateful if you could tell me the exact dates of the course and whether I would have to pay the enrolment fee in advance.
5 As soon as the class had finished, Molly rushed out of the school and headed straight for the park. She desperately hoped it wasn't too late.
6 But my favourite moment of all was at the very end of the musical when the entire cast was on stage singing the title song.
7 To sum up, although the food in both restaurants is of the highest quality, Cagney's offers a greater selection of dishes and provides its customers with better service.
8 The person I most look up to is my Uncle Fred. Despite the difficulties he's faced, he is always very cheerful and his piercing blue eyes seem to light up when he smiles.
9 The two short stories from 'Crime Never Pays' which I enjoyed most have many similarities. To begin with, 'Ricochet' and 'Three is a Lucky Number' are both about unsuccessful attempts to murder someone.

Formal or informal?

1 The following comments were made about extracts similar to those on page 118. Circle the appropriate alternative and match each sentence to the feature of language which is being commented on.

1 The use of 'can't' and 'isn't' show that the letter is *formal/informal*.

a phrasal verbs

2 'Furthermore' is a very *formal/informal* word.

b question forms

3 'Make up for' is a more *formal/informal* word for 'compensate'.

c punctuation

4 An exclamation mark would not be used in *formal/informal* writing.

d contractions

5 'Would you mind telling me when it starts?' sounds quite *formal/informal* to me.

e linking words

2 Now look at the extracts again and decide whether each one is formal, informal or neutral. Give reasons for your decisions, commenting on the language used.

Example: *Extract 1 is informal. There is a contraction and a phrasal verb is used: 'put you up'. Starting a sentence with 'anyway' is informal, as is the use of the dash.*

Answering questions

Part 1: Emails

1 Read the following Part 1 question and the two sample answers on page 120. Which answer do you think is better?

You have seen the advertisement below in an international newspaper and you are considering applying for the job. You know your English-speaking friend, Elisa, worked in the same place last year and you have decided to write and ask her about it. Read the advertisement and the notes you have made. Then write an email to your friend telling her about your plans and asking for information and advice.

WORKING HOLIDAYS
in the South of England

Jobs available picking fruit in the county of Kent from June to September.

Strawberries, apples, pears, plums or cherries – depending on the month

- *Cooking facilities available*
- *Bring a tent*

Ask about:
Go July – which fruit?
Work 1 month/travel the next
*   – earn enough?*

Days off?
Any more advice?

Write an **email** of between **120 and 150** words. You must use grammatically correct sentences and accurate spelling and punctuation in a style appropriate for the situation.

A

| **To:** | Elisa Barba |
| **Subject:** | Fruit picking in England |

Dear friend

Thanks for writing. I was really upset to hear about the argument you had with Marco last week. Even though you have fallen out with him I would recommend you to make it up with him. He's really easy-going and you were made for each other.

Anyway, this summer I am thinking in going fruit picking in the south of England. I know you have worked in the same place last year and I have decided to write and ask you about it. I would be grateful if you could to tell me which fruit it is picked in July and how many days a week I would have to work. Furthermore, I'm going to work one month, then travel. I would be grateful if you could tell me wether you earned enough money?

Anyway, I must to go now. If you can think in anything else that is worth knowing, please do not hesitate to contact me.

Kisses

Lola

B

| **To:** | Elisa Barba |
| **Subject:** | Fruit picking in England |

Dear Elisa,

How are you? As you know, I'm starting university in September, but in summer I hope to go fruit picking in England for a month, like you did last year. I'm planning on going in July when my exams have finished. Can you tell me which fruit is picked in that month? When I'm not working, I really want to go sightseeing in London so if you can remember how much free time you had, I'd like to know that, too. Then, after the job has finished, I'm thinking of setting off on a month's tour of England. It depends on how much money I can earn – do you think I'd have enough to do that? Anyway, that's all for now. Let me know if you have any other advice, such as suggestions on how to get there and what clothes to take.

Hope to hear from you soon.

All the best

Tania

2 Now read the two emails again and answer the questions in the categories below. First Certificate examiners use these categories when marking Writing Part 1 answers.

Content:	**a** Has the writer included all the main points in the notes? **b** Is the content of the email relevant?
Organization and cohesion:	**a** Is the email organized into suitable paragraphs? **b** Are ideas connected with appropriate linking words and presented in a logical order? **c** Does the email have an appropriate opening and ending?
Range and accuracy:	**a** Is there a good variety of vocabulary and structures? **b** Has the writer managed to avoid repetition of language? **c** Has he/she copied whole phrases from the question?
Style and format:	**a** Is the style appropriate to the task/reader? Is it consistent? **b** Is the answer clearly set out as an email?
Target reader:	Would the reader understand the writer's plans and be clear about what he/she wants to know?

3 Answer the following Part 1 question.

You and your family have decided to go on a family activity holiday in the UK and you have found the following advertisement. You would like to have more information, but could not find answers to all your questions on the company's website. Write an email to Trident Adventure Holidays, covering all the points in your notes.

> ### Don't forget!
>
> Answer these questions about the writing task before you begin.
>
> - Who is the target reader?
> - Will you use a formal or an informal style?
> - Will your questions be direct or indirect?

would arrive Fri. July 26th – OK?

all the time?

sailing?

FAMILY ADVENTURE HOLIDAYS
in the picturesque Lake District

Activities include:

● canoeing

● mountain biking

● climbing

Parents are encouraged to participate with their children in the activities.

Holidays run from Saturday to Saturday throughout July and August.

£230 – includes all activities, accommodation and meals

For more details consult our website.

cost of extra night?

Write an **email** of between **120 and 150 words**. You must use grammatically correct sentences with accurate spelling and punctuation in a style appropriate for the situation.

4   When you have written your email, check it using the questions in exercise 2.

Part 2: Article, essay, letter, report, review, story

1   The following questions are typical of those you might be asked in Part 2 of the Writing paper. There is one example of each task type: article, essay, letter, report, review and story. Read each of the questions and put a tick (✓) next to those you feel you would be most able to answer. Give reasons for each of your ticks.

   1   Your college magazine has invited you to write an **article** about a member of your family who helped you in some way. Describe the person and explain what they did that was helpful to you.

   2   You have had a class discussion on the following statement:
       It should be illegal for parents to smack their children.
       Your teacher has asked you to write an **essay** giving your views on the statement.

   3   You recently visited a place which you had not been to for a long time. Your cousin, who now lives abroad, also knew this place very well. Write a **letter** to your cousin, describing the changes and your feelings about them. Do not write any postal addresses.

   4   You have a part-time job in a games centre, where people can go to play computer games. The owner would like to buy some new software and he has asked you to write a **report**, suggesting two games for the centre. You should briefly describe each game and explain why you think the customers would enjoy both games.

   5   Your school's English language magazine has invited readers to write a **review** of a holiday they spent recently in a seaside resort. You should include information on your accommodation and what there is to do in the resort, and say whether you would recommend the holiday to other people.

   6   You have decided to enter a short-**story** competition. The competition rules say that the story must begin or end with the following words:
       They were sad to leave, but they had no choice.

2   Write an answer to one of the questions above in **120–180** words in an appropriate style.

How to go about it

• To ensure your answer is relevant, underline the key words in the question. Find the answers to the following questions for number 1 above, underlining the relevant words.
   1 What do you have to write?   **4** What is special about this person?
   2 Who for?   **5** What two things do you have to include in
   3 Who do you have to write about?   your answer?
• It is important to write your answer in an appropriate style. Look at question 1 again. Think about the target reader. Will you write in a formal, neutral or informal style?
• Now underline the key words in each of the other questions and decide which style would be most appropriate.

⑩ Nothing but the truth

Vocabulary 1: Crime and punishment

A Crimes and criminals

1 Match each of the following definitions with the word for a criminal from the box. There is one extra word which you do not need to use.

vandal	kidnapper	arsonist	blackmailer	shoplifter	smuggler
mugger	drug trafficker	hijacker	pickpocket	murderer	

A person who...
1 kills someone.   _____
2 takes goods into or out of a country illegally.   _____
3 deliberately sets fire to a building.   _____
4 steals things from people's pockets or bags in public places.   _____
5 threatens to give away secrets unless he/she is given money.   _____
6 takes things from shops without paying for them.   _____
7 holds someone prisoner until he/she is given money.   _____
8 takes control of an aeroplane by force.   _____
9 deliberately damages other people's property.   _____
10 attacks people in the street and steals their money.   _____

2 Write the name of the crime committed by each of the criminals in exercise 1. Which of the crimes involve theft of some kind?

Example: mugger – *mugging*

3 Match each verb from the box with an appropriate pair of nouns.

burgle   rob   steal

a _____ an office/a house
b _____ money/jewellery
c _____ a bank/a person

B Punishment

1 Look at the following types of punishment which can be given by courts. Put them in order from the least to the most severe.

a to sentence someone to life imprisonment
b to order someone to do 200 hours of community service
c to sentence someone to death
d to order someone to pay a £200 fine
e to give someone a two-year prison sentence

2 Decide what punishment, if any, should be given to the person or people below. Discuss your ideas using some of the language of agreement and opinion in the box.

- a 73-year-old woman who stole a scarf from a department store
- three 16-year-old vandals who set fire to litter bins and sprayed paint on parked cars
- a gang of armed men who hijacked a plane with 135 passengers on board and threatened to blow it up
- two men who mugged another, robbing him of £10 and breaking several of his teeth
- a businessman who has earned millions from drug trafficking

Giving opinions	Agreeing and disagreeing
In my opinion…	*I totally agree.*
To my mind…	*I think so, too.*
From my point of view…	*I agree up to a point.*
Personally, I think…	*I really don't think so.*
I strongly believe…	*I completely disagree.*

Listening 1:
FCE Part 2

Sentence completion 👁 1.42

1 What are the best ways to protect your house from burglary?
How well is your house protected?

2 Read the following Listening Part 2 instructions. Try to predict the type of information you will hear for each question before you listen.

You will hear part of a radio programme, in which a police officer talks about burglary. For questions **1–10**, complete the sentences.

1 Almost a half of burglaries occur [_____ **1**] .

2 Most burglaries take [_____ **2**] minutes.

3 'Operation Bumblebee' targets criminals who
[_____ **3**] .

4 The operation led to a [_____ **4**] decrease in
burglary in its first year.

5 Officer Woodcock warns householders not to hide keys
[_____ **5**] .

6 A [_____ **6**] will help to deter burglars.

7 Locks should be fitted to the [_____ **7**] .

8 Neighbourhood Watch Schemes give everyone the chance to
[_____ **8**] .

9 The schemes particularly help protect people like the
[____ *and* ____ **9**] .

10 Over [_____ **10**] people benefit from the schemes.

Speaking 1:
FCE Part 3
Collaborative task

Here are some different methods of tackling crime. Talk to your partner about the advantages and disadvantages of each approach and then choose which you think are the least and most effective.

> • What are the advantages and disadvantages of each approach?
> • Which are the least and most effective approaches?

Speaking 2:
FCE Part 4
Further discussion

Discuss these Speaking Part 4 questions with your partner. Try to develop your answers and give reasons and examples to support your opinions.

• What do you think are the main causes of crime in your country?
• Do you have any other suggestions for reducing crime in your local area?
• Do you think the police should carry guns?
• Do you think the death penalty is a valid form of punishment?

When she saw the broken chair the teacher said she wouldn't let us go home until the person who was responsible for the damage **(1)** <u>owned up</u>. In the end Brian Ogilvie said he'd done it, but that it had been an accident. He **(2)** <u>made up</u> a story about falling over backwards onto it and the chair just falling apart under his weight. Our teacher will believe anything and she was completely **(3)** <u>taken in</u> by his words, totally unaware that the chair had been broken in an act of pure vandalism. She **(4)** <u>let him off</u> with nothing more than an unconvincing warning.

But he didn't **(5)** <u>get away with</u> it. The next day the teacher **(6)** <u>found out</u> the truth when she overheard Ogilvie **(7)** <u>showing off</u> to his friends in another class about how he'd managed to deceive the teacher. The headteacher was informed, and after **(8)** <u>looking into</u> the incident, decided to suspend him for a month.

Vocabulary 2: Phrasal verbs

1 Read the story and decide whether you feel the punishment was suitable.

2 Read the story again. Work out the meaning of each of the underlined phrasal verbs using the context of the sentence and of the story as a whole.

3 Write four sentences, each one including one of the phrasal verbs from the story. Then rewrite the sentences, leaving a space where the verb should be. Ask your partner to complete the spaces with an appropriate phrasal verb.

Writing 1:
FCE Part 2

Choose **one** of the following questions and write **120–180** words.

1 You have been doing a class project on crime. Your teacher has asked you to write a contribution for the school's English language magazine with the following title:

What can ordinary people do to help in the fight against crime?

Write your **article**, giving other students practical suggestions for beating crime.

How to go about it

Style
- Who is the target reader?
- Should the style be formal, neutral or informal?

Organization and ideas
- Introductory paragraph:
  Why is it important for ordinary people to help in the fight against crime? Can they do very much to help?

- Paragraphs two and three:
  Think of your discussion in the speaking activity.
- To finish your article you could:
  encourage readers to take action.
  and/or give them advice on the first thing they should do.
  and/or ask them to consider the consequences of not doing anything.

2 Your teacher has asked you to write a story for the school's English language magazine. It must begin with the following words:

He quickly put the tin of soup into his pocket and moved towards the checkout.

Write your **story**.

How to go about it

- Plan your story before you start writing
- Look again at pages 50 and 51 in Unit 4 for the ingredients of a good narrative.
- Use a range of past tenses:
  Past perfect to describe what had happened before the main events of the story.
- Past continuous and past simple to describe the main events of the story.
- Use some of the vocabulary you have learnt in this unit.
- Begin with the words in the question.

Reading:
FCE Part 1

Multiple choice

1 Why might somebody hire a private detective?
What image do you have of private detectives?
What qualities do you think are required to do the job well?

2 Read through the newspaper article on page 126 and compare your ideas in exercise 1.

Private investigators investigated

David Lee investigates the world of the private eye – and uncovers some surprising truths.

When I walk into the offices of *Wright & Wrong Ltd*, a predominantly female firm of private investigators, I have to say I am a little disappointed. My only previous contact with private detective agencies has been through crime novels read during my far-off student days, or black and white films from the golden age of Hollywood. So I am half expecting to see a small, dark, smoke-filled room, a single desk with an empty in-tray and a long, scruffy raincoat hanging from a hat stand in the corner.

Clearly, my romantic image of the profession needs updating. *Wright & Wrong Ltd*'s offices are light and spacious and there are no ashtrays in sight on any

14 of the dozen or so desks. These are tidy and free of paper, but concentrated faces at large computer screens give the place a busy feel.

Jenny Wright, founder of the agency, is not surprised at my error, and with a note of irritation in her voice, points to further misconceptions. 'Cinema and television are mostly to blame for our reputation. Contrary to popular belief, we always work very strictly within the law – there's no violence, no break-ins, and certainly no guns. The laws relating to our activities are very tight, and if we don't stick to them there's a very real danger that the evidence we obtain will not be accepted in court.'

The types of cases her agency deals with are varied but the day-to-day work is often far from stimulating. *Wright & Wrong Ltd* handles anything from infidelity in a marriage or tracing a missing person to insurance fraud, employee theft and advising companies on security measures. 'Resolving a case is very rewarding,' says Jenny, 'but the actual investigation can be rather dull. When we're not dealing with paperwork or Internet searches, we're usually involved in surveillance. And that normally means just sitting around in cars or cafés for hours, waiting for something to happen.'

Not surprisingly, then, patience is an important asset for anyone doing this kind of work. Is that why nine of the twelve investigators in her team are women? 'Obviously, women don't have a monopoly

43 on patience,' replies Jenny diplomatically, for my benefit, I sense, 'but perhaps it's no coincidence that they tend to stay in the job a lot longer than men – at least in my experience, anyway.'

Jenny tells me that people's perceptions of women make them popular with clients, and also, consequently, with her as an employer. Women are often considered to be more sensitive than men. They're looked upon as less threatening when it comes to making inquiries or serving court papers. 'People open up to women more readily,' she says, 'and are relieved when a woman picks up the phone to speak to them. We're also good at breaking bad news. What may be a victory for the agency – filming someone doing something they shouldn't be doing, for example – tends not to be such a pleasant discovery for the client, and there's a right way and a wrong way of handling that information.'

Most of Jenny's clients are wealthy. The hourly rate is anything between fifty and eighty pounds, so the cost of a single case will often run into thousands of pounds. Even with the latest hi-tech equipment, such as GPS and long-range listening devices, a surveillance campaign can last several days. 'The technology is freely available and most of what we do could be done by the clients,' explains Jenny, 'but they're reluctant to get involved. Finding out the truth is often just too painful to do on your own.'

I ask Jenny, a former night club owner, how she came to be a private detective. Her face turns red, she gives a slight grin and drops her voice to a whisper so as not to be overheard by her staff. 'I used to read a lot of crime novels during the daytime,' she confides, 'and I started to think 'I could do that'. I went on a training course and realized I was in the wrong job.' I am about to ask her whether she ever wears a long, scruffy raincoat, when her mobile phone rings and she is called away on business.

---

3 For questions **1–8**, choose the answer (**A**, **B**, **C** or **D**) which you think fits best according to the text.

1 What does the writer discover on his visit to the offices of *Wright & Wrong Ltd*?

A The firm is not as dynamic as he had been told.

B The offices have recently been modernized.

C All the private detectives in the firm are women.

D He has an old-fashioned idea of private detectives.

2 What does 'these' in line 14 refer to?

A offices

B ashtrays

C desks

D computer screens

3 Jenny Wright is annoyed by

A the strict laws controlling private detectives.

B the inflexibility of the law courts.

C the way her profession is represented in films.

D the violence used by other detective agencies.

4 According to Jenny, most of the work of a private
detective is

A monotonous.

B challenging.

C exhausting.

D enjoyable.

5 The writer uses the word 'diplomatically' in
line 43 to imply that Jenny

A had no strong views of her own.

B was trying not to offend him.

C was being oversensitive.

D was unsure of her answer.

6 Jenny is influenced in her decision to take
on women by

A women's ability to get results.

B the speed at which women work.

C women's tendency to speak openly.

D the way clients see women.

7 What do we learn about Jenny's clients?

A They cannot afford to buy the surveillance
equipment.

B They object to paying such high prices for
the work.

C They do not want to do the detective work
themselves.

D They prefer more than one detective to work
on a case.

8 How does Jenny feel about telling her story in
the last paragraph?

A embarrassed

B frightened

C proud

D angry

Reacting to the text

Do you think you would make a good private
detective? Why/Why not?

Language focus 1: Passives

1 Read through the text in the next column ignoring the gaps,
and answer the following questions:

  a What methods do private detectives use to spy on
children?

  b Why is the charity Childlook concerned about this
practice?

2 Complete each space in the text with one of the verbs in the
box. You may use some verbs more than once. There is an
example at the beginning (**0**).

be	to be	being	been
is	are	was	were	has	have

3 Most of the numbered verbs in exercise 1 form part of
passive constructions. Arrange these passives in the table
below.

How is the passive formed?

Tense	Example
Present simple	
Present continuous	*are being used*
Present perfect	
Past simple	
Past perfect	
Future simple	
Infinitive	
Gerund	

4 Do you share Childlook's concerns about parents
hiring private detectives to follow their children? Why/Why
not?

G Read more about passives in A and B on pages 213 and
214 of the Grammar reference.

Spying on children

Private detectives are (**0**) _being_ used in increasing numbers
to spy on children, according to a new report by the children's
charity Childlook. Investigators (**1**) _____ hired by anxious
parents worried about what their children are up to and who
they might (**2**) _____ hanging around with. The charity has
expressed concern at the trend, which it says (**3**) _____ been
caused by the growing lack of communication between parents
and teenagers. 'In the past, youngsters (**4**) _____ kept under
close control by their parents,' said Andrew Hird, a spokesman
for Childlook. 'Now, both parents are often too busy and
increasingly they (**5**) _____ to involve a third person to watch
over their children.'

The report, which will (**6**) _____ published later today,
describes some of the methods used. In some cases, parents
allow their telephones (**7**) _____ bugged to enable detectives
to listen in on their children's conversations. However, since
most youngsters nowadays have their own mobile phones,
this (**8**) _____ not done as much as it used (**9**) _____
Instead, teenagers (**10**) _____ followed and anything illegal
or irregular (**11**) _____ captured on film. One investigator
who (**12**) _____ interviewed for the report said that once
teenagers had (**13**) _____ caught, they were reluctant to
repeat their act for fear of (**14**) _____ subjected to more
surveillance.

Whilst these methods are perfectly legal, Andrew Hird said he
was 'alarmed' by the practice of young people (**15**) _____
filmed without their knowledge. He said it was 'an invasion of
privacy' and urged parents to talk to their children first before
resorting to such methods.

Passive constructions with the infinitive

*Women **are often considered to be** more sensitive than men.*

This phrase has the same meaning as:

***It is often considered that** women are more sensitive than men.*

Change the following sentence in the same way:

They are believed to have stolen £3 million.
It _____ .

The infinitive (*to do*) or the perfect infinitive (*to have done*) can be used after the passive of these verbs:

believe   consider   expect   know   say   think

Transformations

For questions **1–6**, complete the second sentence so that it has a similar meaning to the first sentence, using the word given. **Do not change the word given.** You must use between two and five words, including the word given.

1 It is forbidden to take cameras into the courtroom.
must
Cameras _____ into the courtroom.

2 It is known that Smith broke into several houses.
known
Smith _____ into several houses.

3 They do not think he is dangerous.
be
He _____ dangerous.

4 They'll make you pay a fine if they catch you smoking.
made
You _____ pay a fine if they catch you smoking.

5 I told nobody about our conversation so I'm sure someone tapped my phone.
must
I told nobody about our conversation so my phone _____ _____ by someone.

6 The lawyer is still waiting for his client to contact him.
contacted
The lawyer _____ his client yet.

(G) Read more about this type of passive construction in **C** on page 214 of the Grammar reference.

Further practice: Passives

Complete each of the spaces in the following text with an appropriate active or passive form of the verb in brackets. You may need to use more than one word in each space.

Man fined £800 for not clearing his dog's mess

A dog owner (**0**) _has been ordered_ (order) to pay a record £800 after (**1**) _____ (let) his pet foul a grass verge within yards of a waste bin. Paul Humphris, 52, who got his black Labrador, Billy, from a rescue centre 13 years ago, (**2**) _____ (find) guilty of failing to clean up after him.

Sue Bell, the association's president, said: 'I hope this case (**3**) _____ (send) out a strong message against dog fouling, but I do feel sorry for the man concerned.'

Mr Humphris, a purchaser from Banbury, said: 'This is the first time I (**4**) _____ (fine). I cannot believe what has happened. Usually I (**5**) _____ (put) my dog's mess in one of the council bins. On this particular evening it was freezing cold, wet

and raining and I was lazy, I have to admit that. But normally people (**6**) _____ (fine) about £50 for dog fouling.'
Cathy Wainwright, the warden who (**7**) _____ (catch) Mr Humphris in December, said she was pleased with the result. 'The high fine imposed reflects the severity of the offence and will hopefully serve as a warning to other irresponsible people who (**8**) _____ (not/clean) up after their pets.'

Yesterday the court (**9**) _____ (tell) how Ms Wainwright followed Mr Humphris on foot to his home after seeing him let his dog foul the verge. Soon afterwards Mr Humphris (**10**) _____ (invite) to meet Ms Wainwright to discuss the matter, but he declined, claiming he was unhappy about (**11**) _____ (follow). The case then went to court three times, with Mr Humphris eventually (**12**) _____ (order) to pay £400 costs as well as a £400 fine.

Writing 2:
FCE Part 2

Articles

1 Look at these sentences from the article on page 126.

Clearly, my romantic image of the profession needs updating.
Not surprisingly, patience is an important asset for anyone doing this kind of work.
Obviously, women don't have a monopoly on patience.

Each one begins with an adverb which expresses the writer's attitude to or opinion of what follows. In **1–8** below replace the underlined phrase with an adverb from the box.

Astonishingly	Interestingly	Curiously	Personally
Happily	Sadly	Worryingly	Unfortunately

1 <u>In my opinion</u>, I think that any form of physical punishment is unacceptable.
2 <u>I'm absolutely amazed that</u> he was released after only two years in prison.
3 <u>It is sad that</u> there is a growing trend towards violence in our schools.
4 <u>It is regrettable that</u> many parents just don't communicate with their children.
5 <u>It's strange that</u> some kidnap victims end up sympathizing with their captors.
6 <u>It is of some concern that</u> many drivers still do not wear their seat belts.
7 <u>It's worth noting that</u> most children don't leave home until they get married.
8 <u>I'm pleased to be able to say that</u> this is an exception rather than the rule.

2 Read the following Writing Part 2 instructions and discuss with your partner how you might answer the question.

You see this announcement in an international magazine:

> We invite you, our readers, to write an article giving your opinions on:
>
> **DEALING WITH LITTER**
> - How serious a problem is litter in your area?
> - What can be done to stop people dropping litter in the street?
>
> The best articles answering this question will be published next month.

3 Now read the following article and compare the writer's ideas with those you discussed in exercise 2.

A load of rubbish

I'm sure the people of Brenton don't drop crisp packets and drink cans on the floor in their own home. So why do so many think it's acceptable to do so on the streets of our town?

A walk in the area around the cathedral reveals how serious the problem has become. Litter lines the pavements outside some of our most picturesque buildings, giving tourists a poor impression of the town and its residents. And incredibly, there are sometimes more plastic bags in our parks and playgrounds than there are people. Clearly, something needs to be done.

More litter bins won't solve the problem - there are already plenty of these, but most people ignore them. What we need is an awareness campaign organized by the council encouraging people to use the bins or take their rubbish home. Also, heavier fines should be imposed on anyone who is caught dropping litter - the current maximum of £100 is not enough.

Unfortunately, the council seem reluctant to act. But surely they, more than anyone, want a town they can be proud of, don't they?

4 Read the model answer again and find examples of the following common features of articles:

    a Title
    b Interesting beginning
    c Direct questions
    d Adverbs which express the writer's attitude or opinion
    e More informal use of linking words
    f Leaving the reader something to think about at the end

5 How are the writer's ideas organized in the model answer? What information is contained in each paragraph?

    Paragraph 1: _____
    Paragraph 2: _____
    Paragraph 3: _____
    Paragraph 4: _____

6 Read the following Writing Part 2 instructions.

You see this announcement in an international magazine:

> We invite you, our readers, to write an article giving your opinions on:
>
> **DEALING WITH GRAFFITI**
> - How serious a problem is graffiti in your area?
> - What can be done to stop people covering walls with graffiti?
>
> The best articles answering this question will be published next month.

Write your **article** in **120–180** words.

Don't forget!

- Give your article a title. It may be better to do this after you have written your answer.
- Organize your ideas into logical paragraphs.

- Include the techniques and language features you saw in exercise 4.
- Do not copy whole phrases from the article in exercise 3.

Listening 2:
FCE Part 3

Multiple matching 1.43–1.47

 1 Have you ever failed to tell the whole truth to your parents?
Did they find out? What were the consequences?

2 You will hear five people talking about how they were 'economical with the truth' to their parents. Match the speaker to the correct description in the list **A–F**. Use the letters only once. There is one extra letter which you do not need to use.

A property was stolen   Speaker 1 [   ]
B some money was stolen   Speaker 2 [   ]
C the lie was unnecessary   Speaker 3 [   ]
D helping the father brought results   Speaker 4 [   ]
E the mother found the evidence   Speaker 5 [   ]
F a telephone call spoiled the fun

Language focus 2: Past necessity

Compare the use of *need* by Speakers 1 and 5 in these extracts from the listening.

Speaker 1:
*I **needn't have lied** after all – I found the money in the bottom of my jacket pocket.*

Speaker 5:
*I **didn't need to tell lies**. I knew how to get round my dad.*

Which of the following sentences applies to which speaker?

a She didn't lie because she knew it wasn't necessary.
b She lied but she only realized it wasn't necessary afterwards.

[G] Read more on page 214 of the Grammar reference.

Practice
Complete each of the following spaces using the verb in brackets and the correct form of *need*.

1 I wrote 250 words in my composition but noticed later that the word limit was only 180. I _____ (write) so much.

2 Today's a public holiday so last night I _____ (set) my alarm clock. This morning I got up at 11.30!

3 Last summer I had my head shaved. It was great – I _____ (go) to the hairdresser's for ages after that.

4 I stayed up until midnight last night to get my homework finished. I _____ (bother) – the teacher is off sick today.

5 I was a bit concerned that my mum wouldn't like the earrings I bought her, but I _____ (worry) – she wears them every day.

⑩ Review

The passive

Complete each of the following spaces with the correct passive form of the verb in brackets.

1 This bank _____ (rob) twice since it opened in January this year.
2 Two men _____ (arrest) yesterday in connection with the theft.
3 I think people who commit acts of vandalism should _____ (make) to pay for the damage they cause.
4 We're getting used to _____ (burgle): that's the third time it's happened to us this year.
5 Millions of pounds' worth of drugs _____ (smuggle) into the country each year.
6 I don't think he _____ (give) a prison sentence; he'll probably just have to pay a fine.
7 The causes of the fire _____ (currently/look) into by the police.
8 I was shocked when the teacher shouted at Sue. She _____ (never/tell) off before that in her life.

Vocabulary

Phrasal verbs

The following phrasal verbs have appeared either in this unit or in previous units.

1 In A and B complete each sentence beginning 1–6 with an appropriate ending **a–f**. The first one has been done for you.

A Phrasal verbs with *off* and *out*

1 The judge let him off   a for being rude.
2 He told her off   b the truth about him.
3 He was showing off   c with a fine.
4 I found out   d over something stupid.
5 He gave out   e to his classmates.
6 They fell out   f the books.

B Phrasal verbs with *up* and *away*

1 He made up   a in the south of England.
2 She owned up   b with that noise any more.
3 I grew up   c the whole story.
4 I can't put up   d with it again, hasn't he?
5 He's got away   e by the gun in his car.
6 He was given away   f to doing it.

2 Choose four phrasal verbs from the box below and write an example sentence for each verb you have chosen.

split up with	set up	turn up	give up
take up	bring up	come up	make up for

Use of English:
FCE Part 1

Multiple-choice cloze

For questions **1–12**, read the text below and decide which answer (**A**, **B**, **C** or **D**) best fits each gap. There is an example at the beginning (**0**).

Ex-athlete taken in … again.

The home of **(0)** ____ athlete Helen Barnett was burgled this weekend and a large number of sporting medals and trophies were **(1)** ____ , including the five Olympic golds she won in a career spanning three decades. Ms Barnett, who now **(2)** ____ a successful sportswear company, is **(3)** ____ to be 'devastated' at the loss.

The burglary is believed to have taken **(4)** ____ on Saturday afternoon when Ms Barnett went into her large, two-acre garden in order to investigate smoke coming from a wooded **(5)** ____ near her summerhouse. The burglar is thought to have **(6)** ____ fire to undergrowth in order to lure Ms Barnett out of the house. A young man carrying a large bag was seen climbing over a wall bordering the garden **(7)** ____ before the fire brigade arrived. He apparently made his **(8)** ____ in a sports car.

The theft **(9)** ____ just ten months after a similar incident in which Ms Barnett was robbed of several items of jewellery. On that **(10)** ____ , a man posing as a telephone engineer had **(11)** ____ the ex-athlete into leaving the house while another helped himself to her jewels. The thieves were eventually caught and **(12)** ____ to four years in jail.

0	**A** earlier	**B** sooner	**C** <u>former</u>	**D** preceding
1	**A** robbed	**B** mugged	**C** pickpocketed	**D** stolen
2	**A** runs	**B** overtakes	**C** works	**D** holds
3	**A** spoken	**B** said	**C** felt	**D** told
4	**A** part	**B** hold	**C** place	**D** time
5	**A** land	**B** earth	**C** ground	**D** area
6	**A** made	**B** given	**C** set	**D** put
7	**A** shortly	**B** firstly	**C** initially	**D** previously
8	**A** runaway	**B** getaway	**C** hideaway	**D** takeaway
9	**A** comes	**B** arrives	**C** gives	**D** takes
10	**A** time	**B** situation	**C** occasion	**D** circumstance
11	**A** succeeded	**B** managed	**C** tricked	**D** obtained
12	**A** imprisoned	**B** ordered	**C** given	**D** sentenced

Writing:
FCE Part 2

Short stories

You have decided to enter a short-story competition organized by an international young people's magazine. The competition rules say that the story must end with the following words:

I swore then that I would never tell another lie as long as I lived.

Write your **story** in **120–180** words.

Don't forget!

- Look again at the 'ingredients' of a good narrative on pages 50 and 51 in Unit 4.
- Try to include two or three phrasal verbs.

(11) What on Earth's going on?

Vocabulary 1: Weather

1 All the words in each of the groups **1–7** below can be used with one of the nouns in the box to form strong collocations. For each group of words write the noun which can be used in the appropriate space. There is an example at the beginning **(0)**.

sunshine
showers
~~sky~~
sea
storm
clouds
rain
wind

0 overcast
clear   *sky*
stormy

1 violent
severe   _____
electric

2 fine
heavy   _____
torrential

3 strong
gale-force _____
light

4 warm
brilliant   _____
glorious

5 rough
calm   _____
choppy

6 thick
storm   _____
angry-looking

7 light
scattered   _____
snow

2 Study the words in exercise 1 for two minutes. Then cover up the adjectives and see how many you can remember for each noun.

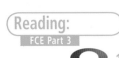 3 Describe the photos above using as many of the adjective + noun collocations as possible. What types of weather do you prefer? What weather conditions do you least like?

Reading:
FCE Part 3   Multiple matching

1 Which of the following occur in your country?

droughts   floods   avalanches   hurricanes   earthquakes   tornadoes

Have you experienced any of these? What was it like?
What are the worst weather conditions you have had to endure?

2 You are going to read a magazine article in which people describe their experiences with natural disasters. For questions **1–15**, choose from the people **(A–D)**. The people may be chosen more than once. When more than one answer is required, these may be given in any order.

Don't forget!

● Before doing the matching task, underline key words in the statements **1–15**.

Which of the people suggest the following?

I was impressed with how people reacted.	**1** ☐
Preparations were made for the disaster.	**2** ☐
I didn't think it could happen here.	**3** ☐
We didn't think we would be in any danger.	**4** ☐ **5** ☐
The experience had a long-lasting effect on me.	**6** ☐
Disaster had struck in the same place before.	**7** ☐
I tried unsuccessfully to see it happening.	**8** ☐
We were without electricity.	**9** ☐ **10** ☐
We were saved by someone's warnings.	**11** ☐
It has not affected my feelings for the place.	**12** ☐
We had to hide our real feelings.	**13** ☐
I slowly became aware of how serious it had been.	**14** ☐
I cried after the event	**15** ☐

LUCKY TO BE ALIVE

A

David Crossland, 50, was on holiday with his wife, Louise, in the Bahamas when the giant Hurricane Floyd hit New Providence Island.

'We were on holiday on Providence Island last year when Hurricane George was due to hit, but it changed direction. So this year, when Hurricane Floyd was heading towards us, Louise and I were convinced it would change course. But a week into our holiday the island was in the direct path of the hurricane and the hotel staff feared the worst. All of the ground-floor windows and balcony doors in the hotel were boarded up. At one point I tried to open the balcony door in our bedroom to catch a glimpse of the hurricane but the winds were so strong I couldn't move it. All we could do was lie in our bed in the candlelight and wait.

When the all clear was given at 2 pm we were able to go out and see the devastation. It was shocking. There were parts of houses, trees and debris everywhere and a tidal wave had destroyed many homes on the island. Such a shame for the island, but hurricanes could never put us off going back there.'

B

When Pat Beddows reached 40, she set herself a mountainous challenge in the Himalayas. During the trek disaster struck.

'I set off in a group of 20 from Gangotri, a village at 4,000 metres in the foothills of the Himalayas. As we sat having lunch, we watched huge chunks of ice break away from a glacier, then fall into the water. Unaware of the risk we were taking we climbed down into the glacier to take a closer look. Suddenly, I heard a thundering noise and our guide started screaming: "Run! Run! Climb up!"

A tidal wave of water and ice was heading straight for us and we scrambled up the rocky slopes to safety. Chunks of ice the size of cars were being thrown into the air barely five metres away. If the guide hadn't shouted at us to get out of the way, the consequences would have been tragic. When we got back to camp we were told that, three years earlier, 16 people had died

there in a similar incident. I realized how lucky we all were and I burst into tears.'

C

Teacher Caroline Casterton, 25, was visiting friends in Istanbul when an earthquake struck.

'I was fast asleep in my friends' apartment when the tremor shook. At first it was total confusion. There was a power cut so it was pitch black and everything inside the building was shaking and moving. It lasted only 45 seconds but it felt like an eternity. It was absolutely terrifying. For the next four days and nights I slept on the streets with thousands of others and the scale of the devastation gradually began to sink in.

Yet out of the chaos there was the most incredible sense of camaraderie. Everyone seemed so united and I witnessed so much courage and kindness. Since that day I have taken far less for granted and I really do feel life is for living in the present. Now I'm teaching the pupils at my school to be far more aware of the misfortunes of other people.'

D

Doug Glenwright, 33, was sitting in his front room in Birmingham, England, when he had the shock of his life.

'Last week we were watching on the television how tornadoes wrecked Oklahoma, where you'd expect to see them. Then suddenly last night one of them came down our street. The first I became aware of it was when I saw a dustbin bag come up from the street and fly past the window like a kite. Then branches of trees and all sorts of other debris were pulled up into the air. Telephone lines were knocked down by the hurricane-force winds and the heavy rain caused four feet of flood water in some people's kitchens.

Naturally my wife and I were both nervous, but we couldn't let the children see so we laughed and joked our way through it. We didn't think it was very funny, though, when we saw the massive hole it had made in our roof.'

Reacting to the text

How do you think you would have felt in each of the situations in the text?
Can you remember a time when you were frightened or concerned for your safety?

Language focus 1: Conditionals

A Real or imaginary?

Look at the following statement from text B of the reading.
If the guide hadn't shouted at us to get out of the way, the consequences would have been tragic.

Read the following explanation and underline the correct alternatives.

In this sentence the speaker is referring to a situation in the *present/past/future*. The situation she describes is imaginary because we know that the guide *shouted/didn't shout* at them to get out of the way and that the consequences *were/were not* tragic.

B Context

1 In which of the four situations described in the reading do you think each of the following were said?

Zero conditional:	*This **occurs** if the 'plates' underneath the earth's surface **rub** together or **pull** apart.*
First conditional:	*You **will be** much safer if you **stay** in the hotel.*
Second conditional:	*If we **lived** in Oklahoma, we **would see** a lot more of these.*
Third conditional:	*If we **had known** it was going to happen, we **would have got** out of the building earlier.*
Mixed conditional:	*If we **had ignored** his warnings, we **wouldn't be** alive today.*

2 Identify the verb forms in **bold** in each of the conditional sentences in exercise 1.

C Meaning

1 Match each of the explanations **a–e** to a conditional sentence in exercise B1.
   a an imaginary situation in the past
   b an imaginary situation in the present
   c a possible future situation and its likely result
   d the likely present result of an imaginary situation in the past
   e a scientific fact, or something that is always true (*if* means *whenever*)

2 Do the following two sentences refer to past, present or future situations?
   a *If we have another tornado here, we'll sell the house and move to a different area.*
   b *If we had another tornado here, we'd sell the house and move to a different area.*

Why are different tenses used in each sentence?
What does each sentence tell us about how the speaker views the possibility of the event occurring?

3 Explain the difference in meaning between the following pairs of sentences.
   1 a If it doesn't rain tomorrow, we'll go for a picnic.
      b If it doesn't rain tomorrow, we may go for a picnic.
   2 a If it didn't rain so much, we would all be a lot healthier.
      b If it didn't rain so much, we might all be a lot healthier.

4 a Which of these words and expressions can be used in place of *if* in the following sentence without changing the meaning?

   as long as   as far as   provided   providing
   promising   on condition

   *You can watch the film on TV **if** you help me do the washing up first.*

   b Which word meaning *if not* can be used in the following sentence?
   We'll probably go to the beach tomorrow _____ it rains.

 Read more about conditional sentences on page 214 of the Grammar reference.

Practice

1 Each of the following sentences contains a mistake. Find the five mistakes and correct them.
   1 If you'd have asked me, I would have lent you some money.
   2 I'll give you a ring if I'll find out what time he's arriving.
   3 What would you do if she doesn't come to your party?
   4 If I would drink coffee after six in the evening, I can never sleep.
   5 If they lose another match, I'd never go to see them play again.

2 **Student A:** On page 202 you will find the second half of four conditional sentences. For each one, write three possible beginnings.

   Example:
   a *If I could speak English fluently,*
   b *If I went to live in the capital,*   I'd get a good job.
   c *If my dad asked the right people,*

   Student B: On page 200 you will find the first half of four conditional sentences. For each one, write three possible continuations.

   Example:
                                    a *I'd probably be married.*
   If I were 10 years older, b *I wouldn't have to go to school.*
                                    c *I'd be able to vote.*

Read out the sentence halves you have written and your partner will try to guess the sentence half you were given.

Conditionals: Expressing regret

The third conditional can be used to express regrets. For each of the following situations imagine what the person might be thinking. Write a third conditional sentence for each picture.

0 *If I'd brought my umbrella, I wouldn't have got so wet.*

1 _____

2 _____

3 _____

4 _____

5 _____

Listening 1:
FCE Part 2

Sentence completion 🔘 2.1

1 Which parts of the world suffer hurricanes and earthquakes?
   How do rescue teams find and save earthquake victims?

2 You will hear part of a radio interview with Paul Murphy, a member of IRC, the International Rescue Corps. For questions **1–10**, complete the sentences.

Paul Murphy worked with a founder member of the IRC as a [1].

In the United Kingdom, the IRC is frequently asked to [2].

A disaster-struck country usually asks for help from the [3].

Unlike other rescue agencies, the IRC has its own [4].

All of the members of the IRC are [5].

Apart from the heat, the main problems for Paul in Nicaragua were the [*and*   6].

The rescue of the woman in Japan took [7].

The woman owed her survival to a [8].

She said she felt [9].

In order to prevent loss of life in earthquakes, Paul says that governments should construct [10].

What qualities do you think you need to become a member of a rescue team?

Vocabulary 2: *Put*

A Phrasal verbs with *put*

1 Look at this sentence from section A of the reading text 'Lucky to be alive'.

Such a shame for the island, but hurricanes could never put us off going back there.

What is the meaning of *put off* in this sentence? Choose from the following:

A postpone   **B** distract   **C** discourage   **D** cause to dislike

Now match the remaining three meanings to each different use of *put off* in the following sentences.

1 Because of the rain they had to **put** the cup final **off** until the following week.
2 Turn the TV down. I'm trying to read and the noise is **putting** me **off**.
3 I soon realized that all he ever talked about was football. It **put** me right **off** him.

2 In A and B below, the particle required for the spaces in each of the three sentences is the same. Decide what the missing word is and then choose the appropriate meaning **A**, **B** or **C** for each of the three phrasal verbs.

A
1 It's too quiet for me. Why don't we **put** the radio _____ ?
2 All the clothes which fitted me last summer are too tight for me now. I must have **put** _____ weight.
3 If you're cold, you should **put** your coat _____ .

   A place on your body   **B** increase   **C** start something working

B
1 Don't shout out the answer. If you want to say something, **put** your hand _____ .
2 If they keep **putting** _____ the price of cigarettes, I'll have to stop smoking, I just can't afford it.
3 If you want people to come to the concert, you should **put** posters _____ around the school to advertise it.

   A increase   **B** fix to a wall or board   **C** lift into the air

B Expressions with *put*

1 Complete the spaces **1–12** in the following short texts (**A–D**), using the words in the box. The first one has been done for you.

effort	~~night~~	cigarette	touch
position	blame	money	feet
risk	book	smoking	pressure

A
When Anne first came to London she had nowhere to live so I offered to put her up for the **(1)** _night_ at my house and then help her to find a flat of her own. The next morning I put her in **(2)** _____ with my friend Richard, who was looking for a flatmate, and she went to see him. Unfortunately, Anne gets through 30 cigarettes a day and I'd forgotten that Richard won't put up with anyone **(3)** _____ in his flat. He doesn't see why other people should put his health at **(4)** _____ as well as their own, he always says. When he opened the door and saw Anne there smoking, he told her she'd have to put out her **(5)** _____ before she went in. Needless to say, Anne decided to look elsewhere for accommodation.

B
My parents used to put **(6)** _____ on me to study harder. They said I wouldn't get into university if I didn't put more time and **(7)** _____ into my school work.

C

After a hard day at work I like nothing more than to put my **(8)** _____ up as soon as I get in and read a good novel. This particular story is so well written I just can't put the **(9)** _____ down.

D

Naturally I was upset. I'd been putting some **(10)** _____ aside each week in order to pay for our holiday and during the night someone broke in and stole it. And then the policeman who came had the cheek to put the **(11)** _____ on me; he said it was my fault for leaving such a large amount of cash in the house. I know it was wrong to shout at him, but put yourself in my **(12)** _____ ; I'm sure you'd have done the same.

2   Underline the phrases with *put* in exercise 1 and try to work out the meaning using the context.

Speaking

What do you think the picture shows?
Who are these people and why are they there?

Use modal verbs of speculation and the Useful language on page 98 to say what you think:
- may have happened
- might be happening now
- could happen next

Reading

Read the following text about Christiana Tugwell and answer the following questions.
What is she protesting against? How is she doing this?
How does her mother feel about her protest?

Teenager Christiana Tugwell and a small band of fellow school-age environmentalists have spent the past five months fighting proposals being put forward by the property developer, Countryside Residentials, to build 66 luxury detached houses in an area of woodland. They have received support at their protest camp from other residents who want to save the wood and the wildlife it contains. They have built a network of underground tunnels, which they will occupy to prevent the developers from starting work. Countryside Residential said it had been careful to preserve wildlife on the site, employing ecologists to do surveys and spending tens of thousands of pounds protecting animal and plant life.

'I began organizing the local campaign when I realized just how many local residents were against the developments. They were writing letters of protest to the council but this was simply not enough. So in order to put more pressure on the council and to raise national awareness, I started camping on the proposed development site. I was the ring-leader and had to bully some friends to join me. They weren't keen on sleeping rough and neither was I, but something had to be done.

My mum's initial reaction was "you're going to get cold" and "are you sure you want to do this?" After the first week she sent some friends to try to make me come home. They said I'd get into trouble, but I was determined to stay. I even spent three nights at the camp on my own. Even though she wanted me home, mum was always supportive and even brought us vegetarian sausages.

'Mum and I don't always see eye to eye on everything. But we agree that as long as what I want to do is not completely stupid, she lets me do it. I'm very stubborn and if I think I can do it, normally I can. I'd never done anything like this before, apart from a few anti-McDonald's demonstrations. Although we both support the campaign, our methods are very different: I believe in direct confrontation but she doesn't. She can't climb trees, dig tunnels or camp out, whereas I can. Her way is to raise awareness by writing letters and distributing leaflets, which also has its place.

'She worries about possible violence from the people trying to evict us and so do I, but there won't be any violence on our part: we are pacifists. I don't want to worry her, but stopping the development is more important.'

Reacting to the text ⬤

What is more important: defending woodland for wildlife or building houses?
Christiana says she is a pacifist. Do you think violence can ever be justified as a way of protesting?
She says she has taken part in anti-McDonald's demonstrations. What do you think were her reasons?

Language focus 2: *So, neither* and *nor*

1 Look at the ways in which Christiana expresses how people's feelings, behaviour or abilities are the same or different.

a The same
They weren't keen on sleeping rough and *neither was I.*
She worries about possible violence from the people trying to evict us and *so do I.*

b Different
I believe in direct confrontation but *she doesn't.*
She can't climb trees, dig tunnels or camp out, whereas *I can.*

When is *neither* or *so* used?
How do you decide which auxiliary verb to use?

Ⓖ Check the formation of *so, neither* and *nor* phrases on pages 214 and 215 of the Grammar reference.

2

a Match each statement **1–8** with a reply **a–h**.

1 I'm not very interested in <u>politics</u>.	**a** So would I.
2 I don't know how to <u>play chess</u>.	**b** I don't.
3 Last night I didn't <u>sleep very well</u>.	**c** Neither are we.
4 Next week I'm going to <u>start revising for the exams</u>.	**d** So is mine.
5 I'd like to <u>go for a drink</u> now.	**e** Mark does.
6 I've never <u>been windsurfing</u>.	**f** Nor did I.
7 I really enjoy <u>going for long walks</u>.	**g** So are we.
8 My favourite TV programme is '<u>Friends</u>'.	**h** Neither have I.

b Change the underlined part of each statement **1–8** to make sentences that are true for you.

c ◯ Read out the sentences you wrote in **b**. Respond to your partner using *so, neither* and *nor*.

Use of English:
FCE Part 2

Open cloze

1 You are going to read a text about World Carfree Day. What do you think happens on this day and why?

2 Read the text through quite quickly, ignoring the gaps. Compare what it says with your own ideas in exercise 1.

World Carfree Day

Each year, **(0)** <u>_on_</u> September 22nd, people in over 1,500 cities in 40 countries around the globe celebrate World Carfree Day. **(1)** _____ annual event, which **(2)** _____ coordinated by the World Car Network in Prague and supported by the European Union and the United Nations, aims **(3)** _____ raise awareness of the problems caused by our dependence on private cars. Streets are closed to traffic and opened instead to street parties, theatre, bicycle demonstrations or outdoor cafés, in **(4)** _____ to show people what their city might look like **(5)** _____ there were fewer or no cars. Over one hundred million people are believed to take **(6)** _____ in the celebrations, **(7)** _____ this figure is difficult to verify.

The hope of the organisers is that the initiative will serve as a catalyst and lead to more permanent changes **(8)** _____ will promote and encourage more environmentally friendly alternatives to the car, **(9)** _____ as walking, cycling and public transport. **(10)** _____, with increasing global car production and a world which **(11)** _____ grown used to the benefits of private transport, sceptics of the event say the battle is already lost. One can only hope they are wrong, and even if it is unlikely we will see cities **(12)** _____ any cars at all, people may at least begin to change their habits and leave their car at home more often.

3 Read the text again and for questions **1–12**, think of the word which best fits each gap. Use only **one** word in each gap. There is an example at the beginning (**0**).

What to expect in the exam

- The Open cloze task focuses mainly on grammar (see page 80). However, occasionally your knowledge of vocabulary may be tested (eg question 6 above).

◯ **4** Do people in your country celebrate World Carfree Day? If so, how successful is it? How dependent are you and your family on the car?

Speaking:
FCE Part 3

Collaborative task

1   One vocabulary item has been given for each of the six categories below. Add two more items from the box to each category.

dropping litter
dumping waste
nature reserve
endangered
    species
unleaded petrol
global warming
exhaust fumes
cigarette butts
oil slick
greenhouse effect
plastic containers
bottle bank

Recycling
recycled paper

Keeping cities clean
dog mess

River and sea pollution
toxic effluent

Traffic pollution
carbon monoxide

Climate change
rising sea levels

Animal welfare
facing extinction

How to go about it

- Appropriate use of some of the vocabulary from exercise 1 would impress the examiners.
- When commenting on your partner's opinions you can use *so*, *neither* or *nor* and the language you saw on page 123 of Unit 10 for agreeing and disagreeing.

2   Read the following Speaking Part 3 instructions.

Imagine that you belong to an environmental group and you want to inform people of current environmental problems. Talk with your partner and decide which three categories are the most important for your local area. Then discuss what ordinary people can do to help.

Writing:
FCE Part 2

Essays

Your class has been doing a project on the environment. Your teacher has asked you to write an essay about the following statement:

Nothing can be done to save the environment.

You should state whether you agree or disagree with this statement, explaining your reasons clearly.

How to go about it

- Decide whether you agree or disagree with the statement.
- Use the categories in the speaking activity and make notes under some of them.
- Remember that the maximum number of

words is 180, so you will only be able to write about two or three of the issues.
- Look at the information on pages 102 and 103 of Unit 8 and write a plan.
- Use appropriate linking devices.

Now write your **essay**. You should write between **120 and 180** words.

Listening 2:
FCE Part 1

Multiple choice ⊙ 2.2–2.9

You will hear people talking in eight different situations. For questions **1–8**, choose the best answer, **A**, **B** or **C**.

What to expect in the exam

- In Unit 4 you saw how contrast linkers such as *although, whereas* and *but*, as well as other words and expressions, can be used to create distractors in listening exercises.

- Look at question 1, together with the tapescript and choose the best answer. Which structure is used to create distractors? Which words help you to choose the answer?

1 You hear a man talking about a new fire station that has just been built. Where was it built?

    A in the city centre

    B in the countryside

    C on the outskirts of the city

Tapescript

I really can't understand why they put it all the way out there. They maintained that if they'd built it in the heart of the city there would have been problems getting out to fires in the rural areas. Too far and too much traffic, they said. But that's exactly why it would have made more sense to build it in the centre instead of on the edge. You know, it takes a fire engine nearly 20 minutes to get from that suburb to the other side of the city.

Now do questions **2–8** below. In questions 2, 3 and 4 you will hear conditional sentences. These are used to create distractors as in question 1 above.

2 Listen to this man speaking. Who is he?

    A a shopkeeper

    B a town councillor

    C a local resident

3 You hear an environmentalist speaking on the radio about a recent project. How does she feel?

    A pessimistic

    B disappointed

    C pleased

4 You overhear this woman talking to her friend about her holiday. Why did she enjoy it?

    A She liked the beaches.

    B There wasn't much traffic.

    C There weren't many people.

5 You hear a conversation between two people. What is the relationship between them?

    A They are married.

    B They are teachers in the same school.

    C They are neighbours.

6 You are listening to the radio when you hear the following being read. What is it?

    A a story

    B a news report

    C a weather forecast

7 You overhear this conversation between a man and his neighbour. What is he doing?

    A asking for help

    B apologizing

    C complaining

8 You hear Brian talking about a recent environmental disaster. What is he going to do?

    A help clean up

    B take part in a protest demonstration

    C write to his Member of Parliament

11 Review

Vocabulary

A Weather

1 Match the adjectives **1–3** with the nouns **a–d** to make appropriate adjective + noun collocations. Each adjective may be used with more than one noun.

1 light   **a** storm
2 heavy   **b** wind
3 strong   **c** showers
              d rain

2 Add an appropriate noun from the box to each of the adjectives **1–10** below. The first one has been done for you.

sea	sky	wave	showers	storm
rain	clouds	~~breeze~~	sunshine	wind

1 gentle _breeze_
2 angry-looking _____
3 rough _____
4 torrential _____
5 scattered _____
6 brilliant _____
7 overcast _____
8 tidal _____
9 violent _____
10 gale-force _____

B Put

Complete each of the spaces in sentences **1–6** with one of the words from the box.

in	down	off	out	up	on

1 This is a great book. I just can't put it _____ .
2 I'm afraid you'll have to put _____ your cigarette. This is a non-smoking area.
3 When I'm next in London, could you put me _____ for the night?
4 Could you put the radio _____ ? I want to listen to the news.
5 My bank manager put me _____ touch with a very good accountant.
6 Never put _____ until tomorrow what you can do today.

Conditional sentences

Complete the spaces in the following sentences with the appropriate form of the verb in brackets.

1 If the weather _____ (stay) good next weekend, we _____ (probably/go) away somewhere.
2 Why didn't you phone us? If I _____ (know) you were coming, I _____ (could/prepare) something special to eat.
3 Absolutely no way! I _____ (not/do) a bungee jump even if you _____ _____ (pay) me.
4 I thought this might happen. If you _____ (take) my advice, you _____ _____ (not/be) in this mess now.
5 If you ever _____ (do) that again, I _____ (make) you pay for it!
6 That was very kind of you. I don't know what I _____ (do) if you ____ _____ (not/help) me.
7 If I _____ (be) at home on Sunday afternoon, I _____ (always/watch) the film on telly.
8 I _____ (go) to the cinema more often if I _____ (have) the time, but unfortunately it's just not possible.

Use of English:
FCE Part 4

Transformations

Complete the second sentence so that it has a similar meaning to the first sentence, using the word given. **Do not change the word given.** You must use between two and five words, including the word given.

1 It's too wet to play tennis today.
if
We could play tennis _____ wet today.

2 It's a good thing I spoke to you or I would have forgotten her birthday.
if
I would have forgotten her birthday _____ to you.

3 I only wrote the letter because my mother made me do it.
not
If my mother hadn't made me do it, _____ the letter.

4 I will help you only if you tidy your room.
not
I will _____ tidy your room.

5 I got soaking wet because I forgot to take my umbrella with me.
remembered
If _____ my umbrella with me, I wouldn't have got soaking wet.

6 Some people say that giving up smoking causes your weight to increase.
you
Some people say that if you _____ on weight.

7 I've had enough of the neighbours' noise.
put
I refuse _____ the neighbours' noise any more.

8 The factory fumes are endangering the health of local residents.
put
The health of local residents _____ risk by the factory fumes.

9 I eat meat, but it has to be well cooked.
provided
I eat meat _____ well cooked.

10 You can borrow it, but you must give it back next week.
long
You can borrow it _____ it back next week.

Writing:
FCE Part 1

Formal letters

You are a member of an environmental group. Last weekend you attended a demonstration against a proposed by-pass for the town of Oldbury. You have just seen a newspaper report about the event, which is incorrect.

Read the newspaper report below, together with your own comments. Then write to the editor, correcting the errors and asking the newspaper to send a reporter to interview you. Write your letter in **120–150** words.

DEMONSTRATION LEADS TO ARRESTS

Last weekend police arrested six demonstrators who were protesting against the building of a by-pass for Oldbury. The protesters claim that the construction of the road will lead to the extinction of a rare species of snail.
An estimated 200 people gathered on the outskirts of the town to express their disapproval and prevent the construction company from starting work. A small group of protesters sat in the road and chanted slogans at workers and police, blocking access to the site. A spokesman for the council said that the 'troublemakers' were all unemployed youngsters from other parts of the country, 'who had nothing better to do with their time'.

and the destruction of woodland!

over 2,000!

no – a silent demonstration

not true – many were local residents

Speaking

Compare what these two people eat.
Who do you think eats more healthily?
Does their diet tell you anything about their lifestyle?
What does 'a balanced diet' consist of?
How well does this term describe what *you* eat?
What are the advantages and disadvantages of fast food?

Language focus 1: Countable and uncountable nouns A

1 The word *plate* is usually countable: we can say 'a plate', 'two plates', 'three plates' and so on.

The word *bread* is usually uncountable: we say 'bread' or 'some bread', rather than 'a bread' or 'two breads'.

Decide which of the following words are countable, and which are uncountable. Some of them can be both countable and uncountable. How does this affect the meaning?

milk	diet	chicken	health	chip
chocolate	meal	pepper	spaghetti	cake

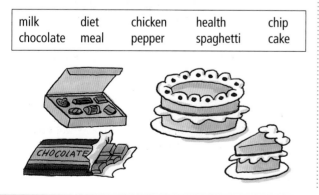

2 The word *bread* can be made countable by saying 'a loaf of bread' or 'two slices of bread'. Write the following uncountable nouns next to an appropriate expression to make them countable. Some of the nouns can be used with more than one expression.

sugar	cheese	jam	milk	toast
cake	spaghetti	salt	chocolate	

1 a piece of _____
2 a slice of _____
3 a plate of _____
4 a teaspoonful of _____
5 a pinch of _____
6 a bar of _____
7 a jar of _____
8 a carton of _____

G See page 216 of the Grammar reference.

Multiple matching 2.10–2.14

1 Have you ever been on a diet?
What type of diet was it? How effective was it?

2 You will hear five people talking about food and dieting. For questions **1–5**, choose from the list **A–F** what each speaker says about the subject. Use the letters only once. There is one extra letter which you do not need to use.

Don't forget!

● Underline the key words in each of the six different statements. This helps you to focus on what to listen for. Are any of the statements similar to each other?
● Listen carefully both times to everything each speaker says. Then make your final decision.

A I follow the advice given in books.   Speaker 1 ☐
B One form of dieting was too expensive.   Speaker 2 ☐
C I used to feel under pressure to lose weight. Speaker 3 ☐
D I have never been on a diet.   Speaker 4 ☐
E I had to change my eating habits.   Speaker 5 ☐
F I don't follow all the advice I am given.

3 The last woman said: *We are constantly under attack from advertising and the media, who tell us that 'thin is beautiful'.*

To what extent is this the case in your country?
What are the dangers of dieting?

Language focus 2: Countable and uncountable nouns B

Why does the woman say 'Just a few' and not 'Just a little'?

The following sentences are all from the listening activity. Complete each of the spaces with one of the words from the box. Some words will be used more than once and more than one answer may be possible for each space.

little	few	much	many	some	any	no
deal	number	piece	lot	plenty	several	

Speaker 1
You drink nothing but lemonade with **a)** _____ salt and pepper for about seven days without **b)** _____ food.

I wasn't earning a great **c)** _____ of money and I simply couldn't afford to keep it up.

Speaker 2
I used to eat a **d)** _____ of junk food.
I ate very **e)** _____ fresh food and this had a serious effect on my health.

And now if I get hungry between meals, I have a **f)** _____ cheese or **g)** _____ nuts, just to fill the hole.

Speaker 3
When I want to treat myself I have a **h)** _____ of cake or a **i)** _____ biscuits.
As long as you eat sweet things after a meal, then there's **j)** _____ problem.
I only ever eat chocolates after lunch or dinner. And never too **k)** _____ of course – just one or two.

Speaker 4
A sensible, balanced diet: **l)** _____ of fresh fruit and vegetables… **m)** _____ glasses of water a day – and **n)** _____ snacks between meals.

Speaker 5
A large **o)** _____ of people follow diets, but very **p)** _____ of them are happier as a result.
I don't pay **q)** _____ attention to what others think or say.

Multiple matching

1 How much water do you drink each day?
What are the benefits of drinking water? What do you think the effects of not drinking enough are?

2 You are going to read a newspaper article about the importance of drinking water. For questions **1–15**, choose from the paragraphs (**A–E**). The paragraphs may be chosen more than once. When more than one answer is required, these may be given in any order.

Which paragraphs mention the following?

the effects of excessive water consumption	**1** ☐
a local scheme to improve water provision	**2** ☐
the effects of dehydration on appearance	**3** ☐
evidence of improved brain activity	**4** ☐
the recommended daily intake of water	**5** ☐
a denial that any problem exists	**6** ☐
harmful alternatives to water	**7** ☐
free gifts to encourage the drinking of water	**8** ☐
a survey result revealing how few of us drink enough water	**9** ☐
the improbability of a particular health problem occurring	**10** ☐
a general lack of awareness of the full extent of the dangers	**11** ☐
difficulty in implementing a national scheme	**12** ☐
informing people of the need to drink water	**13** ☐ **14** ☐ **15** ☐

Water: are you drinking enough?

Drinking water can protect your health, improve your concentration and even prevent depression. Kate Hilpern reports on the dangers of dehydration.

A Practically the only time I drink water is when I'm working out at the gym and can feel my body crying out for it. Like millions of people, the rest of the time I prefer some flavour to my beverage. Insufficient consumption of water is a serious problem, according to scientists, who claim that anyone drinking less than eight glasses of pure water per day is at risk of dehydration. The consequences, they say, include poor performance at work, depression, allergies and even some cancers. Adding to the problem of getting this message across to the public is the fact that recent studies show drinking too much water can also jeopardize your health, causing 'acute water intoxication.' Salt in the blood is diluted, depriving the brain, heart and muscles of the amounts they need to function properly. But, according to Dr Wendy Doyle of the British Dietetic Association, 'It's very unlikely to happen except in the most extreme circumstances.'

B One recent poll suggests that only one in 10 of us drinks the right amount to meet the body's needs. And it's not only adults who are affected. A quarter of children drink no water during the school day and their performance is affected as a result. Indeed, thirst can cause mental performance to drop by at least 10 per cent. Studies of primary schools have found that test results significantly improve when pupils are encouraged to drink water throughout the day. There are also risks of longer-term damage, with paediatricians treating increasing numbers of children with bladder and kidney problems relating to dehydration.

C Fizzy drinks are four and a half times more popular than water among children, it seems. 'But soft drinks, including fizzy drinks and fruit juices, contain high levels of sugar,' says Barrie Clarke of Water UK, the umbrella organization for water suppliers. 'This means they are absorbed much more slowly than water so they don't hydrate the brain as quickly.' Really high sugar drinks cause a rapid rise in blood sugar level, followed by a sudden dip, which can cause lack of concentration, he adds. 'Most people know that drinking water is good for you but few realise the huge range of risks that can affect us every day, including lack of concentration, fatigue and irritability.' Then there's your vanity to think of. Lack of water leads to dry and tired looking skin as well as ageing.

D Recognizing that dehydration is a major health issue, primary schools in one region are taking action by providing water coolers. 'One of the major reasons seemed to be that, as in schools nationwide, the only water provided was through water fountains situated in the toilets. Many didn't work very well and the water was very often not that cold,' explained Jackie Abusin of the 'Cool Schools' campaign. For every cooler installed in a school, the regional water authority gives away refillable water bottles which children can take into classes with them. 'There is still a lot of work to be done around explaining to teachers about the importance of drinking water,' said Abusin. 'So part of our campaign is getting them not only to allow children to have water bottles on their desks, but to encourage them to drink from them before they get thirsty.'

E But what about adults? Water fountains in public places, as in schools, often offer nothing but a dribble of tepid water and appear less than hygienic. Water UK is currently working with shopping centres and public parks, among other places, to address the problem nationwide, but admits it is a slow process. Clarke is also working with the Institute of Directors, as well as individual employers, to persuade offices to provide water coolers for their employees. 'We're trying to get the message across that it's not an act of generosity, but that it's in their business interests as dehydrated employees are unproductive.' Not everyone agrees with the current panic, however. Dr Doyle believes that most forms of fluid are as good as water and that most of us get enough of it anyway. 'Let's not forget that food contains a lot of water. According to research, a quarter of the water we need to replace in our bodies each day comes from food.'

Reacting to the text ⬤

How much importance is attached to drinking water in your country?
How effective would campaigns such as those described in the last two paragraphs be?
What other measures might usefully be introduced?

Language focus 3: Reported speech

1 Look at the following example from the text, together with the reported speech version. What change is made to the verb when it is reported?

Direct speech: *'There **is** still a lot of work to be done,' said Abusin.*

Reported speech: *Abusin said there **was** still a lot of work to be done.*

Under what circumstances would the following reported speech version be possible?
*Abusin said there **is** still a lot of work to be done.*

2 Complete the columns below to show how verb tenses and other words and expressions can change in reported speech.

Direct speech	Reported speech
a 'We're meeting her tomorrow.' →	They said they _were meeting_ her _the next_ day.
b 'I've seen him twice today.' →	She said she _____ him twice _____ day.
c 'She's been living here for years.' →	He told me she _____ living _____ for years.

d 'I spoke to her last week.' →	He said he _____ to her _____ week.
e 'I was working yesterday.' →	He told me he _____ working _____ before.
f 'We'd asked her several times.' →	They said they _____ her several times.

3 Name the tense in each sentence in exercise 2.
Example: a *present continuous → past continuous*

4 What happens to the modal verbs *will, may, can* and *must* in reported speech?
What happens to *would, might, could, should* and *ought to*?

5 What happens to these time expressions in reported speech?
two days ago   next month   tonight
this morning   now

Ⓖ Check your ideas on page 215 of the Grammar reference.

6 ⬤ Write down at least five things that different people have said recently. Then report the different statements to the class using reported speech.

Speaking:
FCE Part 2

Speaking: **Talking about photos**

Look at the photographs, which show people eating in different places.

Student A: Compare photographs 1 and 2 and say how you think the people are feeling in each of them.

Student B: When your partner has finished, say whether you have eaten in situations like this.

Now change roles. Follow the instructions above using photographs 3 & 4.

Language focus 4: Reporting verbs

1 Look at these different ways of reporting what people say:

a 'I'll get you a drink,' said Jan to Tom.
   Jan told Tom she would get him a drink.
   *Jan **offered to get** Tom a drink.*

b 'You should go and see a doctor,' said Tim.
   Tim said I should go and see a doctor.
   *Tim **advised me to go** and see a doctor.*

2 Which of the following verbs follow the same pattern as *advise* (verb + object + infinitive) and which are like *offer* (verb + infinitive)?

order	urge	refuse	threaten
persuade	warn	tell	remind
ask	promise	encourage	recommend

3 Report the following sentences using an appropriate verb from exercise 2. There is an example (**0**) at the beginning.

0 'I'll give you the £5 back next week,' he told her.
   He *promised to give her the £5 back the following week.*

1 'I'm not going to clean my room!' she said.
   She _____ .

2 'Don't forget to take your sandwiches, John,' said his father.
   John's father _____ .

3 'If you don't turn your music down, I'll call the police,' said my neighbour.
   My neighbour _____ .

4 'Don't take the car out. The roads are very icy,' said her friend.
   Her friend _____ .

5 'Get out of my office immediately!' shouted his boss.
   His boss _____ .

6 'You really ought to report the theft to the police,' my friend told me.
   My friend _____ .

4 Look at the following structures which can follow the verb *recommend*.

The doctor recommended me to do exercise.
The doctor recommended (that) I (should) do exercise.
The doctor recommended doing exercise.

Which structure is not possible with the verb *suggest*?

5 ⬤ Work with a partner. You each have various problems and you would like your partner's suggestions and advice. Student A should turn to page 200 and Student B should turn to page 202 to find out what your problems are.

Use of English 1: **Multiple-choice cloze**
FCE Part 1

1 Apart from dieting, what other ways do you know of controlling weight?

2 Read through the following text, ignoring the spaces for the moment, and answer the following questions.

What does the 'alternative diet' consist of?
How effective is it?

3 For questions **1–12**, read the text below and decide which answer (**A, B, C** or **D**) best fits each gap. There is an example at the beginning (**0**).

An alternative diet

Karaoke enthusiasts can now enjoy their sometimes nervous (**0**) _____ safe in the knowledge that they are at least losing some weight. Thanks to Tokyo-based Daiichikosho, which sells and (**1**) _____ out karaoke equipment, karaoke machines can now (**2**) _____ how many calories the singer has burnt while singing the song. (**3**) _____ 40,000 users of its karaoke song-broadcasting service throughout Japan have now (**4**) _____ up for the company's 'Karaoke diet'.

Such factors as the volume and pitch of the singer's voice and the tempo and length of the song were (**5**) _____ into consideration before assigning calorie burning values to more than 1,000 favourite tunes. 'Naturally, the longer and livelier one sings, the (**6**) _____ calories are burned,' said a company spokesman.

(**7**) _____ to Daiichikosho, the Beatles' *Let It Be* burns up 11.4 kcal; but for those (**8**) _____ in shedding a little more weight, a rendition of Frank Sinatra's classic *My Way* will (**9**) _____ in the loss of 15.6 kcal. An average man will burn up approximately 81 kilocalories (**10**) _____ a ten-minute walk, suggesting that karaoke may not be the ideal weight loss programme.

In fact, indulging in karaoke (literally 'empty orchestra') can be counterproductive to any diet as the singing of such songs usually (**11**) _____ a drink – causing the singer to (**12**) _____ back on the same calories they may have just lost.

0 A <u>performances</u>	**B** representations	**C** productions	**D** realizations
1 A borrows	**B** hires	**C** hands	**D** spends
2 A turn up	**B** come across	**C** put down	**D** work out
3 A Over	**B** Several	**C** Many	**D** Various
4 A gone	**B** taken	**C** signed	**D** registered
5 A taken	**B** brought	**C** held	**D** put
6 A most	**B** other	**C** many	**D** more
7 A Regarding	**B** Concerning	**C** Believing	**D** According
8 A enthusiastic	**B** interested	**C** keen	**D** concerned
9 A lead	**B** cause	**C** provide	**D** result
10 A during	**B** while	**C** meanwhile	**D** until
11 A requires	**B** requests	**C** asks for	**D** wants
12 A bring	**B** place	**C** put	**D** get

Writing 1:
FCE Part 2

Reports

1 Read the following Writing Part 2 instructions.

What would *you* recommend the manager should do?

You have a part-time job in a restaurant. The manager wants to make the restaurant more popular with families and has asked you to carry out a survey among people of various ages and write a report.

Write your **report** in **120–180** words summarizing the findings of your survey and making one or two recommendations of your own.

2 Read the model answer and give each section a heading. There is one extra heading which you do not need to use.

A What their children want to eat   **D** Most popular dishes
B Further recommendations   **E** Parents' views on food
C Introduction   **F** Facilities

3 Who is the target reader and what style has the writer used?

1 _____
The aim of this report is to show what different family members expect from a restaurant. The report is based on a survey of 50 people aged between 8 and 45.

2 _____
Several younger parents agreed that a family restaurant should have nappy-changing facilities. Many of those under 16, on the other hand, felt that a non-smoking area was an important feature.

3 _____
Most parents expected to see a wide range of dishes on the menu, catering for all ages and tastes. Understandably, price is a significant factor and 80 per cent of those interviewed said they preferred restaurants which offered cheaper children's portions.

4 _____
Not surprisingly, over 90 per cent of those under 12 wanted chips with everything, whereas a large number of teenagers thought that a visit to a restaurant was an ideal opportunity to try new dishes.

5 _____
As a result of the survey, I would recommend that the restaurant should offer reduced prices for large families. I also suggest extending the menu to include meals which are suitable for young children.

4 Find examples of:

    a words and expressions used with countable and uncountable nouns
       eg *Several younger parents*

    b reported speech
       Which verbs are used to introduce the reported speech? eg *agreed*

    c making recommendations
       Which two verbs are used?

5 Find words or phrases which are used to:

    a introduce the report   eg *I was asked to write a report on...*
    b contrast ideas   eg *However,*
    c comment on the findings   eg *Interestingly,*

6 Read the following Writing Part 2 instructions.

As part of your town's cultural exchange programme, a group of foreign students will be visiting your area for two weeks. You have been asked to write a report for the group leader about regional and/or national dishes. You should give information about what the students can expect to eat in your area and comment on the popularity of the different dishes with young people.

7 Before you do the task consider this possible plan.

Introduction:	Explain the purpose of your report and how you obtained the information contained in it.
Most popular dishes:	Briefly describe at least two dishes and mention how popular they are with young people. Give reasons if appropriate.
Least popular dishes:	Give examples and say why they are not popular.
Recommendation:	Recommend your favourite regional and/or national food.

Look at the Wordlist on page 205 for useful vocabulary.

8 Who is the target reader? What style will you use for the report?
Look at page 202 to see how an English person answered the question.

Now you are ready to write your report in **120–180** words.

Language focus 5: Reported questions

1 Look at these examples of reported questions from the person who wrote the report on the opposite page. Write down the original direct questions that were asked.

1 I asked everyone what facilities a family restaurant should have.
'What _____ ? '

2 I asked them whether they thought it was important to have a non-smoking area.
' _____ ? '

2 What changes are made to direct questions when we report them? Consider the following:

- word order
- auxiliary verbs *do, does, did*
- verb tenses
- yes/no questions

   Ⓖ Check your answers on pages 215 and 216 of the Grammar reference.

3 Report the following questions which the interviewer asked.

1 'What type of food do you expect to see on the menu?'
I asked everyone _____
_____

2 'How important is the price of the food?'
I asked parents _____
_____

3 'Do you always eat the same things when you go to a restaurant?'
I asked teenagers _____
_____

4 'What other things would you like a restaurant to offer?'
I asked everyone _____
_____

Vocabulary: Health matters

1 In parts **A** and **B** below complete the spaces with one of the words from the box.

A | ear   stomach   ~~nose~~   heart   blood

0 If you get a...   _nose_   **bleed,**   pinch it with two fingers until it stops.
1 She'll have a...   _____ **attack**   when she sees what you've done!
2 Of course he has a... _____ **ache.**   He ate far too many cream cakes.
3 With such high...   _____ **pressure**   you should eat less salt.
4 She's got a bad...   _____ **infection**   so she can't come swimming.

B | ankle   nose   eye   throat

1 That's a nasty...   **black** _____ . Did somebody hit you?
2 She's got a very... **sore**   _____ . She can hardly speak.
3 You've got a...   **runny** _____ . Would you like a handkerchief?
4 It's just a badly... **sprained** _____ . You haven't broken anything.

2 Cover up the words on the right in exercises 1A and B. How many can you remember?
Now cover up the words on the left. Can you remember more the second time?

3 Choose the correct alternative in each sentence.

1 My father wrapped a *bandage/band* round my sprained wrist.
2 You've cut your finger. You should put *a plaster/plaster* on it.
3 The doctor gave me a *receipt/prescription* for a course of antibiotics.
4 When I broke my arm, I had it in *a plaster/plaster* for about five weeks.
5 The nurse gave him an *infusion/injection* in his arm to help him sleep.

4 When was the last time you were ill?
Do you often have accidents? What about when you were younger?
Which of the conditions in exercise 1 have you suffered?

Word formation: Noun suffixes

1 Use the examples in **A** to help you complete the appropriate noun forms in **B**.

A Verb	Noun	Adjective	Noun
improve	*improvement*	sore	*soreness*
infect	*infection*	sensitive	*sensitivity*

B treat	_____	weak	_____
prescribe	_____	severe	_____

2 Write the noun form of the following verbs and adjectives. Use the suffixes *-ion, -ity,* *-ment, -ness, -ance* and *-ence*

Verbs	Nouns	Adjectives	Nouns
amuse	_____	important	_____
decide	_____	fit	_____
appear	_____	sincere	_____
entertain	_____	happy	_____
explain	_____	secure	_____
perform	_____	evident	_____
imagine	_____	careless	_____
develop	_____	original	_____

3 Mark the stress on the verbs, adjectives and nouns in exercise 2.

Use of English 2: Word formation
FCE Part 3

For questions **1–10**, read the text below. Use the word given in capitals at the end of each line to form a word that fits in the gap **in the same line**.

A knee injury

My brother hurt his knee in a skiing **(1)** _____ recently. He didn't
think it was serious at the time but it soon began to affect his **(2)** _____
to walk properly and he complained of **(3)** _____ in his leg. It slowly got
worse and he eventually had to go into hospital for an **(4)** _____ . He's
resting at home now and the doctors say that in the **(5)** _____ of cases
like this, as long as there are no **(6)** _____ , people are able to resume
their normal **(7)** _____ within a few weeks. They gave him a few gentle
exercises to do and he's already beginning to notice an **(8)** _____ .
Sudden **(9)** _____ obviously have to be avoided and he often complains
of **(10)** _____ , but he'll be as right as rain soon.

COMPETE
ABLE
STIFF
OPERATE
MAJOR
COMPLICATE
ACTIVE
IMPROVE
MOVE
TIRE

Writing 2: Letters: Giving information
FCE Part 1

1 Read the following Writing Part 1 instructions.

You have received a letter from your friend, Trevor, asking for information about a health spa. Read his letter and an advertisement for the health spa, on which you have made some notes. Then write a letter to Trevor, using **all** your notes.

Write your **letter** in **120–150** words in an appropriate style. Do not write any postal addresses.

These exams have left me feeling exhausted. I know I laughed last year when you went to a health spa but it doesn't seem such a bad idea now. What were the facilities and food like in the place you went to?

My main worry is that I might get bored. Could you let me know what there is to do there and whether you think I'd enjoy it?

Hope to hear from you soon.

All the best,
Trevor

Definitely!

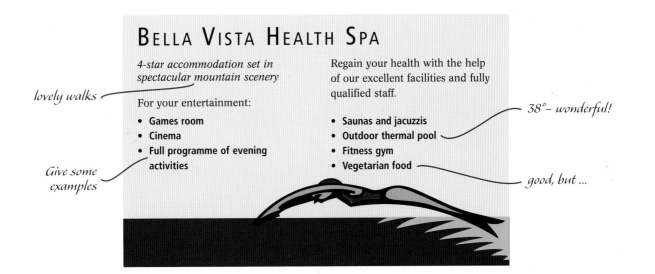

BELLA VISTA HEALTH SPA

4-star accommodation set in spectacular mountain scenery

Regain your health with the help of our excellent facilities and fully qualified staff.

lovely walks

For your entertainment:
- **Games room**
- **Cinema**
- **Full programme of evening activities**

- **Saunas and jacuzzis**
- **Outdoor thermal pool**
- **Fitness gym**
- **Vegetarian food**

38°– wonderful!

good, but …

Give some examples

12 Review

Use of English:
FCE Part 2

Open cloze

For questions **1–12**, read the text below and think of the word which best fits each gap. Use only **one** word in each gap. Here is an example (**0**).

Roast ghost

New Zealander Kay Martin got the fright of (**0**) _her_ life a (**1**) _____ weeks ago. According to the *Auckland Sunday Star*, she and a friend were chatting over a drink (**2**) _____ they heard a chicken squawking. They came (**3**) _____ the conclusion that it (**4**) _____ escaped from a neighbour's garden and they went outside to catch it. But there were (**5**) _____ chickens anywhere.

Then Kay realised with horror that the sound was coming from (**6**) _____ own kitchen – coming, in fact, from the oven, (**7**) _____ she had put a chicken to roast half an hour earlier. 'It was (**8**) ____ if it was calling to me from its grave,' she said. 'I was (**9**) _____ amazed I couldn't speak.'

As they approached, the squawking noise reached a crescendo. They removed the tray from the oven, and as the chicken began to cool, the squawking died away. Ms Martin chopped the neck (**10**) _____ and threw it in the sink. She noticed that the vocal chords were (**11**) ____ perfect condition. 'Steam was coming up the neck from the stuffing inside the chicken,' she said, 'and this had caused the dead bird to squawk.' She has (**12**) _____ eaten any chicken since.

Use of English:
FCE Part 4

Transformations

For questions **1–8** complete the second sentence so that it has a similar meaning to the first sentence, using the word given. **Do not change the word given.** You must use between two and five words, including the word given.

1 'Did you buy a bandage, Roy?' asked Graham.
  he
  Graham asked _____ a bandage.

2 His condition improved so rapidly he went home four days after the operation.
  such
  There _____ in his condition he went home four days after the operation.

3 'I wouldn't go to that restaurant if I were you, Matt,' I said.
  advised
  I _____ to that restaurant.

4 I'm amazed by how much English he knows.
  of
  His _____ me.

5 'Can you swim, Sarah?' asked her teacher.
  her
  Sarah's teacher asked _____ to swim.

6 'I'll drive you to the station, Dawn,' he said.
  offered
  He _____ a lift to the station.

7 'There'll be very few people at the party,' she told Roger.
  not
  She told Roger there _____ people at the party.

8 'Let's eat out tomorrow,' said Chris.
  suggested
  Chris _____ day.

Vocabulary: Health matters

Complete each of the following collocations by writing an appropriate part of the body in each of the spaces.

1 a black _____
2 a sore _____
3 a sprained _____
4 a runny _____

5 an _____ infection
6 a _____ bleed
7 a _____ attack
8 a _____ ache

Use of English:
FCE Part 3

Word formation

For questions **1–7** use the word given in capitals at the end of each line to form a noun that fits in the gap in the sentence. In each case a different suffix from the box is required to form the noun. There is an example at the beginning **(0)**.

| -ment | -ity | -ion | -ness | -ship | -ence | -ance | ~~-or~~ |

0 Alexander Graham Bell, the _inventor_ of the telephone, was born in Edinburgh in 1847.   **INVENT**
1 It is our _____ to speak which makes us so different from other mammals.   **ABLE**
2 Juliet had not been getting on well with her boyfriend, so she decided to end
their _____ .   **RELATE**
3 I wouldn't have the _____ to go fishing; I'd hate the idea of sitting there all day
waiting for something to happen.   **PATIENT**
4 The couple next door had another _____ last night; we could hear them shouting
at each other.   **ARGUE**
5 Russell Crowe gave an impressive _____ as a gladiator in the film of the same name.   **PERFORM**
6 He could not hide his feeling of great _____ at the death of his dog, Georgia.   **SAD**
7 She told the teacher that someone had stolen her book, but he didn't believe her
_____ .   **EXPLAIN**

Collocation revision: Units 1–12

1 In each of the spaces below write one word which collocates with *all* three of the other words. The question numbers also refer to the relevant units of the book where the words you require appeared. If you can't think of a word, look at the contents map on pages ii and iii. The topic areas will give you a clue.

1 second-hand shabby trendy	_____	**5** challenging monotonous badly-paid	_____	**9** a piercing scream a nervous laugh a broad smile	_____	
2 talented session rock	_____	**6** flowing shoulder-length spiky	_____	**10** death life two-year prison	_____	
3 handy labour-saving useful	_____	**7** prosperous bustling run-down	_____	**11** strong gale-force light	_____	
4 horror action science-fiction	_____	**8** business day weekend	_____	**12** fast junk fresh	_____	

2 Use other collocations from the first 12 units of the book to help you create your own exercise. Write three words or expressions which can all be used with the same verb or noun, in the same way as the exercise in 1 above. Write four examples like this for another student to complete.

Part 1: Multiple choice

Part 1 contains eight short unrelated extracts with multiple-choice questions. In each extract you will hear either a monologue or a conversation between two or more people. There are several different types of questions which test your ability to understand, for example, the general idea or main points of the extract, *what* people's opinions are, *how* they feel, *where* they are or *who* they are speaking to.

Predicting

In all parts of the listening paper it is important to use the questions to help you predict what you will hear. This will then help you in your understanding of what you actually do hear. Look at this question from Part 1:

1 You are on a bus and you overhear a conversation between two women.
   What has one of the women just bought?
   A a blouse
   B a skirt
   C a dress

Discuss the similarities and differences between each of the three options.

Example: 1
Both a skirt and a dress are worn over the lower part of the body, whereas a blouse is not.

Distractors

Simply hearing the same word or phrase which is in one of the alternatives will not guarantee that you have found the right answer. These words could be distractors.

Read the following tapescript for question 1 above. What is the answer?

Woman 1: That's lovely. Celebrating something, are you?
Woman 2: Yes, well, my nephew's getting married next week, so I needed something a bit special. It's pure silk, you know.
Woman 1: Yes, I can see that. Must have cost a fortune!
Woman 2: Not really. Cheaper than getting a dress, that's for sure, and I'll probably wear it a lot more, too. It'll go really well with a skirt I bought last week. The sleeves are a bit short, but if I wear a jacket over it, no one'll notice.

Which key words and expressions helped you decide on the answer?
Which are used to create distractors?

Listening 🔘 2.15–2.21

You will hear people talking in seven more situations. For questions **2–8**, choose the best answer, **A**, **B** or **C**.

What to expect in the exam

• In Part 1, you will hear the questions being read out before each extract. As you listen to the question consider the similarities and differences between each alternative and try to predict what you might hear.

2 You hear part of a sports commentary on the radio. What sport is it?
A tennis
B basketball
C football

3 Listen to this man on the telephone. Who is he phoning?
A a friend
B his doctor
C his boss

4 Listen to this man and woman speaking. Where are they?
A in a cinema
B in a restaurant
C at home

5 You hear this woman telling her friend about a restaurant.
What does she say about it?
A The waiters were rude.
B The food was badly cooked.
C It was too formal.

6 You hear a woman talking to her husband in a supermarket.
How does she feel?
A confused
B annoyed
C disappointed

7 You hear this man talking to his friend on the phone about a day trip to London. What is he going to do at the end of the day?
A stay in a hotel
B stay at his friend's house
C travel back home

8 You hear this man talking. Who is he?
A a policeman
B a social worker
C a teacher

Part 2: Sentence completion ◉ 2.22

1 Look at the statements **1–8** about Part 2 of the listening paper and decide which are True and which are False. If a statement is false, give reasons for your answer.

1 You only hear the Part 2 recording once. _____
2 You have 45 seconds to read through the questions. _____
3 You should use this time to predict the type of information which is missing from each space. _____
4 You have to write between three and five words in each space. _____
5 You have to rephrase the words you hear so that they fit into the sentence. _____
6 You do not usually hear the answers in the same order as the questions. _____
7 For difficult questions, keep listening as you'll hear the answer sooner or later. _____
8 You should check the spelling of your answers. _____

2 Now read the following Listening Part 2 question.

You will hear a man talking on the radio about Welsh speakers in Patagonia, Argentina. For questions **1–10**, complete the sentences.

Before you listen, predict the type of information you might hear for questions **1–10**.

Example: 1 This might be a type of building, like a school or a church.

What to expect in the exam

- The words and the sentence structure in the question may not be the same as those in the recording. For question 8 for example, you will hear the following: *'every year, as part of a programme administered by the National Assembly for Wales, groups of ... come to Patagonia'.*

- You can also expect to hear some distractors. For number 2, for example, you will need to choose between two different numbers that you hear. And for number 4, several different types of people are mentioned.

A popular place for tourists to visit in Patagonia is a Welsh [1].

There are estimated to be [2] speakers of Welsh in Patagonia.

The first settlers wanted to establish a colony in an area which was [3].

There were very few [4] among the first Welsh settlers.

The settlers soon became friendly with the [5].

The name for the Andean region where the Welsh settled means ' [' 6].

A Welsh [7] festival is held each year in Patagonia.

The National Assembly for Wales sends [8] to Patagonia each year.

The streets and houses of Gaiman are decorated with [9].

The speaker decides to eat [10] with his tea.

Part 3: Multiple matching

1 In Part 3 you will hear five short monologues which are all related in some way. You have 30 seconds to read the questions and see what makes each question similar to or different from the others. Read the Part 3 task below and study this example:

Example: **A**   I will need a specific qualification to do this job.
You often get qualifications by taking exams, for which you have to study.
***B** and **F** also mention aspects of studying. **E** is different from **A** because...*

2 Complete the example sentence in 1 and then discuss questions **B–F** in the same way. Underlining key words may help, but be careful of distractors when you listen.

Can you predict any of the language you might hear for each of the sentences?

Example: **A** What words do you know which are related to *qualification*?

What to expect in the exam

- You may hear the language which guides you to the correct answer:
  a at the beginning of the extract
  b in the middle of the extract
  c at the end of the extract.
  d in more than one part of the extract
- Listen *both times* to *all* of what the speaker says before making your final decision.

3 👁 2.23–2.27 You will hear five young people talking about the job they would like to do. For questions **1–5**, choose from the list **A–F** what each speaker says. Use the letters only once. There is one extra letter which you do not need to use.

A I will need a specific qualification to do this job.   Speaker 1 [   ]

B I combine work with studying.   Speaker 2 [   ]

C I disagree with the careers advice I have been given.   Speaker 3 [   ]

D I heard about this job from someone in my family.   Speaker 4 [   ]

E I think I have the necessary personal qualities.   Speaker 5 [   ]

F I am studying a relevant subject.

Part 4: Multiple Choice

1 In Part 4 you will hear either a monologue or an interview lasting approximately three minutes. You have to answer seven multiple-choice questions, each with three options.

2 Now read the following Part 4 instructions.

2.28 You will hear an interview with an organizer of the Tall Person's Club conference. For questions **1–7** choose the best answer (**A**, **B** or **C**).

3 Read question 1 and the interviewer's introduction from the recording. Decide on the correct answer, underlining the part or parts of the text which justify your choice.

1 What comment does the presenter make about his height?
A He is below average height for a British male.
B He is the tallest person in his profession.
C He feels tall in comparison to his colleagues.

Tapescript
At one metre 84 I've always thought of myself as being a little on the tall side, particularly when I stand next to the people I work with here in the *Round Britain* studio. Rather curiously, most of them are below the national average height of one metre 78 for men and one 62 for women. But when I popped in yesterday to the annual conference of the TPC – that's the Tall Person's Club of Great Britain and Ireland – I felt decidedly small.

4 With your partner explain with reference to the text why the other options are wrong.

5 Now read questions **2–7**. Then listen to the recording and choose the best answers.

What to expect in the exam

- You are given one minute to read all seven questions before you hear the recording.
- Although a particular option might be mentioned, it may not be the correct answer to the question you are asked. In question **3** below, for example, **A**, **B** and **C** are all mentioned as problems, but only one answers the question: 'What is the biggest problem faced by tall people?'

2 Jenny says that the Tall Person's Club conference
A is usually held in a countryside hotel.
B is one of many events they organize.
C is very different to other club conferences.

3 According to Jenny, what is the biggest problem faced by tall people?
A buying clothes that fit
B travelling on public transport
C sleeping in normal size beds

4 How does Jenny feel about some people's reactions towards her height?
A irritated
B amused
C offended

5 Jenny says that at their first meeting, new club members
A are encouraged to change their posture.
B very quickly grow in confidence.
C have to talk to everyone in the room.

6 According to Jenny, one advantage for tall people is that
A they are naturally talented at certain sports.
B they always have a good view at spectator events.
C they are more suited than others to certain professions.

7 What does Jenny say about membership of the Tall Person's Club of Great Britain and Ireland?
A It includes membership of the American club.
B A special committee decides who can join.
C There is no minimum height requirement.

6 Look at the listening script on pages 230 and 231 and for questions **2–7** follow the same procedure as in exercises **3** and **4** above.

Vocabulary 1: Money

1 Name the items shown in the photographs above.
Which of them are used most in your country?
What are the advantages and disadvantages of each method of payment?

2 For **1–5**, complete each of the spaces with one of the items from the box.

rate of interest	rate of exchange	stock market	account	currency

1 He made all his money on the Wall Street _____ .
2 I can't afford to borrow any money from the bank; the _____ on a personal loan is 15 per cent!
3 You get a free mobile phone if you open a savings _____ with the Western Bank.
4 She tried to buy something in a Dublin shop with British pounds, but of course, Ireland has a different _____ .
5 I never change my money at the airport. I usually find that town centre banks offer a better _____ .

3 Complete each of the spaces with an appropriate preposition from the box. In each section **1–4** the preposition required for both spaces is the same.

on	in	for	to

1 Are you saving up _____ anything at the moment?
How much will you have to pay _____ it?
2 What do you like spending your money _____ ?
How common is it for people to buy things _____ credit
a in your country?   **b** in your family?
3 Imagine you were seriously _____ debt. How many possible ways are there of solving your problem?
Do you know anyone who has invested _____ shares on the stock market?
4 If a friend of yours asked to borrow £50 from you, would you lend it _____ them?
Does anyone owe any money _____ you at the moment?

4 Work with a partner and discuss each of the questions in exercise 3.
Don't forget to ask each other further questions and develop your answers.

Reading 1: Multiple choice
FCE Part 1

1 You are going to read an article about a 14-year-old boy who set up his own business importing motorized skateboards and scooters.

Read the title, introduction and first paragraph and predict the type of information the article will include.

Example: *It might talk about the boy's personality and the qualities needed for a teenager to be successful in business.*

2 Read the article quite quickly and check your predictions in exercise 1.

Life in the fast lane

Henrietta Lake talks to a remarkable 14-year-old entrepreneur who is certainly going places.

Between studying for nine GCSEs, including business studies, 14-year-old Dominic McVey has set up his own company, Scooters UK. The business, which imports motorized scooters and skateboards from the United States, has already made a profit of over £5,000 on sales of the equipment.

Dominic needed £3,000 to set up his business and pay for the initial stock. He used savings from birthday and Christmas money and cashed in some investments that his father had made when Dominic was born. The young entrepreneur had also invested in shares on the stock market. 'I had to do the deals in my dad's name because I was too young,' he says, 'but he doesn't know anything about the market, so I told him what to buy and sell.'

'I realized the potential for the business when I noticed that a lot of inner-city streets were being closed to cars or they were chock-a-block with traffic,' he explains. 'I thought there would be a great market for these scooters and skateboards, particularly now that more restrictions on cars in town centres have been introduced.'

'You can take a smaller one with you on a train in a backpack and then unfold it and use it when you get into town. Men in suits are riding them up and down Wall Street in the US and it is my aim to get them to do the same in this country. I approached the American manufacturer and, after doing some research into their company and the scooters, I was allowed to become their UK distributor.'

The motorized scooters, which sell for £499 and can travel at up to 22 mph, are not classified as motor vehicles and do not need a licence or tax. He also sells unmotorized skateboards for £129. They have special high-speed wheels and are capable of reaching 10 mph.

'I ride them around town in busy areas and usually end up with a crowd of people running down the street wanting to know where to buy them, or winding down their car windows at traffic lights,' he says. Recently he went with his mother on a sales trip to Paris. 'The scooters are really popular there because the centre of the city is pedestrianized at the weekend. I went out with 500 leaflets and came back with none.'

In the early stages Dominic had to overcome one or two obstacles. When he tried to open a business account at his bank, he made an appointment to see the manager. However, the bank thought it was a joke, and when he arrived there they had not set up any time for the meeting. 'This really upset me,' says Dominic, 'but I managed to get a good rate of interest on the account because they were so embarrassed. I think people should take children more seriously.'

Now that he has succeeded in setting up the business Dominic wants to expand it. At the moment, the company is still importing scooters in small numbers. 'But business is picking up and so I am ordering a big container of 106 scooters in the new year.' Dominic is aiming to sell 500 scooters over the next 12 months. 'I think it is worth taking the risk when you are young: if the worst happens, I have my parents' support and I am still at school.'

He also plans to open a showroom for his scooters in the City of London, 'right by some traffic lights so people stop and look'. His idea would then be to sell the business and look for further opportunities to make money. 'I'd like to be able to retire before I'm 40,' he tells me.

3 Read the article again and for questions **1–8**, choose the answer (**A, B, C** or **D**) which you think fits best according to the text.

1 How did Dominic raise the necessary money to set up his company?
   A He invested all his savings on the stock market.
   B He borrowed it from his father.
   C He used money from a variety of sources.
   D It was a birthday present.

2 What does Dominic mean when he says that streets were 'chock-a-block with traffic' in paragraph 3?
   A Cars were not allowed to enter them.
   B They were full of vehicles.
   C Traffic prevented scooters from entering them.
   D They had street markets in them.

3 What type of people does he want to buy his scooters?
   A fashionable people
   B Americans
   C business men
   D people who do not own a car

4 The motorized scooters that Dominic sells
   A require no special driving skills.
   B cannot legally be ridden on the road.
   C have specially designed wheels.
   D cannot travel very long distances.

5 Why did Dominic go to Paris?
   A He went shopping with his mother.
   B He wanted to see the new pedestrian precinct.
   C He took some scooters to sell there.
   D He wanted to distribute information about his scooters.

6 Dominic believes that being young
   A prevents him taking himself too seriously.
   B means that things are more likely to go wrong.
   C is a good time to be adventurous.
   D is a source of concern to his parents.

7 What upset Dominic about his visit to the bank?
   A The manager laughed at him.
   B The manager refused to see him.
   C The meeting with the manager was very short.
   D The manager did not expect him to turn up.

8 In the future, Dominic intends to
   A work beyond normal retirement age.
   B find an alternative way to earn a living.
   C hold an exhibition of scooters.
   D bring in partners to help him run his business.

Reacting to the text

Would the motorized scooters and skateboards be popular in your country?
What qualities do you think you need to be a successful entrepreneur at 14?
If you could have your own business, what type of business would it be?
What would be the advantages and disadvantages of being your own boss?

Language focus 1: Ability

1 In the following sentences from the text, complete each of the spaces with the correct form of the verb in brackets.

  a The motorized scooters… *can* _____ (travel) at up to 22 mph.

  b They have special high-speed wheels and *are capable of* _____ (reach) 10 mph.

  c I'd like to *be able* _____ (retire) before I'm 40.

  d I *managed* _____ (get) a good rate of interest on the account because they were so embarrassed.

  e Now that he has *succeeded in* _____ (set) up the business Dominic wants to expand it.

2 Appropriate forms of *be able to* can be used in all five sentences in exercise 1. For example:

  a The motorized scooters *are able to* travel at up to 22 mph.

  e Now that he *has been able to* set up the business Dominic wants to expand it.

Can you explain the following in relation to *can* and *could*?

- *Can* is possible in **a** and **b** but not in **c**.

- *Could* is possible in the following sentence, but it is not possible in sentences **d** and **e**.
  Dominic could read and understand financial newspapers when he was only eight.

- However, four forms are possible in this sentence:
  They *couldn't find/didn't manage to find/didn't succeed in finding/weren't able to find* the missing climbers, so they abandoned the search.

  Ⓖ   Check your ideas on page 216 of the Grammar reference.

3 Rewrite the underlined parts of the sentences in **1–6** using the verb given in **bold**.

  1 When he was younger he <u>was able to swim</u> a length of the pool underwater.
    capable _____

  2 After trying for several years he <u>finally succeeded in giving up</u> smoking.
    managed _____

  3 I ran out of time so I <u>didn't manage to finish</u> both parts of the Writing Paper.
    unable _____

  4 We <u>managed to find out</u> what was wrong with the computer.
    succeeded _____

  5 One day you'll <u>manage to find</u> a job you like.
    able _____

  6 I'm afraid I <u>wasn't able to buy</u> the brand of dog food you asked for.
    manage _____

4 In which sentences in exercise 3 is it possible to rewrite the underlined part using *can/can't* or *could/couldn't*?

5 ◯   Tell your partner about something:
- you could do when you were younger but can't do now.
- you couldn't do when you were younger but can do now.
- you managed to do last weekend.
- you would like to be able to do.
- you don't think you'll ever succeed in doing.

Vocabulary 2: *Make* and *do*

A *Make* or *do*?

1 Complete each of the spaces with the correct form of either *make* or *do*. When you have finished, check your answers in the article about Dominic McVey. The numbers in brackets refer to the paragraphs in which the answers appear.

1 The business has already _____ a profit of over £5,000. **(1)**
2 He cashed in some investments that his father had _____ . **(2)**
3 I had to _____ the deals in my dad's name because I was too young. **(2)**
4 After _____ some research into their company and the scooters, I was allowed to become their UK distributor. **(4)**
5 When he tried to open a business account at his bank, he _____ an appointment to see the manager. **(7)**
6 His idea would then be to sell the business and look for further opportunities to _____ money. **(9)**

2 For each of the following groups of words and phrases decide which one is not usually used with the verb in capital letters. What do the other three have in common?

Example: 0
'Make a profit', 'make money', 'make a loss' are to do with increasing or decreasing the amount of money you have. This is also true of business, but we say 'do business with someone'.

0 MAKE
a profit
money
business
a loss

1 MAKE
a plan
damage
an appointment
an arrangement

2 DO
homework
a course
an effort
a degree

3 MAKE
up your mind
someone a favour
a decision
a choice

4 DO
the housework
the washing-up
the ironing
the beds

5 MAKE
a speech
a phone call
an experiment
a complaint

6 MAKE
an exercise
a film
a cake
a cup of tea

7 DO
badly in an exam
well at school
your best
progress

8 MAKE
a mistake
a mess
a job
a lot of noise

B Phrasal verbs with *make* and *do*

1 In each of the sentences **1–8** work out the meaning of each underlined phrasal verb. Use the context of the sentence to help you.

1 Put your coat on and <u>do it up</u>, Sofia. Otherwise you'll catch a cold.
2 They had a row, but the next day they <u>made it up</u> and they're closer than ever now.
3 Is that story true, or did you <u>make it up</u>?
4 They bought an old run-down cottage and <u>did it up</u>. Now it looks as good as the day it was built.
5 The quality of the recording was so bad we couldn't <u>make out</u> what the speakers were saying.
6 When the guard asked to see her train ticket my American friend Mary <u>made out</u> she couldn't understand English.
7 I'm really hungry. I <u>could do with</u> something to eat.
8 A mobile phone is essential for my job. I really <u>couldn't do without</u> it.

2 Write a short story of about 80 words including a total of six phrasal verbs and expressions with *do* and *make*.

Writing:
FCE Part 2

Formal letters: An application

1 Read the advert and the letter of application and answer the following questions.

Who is the target reader?
What effect do you think the letter would have on that person?

STUDY GRANTS in the UK

St George's House is offering grants to students wishing to study English in one of their three UK centres this summer. Grants cover:

- **two months' tuition fees**
- **full board and accommodation**
- **help towards travel costs**

Write to the address below, stating why you are applying and how you would expect to benefit from the grant.

The Director
St George's House
13 Southdown Road
York, YO12 4XJ

Dear Sir or Madam,

I saw your advertisement in Monday's issue of the 'Guardian' and I would like to apply for a grant to study English in one of your schools this summer.

It would be better for me if it was in your Manchester school as I have a cousin living there, who I have never met. Furthermore, the night life in Manchester is said to be excellent and I would be able to go clubbing every night after class. Manchester would also be a good base for travelling and I could visit Wales, the Lake District and the birthplace of the Beatles, Liverpool.

I would be grateful if you could put me in a class of no more than six students as it is difficult to learn if the class size is larger. I would particularly like to have help with idiomatic expressions in order to sound more like a native English speaker.

I know you offer free unlimited access to the Internet and that would be very useful to me, too. I hope you will consider my application.

Yours faithfully
Ausra Zeronys

2 You are going to write your own application for one of the advertised grants at St George's House. Here is a possible paragraph plan.

Paragraph 1:	A short opening paragraph stating your reasons for writing.
Paragraphs 2 and 3:	Give relevant information about yourself, explaining why the grant would be useful and how you would benefit from studying English in the UK.
Paragraph 4:	A suitable, brief closing paragraph, re-stating your interest in obtaining the grant.

3 Here are four reasons to support your application. Can you add at least four more?

- *You could not afford to study in the UK without the grant.*
- *A period of study in the UK would help you to get a job in your own country.*
- *A recent illness has caused you to fall behind in your studies.*
- *You are interested in learning about British culture and the British way of life.*

What further details could you add to each of the reasons?

Example: You could not afford to study in the UK without a grant.
Although you have saved up enough money to pay the travel costs, both of your parents are unemployed and would be unable to pay for tuition or accommodation.

4 Now you are ready to write your letter of application. Write **120–180** words.

Don't forget!

- Use formal language throughout the letter.
- Provide relevant personal information together with an explanation of the different ways in
- which you will benefit from the grant.
- The information you give does not need to be true.

Listening 1:
FCE Part 2

Sentence completion

1 Which of the following jobs could you *not* do if you were blind? Give reasons for your answers.

What difficulties would you face in those jobs you *could* do?

2 Read the following Listening Part 2 instructions.

You will hear part of a radio interview with Grace, a singer who suffers from an eye disease. For questions **1–10**, complete the sentences.

Grace has been partially sighted since she was about [_____ **1**].

She is only able to see out of her [_____ **2**] eye.

She says that her eyesight will not get [_____ **3**].

During a check-up, Grace was found to have [_____ **4**] vision.

When she was younger, Grace wanted to go to a [_____ **5**] school.

At school she was [_____ **6**] and bullied by other children.

She says that many of these children [_____ **7**].

After she left school, Grace's father persuaded her to [_____ **8**].

She enjoys her career, particularly [_____ **9**].

She says her experiences at school helped her overcome her [_____ **10**].

 Do you know of anybody else who has managed to overcome their disability and achieve success?

Word formation: Miscellaneous nouns

1 In the listening exercise Grace says:

*My **sight** didn't develop until I was about a year old.*

The noun *sight* comes from the verb *see*.
What is the noun form of the following verbs?

choose   lose   complain   speak

Check your answers in exercise 2 of *make* and *do* on page 166 in this unit.

2 Use the verb given in capitals at the end of each line to form a noun that fits in the space in the sentence. You may need to use a plural form.

1 _____ of mobile phones have fallen recently.	**SELL**
2 Don't forget to print your name below your _____ .	**SIGN**
3 I roared with _____ the first time I heard that joke.	**LAUGH**
4 You'll find yourself in trouble if your _____ doesn't improve.	**BEHAVE**
5 Communications were revolutionized with the _____ of the Internet.	**ARRIVE**
6 The capacity of human _____ to overcome illness is remarkable.	**BE**
7 Many foreign students are asked to show _____ of their age in pubs.	**PROVE**
8 I'm not sure I agree with the _____ that 'Money is the root of all evil'.	**SAY**

Reading 2: Gapped text
FCE Part 2

1 Discuss how you might react in the following situations:

- You see someone drowning in a freezing cold river.
- You hear some people shouting that they are trapped in a building.
- You see an old man being attacked in the street late at night.
- You are in the mountains when your friend falls and breaks his leg.

2 You are going to read a magazine article about a rescue. Seven sentences have been removed from the article. Choose from the sentences **A–H** the one which fits each gap **(1–7)**. There is one extra sentence which you do not need to use.

My river hero

It was just after 9.30 on a cold, wet February morning that I got a call from my 17-year-old son Matthew. **[1]** _____ Terrible thoughts started going through my head but before I really had a chance to worry, he added very matter-of-factly, 'I've just saved a baby girl from drowning.' **[2]** _____

Matthew loves fishing and you'll find him by the River Medway in Maidstone in his spare time. That day the water was high and dangerous because there'd been a lot of rain. Matthew was sitting by the river when he heard a woman scream, 'My baby, my baby, she's dying!' **[3]** _____

He ran up to them to see if there was anything he could do to help. In the water he saw an upside down pushchair. **[4]** _____

At the local hospital, the doctors praised Matthew for reacting so quickly. **[5]** _____ But it wasn't only Emily that was lucky to be alive. A few days later I was reading the local paper when I saw a danger warning for the river. It was only then that I realized I could have lost my son, too.

Soon afterwards, Matthew, myself and my two younger daughters went along to Emily's second birthday party. There, her grandmother drank a toast to Matthew. **[6]** _____ It sent a shiver down my spine and it still makes me go all funny thinking about it now.

[7] _____ He made the front page of the local paper and even appeared on television. I'm proud of my son. He's a caring lad who puts other people before himself. And he has obviously got a level head – I think I'd have panicked. He'll always be my river hero.

A Without thinking, Matthew dived in and went underwater to push the chair up towards the little girl's mum.

B He was hailed as a hero and received a lot of attention from the media.

C She thanked him for saving Emily's life and said they'd think of him on every one of her birthdays.

D He was warned against going fishing again until the river water had gone down to its normal level.

E 'Mum, I'm at the hospital,' he said.

F They said that if little Emily had been in the freezing water for just another three seconds, the outcome could have been horribly different.

G He looked over to see a woman and a young girl by the water's edge.

H What I didn't know at that stage was that he had put his own life at risk in order to save her.

Reacting to the text

Have you ever been in a life-threatening situation?
Have you ever rescued someone or had to be rescued yourself?

Language focus 2: Verbs followed by prepositions

1 Write an appropriate preposition in each of the following sentences.

1 The doctors praised Matthew _____ reacting so quickly.
2 She thanked him _____ saving Emily's life.
3 He was warned _____ going fishing again.

Check your answers in the reading text.

2 Match each sentence beginning **1–7** with a suitable ending **a–g**. Complete each of the spaces with an appropriate preposition.

1 The other driver blamed me *for* ☐ *d*
2 I really must apologize ____ ☐
3 She'll never be able to forgive him ____ ☐
4 My parents tried to prevent me ____ ☐
5 In order to discourage children ____ ☐
6 I'm just phoning to congratulate you ____ ☐
7 My aunt in London insisted ____ ☐

a …being late. It won't happen again, I promise.
b …seeing him again, but we met secretly after school every day.
c …smoking, parents should set a good example and give it up themselves.
d …causing the accident, but it really wasn't my fault.
e …putting me up for the night, though I'd have preferred to stay in a hotel.
f …leaving her to bring up the children on her own.
g …passing all your exams. You deserved to do well.

What form of the verb is used after prepositions?

3 🔘 Talk to your partner about the last time you:

• apologized
• thanked someone
• were congratulated
• were prevented from doing something.

Vocabulary 3: Ways of looking

1 Read the following sentences. What is the difference in meaning between the three underlined verbs?

a In the water he <u>saw</u> an upside down pushchair.
b <u>Look at</u> my new dress. Do you like it?
c He <u>watched</u> her open her bag and take out a gun.

2 Underline the most appropriate alternative in the following sentences.

1 I think I'll get the mechanic to *see/look at* the engine. It doesn't sound very healthy.
2 Could you turn the light on? I can't *see/look at* what I'm doing.
3 You spend far too much time *looking at/watching* television.
4 Isn't it beautiful? I've never *seen/looked at* a fox before.
5 *See/Watch* carefully how I do it first, then you can have a go.

3 Match each verb **1–5** with its definition **a–e**.

1 gaze   **a** look rapidly and then look away again immediately
2 stare   **b** see for a short moment and not very well
3 glimpse   **c** look very closely and carefully (often with difficulty)
4 glance   **d** look for a long time, especially with interest or admiration
5 peer   **e** look for a long time, eg because you are surprised or shocked

4 Complete the following sentences with a word from exercise 3. The words in **bold** are commonly used with the missing words.

1 He _____ **inquisitively** into the box to see if there was anything interesting in it.
2 Bored with the lesson, I _____ **quickly** at my watch to see how long was left.
3 He _____ **admiringly** at her as she spoke.
4 For several minutes the young child _____ **open-mouthed** in amazement at the enormous cake.
5 She **caught a brief** _____ of her idol as he drove past in his limousine.

Listening 2:
FCE Part 1

Multiple choice

2.30–2.37 You will hear people talking in eight different situations. For questions **1–8** choose the best answer, **A**, **B** or **C**.

What to expect in the exam

- Two very typical types of question in Part 1 of the Listening Paper focus on:
  a the feelings, attitude or opinion of the speakers (see questions 1–4 below).
  b the identity of the speakers or the relationship between them (see questions 5–8 below).
- Remember that the tone of voice of the speakers may be important, as well as the language they use.

- As you listen to the questions being read out, think about the similarities and differences between each of the three alternatives and how the speaker might sound in each case. Look at question 1 below, together with the comments, and then talk about questions 2–8 in the same way.
- You will hear each recording twice. Listen carefully both times.

1 You hear this woman talking to a friend about her husband's work situation.
   How does the speaker feel?
   A annoyed   *she'd probably talk in an angry tone about something negative that has happened*
   B worried   *she might sound concerned about possible future problems*
   C relieved   *the tone would be more positive, as something bad has come to an end*

2 You overhear this man talking to his wife about a friend.
   What does he say about their friend's success?
   A He was lucky.
   B He worked hard for it.
   C He didn't deserve it.

3 You hear this woman talking to her friend about going rock climbing.
   How does she feel about it?
   A She thinks she'll enjoy it.
   B She does not want to do it.
   C She is nervous about it.

4 Listen to this woman talking to her son on the phone.
   What is she doing?
   A giving him advice
   B criticizing him
   C congratulating him

5 You overhear this young man talking on the phone.
   Who is he talking to?
   A his girlfriend
   B his mother
   C his sister

6 You hear a woman talking to a young man.
   What is the woman's relationship to the man?
   A his neighbour
   B his boss
   C his mother

7 You hear this man giving part of a speech.
   Who is he?
   A a politician
   B a sportsman
   C the manager of a sports centre

8 You hear someone being interviewed on the radio.
   Who is the speaker?
   A an explorer
   B a lorry driver
   C an inventor

Word formation

For questions **1–10**, read the text below. Use the word given in capitals at the end of some of the lines to form a word that fits the gap **in the same line**. There is an example at the beginning (**0**).

Business Profile: Jack Warren

'Money can't buy you (**0**) _happiness'_, or so, at least, goes the	**HAPPY**
(**1**) _____ , but several times millionaire Jack Warren, head of Aadvark	**SAY**
(**2**) _____ Agency, would probably disagree. His broad, toothy	**ADVERTISE**
smile has become his trademark (**3**) _____ and his frequent outbursts	**SIGN**
of (**4**) _____ mean there's never a dull moment when he gives	**LAUGH**
one of his renowned motivational (**5**) _____ at business conferences.	**SPEAK**
In true rags-to-riches tradition, Warren rose from (**6**) _____ to become	**POOR**
one of the five (**7**) _____ businesspeople in the country. He attributes	**WEALTH**
the rapid (**8**) _____ of his company and its continued	**GROW**
(**9**) _____ to a combination of factors, but insists that 'making all the	**SUCCEED**
right (**10**) _____ when recruiting staff has been key'.	**CHOOSE**

Transformations

In **1–8** below complete the second sentence so that it has a similar meaning to the first sentence, using the word given. **Do not change the word given.** You must use between two and five words, including the word given.

1 Mr Yates said it was Helen who had started the fight.
   blamed
   Mr Yates _____ the fight.

2 'I'm sorry I'm late,' said Adrian.
   apologized
   Adrian _____ late.

3 She warned us not to go out alone after dark.
   warned
   She _____ going out alone after dark.

4 The immigration officials did not let him come into the country.
   prevented
   The immigration officials _____ into the country.

5 We demanded to see the manager.
   seeing
   We _____ the manager.

6 The rescue team was unable to find the missing climbers.
   succeed
   The rescue team _____ the missing climbers.

7 We got to the theatre after the play started.
   manage
   We _____ to the theatre before the play started.

8 You really ought to complain to the manager about the service.
   make
   You really should _____ to the manager about the service.

Vocabulary

A Make and do

1 Complete each of the following spaces with the correct form of either *make* or *do*.

1 Do/Did you always _____ your best at school?
2 When and where do you usually _____ your homework?
3 Do you learn from the mistakes you _____ in your homework?
4 Have you _____ any plans for next weekend?
5 Are you good at _____ decisions?
6 Think of three things that you would find it difficult to _____ without.
7 How often do you _____ phone calls? How long do you spend on the phone?
8 What would you like to _____ for a living?

2 Write answers for each of the questions in exercise 1.

B Ways of looking

Match a sentence beginning **1–5** with an appropriate ending **a–e**.

1 For several minutes she sat gazing...
2 Once in the street she could only stare...
3 Every couple of minutes she glanced...
4 She put on her glasses and peered...
5 She only caught a very brief glimpse...

a with difficulty at the tiny writing on the poster.
b of her attacker, so she couldn't describe him very well.
c in wonder at the beautiful mountain scenery.
d in disbelief as the fire destroyed her house.
e anxiously up at the clock, wondering when he would phone.

Writing:
FCE Part 1

Email

You are studying English in Hastings and your cousin is coming to live and work in England. She wants to open a savings account and has asked you to send her information from two banks.

Using your notes below, write an email to your cousin giving her the information. You should also suggest which account you think is better and explain why.

Write an **email** of between **120 and 150** words. You must use grammatically correct sentences and accurate spelling and punctuation in a style appropriate for the situation.

	Phone Bank	Royal Savings Bank
Rate of Interest	3.1%	2.9%
No. of UK branches	none: all operations by phone	over 650
Gifts to new account holders	diary	full set of saucepans
Credit card	no annual charges	£12 p.a. service charge

Vocabulary 1: The Arts

1 Both words in each of the pairs below can be used in combination with one of the words in the box. Write an appropriate word from the box in each of the spaces. There is an example at the beginning **(0)**.

novel	opera	~~concert~~	painting	stone	classical	gallery

0 open-air   *concert*   **1** _____   ballet   **4** portrait   _____
    jazz   music   art

                             2 _____   singer   **5** abstract   _____
                                       house   priceless

                             3 _____   sculpture   **6** detective   _____
                                       statue   historical

2 Which people do you associate with each of the following areas of the arts?

music	literature	art	opera	ballet	sculpture

Example: Theatre: *actor, actress, director, cast, playwright, audience*
Check your answers in the Wordlist on page 205.

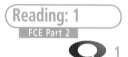

Reading: 1
FCE Part 2

Gapped text

1 Look at the work of art in the photograph and discuss the following questions.
What type of person might want to own such a work of art?
Where might they put it on display?

2 You are going to read an article about British artist Damien Hirst, who created the work in the photograph. Seven sentences have been removed from the article. Choose from the sentences **A–H** the one which fits each gap (**1–7**). There is one extra sentence which you do not need to use.

The most successful living artist

**Have you ever thought, 'I wish I could be an artist'? Don't give up hope.
Damien Hirst nearly failed his Art A Level at school and his work now sells for millions.**

Controversial British painter Damien Hirst, who is often mentioned in the same breath as Jackson Pollock and Andy Warhol, has been confirmed as the most successful artist alive, thanks to a huge increase in the prices paid for his work recently. The forty-something from Leeds changed the face of contemporary art in the nineteen nineties with his *Natural History* series, in which dead animals are preserved in formaldehyde and displayed in glass cases.

The first of these, his four-metre shark entitled *The Physical Impossibility of Death in the Mind of Someone Living*, recently fetched an incredible £6.5 million when it was sold to an American collector. **1** [   ] After that came a string of similarly provocative works, which included a pickled lamb in *Away from the Flock*, as well as dissected cows and rotting animal carcasses.

2 [   ] In 2003, he was labelled a 'sadist' by some animal rights activists, who objected strongly to his *Amazing Revelations*, a triangular collage made of thousands of dismembered butterfly wings. Earlier, in 1994, *Away from the Flock* became the focus of attention when Mark Bridger, an artist from Oxford, poured black ink into the tank containing the dead lamb. However, Bridger claimed he was contributing to the artwork, not protesting against it and he renamed it *Black Sheep*. It cost £1,000 to remove the ink.

The considerable controversy surrounding Damien Hirst's work inevitably raises the question of whether or not it constitutes art. **3** [   ] Charles Saatchi, former advertising mogul and a formidable collector of YBA works, describes Hirst as 'a genius', and former arts minister Virginia Bottomley has called him 'a pioneer of the British art movement'. He also enjoys the support of stars such as David Beckham and former *Friends* actress Courteney Cox, who are both proud owners of his work.

However, others have been equally swift to condemn the artist. When Hirst won the prestigious Turner prize in 1995, Conservative politician Norman Tebbit, writing in *The Sun* newspaper, asked: 'Have they gone stark raving mad?' **4** [   ] But there are also many people within the art world who have attacked and ridiculed the artist, accusing him of producing work which is exaggerated and silly.

5 [   ] He, too, has used the word 'silly' to describe his spin paintings, a series of works created by dropping paint onto a spinning canvas. 'You do turn round after a few years and look at your stuff and you think it's embarrassing,' he confessed at an exhibition in 2005. 'Certainly everything you make is not a masterpiece.'

He also freely admits to using assistants to do most of his spot-paintings, which consist of rows of randomly coloured dots. Of the 500 or more such works produced, he is said to have painted only five himself, the rest being attributed to assistants like Rachel Howard, his 'best ever' spot-painter. **6** [   ] And indeed, there is nothing new about artists getting others to do some of the work for them: Rembrandt, for example, had very large workshops with pupils to help him, and they had to pay for the privilege.

In recent years Hirst has branched out and taken on new challenges. He has made short films, opened a restaurant, set up a publishing company and even recorded a pop music single with Fat Les, a group he formed with Blur bassist Alex James. **7** [   ] But of course, it's his art for which he will be best remembered. Whether his memory will live on as long as that of Pollock, Warhol or even Rembrandt, only time will tell. In the meantime, his paintings continue to sell.

A Indeed, the tabloid press is one of Hirst's strongest critics.
B Entitled 'Vindaloo', it reached number two in the UK charts in 1998.
C The work caused a sensation when it was first shown in 1992 and quickly became a symbol for the circle known as the Young British Artists, or YBAs.
D For some, there is absolutely no doubt.
E In defence of this practice he is quoted as saying, 'But then architects don't build their own houses.'
F *Mother and Child Divided*, a cow and calf cut in half, certainly fits this description.
G Predictably, the artist has come in for criticism for his use of real animals.
H Surprisingly enough, though, Hirst seems to agree with some of this criticism.

Reacting to the text 🔘

Do you think Damien Hirst's work constitutes art? Why/Why not?
Why do some people pay vast sums of money for artworks? Would you?

Language focus: Hypothetical situations

A Wishes

1 The reading text began with this sentence:

Have you ever thought, 'I wish I could be an artist'?

We use *wish* (or for more emphasis *if only*) to express how we would like things to be different if we had the power to change them.

2 Look at the following sentences and then complete each of the three rules below with words from the box.

1 I wish it wasn't/weren't so cold here in winter.
2 If only I had more time to study.
3 I wish you would stop interrupting me!
4 I wish he wouldn't drive so fast.
5 I wish I hadn't gone to see that boring play last night.
6 If only you'd told me earlier.

> *would*   the past perfect   the past simple

a We use *wish/if only* + _____
to express wishes about present states.

b We use *wish/if only* + _____
to express irritation at other people's actions or behaviour.

c We use *wish/if only* + _____
to express wishes and regrets about the past.

3 a Reword the following sentence so that it sounds more natural.
I wish I would give up smoking.

b What is the difference in meaning between these sentences?
I wish she could come to my party on Saturday.
I hope she can come to my party on Saturday.

 Check your ideas on page 217 of the Grammar reference and read more about expressing wishes.

Practice

1 In **1–5** below underline the correct alternative in each sentence.

1 I wish I *could/would/did* remember where I put my reading glasses.

2 I wish I *don't/didn't/won't* have to do so much homework. I never have any time to myself.
3 The car has broken down again! I'm beginning to wish we *wouldn't buy/didn't buy/hadn't bought* it.
4 I wish they *didn't/would/had* turn their music down next door. I can't hear myself think!
5 If only *you'll listen/you'd have listened/you'd listened* to me! None of this would have happened.

2 In **1–5** below complete each space with the correct form of the verb in brackets.

1 What glorious sunshine! I bet you wish you
_____ (be) on the beach right now, don't you?
2 I wish you two _____ (stop) shouting! You're driving me mad!
3 It has rained every day of this holiday. If only we _____ (go) to Greece instead!
4 I can't afford to buy any new clothes. If only I _____ (have) a job!
5 One minute you want to come, the next minute you don't. I wish you _____ (make) up your mind!

B *It's time* and *would rather*

Choose the correct alternative in the following sentences.

1 I'd rather you *didn't/wouldn't/don't* bring a mobile phone to school.
2 It's time you *went/will go/go* to bed now.

[G] Check your ideas in sections B and C of the Grammar reference on page 217 and read more about *it's time* and *would rather*.

Practice

You have decided to spend the day complaining, telling different people how you would like them to change! The people you are going to speak to are:

- your mother or father
- your brother, sister or cousin
- your best friend
- a neighbour
- the leader of your country
- another person of your choice

Write one sentence for each person beginning with one of the following phrases:

I wish you...
It's time you...
I'd rather you...

Then compare your sentences with those that your partner has written. Are you unhappy about any of the same things?

Word formation: Adjective suffixes *-ible* and *-able*

The suffixes *-ible* and *-able* are used to form a number of adjectives, as in the following two examples from the text.

*the **considerable** controversy surrounding Damien Hirst's work*
*his four-metre shark … fetched an **incredible** £6.5 million*

1 Add an appropriate prefix and/or suffix to the part of the word in bold in the sentences below. The completed word may be an adjective, an adverb or a noun. Nouns may be singular or plural. There is an example at the beginning (0).

0 This chair is a little <u>un</u> **comfort** <u>able</u>. I'm going to sit somewhere else.
1 The weather in Britain is so _____**predict**_____ : you should always take an umbrella with you, just in case.
2 We know it will be a difficult match, but we are **reason**_____ confident of success.
3 No one can touch their right elbow with their right hand. It's a physical _____**poss**_____ .
4 I wouldn't say I was **incred**_____ rich, but I'm certainly **comfort**_____ well-off.
5 Please do not leave any **valu**_____ in your room. The management will not accept **respons**_____ for theft.
6 We usually get away to the coast or the mountains in summer. It can get _____**bear**_____ hot in the city.
7 We'll have to walk to the village. It's _____**access**_____ to cars.
8 The accuracy of her written work has improved **consider**_____ since she started the course.

2 What for you would be the most *enjoyable* way to spend a weekend?
What would be the worst *imaginable* way to spend a Sunday?
Do any of the following describe your last weekend? What did you do?

forgettable   unbelievably boring   reasonably enjoyable
remarkably good   memorable

Speaking:
FCE Part 3

Collaborative task

Imagine that some friends are coming to visit you for the weekend. Your friends have two young children and you would like to take the whole family out for the day. Discuss with your partner the potentially good and bad points about each of the options below and then agree on three of the places or events that you might take your visitors to.

- What are the good and bad points about each option?
- Which three of the places or events might you take your visitors to?

a modern art exhibition   a swimming pool

a funfair   a zoo   a shopping centre

a natural history museum   a puppet show

Vocabulary 2: Animals

1 Complete each of the spaces with the names of animals from the box to complete these well-known similes.

| a fox   a mule   a bat   an owl   a mouse   a peacock   a bee |

1 as blind as _____
2 as busy as _____
3 as quiet as _____
4 as cunning as _____
5 as stubborn as _____
6 as wise as _____
7 as proud as _____

2 Complete these expressions using the names of the animals from the box.

| bear   fish   cat   fly   dog   frog   horse |

1 She's so kind and gentle. She wouldn't hurt a _____ .
2 I'm so hungry I could eat a _____ .
3 She's upset about splitting up with Gary, but I told her there were plenty more _____ in the sea.
4 My two kids don't give me a moment's peace. They fight like _____ and _____ all the time.
5 I was so pleased to see him again. I rushed up and gave him a really big _____ hug.
6 I'm sorry I can't speak any louder. I've got a bit of a _____ in my throat.

3 Match each of these groups of nouns to an animal from the box.

| horse   bird   cat   fish |

a _____   **b** _____   **c** _____   **d** _____
 feathers   gills   whiskers   hooves
 beak   scales   paws   tail
 wings   fin   fur   mane

 4 Discuss the following with your partner, giving reasons for your answers.
Which of the animals in exercises 1 and 2:
• makes the best pet?
• is the most useful to humans?
• makes the most noise?
• is the ugliest?
• is the most attractive?

Multiple choice 2.38

1 The following animals can all be kept as pets. Look at the list then discuss the questions below.

- ants
- tarantulas
- snakes
- rats

What dangers might there be in keeping these animals as pets?
What conditions do you think they each need to be kept in?
Why do you think some people prefer these animals to more traditional types of pets?

2 You will hear an interview with a pet shop owner. For questions **1–7**, choose the best answer (**A**, **B** or **C**).

1 According to Sally what is the main reason people buy insects and spiders?

  A Cats and dogs are expensive to look after.

  B Owners want to impress their friends.

  C Insects and spiders require little attention.

2 Sally says that ants can teach us the importance of

  A working together.

  B keeping clean.

  C building relationships.

3 Sally says that some children

  A get bitten by the ants.

  B lose interest in the ants.

  C like playing with the ants.

4 What is the main reason Sally gives for not handling the tarantulas she sells?

  A Their bite is deadly.

  B They can easily be injured.

  C They might try to escape.

5 What warning does she give about snakes to potential owners?

  A They can live for a long time.

  B They are difficult to feed.

  C They are very different to other pets.

6 Sally recommends feeding pre-killed animals to snakes because

  A dead animals are more nutritious.

  B dead animals are cheaper than live ones.

  C live animals can harm snakes.

7 What do we learn from Sally about rats as pets?

  A They are very easy to tame.

  B They are social animals.

  C They are only ever active at night.

3 Do you think it's right to keep animals such as those mentioned in the listening as pets? Why/Why not?
Which pets have you owned? What advice would you give to someone thinking of buying the same animal?
If you have never owned a pet, which animal would you most like to have? Why?

Writing 1:
FCE Part 2

Set books

1 If you have read one of the set books you may decide to answer the relevant question, either 5a or 5b, in Part 2 of the Writing Paper (Paper 2). You may be asked to write an article, an essay, a letter, a report or a review. Rank questions 1–8 below from the one you would most like to answer about the set book you have read (1), to the one you would least like to answer (8).

What to expect in the exam

- Each year there are two set books for the First Certificate exam.
- In the Writing Paper there are two optional set text questions, each related to a specific book.

1 Write a **review** for your school's English magazine about the book you have read. Tell readers what you did and did not enjoy about the book and say whether you would recommend it.

2 Write an **essay** explaining how the beginning of the book you have read is important to the development of the rest of the story.

3 Your local English language bookshop wants your help in designing a poster to advertise the book you have just read. They have asked you to write a **report** suggesting two pictures showing different scenes from the book and explaining why they should be included on the poster.

4 Your school magazine has asked students for articles on unpopular characters in literature. Which character in the book you have read did you like the least? Write an **article** saying who the person is and giving reasons for your choice.

5 A friend has written to you asking about the book you have read. Write a **letter** to your friend explaining what you learnt from your reading about the time and/or place in which the story is set.

6 'The ending of a story is crucial to the reader's enjoyment of a book.' Write an **article** for your college magazine briefly describing the ending of the book you have read and explaining how much it contributed to your enjoyment of the book as a whole.

7 Write an **essay** briefly describing a place or building which appears in the book you have read and explaining its importance to the story.

8 Write an **essay** describing the development of the relationship between two of the characters in the book you have read. Explain how the relationship affects the events of the story.

2 Look at the following example answer. Which of the above questions is it answering?

Animal Farm

After overthrowing Jones at the beginning of 'Animal Farm' the animals enter the farmhouse quietly and carefully. They are amazed at 'the unbelievable luxury' of the rooms and the furniture, such as the horsehair sofa and the soft feather beds. They decide never to live there and it is turned into a museum as a symbol of the terror and oppression of Jones's reign.

However, the pigs eventually move into the farmhouse and it soon symbolizes the inequality between themselves and the other animals. They grow fat there, drink whisky and even sleep in the beds, while the others do all the work. As in Jones's time, the leaders live comfortably whereas the workers suffer.

Furthermore, Napoleon spends most of his time in the house, waited on by dogs in his own private apartments. In this way, the new dictator separates himself from the other animals, including the pigs.

At the end we see him talking to the humans as equals in the dining room. It is in the farmhouse, then, that we see best how Napoleon occupies Jones's position.

3 Has the writer answered both parts of the question satisfactorily?
What is the purpose of each of the four paragraphs?
Which words are used to link ideas?
Has the writer quoted directly from the text?

4   Choose one of the example questions and write your answer in **120–180** words, with reference to one of the set books.

How to go about it

- Underline the key words in the question.
- Write down as many ideas as you can which will be relevant to the question.
- Check in the book that your information is correct and add any further ideas which might be useful. If you notice any short, relevant quotations, make a note of them.
- Decide which of your ideas you will include in your answer. The word limit is 180 words, so be selective.
- Organize your ideas into a paragraph plan which is relevant to the task type.

- Four paragraphs should be enough if you are writing an **essay**.
- If you are writing a **letter**, decide how you will begin and end it.
- If you are writing a **report**, consider what headings, if any, you will use.
- If you are writing an **article**, interest the reader from the very beginning.
- If you are writing a **review**, make sure there is a balance of information and opinion.

Vocabulary 3: Television

1   Can you give an example of each of the following types of TV programme?

sitcom   sports programme   quiz show   soap opera music programme   chat show   documentary   comedy programme game show   news broadcast   current affairs programme   detective series

2   What are your three favourite types of programme?
Which three types do you like the least? Why?

Reading 2:
FCE Part 3

Multiple matching

1   Look at the following challenge from the 'Kill Your TV' website.
Would you accept the challenge?
Do you think you would be successful?

2   You are going to read various emails sent to the website by people who took up the challenge. For questions **1–15** on page 182, choose from the people (**A–F**). The people may be chosen more than once. When more than one answer is required, these may be given in any order.

The kill your TV challenge

If you want to experiment with a TV-free life and prove that TV is not addictive, take up this challenge:

Go entirely without TV for a month. No news, no sports, no cartoons – absolutely nothing. If you decide to take up the challenge, email me at the end of the month and let me know how it went. I'll post your comments on this page. Good luck!

Don't forget!

- Read the emails through quite quickly to get a general idea.
- Underline the key words in the questions. The first two have been done for you.
- Read the text again and underline the parts of the text which give you the answers.

- Do not leave any questions unanswered. **Be careful!** Just because a word in the text is the same as a word in the question, this does *not* necessarily mean that this is the correct answer.
  eg The word 'education' or 'educational' appears in texts **D**, **E** and **F**, but only one answer is correct for question 11.

Television was <u>dominating</u> our lives. | 1 |

I <u>nearly didn't succeed</u> in the challenge. | 2 | 3 |

I feel healthier as a result. | 4 |

I managed to do some home improvements. | 5 |

Some alternatives are no better than television. | 6 | 7 |

I'll probably continue to watch too much television. | 8 |

We speak to each other more now. | 9 | 10 |

Television has educational benefits. | 11 |

I wasn't entirely successful in the challenge. | 12 |

You need to achieve a balance. | 13 | 14 |

The rest of my family like watching television. | 15 |

Comments

A Nikki Bowen

After one month without the TV I've become fitter, having spent less time in front of the box and more time outside. Of course, I've also spent more time in front of the computer, which can sometimes be as bad as passively watching television. And now that I'm 'allowed' to watch television, I have no real desire to, apart from the occasional episode of 'The Simpsons'. Not all television is bad, of course. The problem only arises when these activities take up too much of your time and you start to get your priorities wrong. I gave up television, not because it is bad in itself, but because it was eating up time that I could spend doing other, more productive activities.

B Steve Tyler

I really thought I'd have no difficulty in getting by without a telly, so when I took up your challenge I was honestly surprised at how much I missed the ability to watch those shows I truly enjoy. In some respects I failed, as I had some episodes of 'The X-Files' recorded for me so I could watch them when the 30 days were up. In general, though, I discovered that listening to the radio is a better alternative to the television. For one thing it enabled me to get on with the job of doing up the kids' bedroom.

C Pete Simpson

When I scored 18 on your questionnaire I realized I should give up watching TV for a while and try to cure my addiction. Although there were several times when I was on the point of reaching for the 'on' button, I surprised myself by managing to get through the month. I certainly watch less television now than I used to, but I'm sure it's just a matter of time before I'm back to my bad old ways. The only permanent cure would be to throw away the telly – and I don't think my wife and kids would thank me for that.

D Leanne Watson

My husband and I got rid of the TV about a month before we came across your website. We did it to protect our kids from the effects of television and because we felt it was taking over. As a result our daughters are calmer and more relaxed and we're all a lot more communicative. One thing that has been most surprising is other people's reactions to our decision to no longer watch TV. They find it hard to understand why we would want to do such a thing. Most speak of the educational benefits, though few watch anything but soaps and sitcoms.

E Jane Kennedy

I would have given up after a week if my mum and dad hadn't been there to stop me. I'm glad they did, though, as it's had a tremendous effect on my education and my general quality of life. I do my homework better and more quickly without the television on and whereas before there were times when I barely exchanged a word with my family, we've all now become great conversationalists.

F Dave Hamilton

Having successfully completed your challenge, I've now gone back to watching eight or so hours of television a week – which, you have to agree, is not excessive. Like all things, it needs to be taken in moderation. For me, television is as entertaining and educational as reading and is only harmful when you are unable to separate that which entertains and educates from that which simply passes the time. The same is true of the computer. Giving up the television just to spend three hours a day surfing on the Internet cannot be considered an improvement.

Reacting to the text

Do you agree with Dave Hamilton that 'television is as entertaining and educational as reading'? Give examples of programmes to support your opinion.

Do you think there is too much violence on television? Should there be more censorship?

Vocabulary 4: Phrasal verbs

1   What is the meaning of the following underlined phrasal verbs?

I realized I should <u>give up</u> watching television for a while.
If you decide to <u>take up</u> the challenge, email me at the end of the month and let me know how it went.

2   The following sentences all come from the emails about television. Match each of the underlined phrasal verbs with its meaning below, using the context in the sentences to help you make your decisions. The phrasal verbs in **bold** appeared in earlier units of the book.

  1 The problem only arises when these activities **take up** too much of your time.
  2 I gave up television… because it was <u>eating up</u> time that I could spend doing other, more productive activities.
  3 I really thought I'd have no difficulty in **getting by** without a telly.
  4 (Listening to the radio) enabled me to <u>get on with</u> the job of **doing up** the kids' bedroom.
  5 I surprised myself by managing to <u>get through</u> the month.
  6 The only permanent cure would be to <u>throw away</u> the telly.
  7 My husband and I got rid of the TV about a month before we **came across** your website.
  8 We felt (television) was <u>taking over</u> our lives.

  a find by chance
  b start or continue doing something
  c get rid of
  d use or occupy
  e use or consume in great quantities
  f repair or redecorate
  g take control of
  h manage to live or survive (intransitive verb)
  i manage to survive a difficult period of time (transitive verb)

Writing 2:
FCE Part 2

Essays

Your class has been discussing the quality of television programmes. Your teacher has asked you to write an essay giving your opinions on the following statement:

Most of what is shown on television is not worth watching.

Write your **essay**. You should write between **120 and 180** words.

How to go about it

- Write down some ideas for your essay. Consider: entertainment value, educational benefits, violence, cultural relevance, news programmes, advertisements and digital, satellite and cable TV.
- Decide whether you are going to consider both sides of the argument (Unit 3) in your essay or only one (Unit 8). Look again at the relevant unit of the book.
- Select those ideas which you intend to use. The word limit is 180, so be selective. Some examples should be included in your essay to support your ideas.
- Decide which linking devices you will use.
- Remember to check your essay when you have finished writing. Can you make any improvements?

Now you are ready to write your essay.

Use of English: FCE Part 3	**Word formation**

For questions **1–10**, read the text below. Use the word given in capitals at the end of some of the lines to form a word that fits in the gap **in the same line**. There is an example at the beginning **(0)**.

A record-breaking fish

The world's **(0)** _oldest_ known captive goldfish, named Tish, has | OLD
died **(1)** _____ at home in his tank. Tish, who had reached the | PEACE
(2) _____ age of 43, was won by seven-year-old Peter Hand at a fair. | REMARK
He **(3)** _____ shared his bowl with Tosh, who died in 1975; he also | ORIGIN
outlived the family's other pets, **(4)** _____ dogs, rabbits and hamsters. | INCLUDE
When Peter left home his parents took **(5)** _____ for Tish, who moved | RESPONSIBLE
with them to Yorkshire, where they now live in **(6)** _____ . His | RETIRE
(7) _____ in the *Guinness Book of Records* came when he turned 41. | APPEAR
The normal procedure of counting the microscopic growth rings on a fish's
scales could not be used to establish **(8)** _____ of his age. Because | PROVE
he had been kept indoors and was unaffected by **(9)** _____ changes, | SEASON
this method was **(10)** _____ and friends of the family had to sign | RELY
affidavits, written statements supporting the owner's claim.

Vocabulary

A The Arts

Complete the spaces in the following sentences with an appropriate word. The beginning of each missing word has been given to help you.

1 He had a full-length **po**_____ painted of himself.
2 The museum contains several bronze **sc**_____ of animals.
3 I am reading a great **no**_____ at the moment. It's by a contemporary author.
4 There'll be 16 groups playing live the weekend after next at the Bletchley
    op_____-_____ jazz festival.
5 You really can't put a value on this Chinese vase. It's **pr**_____ .
6 Shakespeare is England's best-known **pl**_____ .
7 This piece of music is by a famous 18th century German **co**_____ .
8 We went to a marvellous **ex**_____ of contemporary art at the weekend.

B Animals

1 Which animal is being described below?

> This animal lives in small groups. Its sharp claws and teeth are used for killing and eating other animals, both small and large. It has light brown fur, whiskers on its face and the male can be identified by the beautiful golden mane on its head and neck.

2 Now write descriptions of three other animals. Use the Wordlist on page 205 to help you. When you have finished, give your descriptions to your partner, who will try to guess which animals you have described.

C **Phrasal verbs**

Complete the spaces in the following sentences with an appropriate phrasal verb.

1 Please _____ _____ your rubbish when you have finished your lunch.
2 Some people worry that aliens will come and _____ _____ the world.
3 His new car has a huge engine and is very powerful, but, of course, it _____ _____ petrol.
4 I really must _____ _____ _____ my homework or I'll never finish it!
5 The temperature was -10°C but the climbers _____ _____ the night by keeping a fire burning.

Use of English:
FCE Part 4

Transformations: Hypothetical situations

In **1–8** below complete the second sentence so that it has a similar meaning to the first sentence, using the word given. **Do not change the word given**. You must use between two and five words, including the word given.

1 It's a pity I don't live nearer the school.
wish
I _____ nearer the school.

2 I regret telling her about my new boyfriend.
wish
I _____ her about my new boyfriend.

3 I'd prefer you not to wear those jeans to the wedding.
rather
I'd _____ those jeans to the wedding.

4 We really ought to go home now.
went
It's _____ home.

5 I'd really like to go with them, but there's no room in their car.
wish
I _____ with them, but there's no room in their car.

6 You should have brought your umbrella!
brought
If _____ your umbrella!

7 I don't like you speaking to me like that!
wish
I _____ to me like that!

8 It would be nice to know what my dog was thinking.
wish
I _____ what my dog was thinking.

Writing:
FCE Part 2

Essays

Your class has been discussing the role of zoos in the modern world. Your teacher has asked you to write an essay giving your views on the following statement.

Zoos no longer serve a useful purpose.

Write your **essay**. You should write between **120 and 180** words.

afedersiniz

disculpe

entschuldigen Sie

mi scusi

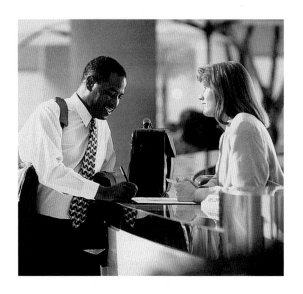

permisi

ursäkta mig

elnézést

excusez-moi

Multiple matching 2.39–2.43

 1 Can you identify any of the languages above? Would you like to learn any of them?
How important is it to learn a foreign language?
In what ways might English be useful to you in the future?
What problems can occur if you don't know the language of the country you go to visit?

2 You will hear five different people talking about how learning another language was useful for them. For questions **1–5**, choose from the list **A–F** what each speaker says about his or her experience. There is one extra letter which you do not need to use.

A Studying abroad brought success.	Speaker 1 [ ]
B Not everyone understands me when I speak.	Speaker 2 [ ]
C Doing things twice worked for me.	Speaker 3 [ ]
D Going to the cinema helped me learn.	Speaker 4 [ ]
E I made more progress the second time.	Speaker 5 [ ]
F Progress was very slow at first.	

Vocabulary 1

A Phrasal verbs with *turn*

1 Speaker 5 in the listening says: *all three French-owned companies that I applied to turned me down at the interview stage*. What is the meaning of *to turn someone down*?

2 Match each sentence beginning **1–7** with an appropriate ending **a–g**.

1 Why are you two still awake? **Turn**
2 They left port at sunrise but were forced to **turn**
3 It's amazing that this small seed will gradually **turn**
4 According to this map we have to **turn**
5 The party starts at 8pm but people won't **turn**
6 We had no reason to be suspicious of him, but it **turned**
7 I can't hear what they're saying. **Turn**

a **off** the motorway at the next exit.
b **out** that he was wanted by the police for burglary.
c **back** by rough seas and strong winds.
d **up** the sound a bit, will you?
e **into** a beautiful rose.
f **up** until much later.
g **off** the light and go to sleep.

3 Now write the infinitive of each of the seven phrasal verbs with *turn* from exercise 2 next to its meaning below.

a become   _____
b increase the volume   _____
c become known   _____
d arrive   _____
e leave a road   _____
f return   _____
g disconnect   _____

B Compound adjectives

Two common types of compound adjectives are formed using either adjectives referring to countries and languages:

Examples: *French-owned companies, Spanish-speaking teachers*

or numbers:

Examples: *a two-month course in Paris, a four-hour flight*

Note that a hyphen is used between the two words in the adjective and that a noun used with a number to form an adjective is singular.

1 For questions **1–8**, complete each of the below with one of the compound adjectives from the box.

Irish-made	one-hour
American-educated	five-minute
English-speaking	11-year-old
Italian-born	1,000-word

1 When I've finished my studies I hope to work in an _____ country, like the States or Australia.
2 The language school is just a _____ walk from the beach.
3 My _____ grandmother used to tell me stories of her childhood in Rome.
4 As part of my language project I have to write a _____ report on the growth of English on the Internet.
5 Our firm has just taken on an _____ accountant: he studied in Boston, I believe.
6 We have four _____ lessons before lunch at my school.
7 I bought this tablecloth in London but it's _____ .
8 This remarkable _____ boy can already speak five languages fluently.

2 What compound adjectives could you use to describe the following? There is an example at the beginning **(0)**.

0 a journey which takes three hours	→	a *three-hour*	journey
1 a bank note which is worth five pounds	→	a _____	note
2 a shift which lasts from 8pm to 8am	→	a _____	shift
3 a team with ten men	→	a _____	team
4 a meal with a starter, main course and dessert	→	a _____	meal
5 a holiday which lasts a fortnight	→	a _____	holiday

3 Use compound adjectives to tell your partner about:

- the age of your brothers and sisters, eg *I've got a seven-year-old sister.*
- the number and duration of lessons each day at your school
- the duration of your last holiday and the length of the journey
- the time taken to get from your house to your school/place of work/town centre
- the length of this book.

Multiple choice

1 What do you think are the advantages of growing up bilingual?
What, if any, are the disadvantages?

2 You are going to read an article on multilingualism. For questions **1–8**, choose the
answer (**A**, **B**, **C** or **D**) which you think best fits according to the text.

> **Don't forget!**
>
> ● Read the text through quite quickly first
> to get a general idea of the content. As
> you read this text, compare your ideas
> in exercise 1 with those contained in
> the text.

Two languages good, three languages even better

Nine-year-old Naomi Gray is like many British children in that when she gets home from school, she loves to lose herself in a Harry Potter book. What makes her different is that she will have chatted to her school friends in French on the bus home, and spent her day with them learning her lessons in Breton.

Naomi is the daughter of Jane and Dug Gray, a translator
and stone-mason who live in Finistère, the heart of Celtic
Brittany in north-west France. They have opted not to bring
up their three children bilingually in French and English, but
5 trilingually, by enrolling them in Brittany's educational system,
Diwan, whereby all lessons, bar English and French, are taught
in Breton. Around 3,000 children in Brittany are educated via
this immersion method that has played an important role in
the revival of the Breton language.

10 Jane admits that the decision was controversial: 'Other British
parents said: 'How dare you do that? Don't your children
have enough to take on?' ' But she had seen how quickly the
girls absorbed French: 'I felt sure they could take in another
language.' The girls' father, Dug, admits to being envious of
15 their abilities. 'After 16 years in France, I'm comfortable with
the language, but the kids still pick me up on my pronunciation
and grammar mistakes,' he says.

It was once thought that forcing a child to learn more than
one language could slow academic development but according
20 to Professor Colin Baker, a world expert on bilingualism,
the effect is the opposite. The evidence is that bi- and
trilingualism actually increases mental capacity and that
multilingual children tend to do better at school. 'The latest
research shows that in intelligence tests, children with two or
25 more well developed languages have higher scores,' he says.
'Bilingual children have two or more words for objects and
ideas, so the links between words and concepts are looser,
allowing more fluent, flexible and creative thinking.' He adds
that children learning languages young also tend to have more
30 confidence and better general communication skills.

Professor Tony Cline is an educational psychologist specialising
in language development in children. He says, 'We used to
think [the brain] had a limited capacity, like a milk bottle,
and that it was impossible to pour two pints of milk into a
35 pint bottle. Now we understand that our brains are capable of

making an infinite number of connections; there is no limit to
what we can take in.' He concedes that there might be minor
disadvantages in having a bi- or trilingual childhood: 'The child
sometimes applies the rules of one language to another, and
40 so makes mistakes - but these grammatical 'errors' are soon
outgrown, as long as the child is exposed to good models of
language.'

It seems that by giving your child the option of becoming
multilingual, you are offering them far more than just the
45 acquisition of a foreign language. That certainly seems to be
the case for the Gray girls. All three are getting top grades
at school and are literate in three languages. Naomi has
also successfully taken on German, where she is proof that
bilingualism increases language-learning aptitude. Says Prof
50 Cline: 'Multilingual children pick up other languages quickly
because they have a more flexible approach and are used to
handling different forms of syntax, grammar and vocabulary.'

Jane thinks her daughters have gained more than just
language; they have also gained culturally. In fact, the girls
55 are all enthusiastic about Breton culture: Naomi does extra-
curricular Breton step dancing and loves singing in Breton and
attending dance evenings known as fest-noz while Nina takes
part in the Breton sport of Gouren, a form of Celtic wrestling.
Says Prof Baker: 'Multilingual children gain the benefits of
60 multiple sets of literatures, traditions, ideas, ways of thinking
and behaving.'

And, he stresses, if parents have the opportunity to give their
child the gift of another language, they should jump at it.
Because in today's global marketplace, on top of all the above,
65 multilinguals are far more employable than monolinguals. 'I
find it a great shame that languages don't have a higher place
in the classroom in the UK because English is a mainstream
language of business but, in the future, that is going to
change.'

1 What does the writer say about the school that Naomi attends?
   A All of the lessons are taught in Breton.
   B English and French are not taught.
   C It is helping Breton to regain its popularity.
   D The pupils are all fluent in three languages.

2 Some people criticized the Grays for
   A not encouraging their children to learn French.
   B helping to promote a minority language.
   C not sending their children to a British school.
   D expecting too much of their children.

3 Dug Gray says that his children
   A sometimes correct him in his use of French.
   B are not as fluent in French as they would like to be.
   C need to improve their French pronunciation.
   D would like to learn another language.

4 Professor Baker says that, compared to other children, multilingual children
   A work harder at school.
   B tend to do better in examinations.
   C have a less rigid way of thinking.
   D are generally more talkative.

5 Professor Cline uses the example of the milk bottle to illustrate
   A our knowledge that the brain has limitations.
   B how much language can be stored in the brain.
   C the link between brain size and intelligence.
   D a previous way of thinking about the brain.

6 What does Professor Cline say about mistakes made by multilingual children?
   A They are only apparent in childhood.
   B Theyare only a temporary issue, given the right conditions.
   C They usually only occur in one of the child's languages.
   D They can increase in number as the child grows older.

7 Naomi's experience is presented as evidence that multilingual children
   A enjoy taking part in group activities.
   B are better equipped to learn foreign languages.
   C take advantage of opportunities they are offered.
   D integrate easily into any new cultural environment.

8 What does 'it' refer to in line 63.
   A the opportunity
   B their child
   C the gift
   D another language

Reacting to the text ⬤

In the last line Professor Baker says 'that is going to change'. What do you think might replace English as the language of business?

How might your life be different now if you had grown up bilingual in your mother tongue and English?

Vocabulary 2: Abbreviations

1 What do the following abbreviations from the text stand for?
   Prof _____   UK _____

2 The following abbreviations, written in **bold**, are often used in written English. Some may appear in the notes in Part 1 of the Writing Paper. What does each one mean?

   1 There are several ways to learn a language, **eg** private classes, books, **etc**.
   2 It gets very crowded during the peak holiday season, **ie** from June to September.
   3 **NB** Examination fees can be paid via our website at **www**.collegefees.com.
   4 **PS** Let me know **ASAP**.
   5 He wrote '**PTO**' at the bottom of the letter, but there was nothing on the other side.

   Check your answers in the Vocabulary section of the review at the end of this unit.

3 The following abbreviations are also used in spoken English. What do they stand for?

   BBC _____   MP _____

   UN _____   FBI _____

   CD _____   EU _____

Language focus: Expressing purpose

A *In order to, so as to* and *so that*

1 The full infinitive or *in order to* + infinitive can be used to show the purpose of an action.

> *Professor Cline uses the example of the milk bottle **to illustrate** a previous way of thinking about the brain.*

> *She studied another language **in order to make** herself more employable.*

In order to can also be used in the negative.
*I set two alarm clocks **in order not to** oversleep.*

So as (not) to + infinitive is another possibility.
*He left work early **so as not to** miss his daughter's birthday.*

So (that) + a clause is yet another way of expressing purpose.

2 Look at the following examples and decide which verb forms are used after *so (that)* to refer to the future and which verb forms are used to refer to the past.

1 I turned the light on so I could see what I was doing.
2 Put your bag by the door so that you don't forget it when you leave.
3 I'm going to buy a phrase book so I can at least order a coffee in Polish.
4 I wore my raincoat so that I wouldn't get wet.
5 I've put an extra blanket on your bed so that you won't get cold again tonight.

G Check your answers in the Grammar reference on page 217 and read more about expressing purpose.

Practice

1 Complete the following sentences in an appropriate way.

1 We've decided to get my grandmother a mobile phone so that…
2 We're going to get to the football match two hours before the start in order…
3 I'm taking the First Certificate exam so…
4 I pretended to be ill so…
5 She logged on to the Internet in order…
6 He went up the stairs very quietly so as…
7 I'm going to do my homework as soon as I get home so…

2 ⬤ Think of three reasons for each of the following. Use clauses of purpose in your answers.

Why do people:
- go to nightclubs?
- do dangerous sports?
- learn languages?
- go on diets?
- get married?
- take exams?

Example:
People go to nightclubs… *so as to* meet new people.
in order to have a good time.
so that they can dance.

B *In case*

*I'll take my credit card **in case** I run out of cash.*

The first action (taking the credit card) prepares for a possible situation or problem in the future (running out of cash). When *in case* is followed by the present simple it has a future meaning.

To refer to past situations we use *in case* + the past simple. *I wore my raincoat **in case** it rained.*

Practice

Complete the following sentences in an appropriate way.

1 Take a spare pen into the exam in case…
2 We decided not to take the car in case…
3 You should insure the contents of your house in case…
4 I'm taking a sandwich to work in case…
5 My mum gave me some extra money in case…
6 We've left a key with the neighbours in case…

Roleplay: Expressing purpose

1 Work in pairs. Decide who is Student A and who is Student B and follow the relevant instructions.

Student A:
You are a rather fussy, over-protective parent whose teen-age son/daughter is going away on a one-week camping trip with some friends. It is the first time he/she has been away on holiday without you, and you are going to give advice on what items he/she should take. Write down eight things which you consider to be essential for the trip, together with your reasons. Use the expressions above (*so that, in case,* etc). Use the prompts in the box below to help you.

Student B:
You are a teenager who is about to go on a one-week camping trip with a group of friends. Your parents always worry too much and one of them is going to give you lots of advice about what to take. You just want to have a good time, so you're not interested in boring details. Write down at least eight items you want to take on the trip, together with your reasons. Use the expressions above (*so that, in case,* etc). Use the prompts in the box below to help you.

food	drink	cooking equipment
emergency provisions		medicines
clothing	entertainment	

2 When you have each prepared your lists, take it in turns to talk about each of the items giving your reasons. Try to agree on at least five items which will be taken on the trip.

Who was the most persuasive?

Writing:
FCE Part 2

Articles

Your college magazine has asked you to write an article giving advice to next year's First Certificate students about how to prepare for the examination throughout the course.

Write your **article** for the magazine, based on your own experience. You should write between **120 and 180** words.

How to go about it

When planning your article, consider the following:

- organizing and learning new vocabulary
- studying grammar
- improving reading, listening, writing and speaking skills
- where and when to do homework
- organizing your time
- watching videos, reading books etc

Clauses of purpose might be useful when giving the reasons for your advice.

Examples:

*I've read several short stories this year **in order to prepare** for the Reading Paper.*
*I'd recommend buying a separate notebook **so that you can organize** new vocabulary.*
*Try to learn as many collocations as possible **in case they come up** in Paper 3.*

Reading 2:
FCE Part 2

Gapped text

1 What aspects of American school life have you seen depicted in films and on television? What impression do you have of American high schools?

2 You are going to read an article on page 192 about an American high school. Seven sentences have been removed from the article. Choose from the sentences **A–H** the one which fits each space **(1–7)**. There is one extra sentence which you do not need to use.

Don't forget!

- Read the whole text through quickly before you begin to do the task. Are any of the aspects that you discussed in exercise 1 mentioned in the article?

- In the exam, you have to write your answers on a separate sheet.

American high

Grades, jocks, security, cheerleaders... just what is life really like at a US high school? Luke Norris visits the States to find out.

Arriving at the start of day at Montclair High School, New Jersey, is like walking on to the set of teen movie *American Pie*. The Blue Crew (as they call the jocks in the school's navy sports shirts) are hanging out by the gym and students are parking cars and meeting friends. Inside, seniors, dressed in the 'uniform' of khakis and T-shirts, slam locker doors as they head to class.

School starts with a buzzer at 8am and ends, after six periods and the all-important lunch, at 2.30pm. Then there's a diary of non-stop club meetings. You're not considered a nerd if you belong to four or five clubs (at Montclair there are more than 50); it all adds weight to your college application. [1 ____]

Years run from 13/14-year-old freshmen (9th grade) to 17/18-year-old seniors (12th grade). Every student has to complete four years of school; they gain credits for taking classes and need 119 to graduate. There's not a big emphasis on exams, which means there's a less disciplined atmosphere. [2 ____]

The teachers also have a lot to do with this. 'They're really approachable people and they're always willing to help,' explains Mona, an 11th grade student. [3 ____]
Freedom is a buzzword, but that doesn't mean 'no rules'.

At Montclair there are plenty, like no hats in school or no mobile phones. [4 ____] Frisking for guns and metal detectors at school gates is still rare, though, even after the recent high school shootings.

One word that comes up again and again is cliques. But pupils do not stick to the same one all the time, as movies like *American Pie* would have us believe. 'Most people drift in and out of cliques and rarely have a single set of friends,' says Mona.

Another myth about American high schools is locker culture. Those who cherish their lockers and put pictures inside are a rare breed. [5 ____] When class is out, the cafeteria, which serves amazingly typical burgers and fries, or a clubroom are the places to hang out.

The formal end-of-year dance or prom, on the other hand, is a big thing, with student councils raising money all year to put it on. So is the yearbook, which comes out at the end of the school year and is full of pictures of pupils taking part in extra-curricular activities. [6 ____] 'Biggest gossip,' 'Best-looking' or 'Most likely to succeed' are just a few of the titles.

The impression I am left with is that students in the US get a lot more freedom than their UK peers. But what do they think British schools are like? [7 ____] Classmate Dani nods: 'Yeah, proper discipline and a lot more serious.'

A Even seniors describe school as 'fun' and 'relaxed'.

B And if they don't manage to get their photo in it, students can always compete for an entry as one of The Superlatives.

C But senior prom is perhaps the most important event of high school.

D There are also security guards in every corridor who check for hall passes.

E 'Strict teachers, smart uniforms,' says Noah, 17.

F Most say they are just a place to leave books and things.

G 'We can email them at home for advice on most things,' she adds.

H Many happily stay until after 6pm doing sport, choir and drama.

Reacting to the text

How does Montclair High School compare to your own school?
Would you prefer to study there?

Vocabulary 3

A American English

1 Look at the following differences between American and British English. The American words appeared in the reading text.

1 The equivalent of **high school** in British English is secondary school.
2 In American English you **graduate** from high school or university, whereas in British English you only graduate from university.
3 Americans talk about seeing a **movie**; British people tend to use the word film.
4 **Jock** is an American word used to describe someone who is very keen on sport.

2 Match the British English words **1–7** with the American English equivalents **a–f**. One has been done for you.

British English
① flat
2 lift
3 wardrobe
4 curtains
5 garden
6 dustbin
7 trousers

American English
a elevator
ⓑ apartment
c pants
d drapes
e trashcan *or* garbage can
f yard
g closet

3 Write the equivalent British English word for the American English word on the right. There is an example at the beginning **(0)**.

British English
0 _____*lorry*_____
1 _____
2 _____
3 _____
4 _____
5 _____
6 _____
7 _____

American English
truck
subway
gas station
freeway
vacation
railroad
parking lot
round trip ticket

4 Write the following in British English. As well as vocabulary, you may need to change the spelling of certain words.

1 She took the garbage out to the trashcan in the yard.
2 The truck driver slowed down and pulled into the gas station on the freeway.
3 'I can't find my pants anywhere, mom!'
   'Try looking in the closet, honey.'
4 No cookies and candies for me, thanks, I'm dieting.
5 It was early fall. The sidewalks in the neighborhood were covered with leaves of different shapes and colors and the summer vacation was just a distant memory.

B Education

1 Explain the difference between each of the following pairs of words.

1 nursery school / primary school
2 a state school / a public school
3 grammar school / a comprehensive school
4 a degree / a career
5 a teacher / a professor
6 a qualification / a title

2 Write down one subject for each of the following. Use the Wordlist on page 205 to help you. If you are no longer at school, think back to when you were.

1 the subject you most enjoy _____
2 your least favourite subject _____
3 a subject which you would like to be better at _____
4 the subject that you think is the most useful for your future _____
5 the least practical subject _____

15 Review

Multiple-choice cloze

For questions **1–12**, read the text below and decide which answer (**A**, **B**, **C** or **D**) best fits each gap. There is an example at the beginning (**0**).

Homestay

When studying a foreign language abroad, a **(0)** ____ majority of students choose 'homestay' accommodation, living with a host family while they **(1)** ____ classes in a nearby language school. Very **(2)** ____, however, once lessons have finished, students speak their mother tongue with other class members of the **(3)** ____ nationality. On a Homestay Language International study trip, we ensure total immersion in the target language environment by arranging accommodation and one-to-one tuition in your teacher's home, **(4)** ____ you are surrounded by the language during every moment of your **(5)** ____.

As you are the **(6)** ____ student, you can learn at your own pace, and lessons are tailor-made to **(7)** ____ your individual interests and objectives. You will also have the chance to **(8)** ____ fully in your host teacher's family and social life, including trips to places of interest in the local area. All of our teachers have a university **(9)** ____ and a relevant teaching qualification, and most have spent time abroad so understand the needs and concerns of their student guests.

Homestay Language International offers a wide **(10)** ____ of general or business courses for young and old alike, with a choice of over 80 **(11)** ____ throughout the world. Whether it's English in New Zealand, French in Canada or German in Austria, you can **(12)** ____ a warm welcome in a relaxed home environment and an unforgettable study experience.

	0	**A** broad	**B** <u>large</u>	**C** grand	**D** high
	1	**A** assist	**B** present	**C** attend	**D** go
	2	**A** more	**B** often	**C** much	**D** well
	3	**A** same	**B** own	**C** personal	**D** equal
	4	**A** because of	**B** in case	**C** in order	**D** so that
	5	**A** halt	**B** pause	**C** stop	**D** stay
	6	**A** only	**B** alone	**C** unique	**D** lonely
	7	**A** agree	**B** adapt	**C** suit	**D** adjust
	8	**A** enjoy	**B** involve	**C** participate	**D** include
	9	**A** title	**B** degree	**C** career	**D** grade
	10	**A** sort	**B** kind	**C** type	**D** range
	11	**A** terminals	**B** destinations	**C** stations	**D** destinies
	12	**A** expect	**B** wait	**C** reach	**D** hope

Vocabulary

A Abbreviations

What are the abbreviations for the following?

1 for example   _____
2 and so on   _____
3 that is to say   _____
4 please note   _____
5 World Wide Web   _____
6 postscript   _____
7 as soon as possible   _____
8 please turn over   _____

B Compound adjectives

Complete each of the spaces with a suitable noun. Choose from the words in the box.

```
lesson    shift    meal    holiday
composition    clock    note    baby girl
```

1 the 24-hour _____
2 an eight-hour _____
3 a two-month-old _____
4 a three-course _____
5 a 180-word _____
6 a 45-minute _____
7 a three-week _____
8 a ten-pound _____

C American English

What are the American English equivalents of the following British English nouns?

1 trousers   _____
2 dustbin   _____
3 wardrobe   _____
4 garden   _____
5 motorway   _____
6 lorry   _____
7 car park   _____
8 pavement   _____

Use of English:
FCE Part 4

Transformations

For questions **1–6**, complete the second sentence so that it has a similar meaning to the first sentence, using the word given. **Do not change the word given.** You must use between two and five words, including the word given.

1 You should put an extra jumper on so that you don't get cold.
   order
   You should put an extra jumper on _____ cold.

2 He left early because he didn't want to miss the last bus.
   as
   He left early _____ the last bus.

3 I've kept the receipt for the shirt because it may not fit you.
   in
   I've kept the receipt for the shirt _____ fit you.

4 She took something to read to avoid getting bored.
   would
   She took something to read _____ get bored.

5 The workers were offered a three per cent pay increase but they didn't accept it.
   turned
   The workers _____ of a three per cent pay increase.

6 What time did Mike eventually get to the party?
   turn
   What time _____ at the party?

Introduction

Paper 5, the Speaking Test, consists of four separate parts and lasts about 14 minutes. You will probably take the test with another candidate, though it is possible to be part of a group of three. There are two examiners: the Interlocutor, who conducts the test and asks the questions, and the Assessor, who listens to the test and assesses your performance. The Interlocutor also assesses and contributes to your final mark.

1 Read the descriptions of the four parts of the Speaking Test below and match each one to a diagram **a–d**. The arrows (◂▸) show who is speaking to whom.

a INTERLOCUTOR	**b** INTERLOCUTOR	**c** INTERLOCUTOR	**d** INTERLOCUTOR
CANDIDATE A ◂▸ CANDIDATE B	CANDIDATE A (◂▸) CANDIDATE B	CANDIDATE A ◂▸ CANDIDATE B	CANDIDATE A CANDIDATE B

Part 1: Interview   Total time: 3 minutes

The Interlocutor asks you questions which require you to give basic personal information about yourself. You may speak with your partner in this part if you want to, though you do not have to.

Part 2: Talking about photographs   Total time: 4 minutes

You have one minute to compare two photographs and add some further comment about them. You also have up to 20 seconds to comment on your partner's pictures. You do not talk to your partner in this part.

Part 3: Collaborative task   Total time: 3 minutes

The Interlocutor listens while you and your partner perform a speaking task together. You may be asked to try to agree or reach a decision by the end of the task.

Part 4: Further discussion   Total time: 4 minutes

The Interlocutor asks further questions related to the topic introduced in Part 3. As well as responding to these questions you should also interact with your partner and comment on what he or she says.

2 The following comments were all made by students who had just taken the Speaking Test of the First Certificate exam. Look at each one and answer these questions:

Does the student set a good example to follow in the Speaking Test? Why/Why not? If not, how would you avoid making the same mistake?

Part 1   **a** 'The examiner asked us some really simple questions at the beginning of the exam. So I just gave some short, simple answers, as I would in my own language.'

           b 'Before the exam, my partner and I learnt and rehearsed some nice long answers to all the typical questions they ask you about yourself in the exam. We knew exactly what we were going to say to each other.'

           c 'I was a bit nervous in this part, but the questions were not difficult so I tried to answer them as fully and as naturally as I could, as if I was talking to someone I knew. It helped me to relax for the rest of the test.'

Part 2   **a** 'I used some really good vocabulary to describe in detail what everyone in the pictures was wearing, what they were doing and so on.'

b 'The examiner stopped me after about a minute and I hadn't finished what I wanted to say!'

c 'I was concentrating so much on the pictures when the examiner gave them to me that I forgot to listen to the instructions! I had to ask her to repeat them.'

Part 3 **a** 'I did really well in this part of the exam. I had lots of ideas and I seemed to be speaking for most of the three minutes. My partner was a bit quiet, though.'

b 'We had to agree on the three most important qualities of a good language learner. It was easy – we did it in about two minutes.'

c 'We had to choose two designs for a new set of postage stamps. We found one we both liked but when the examiner stopped us after three minutes we were still trying to agree on the second.'

Part 4 **a** 'The examiner didn't really say very much in this part. We did most of the talking.'

b 'My partner said that computers would eventually replace books. "Nonsense," I said, "you must be mad." I thought that was really good – an expression of disagreement and a modal verb of deduction in one sentence!'

c 'We had to talk about the environment, which I don't know much about, so I changed the topic of conversation to pets; I've got two dogs and a hamster, you see.'

Part 1: Interview   Total time: 3 minutes

1 Choose three of the following categories and for each one write three questions you could ask another student.

work/study	sport/keeping fit	family	travel/holidays
future plans	English	animals	music
fashion	going out	friends	

Begin your questions with the following words:

What... ?	Where... ?	Who... ?	Why... ?
When... ?	How... ?	How long/often/much... ? etc	

If you write a question which only requires a short answer, write another which will encourage the other student to say more.

Example: *Where do you live? What do you like about living there?*

2 Work with another student. Interview each other using the questions you have prepared. Develop your answers, making sure they are relevant to the question.

3 ⏺ 2.44 Listen to two students, Christina and Paolo, doing Part 1 of the Speaking Test and answer the following questions.
  1 Does the interlocutor ask any of the same questions you prepared?
  2 Why does the interlocutor interrupt Christina at the beginning?
  3 What advice would you give to Paolo to help him improve his performance?

Don't forget!

- Do not learn long pre-prepared answers for this part of the exam. They may not be entirely appropriate to the question you are asked and they will probably not sound very natural.
- Do, however, make sure you know individual items of vocabulary which are relevant to yourself. For example:

Your hobbies and interests.
'I'm really keen on rock climbing and walking.'
The course you have decided to study.
'I would like to study for a degree in aeronautical engineering.'
What your parents do.
'My mother's a systems analyst.'

Part 2: Talking about photographs   Total time: 4 minutes

Useful language

'Fillers' are words or phrases which enable you to think while you are speaking. Look at the following examples and think about the equivalent expressions you would use in your own language.

Buying time	Gathering your thoughts
Well...	*I'm not quite sure, but I think...*
Let me see...	*I haven't thought about it before, but*
What else (can I say)?	*perhaps...*
Is there anything I can add to that?	*I don't really know, but I imagine...*

Don't forget!

● Do not describe the photos in detail.
● Make sure you address both parts of the instructions.

Student A: Look at these two photographs. They show grandfathers with their grandchildren. Compare these photographs and say how important grandparents can be in situations like these.

> **How important can grandparents be in situations like these?**

Student B: When your partner has finished, say if an older relative has taught you to do something. (20 seconds)

For Student B's photographs, turn to page 201.

🔊 **2.45–2.46** Listen to Christina and Paolo doing the Part 2 task. Paolo's two photographs are on page 201. How well does each person compare the photographs?

Part 3: Collaborative task   Total time: 3 minutes

The History Museum in your town would like to attract more visitors and various ideas have been put forward. First, talk with your partner about the proposals shown below saying how they might appeal to different people. Then choose two which you think would be the most successful in attracting new visitors.

How to go about it

- When talking about the different people each activity might appeal to think about: people of different ages, people with different interests and people with different personalities.
- For each activity you could also mention what type of people the activity would not appeal to.
- You will gain marks for using a range of vocabulary. What other words do you know with a similar meaning to these adjectives? *interesting   boring   good*
- Use some of the useful language and expressions of agreeing and disagreeing from page 123 in Unit 10.
- Involve your partner in the interaction, asking questions if necessary.

- **How might the proposals appeal to different people?**
- **Which two would be the most successful in attracting visitors?**

2.47 Listen to Christina and Paolo doing Part 3 and answer questions **1–3**.

1 Which activities do Paolo and Christina choose?
2 At what point in their conversation do they make their decision?
3 How does Christina encourage Paolo to talk?

Part 4: Further discussion   Total time: 4 minutes

Now discuss the following questions with your partner.

Don't forget!

- Develop your answers, justifying your opinions and giving examples if necessary.
- Interact with your partner, listening and responding to each other's comments.

- What do you think makes a good history museum?
- How could the teaching of history in schools be improved?
- Do you agree that learning about the past is important for our future?
- What was the most important moment in the history of the twentieth century?
- What has been the most important moment in your life so far?
- What items from our lives today will be in the history museums of the future?

2.48 Listen to Part 4 and answer the following questions.
1 How well do Christina and Paolo interact with each other:
   a in the first half of Part 4?
   b in the second half of Part 4?
2 Who helps the interaction more, Christina or Paolo?

Additional material

Unit 11
Language focus: Conditionals, page 136
Student B
1 If I lived in Britain, …
2 If I wanted to make new friends, …
3 If you help me with my homework, …
4 If it rains this weekend, …

Unit 12
Language focus: Reporting verbs, page 150
Student A
1 Tell each other your problems (see below) and give each other suggestions and advice. Use the following phrases: *You should…   Why don't you… ?   If I were you, I'd…*

- I'm finding it difficult to sleep at night.
- I'm addicted to the Internet. I spend six hours a day on it.
- I think my best friend is stealing things.
- I get very nervous when I take exams.

2 Change partners and report your conversations using the verbs *suggest*, *recommend* and *advise*.

Unit 2
Writing: FCE Part 2, Articles, page 23
1 Read this model answer to the writing question on page 23 and answer the questions below.

A strange way to enjoy yourself

(1) Have you ever seen a smile on the face of a long-distance runner? Running 10 kilometres or more certainly doesn't sound much fun, but this sport is a powerful addiction and once you've started, you'll find it difficult to give it up.

(2) So what is the attraction of running? For me, whether I'm working or studying, there is no better way of getting rid of stress. I can think my problems through and at the end of the race I have the answers. And simply completing a half or full marathon increases my confidence and makes me feel on top of the world.

(3) If you're thinking of taking it up yourself, don't try to do too much at the beginning. You should set yourself realistic targets and always do warm-up exercises before you run. Also, make sure you buy a good pair of running shoes to protect your knees and back from injury.

(4) And don't be put off by the expressions on the faces of the runners - they're enjoying every minute, and so will you!

2 Match each of these summaries to a paragraph in the article.
   a Benefits of the sport and reasons for liking it.
   b Closing comment.
   c What the sport is and what is special about it.
   d Advice to people who want to do this sport.

3 Who is the article written for (the target reader)?

4 Is it written in a more formal or informal style? Find examples of the following:
   a Contractions: eg *she's, won't*
   b Informal linking words: eg *But*
   c Direct questions
   d Phrasal verbs

5 Match each of the features 1–3 with its purpose a–c.
   1 The title   a to involve the reader
   2 Direct questions   b to encourage the reader to take up the sport
   3 The final sentence   c to attract the reader's attention

6 Now write your own answer to the question on page 23. Read the How to go about it box on the same page before you begin to write.

Ready for Reading
FCE Part 3, page 40
Removed sentences
A Mrs Stevens said: 'I was becoming increasingly desperate because he is 82, and I am 78; I was beginning to think I would never see him again.
B Mr Rider immediately flew back with his wife to England to meet his long-lost sister.
C A search of New York addresses was unsuccessful.
D The Riders had just returned from a six-week break in London, which explained the unanswered calls.
E Mrs Stevens, 78, tried repeatedly to make contact again, but each time her efforts were in vain.
F Mrs Stevens phoned every day for six weeks, but her calls all went unanswered.
G Eileen Stevens lost touch with Percival Rider, a former army bandsman, in 1962.

Unit 5
Writing: FCE Part 2, Application letters, page 62
1 Read this student's answer to the letter of application question on page 63. Would it have a positive effect on the target reader? Give reasons for your answer.

Dear Sir or Madam,
I really liked the sound of the job I saw advertised in the publication 'Summer jobs in the UK'. I'm still quite young and I recently completed a short course on garden design. My level of English is intermediate and I know quite a bit about plants and flowers. I am particularly interested in the cultivation of roses and the use of trees in landscape design. If you have a look at my CV you'll see I've had lots of different jobs. One of them was working for a couple of months on a campsite similar to those mentioned in your advertisement. I've put in a little note from my last boss with this letter. I like being part of a team and I'd love to have a go at working in a foreign country. By the way, how many hours do I have to work? And how long's the contract for? If you want I can start at the beginning of June. Let me know what you think.
Yours faithfully
Pascal Sylvestre

2 Rewrite the letter substituting the expressions below for those parts which are too informal. You should also make the questions less direct and organize the letter into appropriate paragraphs.

a As you will see from my curriculum vitae
b I look forward to receiving your reply
c I am writing to express an interest in
d I have a great deal of experience
e I will be available to work from
f I have a good knowledge of gardening
g I enclose a reference from my previous employer
h I am 25 years old
i I would enjoy the experience of working abroad
j This includes a temporary position

Unit 9
Reading: FCE Part 3, page 112

Answers to Hallowe'en questions

When is Hallowe'en?
The night of the 31st of October.

What does the word 'Hallowe'en' mean?
All Hallows' Eve. The evening before All Hallows Day or All Saints' Day (1st November).

Why is Hallowe'en celebrated?
Hallowe'en was originally a pagan festival of the dead. Celts in Ireland had a festival called 'Samhain' (pronounced 'sow-in'), which marked the official end of summer and the beginning of the Celtic New Year. On this night the souls of the dead were said to come out and move freely in the land of the living. The tradition of Hallowe'en was taken to the United States by Irish emigrants, and it is now spreading in Britain and other European countries.

Why do people dress up as witches and ghosts?
In addition to the souls of the dead, the Devil, witches and numerous spirits are believed to be out, and at the peak of their supernatural powers.

What is 'Trick or treat'?
According to an old Irish peasant practice, villagers would go from house to house to ask for soul cakes (bread with currants) in return for promises of prosperity or protection against bad luck. Now children and teenagers go from house to house asking for small gifts of money, fruit or sweets in return for not playing tricks on the people inside.

Why are pumpkins made into lanterns?
According to Irish legend, when a notorious drunkard called Jack died, he was refused entry to Heaven because of his meanness, and he was banned from Hell because he had tricked the Devil on several occasions. However, the Devil gave him a piece of coal to help him find his way in the dark of purgatory, which Jack put into a turnip to make a lantern. The Irish made similar lanterns to represent the souls of the dead on Hallowe'en, but when they emigrated to America they could not find many turnips so they used pumpkins instead.

Ready for Speaking: FCE Part 2, page 198

Student B: Look at the two photographs below. They show people in an emergency situation. Compare these photographs and say how serious you think each of the situations looks.

> How serious do you think each of the situations looks?

Student A: When your partner has finished, say if you think you could be a policeman/woman. (20 seconds)

Unit 11
Language focus: Conditionals, page 136
Student A
1 ...I'd probably be extremely popular.
2 ...the world would be a happier place.
3 ...I'll never speak to you again.
4 ...he starts to cry.

Unit 12
Language focus: Reporting verbs, page 150
Student B
1 Tell each other your problems (see below) and give each other suggestions and advice. Use the following phrases:
You should...   Why don't you... ?   If I were you, I'd...

- I'd like to go on holiday, but I haven't got much money.
- I want to lose weight, but I don't know the best way.
- No one phones me on my mobile phone.
- I want to go to a concert, but I have to go to a wedding.

2 Change partners and report your conversations using the verbs *suggest*, *recommend* and *advise*.

Unit 12
Writing: FCE Part 2
Model report, page 152

Introduction
This report looks at some of my country's national dishes and their popularity among young people. It is based on a survey of 90 people aged between 14 and 19.

Most popular dishes
Fish and chips is perhaps the best-known food in my country. Interestingly, only half of those interviewed said that it was their favourite dish. However, almost everyone agreed that it was the tastiest fast food available. Nearly 40% felt the best traditional food was roast beef served with Yorkshire pudding, a mixture of flour, eggs and milk, which is baked in the oven. Not surprisingly, desserts are popular with most young people. Trifle was mentioned several times for its rich combination of cream, custard, jelly and fruit.

Least popular dishes
A large majority said that steak and kidney pudding was their least favourite food. Although they like steak, the kidney makes the overall flavour too strong. They said the same of liver, which is fried with onions and mushrooms.

Recommendations
I recommend your students try a full roast beef dinner. Pubs usually serve this, together with a range of other traditional dishes.

Wordlist

Unit 1
Items of clothing
belt
blazer
blouse
boots
bow tie
(baseball) cap
cardigan
dinner jacket
dress
dressing gown
dungarees
fancy dress
hat
helmet
high-heeled shoes
(sports) jacket
jeans
jumper/pullover/
  sweater
overcoat
raincoat
scarf
shirt
shoes
shorts
skirt
slippers
socks
suit
sweatshirt
swimming costume
swimming trunks
top
T-shirt
tie
tights
tracksuit
trainers
trousers
waistcoat

Jewellery
bracelet   necklace
brooch   pendant
earrings   ring

Adjectives: The pattern of clothes
checked   plain
flowery   spotted
patterned   striped

Other adjectives for clothes
baggy
casual
colourful
designer
formal
long-sleeved
loose-fitting
pleated
second-hand
shabby
short-sleeved
smart
tasteful
tight-fitting
trendy
(un)fashionable
waterproof
worn out

Materials for clothes
cotton   nylon
denim   silk
leather   suede
woollen

Verbs for clothing
dress up as sbdy/sthg
fit
get (un)dressed
go with
match
put on
suit
take off
wear

Unit 2
Musical instruments
accordion
cello
clarinet
double bass
drum(s)
flute
guitar
keyboards
organ
electric/grand piano
saxophone
tambourine
trombone
trumpet
tuba
violin
wind/stringed
  instrument

Music: People
backing vocalist
concert audience
DJ/disc jockey
lead singer/guitarist
rock/folk/rap, etc
  band/singer/star
session musician

Playing and performing
a live album/concert/
  gig/performance
a music/rock festival
have a record in the
  charts
be in tune
give a concert
on tour/on stage/on
  the radio
play a tune/a record/a
  track
sing/perform/mime a
  song

Sports

do...
aerobics
athletics
gymnastics

go...
cycling
diving
horse-riding
jogging
running
sailing
skiing
snowboarding
(wind)surfing
swimming

play...
badminton
baseball
basketball
football
golf
handball
hockey
rugby
tennis
volleyball

Sports: People
athlete
baseball/basketball etc
    player
cyclist
diver
golfer
gymnast
jogger
runner
skier
snowboarder
swimmer
(wind)surfer

competitor
opponent
participant
referee (basketball/
    football/rugby)
runner-up
spectator
supporter
team
umpire (badminton/
    tennis/volleyball)
winner

Sports: Places
athletics/cycling track
athletics/football/
    sports stadium
basketball/tennis/
    volleyball court
football/hockey/
    rugby pitch
golf course
gym
ice-skating rink

motor-racing circuit
ski slope
swimming pool

Sports: Events
play/take part/
    compete in...
a football match
a golf/tennis
    tournament
a sporting event
a surfing/swimming
    competition
an athletics meeting
the national/world
    championship

Sports: Equipment
and special clothes
badminton/tennis
    racket
baseball/table tennis
    bat
football/rugby boots
golf clubs
hockey stick
running/tennis shoes
safety helmet
shin/knee pads
shuttlecock
skateboard/surfboard/
    snowboard
skiing/swimming
    goggles
skis and ski poles
sweatband

Sports: Verbs
beat an opponent/
    opposing team
break/hold a record
do/play a sport
draw a match/game
go in for a sport
lose a game/match
practise a shot
take up a new sport
win a medal/match/
    competition/game

Unit 3
Appliances, devices
and gadgets

calculator (D)
coffee maker (A)
cooker (A)
dishwasher (A)
electric carving
    knife (G)
electric pencil
    sharpener (G)
electric
    toothbrush (G)
food mixer (A)
freezer (A)

fridge/refrigerator (A)
hairdryer (A)
juice squeezer (A)
liquidizer (A)
microwave
    oven (A)
remote
    control (D)
toaster (A)
vacuum
    cleaner (A)
washing
    machine (A)

Other inventions and
equipment
cable and satellite TV
clothes steamer
compass
computer
discman/walkman
DVD player
headphones
laptop (computer)
mobile phone
music centre/system
palm top
radar
space blanket
video recorder
word processor

Adjectives for devices
clever
disposable
essential
handy
ingenious
labour-saving
portable
simple
useful/useless
unusual

Equipment and
machines: Verbs
click on (an icon)
dial a number
log on to the Internet
plug in/unplug
print out
save on disc
surf the Net
switch on/off

Unit 4

Types of film
action film
animated film
cartoon
comedy
historical drama
horror film
remake
romance
science fiction film

thriller
western

People and elements
of a film
acting
action scenes
actor/actress
animation
cast
director
film/movie star
main character
make-up artist
photography
plot
producer
screenplay
script
soundtrack
special effects
stuntman/woman
supporting role

Films: Other
vocabulary
a box office hit
a dubbed/subtitled
    film
a film critic
a good/bad review
give a good/bad
    performance
go to an audition
have a part in a film

Unit 5

Jobs
accountant
architect
baker
butcher
chef
childminder
civil servant
company director
cook
dustman
electrician
engineer
firefighter
flight attendant
gardener
hairdresser
journalist
judge
lawyer
librarian
nanny
nurse
photographer
plumber
police officer
politician
receptionist
scientist

secretary
shop assistant
surgeon
teacher
vet
waiter/waitress

Career
apply for a job
get a job
go for an interview
look for a job

change career
devote yourself to a
    career
give up your career
start a career

be dismissed/sacked
be made redundant
be out of work/a job
resign from a job

Earn
earn a good living
earn a high/low salary
earn a lot of money
earn a weekly wage

Work
work as a nurse
work flexitime
work for yourself
work hard
work long hours
work one's way up to
    the top
work overtime
work part/full-time
work shifts

Work: Skills
artistic skills
computer skills
language skills
organizational skills
telephone skills

Adjectives for jobs
badly-paid
challenging
monotonous
responsible
satisfying
stressful
tiring
unpleasant
well-paid

Work: Other
vocabulary
form a new company
go into business
join a company
run a business
set up a company

a colleague
a new recruit

Wordlist

a temporary job
be on/take sick leave
be one's own boss
be promoted
be/go on strike
be self-employed
get paid
retire
take time off (work)

Unit 6
Adjectives for personality
adventurous
affectionate
ambitious
bad-tempered
bossy
brave
caring
cheerful
clever
clumsy
confident
creative
decisive
dull
easy-going
energetic
enthusiastic
fair
fussy
generous
hard-working
honest
intelligent
kind
lazy
lively
loyal
mature
mean
moody
nervous
outgoing
patient
polite
practical
reliable
reserved
responsible
rude
selfish
sensible
sensitive
shy
sincere
sociable
stubborn
sympathetic
tolerant

Adjectives for hair
curly/dyed/flowing/
shoulder-length/

spiky/straight/
thinning/untidy/wavy
be bald/balding
have a beard/
moustache

Adjectives for eyes
almond-shaped/
hazel/piercing/
sparkling

Adjectives for faces
expressive/freckled/
round/tanned/thin/
wrinkled

Adjectives for complexion
dark/healthy/pale/
smooth/spotty

Adjectives for build
fat/overweight/plump
skinny/slim/thin
stocky/well-built

Unit 7
Shops
baker's
bookshop
butcher's
chemist's
clothes shop
department store
florist's
gift shop
greengrocer's
grocer's
hardware shop
jeweller's
local corner shop
newsagent
super/hypermarket

In a supermarket
aisle
cashier
cash register/till
counter
checkout
end of aisle area
receipt
shelf/shelves
shopping basket
shopping trolley

Goods on sale
alcoholic drinks
bakery
confectionery
dairy products
foodstuffs
freezer goods
fresh fruit/vegetables/
meat/fish
household goods
own-brand products

pre-packed meat
soft drinks
tinned/frozen
convenience food
toiletries
well-known brands

Shopping: Other vocabulary
a bargain
a discount
a (money-back)
guarantee
a special offer/be on
offer
ask for a refund
be faulty
be good value for
money
be nearing/past its
sell-by date
be on order
buy sthg in the sales
buy sthg on impulse
charge sbdy £10
have sthg in stock
make a purchase
postage and packing
same-day/next-day
delivery
splash out on sthg

Places
apartment block
building site
housing estate
industrial estate/area/
site
in the city centre
office block
on the outskirts
pedestrian area/
precinct
residential area/estate
shopping centre/
precinct/mall

Adjectives for towns and villages
bustling
depressing
dull
lively
picturesque
pleasant
prosperous
quaint
run-down
shabby

Adjectives for buildings
ancient   huge
attractive   imposing
beautiful   impressive
derelict   magnificent
deserted   tall
historic   ugly

Unit 8
Travel
to go on a/an...
cruise
excursion
flight
journey
package holiday
(business) trip
tour
voyage

be good/great fun
enjoy oneself
go camping
go sightseeing
pack one's suitcase
relax
stay on a campsite

a good view
a holiday/ski resort
brochure
souvenir

Unit 9
Ghosts
a haunted house
a spirit
give a piercing scream
haunt a building
moaning sounds
vanish (into thin air)
walk through walls

Strange phenomena: Adjectives
afraid
bizarre
chilling
frightened/frightening
mysterious
peculiar
scared stiff of sthg
spooky/scary
strange/weird
terrified/terrifying
unnerving

Festivals and celebrations
a bonfire
a custom
a fancy dress party
a firework display
a legend
a parade
a tradition

commemorate sthg
dress up as sthg/sbdy
set off fireworks

Unit 10
Crimes and criminals
arson/arsonist
assassination/assassin
blackmail/blackmailer
burglary/burglar
drug trafficking/drug
trafficker
espionage/spy
hijack(ing)/hijacker
kidnap(ping)/kidnapper
mugging/mugger
murder/murderer
pickpocketing/
pickpocket
robbery/robber
shoplifting/shoplifter
smuggling/smuggler
theft/thief
vandalism/vandal

Crime: Verbs
accuse sbdy of a crime
acquit sbdy of a crime
arrest sbdy for a crime
burgle a house/office
deter sbdy from
committing a crime
find sbdy (not) guilty
of a crime
give sbdy a prison
sentence
order sbdy to do
community service
order sbdy to pay a fine
rob a person/bank (of
£2,000)
sentence sbdy to two
years in prison/life
imprisonment/death
steal money/jewellery
(from a person/shop)

Unit 11
Weather
fine/heavy/torrential
rain
light/scattered/snow
showers
overcast/clear/stormy
sky
rough/calm/choppy
sea
strong/gale-force/light
wind
thick/storm/angry-
looking clouds
violent/severe/electric
storm
warm/glorious/
brilliant sunshine

Weather: Other vocabulary
be struck by lightning
flash of lightning

gentle breeze
gust of wind
hailstones/raindrops/
    snowflakes
it's pouring with rain
weather forecast

Natural disasters
avalanche
drought
earthquake
earth tremor
flood
hurricane
tidal wave
tornado

The environment
air/river/sea pollution
bottle bank
carbon monoxide
cigarette butts
conservation area
dog mess
drop litter
dump waste
endangered species
exhaust fumes
face extinction
global warming
greenhouse effect
natural habitat
nature reserve
nuclear power station
oil slick
ozone layer
preserve wildlife
raise awareness
recycled paper
rising sea levels
toxic effluent
unleaded petrol

Unit 12

Ways of cooking food

bake	poach
boil	roast
fry	sauté
grill	stew
heat	toast

Adjectives for food

bitter	savoury
bland	sickly
creamy	sour
crunchy	spicy
greasy	stodgy
heavy	sweet
hot	tasteless
rich	tasty
salty	

Illnesses and injuries
black eye
bruise (n & v)
chest pain

cold
cough
earache
ear infection
flu
headache
heart attack
high/low blood pressure
nose bleed
runny nose
sore throat
sprained ankle/wrist
stomach ache
toothache

Treatment
cure sbdy of an illness
give sbdy a prescription
give sbdy an injection
have one's arm/leg in
    plaster
have an operation on
    part of body
put a plaster on sthg
put sbdy on antibiotics
take some medicine/a
    pill/painkillers
take sbdy's temperature
treat sbdy for an
    illness/injury
wrap a bandage round
    part of body

**Health: Other
vocabulary**
(un)fit
(un)healthy
(un)well

to bleed
to catch a cold
to feel sick
to heal
to hurt
to injure
to wound

Unit 13

Money
bank/current/savings
    account
cashpoint machine
chequebook
coins
credit card
currency
mortgage
overdraft
personal loan
pocket money
rate of exchange
rate of inflation
rate of interest
stock market

Money: Verbs
apply for/take out/
    repay a loan
be (seriously) in debt
be overdrawn
borrow sthg from sbdy
buy sthg on credit
cash in an investment
have change for £10
inherit money
invest (money) in sthg
lend sthg to sbdy
open/close a bank
    account
owe money to sbdy
pay a bill/a fine/tax/
    the rent
pay by credit card/
    by cheque/by direct
    debit/in cash
pay (sbdy) for sthg
put money into an
    account/deposit
    money
save up for sthg
sell sthg for £100
spend money on sthg
take money out of an
    account/withdraw
    money

Unit 14

Art
abstract painting
art collector
art/portrait gallery
artist
exhibition
landscape
painter
portrait
portrait gallery
priceless painting

Ballet
ballerina
ballet dancer
choreographer
classical/modern ballet

Literature
author
(auto)biography
detective/historical/
    romantic etc novel
novelist
publisher
short story
writer

Music
cellist/pianist/
    violinist
classical music
composer

conductor
concert hall
musician
open-air concert
orchestra
Opera
opera house
opera singer
soprano
tenor

Sculpture
sculptor
stone/bronze
    sculpture/statue

Theatre
Act I Scene II
actor/actress
audience
cast
director
performance
play
playwright
rehearsal
stage

Television
cartoons
chat show
comedy/current
    affairs/music/
    sports programme
detective series
documentary
game show
news broadcast
quiz show
sitcom
soap opera

Animals
Birds: owl/peacock/
    pigeon/sparrow
Farm animals: cow/
    goat/pig/sheep
Fish: cod/shark/trout
Pets: budgerigar/cat/
    dog/goldfish/
    hamster/parrot
Insects: ant/bee/
    beetle/fly/wasp
Other animals: bat/
    bear/fox/frog/mouse/
    rat/snake

Parts of animals
Fish: fin/gills/scales/
    tail
Bird: beak/feathers/
    tail/wings
Cat: claws/fur/paws/
    tail/whiskers
Horse: hooves/mane/tail

Unit 15

Education: Schools
boarding school
comprehensive school
grammar school
nursery school
primary school
public school
secondary school
state school

headteacher
pupil
teacher

Further education

agricultural/teacher
    training college
college of further
    education
(open) university

graduate
lecturer
postgraduate
professor
student
undergraduate

Education: Subjects
art
biology
business studies
chemistry
design technology
drama
economics
games
geography
geology
history
home economics
humanities
information technology
law
literature
maths
modern languages
music
philosophy
physical education
physics
religious education
science
sociology

Qualifications
GCSEs
'A' Levels
degree
BA/MA/BSc/MSc
PhD

Education: Verbs
revise for an exam
do/sit/resit/take an
    exam
pass/fail an exam

Grammar reference

Unit 1

Habitual behaviour in the present

A The present simple is used for habitual actions or permanent situations in the present.
I go for a run twice a week. She lives near the station.

B Frequency adverbs are used to indicate how often an action occurs. They are usually placed:
1 before the main verb.
I always go to bed before midnight.
2 after the verb *to be* or an auxiliary verb.
She is very often late for work.
They have rarely been seen together.
3 *Usually, normally, frequently, sometimes, (very/quite) often,* and *occasionally* can also be placed at the beginning of the sentence or clause.
Occasionally we go out to the cinema, but **usually** we stay in and watch a video.
NB *always, rarely, seldom, hardly ever,* and *never* cannot be used in the same way.

C Variations
1 The present continuous + *always* is used to talk about things which occur frequently and which the speaker finds annoying.
He's always complaining about something!
2 Adjectives can be used as an alternative to *rarely, normally* and *(not) usually.*
It's rare/normal/(un)usual for him to eat meat.
3 *Tend to* + infinitive is used to make general statements about the habitual actions and situations of groups of people or individuals.
British people tend to drink tea rather than coffee.
I tend not to get up very early on Sundays.
4 *Will* + infinitive is used to talk about habitual behaviour. Frequency adverbs can also be added.
She'll sometimes spend the whole day reading.
5 *Keep (on)* + gerund is used to talk about repeated actions, often annoying ones.
Peter keeps on hitting me.

Habitual behaviour in the past

A The past simple is used for regular actions or habitual behaviour in the past, often with a frequency adverb.
I hardly ever went away on holiday when I was young.

B *Used to* + infinitive is used to refer to past habits and situations which no longer occur or exist now.
We used to have a cat, but he died last year.
I always used to walk to work until I bought a car.
Note the negative and question forms:
I didn't use to like cheese. Where did you use to live?
NB *use to* cannot express present habitual behaviour.
I usually (not use to) play tennis twice a week.

C *Would* + infinitive is used to refer to past habits, but not past situations.
Habit: *My dad would often read to me when I was a young boy.*
Situation: *I used to (not would) have a bicycle.*
Stative verbs such as *have* (possession), *be, live, like, believe, think* (= have an opinion), *understand* and *know*

are not used with *would* to refer to the past.

Be used to/Get used to + noun or gerund

Be used to + noun/gerund means 'be accustomed to'.
She's a nurse so she's used to seeing sick people.
Get used to + noun/gerund means 'become accustomed to'.
I want to leave Athens; I can't get used to the heat.

Unit 2

Indirect ways of asking questions

A number of expressions can be used to ask questions in a more indirect way. Indirect questions can sound more polite than direct ones.
Could you tell me what time it is?
Would you mind telling me where he works?
We'd like to know when you first started singing.
When asking indirect questions the same word order is used as when we make statements. The auxiliary verbs, *do, does* and *did,* are omitted.
If or *whether* is used if there is no question word such as *where, what, why, when, who* and *how.*
Could you tell us if / whether you are married..

Gerunds and infinitives

A The gerund is used in the following cases:
1 as the subject/object/complement of a clause or sentence.
Subject: **Reading** *in the car makes me feel sick.*
Object: *I find **shopping** for clothes really boring.*
Complement: *My favourite sport is **swimming**.*
2 after prepositions.
*I'm not very **good at making** things.*
NB *to* is a preposition in the following verbs:
*I **look forward to hearing** from you soon.*
*I can't **get used to living** without her.*
3 after certain verbs.
*Peter **suggested going** for a picnic.*

B The infinitive with *to* is used:
1 to express purpose.
*I'm learning English **to help** me get a better job.*
2 after many adjectives, eg *surprised, delighted, disappointed, easy, happy, important, lucky, necessary, normal, possible, surprised.*
*I was **surprised to hear** she had failed the exam.*
3 after certain verbs.
*He **offered to give** her a lift, but she **decided to go** by train instead.*

C Gerunds and infinitives after verbs
1 Verb + gerund
*Have you **finished cleaning** your room?*
The following verbs, like *finish,* are normally followed by the gerund:
a Certain verbs expressing likes and dislikes: *adore, detest, dislike, enjoy, don't mind, can't stand*
b Other verbs: *admit, avoid, can't help, consider, delay, deny, feel like, forgive, give up, imagine, involve,*

keep, mind, miss, postpone, put off, practise, prevent, resist, risk, suggest

2 Verb + infinitive with *to*
He promised not to tell *anyone what she had said.*

a The following verbs, like *promise*, are normally followed by the infinitive with *to*: *(can't) afford, agree, appear, arrange, ask, attempt, choose, decide, deserve, expect, help, hesitate, hope, learn, manage, offer, prepare, pretend, refuse, seem.*

b The infinitive with *to* is also used after:
would like, would love, would hate, would prefer.

3 Verb + gerund or infinitive
a *Like, love, hate* and *prefer* are usually followed by the gerund. However, the infinitive is also possible with little, if any, difference in meaning.
*I **love going/to go** for long walks in the hills.*

The infinitive is common for specific situations:
*I **hate to interrupt**, but we really must be going.*

b *Begin, start, continue* and *intend* can be followed by the gerund or infinitive with no change in meaning.
*When I arrived it **started to rain/raining**.*

c *Forget, remember, go on, mean, need, regret, stop* and *try* can be followed by the gerund or the infinitive, but with a change in meaning.

- *remember/forget* + gerund = (not) to recall a previous action
  *I **remember coming** here when I was young.*
  *I'll never **forget seeing** U2 in concert.*

  remember/forget + infinitive = (not) to remember what you have to do
  *We must **remember to feed** the cat before we go.*
  *Don't **forget to phone** me if you need any help.*

- *go on* + gerund = to continue with the same activity
  *Some footballers **go on playing** professionally until they're nearly 40.*

  go on + infinitive = to change to a different activity
  *After a successful career as a football player, Johan Cruyff **went on to become** a respected manager.*

- *mean* + gerund = to involve
  *Dieting usually **means giving up** things you enjoy.*

  mean + infinitive = to intend
  *I **meant to phone** the electrician but I forgot.*

- *need* + gerund = (passive meaning)
  *This house **needs painting**. (= needs to be painted)*

  need + infinitive = (active meaning)
  *I **need to get** some new shoes.*

- *regret* + gerund = to be sorry for a previous action
  *I **regret going** to see that film: it was so boring.*

  regret + infinitive = to be sorry for what you are going to say (formal use)
  *We **regret to inform** you that we are unable to repair your washing machine.*

- *stop* + gerund = to stop an activity you are doing
  *I've **stopped smoking**: it's too expensive.*

  stop + infinitive = to stop doing one thing in order to do another
  *If you're driving long distances, you should **stop to have** a rest every two hours.*

- *try* + gerund = to experiment in order to see what will happen
  ***Try resting** for a while: you might feel better then.*

  try + infinitive = to make an effort; to attempt to do something
  *Alan **tried to stop** the thief as he ran away.*

Unit 3 Comparisons

Comparatives and superlatives

A Forms

1 Regular one-syllable adjectives
a add *-er* and *-est* to the adjective:

Adjective	Comparative	Superlative
cheap	cheap**er**	the cheap**est**

Other examples: *clean, dark, light, short, tall, slow*

b add *-r* and *-st* to adjectives ending in *-e*:

late	late**r**	the lat**est**

Other examples: *large, loose, safe, strange, wise*

c double the consonant of adjectives ending in a short vowel and a consonant, and add *-er* and *-est*:

thin	thin**ner**	the thin**nest**

Other examples: *fat, sad, wet, red, big, hot, fit*

2 Regular adjectives with more than one syllable
a use *more* and *most* in front of the adjective:

sincere	**more** sincere	the **most** sincere

Other examples: *boring, careful, modern, comfortable*

b change *-y* to *-i* and add *-er* and *-est* to adjectives ending in *-y* after a consonant:

happy	happ**ier**	the happ**iest**

Other examples: *dirty, friendly, funny, noisy, tidy, silly*

c a limited number of two-syllable adjectives can form the comparative and superlative in two ways:

stupid	stupid**er**	the stupid**est**
	more stupid	the **most** stupid

Other examples: *clever, common, polite, quiet, gentle*

d most adverbs form their comparative and superlative with *more* and *most*:

quietly	**more** quietly	the **most** quietly

a limited number have comparative and superlative forms with *-er* (or *-r*) and *-est* (or *-st*)

fast	fast**er**	the fast**est**

Other examples: *early, hard, late, long, soon*

3 a Irregular forms: adjectives

good	better	the best
bad	worse	the worst
far	farther/further	the farthest/furthest
old	older/elder	the oldest/eldest

b Irregular forms: adverbs

well	better	the best
badly	worse	the worst
little	less	the least
much	more	the most

c Irregular forms: determiners

little	less	the least
few	fewer	the fewest
much/many	more	the most

B Use

1 To talk about people or things that are different in some way we use:

a Comparative forms of adjectives/adverbs + *than*.
*I think listening is **more difficult than** reading.*
For small differences use *a bit, a little, slightly*.
*You need to work **a little harder**.*

For big differences use *much, a lot, far, significantly*.

*My new car's **much faster than** my old one.*

b Superlative forms of adjectives/adverbs:

*That's the **nicest** thing you've said to me all day.*

To emphasize the difference between one person or thing from all the others we can use *by far*:

*This is **by far the best** book I've ever read.*

c *Less … than* and *the least*

*Rugby is **less popular** than football here.*

*That's my **least favourite** track on the album.*

2 *As … as*

a For people or things that are the same in some way we use *as* + adjective/adverb + *as*.

*She's **as intelligent as** her sister.*

Almost, nearly, just, twice, three times, etc can be used to qualify the comparisons.

*There were **nearly twice as many people** at the party **as** last year.*

b *So* can replace the first *as* in negative sentences.

*It's **not so difficult as** I thought it would be.*

Quite and *nearly* can be used to qualify negative sentences of this type.

*Her new film is**n't nearly as bad as** her last one.*

(= her new film is much better than her last one)

*He's **not quite so impatient as** his brother.*

(= he's a little more patient than his brother)

c *The same* + noun + *as*

*My mum's **the same age as** my dad.*

3 *The* + comparative, *the* + comparative

We use this structure for things which occur together.

***The more money** I have, **the faster** I spend it.*

Articles

A The definite article (*the*) is most commonly used:

1 when there is only one of something, either in existence or in a particular context.

*I'd like to speak to **the manager**, please.*

2 when something is mentioned again.

*'I've read three novels and two plays by Camus.'
'What did you think of **the plays**?'*

3 when both listener and speaker know what is being referred to.

*Hurry up! **The film** starts in 10 minutes.*

4 when talking about a specific aspect of something, where the noun is followed by *of*.

*We're studying **the history of** architecture.*

5 to speak generally about certain groups of singular countable nouns.

a Inventions: ***The mobile phone** is thought to pose a serious threat to health.*

b Animal species: ***The whale** is still hunted by some countries such as Japan.*

6 with adjectives referring to general classes of people, eg *the homeless, the blind, the deaf, the rich, the poor, the old, the young, the French, the Spanish*

*Not enough is being done to help **the homeless**.*

7 with superlatives.

*Who is **the greatest footballer** in the world?*

8 with musical instruments.

*I'd love to learn to play **the piano**.*

9 with types of transport which have a fixed timetable.

*Shall we get **the bus** or take **a taxi**?*

10 with some countries, eg *the USA, the UK*

11 with oceans, mountain ranges, deserts, rivers, etc, eg *the Atlantic, the Pyrenees, the Sahara, the Thames*

12 with some geographical areas.

*We're going to **the mountains** rather than **the coast**.*

B The indefinite article (*a/an*) is most commonly used:

1 when a singular countable noun is mentioned for the first time.

***A man** went into **a bar** with **a fish**.*

2 when referring to any one of several things.

*It's quiet in here. Shall I put **a record** on?*

3 when talking about a person's job.

*My father is **a nuclear scientist**.*

4 with some numbers, eg ***a hundred** and one dalmatians, **a thousand** people, **a million** pounds*

5 when it means 'per' in some expressions, eg *twice **a day**, 50 miles **an hour**, £80 **a week***

C No article is used:

1 when referring to nouns in a general sense.

a Plural countable nouns
*Do you think **computers** will replace **teachers**?*

b Abstract nouns
*We sang songs of **love** and **peace**.*

c Other uncountable nouns
*Alan won't eat **cheese** or **meat**.*

2 with most streets, towns, cities and countries.

*I went to **Bond Street** when I was in **London**.*

3 when a town's name is used with a building, eg **Luton Airport, Oxford University**

4 in many common expressions, eg *to go home, to go to work/school/university/prison/hospital/ church/bed, to go on holiday, to be at home/work/ school/university, to be in hospital/church/bed/prison, to go by car/bus/coach/train/plane, to have breakfast/ lunch/dinner (but have **a** meal), at night (but in **the** morning/afternoon/evening)*

Unit 4

Past tenses

A The past simple is used to refer to:

1 completed actions which happened at a specific time.

*I **went** to the cinema last night.*

2 completed actions and situations which happened over a specific period of time.

*I **lived** and **worked** in Germany for three years.*

3 habitual actions or behaviour in the past.

*We **played** football in the street when I was a child.*

4 a series of consecutive events in the past.

*He **kissed** her, **said** goodbye and **closed** the door.*

B The past continuous is used to refer to:

1 temporary activities or situations in progress at a particular moment in the past.

*This time last week **we were sitting** on the beach.*

2 a past activity or situation which was already in progress when another action occurred (the activity or situation in progress may or may not continue).

*I **was reading** to my son when the lights went out.*

3 activities or situations occurring at the same time.

*Ann **was cutting** the grass while **I was cooking**.*

4 the background events in a narrative.

*It **was snowing** heavily and a cold wind **was blowing**. My brother and **I were reading** in front of the fire. Suddenly, there was a knock at the door...*

C The past perfect is used to:

1 show that a past action or situation occurred before another past action or situation.

*When I saw Tim, **he had** just **passed** his driving test.*

2 We use the continuous form to emphasize the duration of the first past action or situation.

*She **had been waiting** for over two hours when he phoned to say he couldn't come.*

D Time linkers

1 The past perfect is often used with time linkers, eg *after, before, by the time, as soon as, once, when, until*

*I couldn't go out **until** I had done my homework.*

2 The past simple can be used if the order of events is clear:

*He sold his house **before** he left the country.*

or if the second event occurred as a result of the first.

When I realized what time it was, I ran outside.

3 *After/afterwards*

After is used to show the order of two or more events in the same sentence.

After he'd cleaned the house, he went shopping.

Afterwards means *after that* and can go at the beginning or the end of a clause.

*We had lunch and **afterwards** we went for a walk.*

*They sent the result slip in September and I received the certificate two months **afterwards**.*

NB *after* would not be correct in these two sentences.

4 *At last/in the end/at the end*

At last suggests that something good happens after a long period of time or more than one attempt.

*I've passed the FCE **at last**! I failed twice before!*

In the end has a similar meaning and may also suggest there have been one or more changes or problems. The result may be good or bad.

*The car broke down several times on the way but we got there **in the end.***

NB *eventually* can also be used in this sentence.

At the end means at the point when something finishes.

*Hand in your books **at the end** of the lesson.*

5 *When/as/while*

These can all be used with the past continuous to introduce an action which was already in progress when another action occurred.

As/When/While I was running, I saw a rabbit.

6 *During/in/for*

These are all used as prepositions when referring to time, and are followed by a noun. *During* and *in* are used to say *when* something happened.

*It rained a lot **during/in** the night.*

For is used to say how long something took or lasted.

*We went to Spain **for** two weeks **during** the summer.*

So and *such*

These 'intensifiers' are used to give emphasis.

1 *So* is used before:

a adjectives and adverbs without nouns.

*I'm **so tired**. I'll have to go to bed.*

b *much, many, little, few*

*You shouldn't eat **so much**, Ian.*

2 *Such* is used with or without an adjective before:

a singular countable nouns (the indefinite article *a/an* is also needed).

*She's got **such a wonderful voice**.*

b uncountable nouns and plural countable nouns (the article is not needed).

*Our neighbours are **such friendly people**.*

3 *So* and *such* can both be used with a *that* clause to talk about the results or consequences

*It was **such a boring place that** we decided to leave.*

*It was raining **so hard** we had to stop the car.*

Unit 5

Obligation and necessity

A *Must/Mustn't* + infinitive without *to*

Must is used:

1 for strong obligations imposed by the speaker. The speaker uses *must* to express his/her authority.

*You **must be** here by 8 am.* (manager to employee)

2 to give strong advice.

*It's a great film. You really **must go** and see it.*

3 to tell oneself what is necessary.

*I **must remember** to phone Roger.*

Must not or *mustn't* is used:

4 to talk about something that is not permitted.

*Passengers **must not smoke** on the aircraft.*

*You **mustn't** drive without your seatbelt on in Britain.*

5 to give strong advice.

*You **mustn't work** too hard. You'll make yourself ill.*

Past form

Must does not have a past form. *Had to* is therefore used to refer to the past.

*We **had to write** a formal letter in the exam.*

Question form

Must is possible in question forms:

***Must you wear** that horrible dress?*

although *have to* is more common:

*What do we **have to do** for homework?*

B *Have to/Don't have to*

Have to is used to refer to strong obligations imposed by another person rather than by the speaker or writer.

*I **have to be** at work by 8 o'clock. The boss will get angry if I'm late.* (employee to a friend)

Don't have to expresses a lack of obligation.

*I'm glad I **don't have to wear** a suit. It's so hot today.*

C *Need to/Don't need to/Needn't*

Need to is used to express necessity.

*Can we go to the baker's next? **I need to get** some bread.*

Don't need to/needn't express a lack of necessity.
We **don't need to/needn't leave** yet. *It's only 2 o'clock.*

D *Should/Shouldn't* + infinitive without *to*

Should and *shouldn't* are used to express obligation or give advice. *Ought to* can also be used with the same meaning as *should.*

You **ought to/should see** *a doctor about your backache.*

If you're on a diet you **shouldn't drink** *beer.*

E *Be supposed to/Had better*

Be supposed to is used to talk about what you should do because of a rule or because it is expected.

Come on, it's 10 o' clock. You **'re supposed to be** *in bed!*

Had better + infinitive without *to* is used to talk about what you should do because you think it's a good idea.

You **'d better ask** *your dad before you borrow the car.*

Permission

To express permission it is possible to use *can, may* (more formal) or *be allowed to.* In the negative these express lack of permission, or prohibition.

You **can order** *another drink but you* **can't have** *any more chips.*

We **aren't allowed to wear** *trainers to school.*

May is not possible in the past. *Could* and *be allowed to* are possible for general permission.

In my last job we had flexitime so we **could arrive** *more or less when we wanted to.*

Could is not used when referring to a particular situation in the past. Only *be allowed to* is possible.

I **was allowed to** *stay up late last night.*

Let and make

Both these verbs are followed by the infinitive without *to.* *Let* is used to express permission.

My dad never **lets me watch** *that programme.*

Let is not normally used in the passive. *Be allowed to* is used instead.

I **wasn't allowed to go** *to the party alone.*

Make is used to express obligation.

The teacher **made her do** *some extra homework.*

In the passive, *make* is followed by the infinitive with *to.*

He was **made to pay** *for the window he had broken.*

Unit 6

Too and enough

A *Too* means 'more than is necessary or desirable'.

1 *Too* + adjective/adverb

This jumper's **too big.** *Can I try a smaller size?*

2 *Too much/Too many* (+ noun)

I can't eat this. There's **too much salt** *in it.*

There are **too many people** *here. Let's go outside.*

3 *Too* + adverb/adjective (+ *for* + object) + infinitive

It's **too cold to play** *tennis today.*

He spoke **too quickly for me to understand** *him.*

B *Enough* means 'as much as is necessary'

1 Adjective/Adverb + *enough*

Are you **warm enough** *or shall I turn the heating on?*

2 *Enough* + noun

We'll have to stand because there aren't **enough chairs.**

3 *Enough* (+ *for* + object) + infinitive with *to*

I haven't got **enough time to see** *you today.*

Causative *have:* 'to have something done'

1 The structure *have* + object + past participle shows that the action is done for the subject by someone else and not by the subject. The subject causes the action to be done. Compare the following:

I cut my hair. (= I did it myself)

I had my hair cut. (= someone did it for me)

All tenses of *have* are possible, eg:

We've just had our washing machine repaired.

I'm having my eyes tested tomorrow.

2 The same structure can also be used for events (usually unpleasant) which are outside of the speaker's control.

John had his car stolen last week.

3 *Get* can be used instead of *have* in this structure. It is slightly more informal.

Where did you get your photos developed?

Relative clauses

Relative clauses give extra information about something or someone in the main clause.

A Defining relative clauses

Defining relative clauses contain information which is essential for our understanding of the whole sentence.

The man who normally comes to clean our windows is on holiday this month.

He's got a computer program which translates texts from Spanish into English.

In each case, the relative clause identifies which person or thing is being talked about.

Features of defining relative clauses

- No commas are required either at the beginning or the end of the relative clause.

- *That* can be used instead of *who* for people and *which* for things, particularly in spoken English.

	For people	For things
Subject:	*who/that*	*which/that*
Object:	*who/that/whom**	*which/that*
Possessive:	*whose*	*whose*

* *whom* is more formal than *who*

- The relative pronoun can be omitted if it is the object of the verb in the relative clause.

I'm enjoying the book (**which/that**) *you lent me.*

- The relative pronoun cannot be omitted if it is the subject of the verb in the relative clause.

That's the shop assistant **who/that** *served me the last time I came here.*

B Non-defining relative clauses

Non-defining relative clauses contain information which is not essential for our understanding of the sentence. We can identify which person or thing is being talked about without the information in the relative clause.

Their new house, which has five bedrooms and a games room, is much larger than their previous one.

At the party she spoke to Mr Peterson, whose father owned the company she worked for.

Features of non-defining relative clauses

- Commas are required both at the beginning and the end of the relative clause (except when the end of the relative clause is also the end of the sentence).
- *That* cannot be used in place of *who* or *which*.

	For people	**For things**
Subject:	*who*	*which*
Object:	*who/whom*	*which*
Possessive:	*whose*	*whose*

- Relative pronouns cannot be omitted from non-defining relative clauses.

  *Her maths teacher, **who/whom** everyone in the class adored, announced that he was leaving the school.*

- Non-defining relative clauses are more common in written English.
- *Which* can be used in non-defining relative clauses to refer to a whole clause.

  *No one phoned him on his birthday, **which** made him feel rather depressed.*

C Relative clauses and prepositions

1 Prepositions usually come at the end of defining and non-defining relative clauses.

   In defining relative clauses the relative pronoun is usually omitted.

   *The town I grew up **in** has changed a lot since I left.*

   In non-defining relative clauses the relative pronoun is never omitted.

   *Keith Rolf, **who** I used to work with, lives in Paris now.*

2 In more formal English, prepositions often come before the relative pronouns *whom* for people and *which* for things (in which case the pronoun cannot be omitted).

   *We shall be visiting the room **in which** Turner painted some of his greatest works.*

   *The head waiter, **to whom** we addressed our complaint, was not particularly helpful.*

D Relative adverbs: *where*, *when* and *why*

   Where, *when* and *why* can be used in relative clauses after nouns which refer to a place (*where*), a time (*when*) or a reason (*why*).

   Where has the meaning 'in/at which'

Defining:	They've booked a week in that campsite **where** we stayed last year.
Non-defining:	She's in Southlands Hospital, **where** you were born.

   When has the meaning 'on/in which' and can be omitted in defining relative clauses.

Defining:	Do you remember that day (**when**) we went to Rhyl and it snowed?
Non-defining:	I'm going on holiday in September, **when** most people are back at work.

   Why has the meaning 'for which' and can be omitted in defining relative clauses.

Defining:	The reason (**why**) I'm phoning is to ask you for Tina's address.

Unit 7

The present perfect

The present perfect links past events and situations with the present.

1 The present perfect is used:

   a to give news of recent past events which have some relevance to the present.

   *Be careful! **I've just dropped** a glass on the floor.*

   b to describe something that started in the past and continues to the present.

   ***My wife and I have lived** in the same house ever since we got married.*

   c to describe events which occurred at some time between the past and the present. Exactly when they happened is not known or not important.

   ***I've been** to Poland three or four times.*

   d to talk about something which occurred in the past, but in a time period which includes the present.

   ***Judy's boyfriend has phoned** her three times this morning – and it's not even 11 o'clock!*

   e after the expression *it/this/that is the first/second/third, etc time*

   *This is the first time **I've seen** this programme.*

2 Time expressions

   a The present perfect is commonly used with *ever, never, just, recently, so far, still, yet* and *already* when referring to a time period up to now:

   *They haven't booked their holiday **yet**.*

   *I've had three cups of coffee **so far** this morning.*

   b *For* is used with periods of time to show how long something has lasted.

   *I've known Eric **for** twenty years.*

   c *Since* is used with points in time to show when something started.

   *I've had this watch **since** 1984.*

3 The present perfect continuous can be used:

   a to emphasize the duration of a situation or activity.

   It's been snowing all day.

   b to suggest that a situation or activity is temporary.

   My mum's not well, so I've been looking after her.

   c to suggest a situation or activity is incomplete.

   I've been painting the house – that's why it's in a mess.

   d to focus on the repetition of a situation or activity.

   He's been getting into trouble at school a lot recently.

4 The present perfect simple and continuous

   a Both simple and continuous forms of the present perfect can be used to talk about the effects in the present of a past event.

   Your new shoes are ruined! You've been playing football in them, haven't you? (an activity)

   I can't do any sport for a few weeks; I've broken my arm. (a single action)

   b The continuous form is not used if we talk about the number of things that have been completed or the number of times a thing has been done.

   She's eaten six chocolate biscuits.

   She's been eating chocolate biscuits.

   c Stative verbs such as *have* (to possess/own), *think* (to have an opinion), *be, like, believe, understand* and *know* are not normally used in the continuous form.

   We've known each other for a long time. ✓

   We've been knowing each other for a long time. ✗

Contrasting ideas

1 *But* contrasts two ideas in the same sentence.

   *The weather was bad **but** she enjoyed the trip.*

2 *Although* and *though* (informal) are also used to contrast ideas in the same sentence. They can go at the beginning of a sentence or in the middle.

Although the weather was bad, she enjoyed the trip.

*She enjoyed the trip **although** the weather was bad.*

Even used before though emphasizes the contrast.

*They managed to communicate, **even though** they couldn't speak each other's language.*

3 *However* contrasts ideas in two different sentences. It often comes at the beginning of the second sentence and is followed by a comma.

*The weather was bad. **However**, she enjoyed the trip.*

4 *Nevertheless* is a more formal alternative to *however*.

The English aren't normally very emotional people. ***Nevertheless**, they get very excited at sporting events.*

5 *In spite of* and *despite* are both followed by a gerund or a noun. They can go at the beginning of the sentence or in the middle.

*She enjoyed the trip **in spite of** the bad weather.*

***Despite** the fact that the weather was bad, she enjoyed the trip.*

***Despite** the weather being bad, she enjoyed the trip.*

If the subject of the verbs in the two clauses is the same, the gerund can be used immediately after *despite* or *in spite of* without a preceding noun/pronoun.

She played tennis despite feeling ill.

***She** paid for the meal despite **me/my** telling her not to.*

6 *Whereas* and *while* are used to contrast two ideas in the same sentence.

*The first photo shows a child having fun **whereas/while** the second one shows a rather sad man on his own.*

Expressing preferences

A *Prefer*

1 *Prefer* + gerund + *to* + gerund

This is usually used to talk about general preferences.

I prefer playing basketball to watching it.

2 *Would prefer* + infinitive with *to* + *rather than* + infinitive without *to*

This is normally used to talk about preferences on a specific occasion.

I'd prefer to walk to school today rather than go by bus.

B *Would rather*

would rather + infinitive without *to* + *than* + infinitive without *to* (same meaning as *would prefer to*)

I'd rather not talk about it at the moment.

I'd rather do nothing all day than go to school.

Unit 8

The future

A Predictions and expectations

Will + infinitive without *to* can be used to make predictions or talk about expectations for the future. These can be introduced by verbs such as *believe, expect, hope* and *think*. Adverbs such as *definitely, (almost) certainly* and *probably* may also be used; they come after *will* and before *won't*.

*United **will probably win** the league again this year.*

*'Where's Anne?' 'I expect she**'ll be** here soon.'*

*She definitely **won't pass** her exams; she's too lazy.*

Alternatives to *will*

1 The following structures can be used to talk about the probability of something happening in the future.

be (un)likely + infinitive with *to*

may/might/could well + infinitive without *to*

*There **may/could/might well be** a cure for cancer in the future. (= there will probably be)*

*They've got a map with them so they**'re unlikely (not likely) to get** lost. (= they probably won't get lost)*

NB *may well* is not usual in the negative.

2 *May/might/could* + infinitive without *to* can be used to talk about the possibility of something happening in the future.

*We **may/might/could see** fewer cars in the future.*

*We **may not/might not have** time to see the exhibition.*

NB *could not* expresses impossibility; see Unit 9.

B Other future forms

1 In addition to making predictions about the future, *will* is also used to talk about:

a decisions made at the moment of speaking, including offers and requests.

***We'll babysit** for you if you want to go out.*

*The phone's ringing. **Will you answer** it?*

b future facts; events which the speaker knows or believes are certain to happen.

***Summer will be** here soon.*

2 *Going to* + infinitive is used to talk about:

a predictions based on present evidence.

*Look at those clouds – **it's going to rain** soon.*

b intentions or plans.

***I'm going to stay** in tonight and read my book.*

Modal verbs can be used to express possible intentions.

***I may/might go** walking in the mountains tomorrow.*

3 The present continuous is used to talk about future arrangements which have already been made.

***Sue and Alan are getting** married on June 21st.*

4 The present simple is used:

a to talk about timetabled or scheduled events.

*The film **starts** at 9.15, just after the news.*

b to refer to the future after time linkers such as *when, before, after, until, by the time, as soon as.*

*Give me a call **as soon as you arrive**.*

5 The future continuous, *will* + *be* + *-ing*, is used to talk about actions or events which will be in progress at a certain time in the future.

*This time next week **I'll be lying** on the beach.*

6 The future perfect simple, *will* + *have* + past participle, is used to talk about actions and events that will be completed by a certain time in the future.

*By the end of today **we'll have driven** over 250 kms.*

7 The future perfect continuous, *will* + *have* + *been* + *-ing*, is used to talk about actions and events which continue to a certain time in the future.

*On 21 May **I'll have been living** here for exactly 10 years.*

8 *Be about to* + infinitive/*be on the point of* + gerund can be used to talk about the immediate future.

*Can I phone you back? I'm just **about to have** lunch.*

*The police say **they are on the point of solving** the crime.*

Unit 9

Modal verbs of speculation

A Certainty

If we are fairly certain about something, *must, can't* and *couldn't* can be used to express this.

1 For present situations the modal verbs *must, can't* and *couldn't* are followed by the infinitive without *to*.

'I haven't slept for two days.' *'You **must be** exhausted!'*

*Everyone here is wearing a football scarf, so we **can't be** very far from the stadium.*

The continuous infinitive can also be used.

*Why is he wearing his uniform? He **couldn't be going** to school – it's Saturday today.*

2 For past situations we use the same modal verbs + *have* + past participle.

*I can't find my book. **I must have left** it at school.*

*This composition isn't very good. You **can't have spent** very long on it.*

The continuous form can also be used.

'And then I lost control of the car.' *'You **must have been driving** too fast.'*

NB *mustn't* is not normally used when speculating about present or past situations.

B Possibility

If we are not certain about something but think it is possible, we use *may (not), might (not)* or *could*.

1 For present situations these modal verbs are followed by the infinitive without *to*. The continuous infinitive is also possible.

'Ed's not answering my emails.' *'He **might be** on holiday.'*

*He **could be telling** the truth, but it's hard to believe.*

2 For past situations we use the same modal verbs + *have* + past participle (the continuous form is possible).

*I think we **may have taken** the wrong road. This doesn't look familiar.*

'Sean looked a little sad.' *'He **might not have been feeling** very well.'*

NB It is not possible to use *can* when speculating about present or past situations.

Question tags

A Form

Question tags are formed using either a modal verb, an auxiliary verb or the verb *to be* + subject pronoun. A negative tag is normally used with a positive statement, and a positive tag with a negative statement.

1 If the verb *to be* appears in the statement, it is repeated in the question tag.

*He **isn't** married, **is he**?*

*I'm late again, **aren't I**? (not **amn't I**?)*

2 If an auxiliary verb or a modal verb appears in the statement, it is repeated in the question tag.

*You've been to Warsaw before, **haven't you**?*

3 If the verb in the statement is a full verb (ie there is no modal verb or auxiliary verb), an appropriate form of the auxiliary verb *do* is required in the question tag.

*You **bought** it last year, **didn't you**?*

4 'Will you?' and 'can you?' are used with imperatives. 'Would you?' and 'could you?' are more formal alternatives.

*Open the window, **will/can/would/could you**?*

'Will you?' is used after a negative imperative.

*Don't forget to write, **will you**?*

5 If *let's* appears in the statement, the question tag 'shall we?' is used.

***Let's** go home, **shall we**?*

6 If the statement contains negative words such as *nothing* or *nobody*, the question tag is positive.

*Nothing frightens you, **does it**?*

NB the pronoun *they* is used with *nobody/no one, somebody/someone* and *everybody/everyone*.

B Use and intonation

We can use question tags to ask a real question if we are unsure if the statement is true or not. In this case we say the question tag with rising intonation.

I've met you before, haven't I?

We can also use question tags when we expect someone to agree with a statement. In this case we say the question tag with falling intonation.

She can't sing very well, can she?

Unit 10

The passive

A Form

The verb *to be* + past participle.

Present simple:	*Goods worth £750 million **are stolen** from shops each year.*
Present continuous:	*A man **is being questioned** in connection with the robbery.*
Present perfect:	*Photos of the suspects **have been put** up around the town.*
Past simple:	*He **was taken** away in a van.*
Past continuous:	*The burglar didn't realize he **was being filmed**.*
Past perfect:	*Two people **had been mugged** there on the previous day.*
Future simple:	*All football supporters **will be searched** at the airport.*
Infinitive:	*He is hoping **to be released** from prison next week.*
Gerund:	*I can't even remember **being hit** on the head.*
Modal verbs:	*He **should be sentenced** to life imprisonment.*

B Use

The passive is used to focus attention on the person or thing affected by the action, rather than on the agent (the 'doer' of the action). If we are interested in the agent, we use the preposition *by*:

*Sue and Mark were brought up **by their grandparents**.*

When we talk about the instrument used by the agent to do the action, we use the preposition *with*:

*He was hit on the head **with a vase**.*

The agent is not usually included when:

1 it is clear from the context who the agent is.

Colin was arrested for dangerous driving. (by the police)

2 we don't know who the agent is or was.

My car was stolen yesterday afternoon.

3 when the agent is not important.

Stamps are often sold in supermarkets in England.

4 The passive is also used in formal notices:

Food may not be consumed on the premises.

C Passive constructions with the infinitive

The infinitive can be used after the passive of verbs such as: *believe, consider, expect, know, say, think*
The President is expected to arrive at 9.30 am.

The perfect infinitive (*have* + past participle) is used to refer to the past.

15 people are known to have died in the accident.

Past necessity

A *Needn't have* + past participle

This structure is used to talk about an action which was unnecessary. It indicates that the subject performed the action.

I needn't have prepared so much food for the party; everyone had eaten before they came. (I prepared lots of food but I realized afterwards that it wasn't necessary.)

B *Didn't need to* + infinitive

This structure is used to talk about an action which was unnecessary. It usually indicates that the subject did not perform the action.

I didn't need to prepare very much food for the party; everyone said they would bring something to eat. (I didn't prepare lots of food as I knew it wasn't necessary.)

Unit 11

Conditionals

Conditional sentences contain a conditional clause (introduced by words such as *if*, *as long as* and *unless*) and a main clause.

If the conditional clause comes before the main clause, a comma is needed (as in this sentence).

A comma is not needed if the conditional clause comes after the main clause (as in this sentence).

A Zero conditional

if + present simple or imperative

We use the zero conditional to talk about situations which are always true. *If* has the same meaning as *when, whenever* or *every time* in such sentences.

Everyday situations:	*My eyes hurt if I spend too long on the computer.*
Scientific facts:	*If you mix blue and yellow, you get green.*
Instructions: (*if* + imperative)	*If you don't know the answer, make an intelligent guess.*

B First conditional

if + present simple, *will* + infinitive without *to*

We use the first conditional to talk about possible situations and their probable results in the future.

She'll be very happy if you phone her.

It can be used for warnings, promises and threats.

I'll send you to bed if you don't behave yourself.

If you pass your driving test, I'll take you out for a meal.

Modal verbs can be used in the main clause in place of *will*. *May, might* and *could*, for example, introduce possible results if a condition is met.

If I finish my homework early, I might call you.

C Second conditional

if + past simple, *would* + infinitive without *to*

We use the second conditional to talk about imaginary, unlikely or impossible situations in the present or future.

If I knew the answer to number six, I would tell you.

If I had wings, I'd fly south in winter.

First or second conditional? Notice the difference in meaning between these two sentences:

First Conditional:
If they give me a pay rise, I'll buy a new car. (I feel there is a real possibility that they will give me a pay rise.)

Second Conditional:
If they gave me a pay rise, I'd buy a new car. (I feel it is less likely that they will give me a pay rise.)

The second conditional can also be used to give advice.

If I were you, I'd complain to the manager.

Both *was* and *were* are possible in the conditional clause after the subject pronouns *I/he/she/it*. *Was* is more common in spoken English.

If he were a little taller, he'd be an excellent goalkeeper.

The modal verbs *might* and *could* can be used in the main clause to indicate possible results.

If you worked a bit harder you might have more success.

D Third conditional

if + past perfect, *would/might/could have* + past participle.

We use the third conditional to talk about imaginary situations in the past.

If we hadn't taken a map, we would have got lost. (We took a map, so we didn't get lost.)

E Mixed conditional

if + past perfect, *would* + infinitive without *to*

Mixed conditionals are a combination of a second and a third conditional. They can express an imaginary past event and a possible or probable present result.

If you'd listened to my advice, you would not be in this situation now.

F Alternative words for *if*

As long as, provided (that), providing (that) and *on condition (that)* can be used in place of *if* to emphasize the condition.

I'll lend you £10 as long as you give it back tomorrow.

We'll go out in the boat tomorrow afternoon provided the sea isn't too rough.

So, neither and *nor*

A Use

To indicate that we have the same feelings, behaviour or abilities as others, we can use *so* (positive statements), and *neither* or *nor* (negative statements).

B Form

so/neither/nor + (modal) auxiliary verb or the verb *to be* + subject noun or pronoun

The rules for deciding which verb is used after *so, neither* or *nor* are the same as those for question tags (Unit 9). The verb is always positive. The clause with *so, neither* or *nor* can appear in the same sentence as the main clause, or it can be said by a different speaker:

She can't play a musical instrument and nor can I.

'I'll phone him tonight.' 'So will I.'

'My mum isn't working tomorrow.' 'Neither is mine.'

C If our feelings, behaviour or abilities are different from those of others, we use the following structure:

subject + (modal) auxiliary or the verb *to be*

He doesn't eat meat but I do.

'We're allowed to wear jeans to school.' 'We aren't.'

Unit 12

Direct and reported speech

When reporting what someone has said or written we can use either direct speech or reported speech.

When we use direct speech we report the exact words which someone has used.

'I'm staying here tomorrow,' said Heather.

When we use reported speech, changes may have to be made to verb tenses, pronouns and certain words indicating place and time.

*Heather said **she was** staying **there the next day**.*

A Reporting statements

1 The following changes are usually made to verbs. In each case the verb 'moves back' one tense.

Direct speech		Reported speech
Present simple	→	Past simple
'I work in an office,' he said.		*He said he worked in an office.*
Present continuous	→	Past continuous
'We are going away on holiday,' she said.		*She said they were going away on holiday.*
Present perfect	→	Past perfect
'I've known her for a long time,' he said.		*He said he'd known her for a long time.*
Present perfect cont.	→	Past perfect continuous
'He's been playing tennis,' she said.		*She said he'd been playing tennis.*
Past simple	→	Past perfect
'I saw Nigel in town,' he said.		*He said that he'd seen Nigel in town.*
Past continuous	→	Past perfect continuous
'We were trying to help him,' she said.		*She said they'd been trying to help him.*

NB the modal verbs *will*, *must*, *may* and *can* change to *would*, *had to*, *might* and *could*.

2 No changes are made in the verb tense:

a if the verb in the direct speech is in the past perfect.

'He had never spoken about it before,' she said.

She said he had never spoken about it before.

b if the direct speech contains one of the following modal verbs: *would*, *might*, *could*, *should*, *ought to*

'You should go to the doctor's,' he said.

He said I should go to the doctor's.

c if the statement being reported is still true.

'I like fish,' she said.   *She said she likes fish.*

d if the reporting verb is in the present.

'It's 40° in Athens at the moment.' (Jeremy to his mother on the phone)

Jeremy says it's 40° in Athens at the moment. (Jeremy's mother to her husband)

3 Pronouns in direct speech may have to change when we use reported speech.

*'I'll see **you** soon,' said Peter.*

*Peter said **he** would see **me** soon.*

4 The following changes may also need to be made to words indicating place and time.

Direct speech		Reported speech
now	→	*then*
today	→	*that day*
this morning	→	*that morning*
tomorrow	→	*the next/following day*
next week	→	*the next/following week*
yesterday	→	*the day before, the previous day*
two days ago	→	*two days before/earlier*
last week	→	*the week before, the previous week*
here	→	*there*
come	→	*go*

5 *This*, *that*, *these* and *those* may change to *the*.

*'**That** book you lent me is really boring,' he said.*

*He said **the** book I had lent him was really boring.*

B Reporting verbs for statements

1 *tell* is used with a direct object

He told me (that) he was getting married.

2 *say* and *explain* are used without a direct object.

She said (that) she was ill. (not *She said me…*)

They can, however, be used with an indirect object.

I explained to them (that) I'd left my passport at home. (not *I explained them…*)

3 Some reporting verbs can be used with an infinitive.

a verb + object noun/pronoun + infinitive with *to*
advise, ask, encourage, invite, order, persuade, recommend, remind, tell, urge, warn

'Don't forget to phone Jim,' he told her.

He reminded her to phone Jim.

b verb + infinitive with *to*
offer, promise, refuse, threaten

'I'll help you mend the car if you like.'

He offered to help me mend the car.

4 The following patterns can be used after both *recommend* and *suggest*:

He recommended/suggested (that) I (should) eat less sugar.

She recommended/suggested joining a youth club.

The infinitive with *to* can only be used after *recommend*.

C Reporting questions

When we report questions we make the same changes to verb tenses, pronouns and words indicating place and time as we do when we report statements. The following changes are also made:

Auxiliary verbs:	auxiliary verbs *do*, *does* and *did* are omitted
Word order:	is the same as that of a statement
Punctuation:	question marks are not used
Yes/No questions:	if there is no question word (*what*, *where*, *who* etc) in the direct question, we use *if* or *whether*.

'Does she smoke?'

He asked if/whether she smoked.

Ask and *tell*

Each of these verbs can be used in two different ways in reported speech.

1 *Ask*

  a Requests (*ask* + object + infinitive with *to*)
  'Can you help me, please?'
  He asked me to help him.

  b Questions
  'Can you ride a horse?'
  She asked me if I could ride a horse.

2 *Tell*

  a Commands (*tell* + object + infinitive with *to*)
  'Put your coat on.'
  She told him to put his coat on.

  b Statement
  'I can't find my coat.'
  He told her (that) he couldn't find his coat.

Countable and uncountable nouns

A Countable nouns are nouns which can be counted.
  one plate   two cats   five chairs

B Uncountable nouns cannot be counted. They are not used with the indefinite article (*a/an*), they do not have a plural and they are used with a singular verb form.
  *Can you get **some bread**?*

  ***A lot of damage** was done to the building.*

  The following nouns are usually uncountable: *news, accommodation, health, progress, advice, homework, research, damage, information, spaghetti, English, work, knowledge, travel, furniture, luggage, weather, graffiti.*

C Nouns which are both countable and uncountable
  1 Many words for food and drink can be used both countably and uncountably.
  I've made a chocolate cake. (C)
  Could I have some more cake? (U)
  Would you like another coffee? (C) (= cup of coffee)
  I don't like coffee. (U)

  2 A word used countably may have a very different meaning from its countable version.
  *I'd like a double **room** for one night.* (C) (= hotel room)
  *There's no more **room** on this bus.* (U) (= space)

D Making uncountable nouns countable
  1 Some uncountable nouns have countable equivalents with similar meanings.
  *There isn't much **work** in this town.* (U)
  *There aren't many **jobs** in this town.* (C)
  *My job involves a lot of business **travel**.* (U)
  *I have to make a lot of business **trips**.* (C)

  2 Some other uncountable nouns can be made countable by using *piece(s) of* or *item(s) of*.
  *Let me give you a piece of **advice**.*
  *Two items of **news** caught my attention.*

  3 Certain other expressions are used with words for food and drink: *a plate of spaghetti, a pinch of salt, a loaf of bread, a slice of cake/toast, a spoonful of sugar, a bar of chocolate, a carton of milk, a jar of jam.*

E **1** Words used with countable nouns: *a/an, few, a few, many, a large number of, each, every, several.*
  2 Words used with uncountable nouns: *little, a little, much, a great deal of, a large amount of.*
  3 Words used with countable *and* uncountable nouns: *some, any, no, a lot of, lots of, all, plenty of, most.*

  Little and *few*
  These two words have more negative meanings. They mean 'not much/many' or 'not as much/many as desired or expected'.

Sue has made little progress since the beginning of term.
There were very few people at the concert.
A little and *a few*
These have more positive meanings. They mean 'some' or 'more than expected'.

I've managed to save a little money to buy Al a present.
I've still got a few eggs – enough to make an omelette.
Plenty of
This means 'a lot of' or 'more than enough'.
Don't hurry – we've got plenty of time.

Unit 13

Expressing ability

A *Can* and *be able to*
  Can and *be able to* are both used to express ability. However, *can* only has present tense (*can*) and past tense (*could*) forms. If another form of the verb is required, *be able to* is used.

Present:	*She can/is able to speak three languages fluently.*
Past:	*She could/was able to read when she was two.*
Infinitive:	*I'd like to be able to ski.*
Present perfect:	*He's never been able to save money.*
Will future:	*She'll be able to drive to work when she passes her test.*

B Present ability
  We use *can* or *be able to* to talk about present ability. *Be able to* is more formal than *can*.
  I can run faster than you.
  He is able to speak without moving his lips.

  The negative form of *can* is *can't* or *cannot*. To form the negative of *be able to*, *not* is used before *able*. You can also use *be unable to*.
  I cannot understand why she married him.
  Many of my students aren't able/are unable to pronounce the word 'taught' correctly.

  Be capable of + gerund can also be used to express ability. It means to have the ability, capacity or potential to do something.
  The team has some excellent players and is capable of winning the championship.

  The negative form *be incapable of* + gerund can be used or *not* can be placed before *capable*.
  She is incapable/isn't capable of looking after herself.

C Past ability
  1 When we talk about general ability in the past, both *could* and *was/were able to* are possible.
  She could sing really well when she was a child.
  My grandfather could play the trumpet when he was 90.
  Be capable of can also be used in the past.
  Joe wasn't capable of making toast without burning it.

  2 When we talk about ability to do something on one occasion in the past, *could* is not possible. Instead, *was/were able to*, *managed to* + infinitive or *succeeded in* + gerund have to be used.
  I managed to/was able to speak to Frank last night.
  Firefighters succeeded in controlling the flames.

  However, *could* can be used for ability on one occasion when it is used with verbs of the senses: *see, smell, hear, feel, sense, taste.*
  I knew my wife had arrived; I could smell her perfume.

When we talk about inability to do something on one occasion in the past, *couldn't*, *weren't/wasn't able to*, *didn't manage to* and *didn't succeed in* are all possible.

I couldn't do the homework; it was too difficult.

I didn't manage to/wasn't able to repair the washing machine.

Verbs followed by preposition + gerund

1 These verbs can be followed by *for* + gerund:
apologize, arrest, blame, forgive, praise, punish, tell off, thank

Have you apologized to Jean for breaking her pen?

2 These verbs can be followed by *from* + gerund:
discourage, prevent, stop

The police prevented him from leaving the country.

3 *Congratulate* and *insist* are followed by *on* + gerund.

He insisted on paying for the meal.

4 *Warn* can be followed by *against* + gerund.

We tried to warn him against driving in the snow.

Warn can also be used with *of* or *about* + noun.

Posters have been put up warning people of the dangers of smoking.

Unit 14

Hypothetical situations

A *Wish* and *if only*

W*ish* or *if only* can express how we would like things to be different if we had the power to change them.

1 Present states

We use *wish/if only* + past simple to express wishes about present states. Stative verbs such as *be, have, know* and *understand* are used.

I wish I was/were taller.

If only I knew how to play the guitar.

2 Present actions

We use *wish/if only* + *would* when we want something to happen or someone to do something. Active verbs (verbs describing actions) are used.

I wish you would turn your music down.

If only this wind would stop blowing.

Wish/If only + *would* is used if we want to express irritation at other peoples' actions or behaviour.

I wish you would stop tapping your foot.

Wish/If only + past simple can also be used if the action occurs habitually.

I wish you didn't (or wouldn't) smoke so much.

3 Present ability

Wish/If only + *would* is used for events which are outside of our control. Consequently, we do not normally say 'I wish I would...'. Instead, we use 'I wish I could...' to indicate our inability to change things.

I wish I could remember where I put my keys.

4 Wishes for the future

Wish/If only + *would* or *could* can be used to express wishes for the future. This use of *wish* suggests that the action will probably not happen.

I wish I could go on holiday with you in summer.
(I know that I can't go with you.)

If there is more possibility that the action will happen, we use *hope*.

I hope I can go on holiday with you in summer. (I don't know if I can or not.)

5 Past situations

We use *wish/if only* + past perfect to express wishes and regrets about the past.

I wish I hadn't left school when I was 16.

The following structures can also be used to express wishes and regrets about the past.

a Third and mixed conditionals (see Unit 11)

If I hadn't been so tired, this wouldn't have happened.

b *should have* + past participle

We should have got the train. This traffic's terrible.

B Would rather

We use *would rather* + past simple when we want someone else to do something in the present or future.

I'd rather you went to get some bread now.

He said he'd rather we didn't arrive too early tomorrow.

If the subject of *would rather* and the following verb is the same, we usually use the infinitive without *to* (see Unit 7).

We'd rather sit in the garden than go to the beach.

C *It's time*

We use *it's (high/about) time* + past simple when we want something to happen or be done now. It implies that the action should have been done already.

It's time you went to bed. You've got school tomorrow.

Unit 15

Expressing purpose

There are several different ways of expressing purpose (saying why people do things).

1 Infinitive with *to*

*I'm writing **to thank** you for the lovely present you sent.*

The negative infinitive, *not to do something*, cannot be used to express purpose.

2 *In order (not) to* + infinitive

*She wore dark glasses **in order not to be recognized**.*

3 *So as (not) to* + infinitive

*We set off early **so as to avoid** the traffic.*

4 *So (that)* + clause

a Future meaning: *so (that)* + *can/will*/present simple
*I'm going to save some money **so I can go** away on holiday.*

*I'll take an umbrella **so that I don't/won't get** wet.*

b Past meaning: *so (that)* + *could/would*
*I sat near the front **so that I could see** the board better.*

5 *In case* + clause

If we do something to prepare for a possible situation or problem we use *in case* + present simple/past simple.

a Future meaning: *in case* + present simple
*Here are some crisps **in case you get** hungry later on.*

b Past meaning: *in case* + past simple
*He made a copy **in case he lost** the original.*

6 *In case* and *if*

Note the difference in meaning between *in case* and *if*:

I'll take my umbrella if it rains. (= I'll take my umbrella only if it is raining when I leave the house.)

I'll take my umbrella in case it rains. (= I'll take it as a precaution, even if it isn't raining when I leave the house.)

Listening scripts

Unit 1 (Page 7)

🔘 1.1–1.5

FCE Part 3 – Multiple matching

Speaker 1

After we got the invitation my mum and I kept having big rows about what I was going to wear for the big event. She's always criticizing me for my taste in clothes and she'd bought me this long, bright red dress to wear on the day. Of course, I refused. I went instead in a short black skirt, trainers and a sports top, thinking I'd look really cool and trendy. But, of course, when we got to the church and I saw all the other guests in their smart new clothes and expensive hats I just felt really, really stupid and embarrassed. The bride and groom looked quite surprised when they saw me so I spent most of the time at the reception trying to avoid them.

Speaker 2

We really had no other option but to send her home to get changed, dye her hair back and take out the nose stud. We have rules and the rules are there to prepare young people for the reality of the world of work. I don't know of many jobs where you could turn up with shabby old clothes, green hair and a pierced nose. We insist on uniform from the first day until the last, and that includes sitting your GCSE exams. It's unfair on other candidates who respect the regulations, and distracting for them at a time when they need maximum concentration.

Speaker 3

Indeed, attitudes to women were already beginning to change. In 1919, the young French star Suzanne Lenglen caused a sensation at the British championships by wearing a calf-length, sleeveless dress. Her unconventional, yet practical clothing shocked spectators who were used to seeing women play in the long heavy dresses which were typical of that period. As a result, Lenglen attracted the kind of attention from the world's press which was normally reserved for the stars of the silent movies. She silenced her critics, however, by beating her opponents and going on to win several major titles.

Speaker 4

He clearly has ability. You only have to look at his examination results to see that. And he used to live in France which means he probably wouldn't mind changing countries, if we needed him to. No, what concerns me is his appearance. If he's prepared to turn up for something as important as this, wearing what can only be described as casual clothes, what would he be like with our clients? If he really is a serious candidate and we decide to take him on, then he will have to get used to wearing something a little more formal.

Speaker 5

They had to have their little joke, didn't they. 'Jane's having a little celebration at her house for her "coming of age" and she wants everyone to go in fancy dress.' That's what they said. So I thought about it for ages, what I was going to go as and everything. I spent more time thinking about my costume than about what present I was going to get for Jane. Of course, when I turned up at the house dressed as Coco the Clown and everybody else was wearing normal clothes, I don't know who was more surprised, me or Jane.

Unit 2 (Page 15)

🔘 1.6

FCE Part 2 – Sentence completion

I = Interviewer   B = Brad Andrews

I: With us today in the studio we have Brad Andrews, one of the most famous names in dance music and club DJ-ing of the moment. Brad, why are club DJs so popular these days?

B: DJ-ing has changed an awful lot since the seventies. People used to go to discos and clubs to drink, talk or pick each other up. Now they come for the music, so whether you have a good time or not depends very much on the skills of the DJ.

I: Do you really need that much skill to put on a few records?

B: It's not that simple. I often operate three turntables at once, sometimes using one or two CD players as well. A lot of DJs are talented musicians, because you need a great deal of co-ordination to play with the records and use these huge decks we have nowadays. The job of DJ-ing is mostly about mixing tracks, using several records at once to create a totally whole new sound. On one record I might use just the high notes and sounds, and combine that with the bass on another record. Then I'll bring in a third one with the bass and treble turned off and use it to mix in vocals or another drum. It's a complex business.

I: And from what I hear, a well paid one, too. Would you mind telling us how much you earn for a single gig?

B: There are probably about three or four DJs in the country earning up to ten thousand pounds for a three-hour gig, that much I can tell you. But you have to understand this is an extremely demanding job. People go to see their favourite DJs like fans go to see bands, except top DJs play live gigs every weekend and not just three or four weeks in the year. Dedicated clubbers will often follow a DJ around the country, or...or even the world. People come from Paris to London just to spend Saturday night in a club, before going back on the train on Sunday morning.

I: Does a gig require much preparation?

B: You're dead right it does. I arrange and build a set at a club like I would do in a concert on stage, or if I was recording a single in the studio. You're basically composing a three-hour piece of music. It's as if you're taking people on a journey, and you want them to enjoy it. I also need to clear my mind before I get out there and do my stuff, so I use a form of meditation to get myself ready for a gig.

I: Looking ahead now Brad, could you tell us what the future of dance music is. How do you think it will develop in the next few years?

B: Well, it's interesting to think that here we are at the beginning of the twenty-first century, still using the old-fashioned vinyl records on old-fashioned turntables to create sophisticated sounds. But obviously computer programmes can now be used to put together a dance track in the same way that I described earlier, and of course much quicker. That could well be the way ahead for DJs. Another trend now is for established, big-name bands to ask DJs to rearrange their music in order to attract a younger audience.

I: A bright future indeed, then. We'll take a break now, but don't go away. Brad's going to do a bit of live DJ-ing for us here on Radio Perfect …

Unit 2 (Page 21)

🔘 **1.7**

FCE Part 4 – Multiple choice

I = Interviewer   L = Liz

I: In today's edition of 'Sports Showcase' we talk to 19-year-old Liz Harris, one of the country's rising stars in the fast-growing sport of snowboarding. How long have you been into snowboarding, Liz?

L: I first did it when I was on holiday with my parents. When I was younger I used to go skiing every year with them and then one year I tried snowboarding, and I haven't skied since then. That was five years ago.

I: And what's the achievement that you're most proud of so far?

L: I suppose it has to be when I entered my first international competition this year. I came first in the Big Air event and won some money.

I: Let's hope you can go on winning! Would you say, Liz, that there are any particular qualities or strengths you need to have to be a snowboarder?

L: Good co-ordination and balance helps, but you don't have to born with it. If you practise for a few days, you'll get it anyway, even if you're not naturally sporty.

I: And have you ever had any nasty falls?

L: I hurt my back a few years ago on a dry slope. I was doing a jump and I fell really badly, but I didn't break anything. So far I've been really lucky, unlike my friends, who've all had bad injuries. Broken limbs, that kind of thing. No doubt I'll break an arm or a leg soon! It's just a question of time.

I: How many boys are there compared with girls who snowboard?

L: There are more guys, that's for sure, but it's a lot more even now. When I first started snowboarding you hardly ever saw any girls, but now there are loads of them. Not as many as the guys, but almost.

I: And how do the male snowboarders treat the girls?

L: Well, as far as my friends are concerned, they couldn't care less what sex you are. But there are certain people that think girls are rubbish, and that they shouldn't get paid as much as guys. On the whole, though, spectators have got used to seeing girls on the slopes.

I: You're professional, aren't you, but you don't get paid.

L: No, I get a few hundred pounds from some of my sponsors just to help me to pay for my lift pass. They also give me a few boards a year and then, you know, when I get photos in a magazine on the board it's basically a free advert for the company. So, yeah, all of my equipment is given to me and that's very useful of course. But I usually just save up the money in the summer and then go and spend it all riding in the winter.

I: What sort of advice would you give to a girl who wanted to take up snow-boarding?

L: If you can't get out to the Alps, then try going along to your local dry slope, where you can get lessons and hire equipment, or you could try the Cardiff Snow Dome, which is like a big indoor fridge with real snow. So wrap up warm because it can get quite cold in there. Anywhere in Britain, though, is fine really. There are dry slopes all over the place.

I: We hear you've been doing some modelling work as well. Is that right?

L: Yes, I have. I was on the cover of a fashion magazine a couple of months ago and I'm hopefully going to get some more work because of that. I didn't actually get paid for doing it. But, of course, it's great exposure, and any part-time modelling work now could be useful for the future.

I: You mean, you might go on to become a full-time model?

L: Who knows? If my luck runs out with the snowboarding, then why not? We'll just have to see.

I: Well, good luck for the moment with the snowboarding, Liz, and we'll certainly be looking out for you on the catwalk.

Unit 3 (Page 31)

🔘 **1.8–1.12**

FCE Part 3 – Multiple matching

Speaker 1
They last for about eight hours, which is about all you need them for really, even during the winter months when the nights are much longer of course. They're absolutely marvellous. Each one has a solar panel, which stores energy during the day, and then they come on as soon as it gets dark. When we moved into the area, we were a little worried about security, so we put them all along the driveway. They certainly seem to keep the burglars away. They also help you to see your way safely back to the front door if you come back after a good night out.

Speaker 2
An amazing gadget. It's solar powered, so it doesn't need batteries. You just attach it to a box which has solar panels on top and leave it by the window. It'll charge itself in a couple of hours – as long as it's sunny, of course! It's handy to have round the house for when you have a power cut and you can't see what you're doing, and it's ideal for camping too. Just leave it outside the tent in the afternoon and it's ready for you to use when you need it later on.

Speaker 3
We ordered it off the Internet. An American company. They said it was the latest in environmentally-friendly appliances. No batteries, no fuel, just sunlight. Take it on camping trips, they said, and enjoy delicious al fresco meals. Use it outside at home, they said, and keep the kitchen cool. What a waste of money. It keeps the kitchen cool alright, but when you live in a country which hardly sees the sun all year, it keeps the food cool, too. It would have been better to order the fridge.

Speaker 4
This one looks good! Clockwork and solar-powered and it comes in translucent red or blue plastic. There's a photo of one here. Cool! A bit expensive, though – sixty quid. Anyway, it says here: 'As well as a handle to wind it up, it comes equipped with a solar panel which automatically takes over when the machine is placed in direct sunlight. Its waterproof beatbox is perfect for the beach.' It also says it's got headphones if you're worried about noise pollution. Can't see why you would be, though, can you?

Speaker 5
Solar-assisted, really. I mean, you still need batteries, but the tiny solar cell means you can use the playback without running them down. Cost an arm and a leg, mind you, but as far as I'm concerned it was worth every penny. I can plug it into my PC and the images are just fantastic. Really clear. Do you want to see where I went on holiday?

Unit 3 (Page 34)

🔘 **1.13**

FCE Part 4 – Multiple choice

P = Female presenter   K = Keith Wells

P: My guest today is robot scientist Keith Wells. Keith's company, *ELA Robotics*, hit the news last year with their *Home Help* robot, the first of its kind to be able to perform more than one domestic task. What are you working on now, Keith?

K: I can't really tell you that, I'm afraid. It's not that I don't want to, it's just that we've all been given our instructions and signed an agreement not to give anything away until it actually comes on to the market. I don't quite know when that will be, but probably some time early next year.

P: OK, well we'll look forward to that. In the meantime, perhaps you could tell us what you think are the most important applications of robots in our lives. Why are they useful?

K: Well, they help us to do what we call 'the 3 Ds'. That's anything which is dull, dirty or dangerous. They can be used in the home or in the car manufacturing industry, to do dull or monotonous work; they're used for doing dirty jobs like mining or cleaning toxic waste; and then they have applications in the military or in the dangerous business of space travel. Of course, that's not an exhaustive list, but it gives you an idea of the range of different uses they have – and also of the variety involved in my line of work.

P: Yes, indeed. Let's talk if we may about one area in particular, though, the more humanoid robots, the ones with a recognizable human form. What are the latest developments there?

K: Yes, the ones being built now are able to see, hear, touch and even smell and taste. In the future they should also be able to display a range of emotions. They might feel happy for example that they have carried out a domestic task particularly well, or sad and guilty because they haven't. That way they will have a reason to go on doing the same task in the future, either to match their last performance or to improve on it. A robot with emotions is a robot with goals.

P: Amazing. But isn't all this a little bit worrying – robots with emotions? Isn't there a danger of science fiction becoming science fact, with robots taking over?

K: Yes, unfortunately, robots do get rather a bad press sometimes, don't they? Particularly in films and video games where they're either objects of humour and ridicule which we laugh at or else they're menacing characters which threaten to destroy the whole human race. But no, there is actually an ethical code which sets out what we can and can't do in robot design – and one thing we won't do is allow ourselves to lose control over our creations.

P: Don't you think, though, that robots will make us lazy, that we'll no longer want to do anything that requires any effort?

K: I think the car's already done that to us. It's made us physically very lazy. We don't walk so much as we used to and our bodies have suffered as a result. I think robots could well have the same effect on our brains. If we let intelligent robots do all of our thinking for us, there is a danger we won't be able to make any of our own decisions, that we'll become mentally lazy. And that, I think, is just as worrying.

P: Do you really think that the day will come when most homes have their own robot?

K: If you think back to just twenty-five years ago, few of us then would have predicted that we'd soon have a personal computer in our home, be logging onto the Internet and downloading hundreds of songs on to a thing called an MP3 player. So why shouldn't we all have robots? The truth is that we've been talking about robots for nearly a century and their development hasn't been quite as fast as we thought it would be, but now with advanced computer technology available, that should all change very soon.

P: How soon?

K: Well, it's changing already. The first humanoid robots at the end of the 1990s could do very little, then later models learnt to sit down and stand up, then talk, walk around, dance and so on. It's rather like watching a child grow. Through television and other media, the public is slowly growing accustomed to the idea of robots as a reality, and when they eventually become widely available, people will be ready for them.

P: Thank you, Keith. It's been fascinating having you on the programme.

Unit 4 (Page 46)

🔘 **1.14–1.21**

FCE Part 1 – Multiple choice

One

I used to think he was so good looking – those sparkling blue eyes and that sexy smile – although now of course the wrinkles have taken over and he's lost it completely. Call me old-fashioned, but I really don't think that somebody of his age should be wearing tight trousers and flowery shirts. It's obscene. And the way he talks to the press! I mean, 'politeness' is just not a word he understands. I'm not surprised they get upset and give him bad reviews.

Two

M = Man   W = Woman

M: So, have you decided which film we're going to see, then?

W: Well, I really wanted to see the new Fiona Miller film which everyone is raving about.

M: Oh, please, no! I couldn't stand another costume drama.

W: No, this one's very different from her others. She plays the part of an out-of-work spy who decides to turn to crime and begin a life as a jewel thief. But anyway, Katie says it's not her cup of tea, so I'm afraid it's 'get your handkerchief ready for another tear-jerker'. You know the plot already: boy meets girl, girl meets another boy, first boy gets upset – all that kind of nonsense.

Three

SO = Shop Owner   C = Customer

SO: I'm afraid I'm going to have to ask you to pay an extra £3.

C: Why?

SO: Well, you're only supposed to have the video out for two days: it says on the box – 48 hours only.

C: Right, and I took it out on Saturday.

SO: And today's Tuesday, so that's one day overdue. Hence the extra £3.

C: But you're not open on Sundays, so that day doesn't count. Saturday to Monday, one day, and Monday to Tuesday, two days.

SO: I'm very sorry, sir, but that's not how we work.

Four

Drained, darling, absolutely drained. And have you read what the critics wrote about it? I don't know how anyone could say it was 'disappointing'. I mean, OK, so it's not the most exciting part I've ever had to play but I gave it my all, absolutely everything. One look at my face will tell you just how utterly exhausted I am. I could sleep for a week.

Five

What do you think we should get him? … An atlas! That's not very much … I know he's interested in geography, but he's been with the company for nearly 25 years. I really don't think an atlas would express our appreciation for all he's done for the firm. He's been like a father to us all … I don't know, something that will remind him of us in his retirement, something he can use every day. How about a palm top or something?

Six

M = Man   W = Woman

M: What was it like?

W: Oh, don't ask. I certainly wouldn't recommend it to anyone.

M: Too violent for you, was it?

W: Quite the opposite. I mean, at first there was the usual dose of gratuitous violence – basically what you'd expect from that type of film, and partly why I went to see it. After that, though, not a great deal happened. From what I can remember – when I wasn't falling asleep, that is – the script seemed to focus on an analysis of the protagonist's inner self.

M: A kind of 'non-action film', then.

W: Exactly.

Seven

Hello, yes, it's about a book I bought in your shop last week. A Katharine Adams novel. I just wanted to point out that there were one or two pages missing … No, no, there's really no need to apologize. I mean it's not as if it was the last page or anything. And I got the gist of what was happening without the pages. I just thought you ought to know so you can check the rest of your stock, or talk to the publishers or something … That's OK … Yes, pages 60 to 64 …

Eight

Well, we were born in the same month, but I'm a Leo, as you know, whereas her birthday's at the beginning of July, which makes her a Cancer. I don't know if that's good or bad. We certainly seem to laugh at the same things; the same jokes, the same comedy programmes … Sorry? … Oh, next Friday. We're going to a jazz concert, although I can't say it's my favourite type of music. She's really into it, and she wanted me to go, so …

Unit 5 (Page 59)

 1.22

R = Richard   L = Louise
True/false

R: Right, let's see, jobs and duties. Where shall we begin?

L: Let's talk about washing up first. Now that's something I really can't stand. My mum makes me do it after every meal at the weekend, and she won't let me go out with my friends until I've done it. I just think that's so unfair. I mean, none of my friends have to do it. I bet you don't either, do you?

R: No, you're right. In fact, no one in my family does. The most I have to do is get the plates out of the dishwasher.

L: Lucky you! I wish we had one. And what about cleaning shoes? You have a machine to do that as well, I suppose.

R: Unfortunately not. If it was left up to me, I wouldn't bother. But my dad says that shoes tell you a lot about a person so he has me brushing and polishing every other day. It's such a pain.

L: Same here. I'm not made to do it that often, but I still dread having to do it.

R: Right, so that could be one of our three. What's next?

L: Well, I honestly can't understand why clothes shopping is there. That's no chore for me. I mean I could spend all day popping in and out of shops. But going to buy food - now that's completely different.

R: I can't bear doing either of them. In fact, even *talking* about them makes me feel funny. Shall we move on?

L: OK. What do you feel about visiting relatives?

R: Oh that's not so bad. I've got a pretty small family so it doesn't happen that often. And I get on really well with my grandparents, the ones that are still alive, that is. In fact, one of my granddads is a real laugh, and I think he enjoys my company when I go to see him, now that he's on his own. How about you?

L: Well, I suppose I'm a bit lazy really. My parents both say I should go and see my grandparents more often, but they live so far away – I always make sure I'm in when they come to see us, and they come round quite a lot, so I don't feel as though I *need* to go and see them. I don't think my mum and dad agree, though.

R: Oh well, that's relatives for you. Let's have a look at the next one.

L: What about looking after animals? Have you got any pets?

R: I've got a couple of fish, but they're not really that much trouble. You just have to change their water once a week, and drop some food into their tank every now and then. But you've got a dog, haven't you?

L: Yeah, don't remind me. Every morning he's there by the front door with his lead in his mouth, looking up at me with his big eyes, as if to say; 'Come on, it's that time again.' And if I ignore him, he starts barking, and my dad gets angry and says, 'He's your dog, no one else wanted one, so you've got to take responsibility for him'. Thanks, dad. You're a great help.

R: Bad luck. Get a fish next time.

L: Oh, I love him really. Anyway, what have we decided so far?

R: Well, we both seem to agree on cleaning shoes, and neither of us likes shopping for food. So that leaves one more. I can't talk about cleaning the car, 'cause we haven't got one.

L: And my dad won't let any of us go anywhere near his. I think he's frightened we might scratch it, or something, so he takes it to the local car wash. That's fine by me.

R: And if you tell me you like tidying your room, I just won't believe you.

L: Well I think we've found the third one – I absolutely …

Unit 5 (Page 60)

1.23

FCE Part 2 – Sentence completion

I = Interviewer   AN = Allan Nicholls

I: With us today on 'All in a day's work' we have Allan Nicholls, station officer at Hove Fire Station, who's here to talk about the job of the much-respected fire-fighter.

Allan, the first thing I'd like to ask you is about the selection procedure. What do you have to do in order to become a fire-fighter?

AN: Well, as you can imagine, it's a fairly rigorous process, with a variety of different tests. Whilst we don't insist on any academic qualifications, potential recruits do have to undergo a short educational test, aimed at assessing basic literacy and numeracy, or in other words, reading, writing and arithmetic. Surprisingly for some, you no longer have to be a minimum height. Instead, there are a series of physical tests, designed to measure such things as how tightly they can grip things, or whether their back and legs are sufficiently strong. If they get through this stage they go on to the next one, the practical awareness day which involves fitness tests, checks to see if claustrophobia is a problem and practical tasks such as ladder climbing.

I: And are women accepted into the force?

AN: Ah yes, indeed, though they are still very much in the minority. At the moment here at Hove we have four women on the workforce.

I: Now, fire-fighters are obviously on call 24 hours a day, but perhaps you could tell us how the shift system operates?

AN: Well, there's an eight-day rota. A fire-fighter works two nine-hour day shifts, followed by two 15-hour night shifts. And then of course we get four days off before starting again. It's a continuous cycle.

I: And what characterizes a typical shift?

AN: We always begin with the Watch Parade, which is where one shift finishes and the next begins. This is a fairly formal affair and it's compulsory for everyone to wear full uniform. And then once the various jobs have been detailed for the shift, there are equipment checks. The breathing apparatus, for example, is a vital piece of equipment and lives can depend on it, so, it's essential that this and everything else is maintained in perfect working order. Nothing escapes attention, including of course the fire engines which also have to be checked from top to bottom. And then after that, if we're not called out to a fire there's the routine work which is programmed into the day. That can be anything from training to the more everyday jobs of cleaning and maintenance. Fitness of course is extremely important, so we also have a kind of mini gym where we work out every day.

I: Many listeners have phoned in saying they would like to know when your busiest period is.

AN: Well, we don't really have a 'busiest period,' despite the fact that most people might think it's November 5th, Guy Fawkes night. We do, however, tend to be busier in the evening, rather than during the day. That's the time when shops and other business premises are left unattended and also when most people are at home, cooking and so on, and as you might expect, the majority of fires are domestic ones. It's worth pointing out that the fires themselves often take only minutes to put out, whereas clearing up afterwards can take several hours. We have to do everything necessary to prevent the danger of a fire re-igniting, so that means taking all the floors up, getting flammable things like carpets out of the building, and so on.

I: Fire-fighting is obviously dangerous work, Allan. Do you ever feel fear?

AN: Any fire-fighter who said that he had never felt frightened would be fooling himself and you. But it's all a matter of control. It's what we've been trained for and

we learn to control feelings such as fear. But rather than the danger and the drama of the job it's very satisfying being out on the street, knowing that you're helping the public. There's also the camaraderie which goes with working as part of a team. I certainly don't think I'd be able to do any other job.

Unit 6 (Page 70)

🔘 **1.24–1.28**

FCE Part 3 – Multiple matching

Speaker 1
My sister was always going out alone on her bike and she'd spend hours cycling along the country lanes. She'd come home with blackberries she'd picked and tales of wild rabbits she'd seen. I couldn't understand how anyone could get so excited about a rabbit. She went on to live on a farm and milked cows for a living. I left home when I was 16 and moved into a flat with a boy who played drums in a punk band. My parents were really upset. I had my hair cut really short and wore clothes that got all the neighbours talking. We're still both like chalk and cheese.

Speaker 2
She'd do anything just to be different. That often caused a lot of friction in the family and I know our parents had a really hard time. If the atmosphere got a bit tense I'd try to smooth things over. I was always there for my sister. Mum and Dad used to get really mad about the way she lived her life, but I'd always make excuses for her. And if she ever got into trouble I never told them the whole truth. I don't think they know half of what she got up to.

Speaker 3
When we first started school my sister used to get teased a lot because of her skin colour. It was never anything unpleasant or spiteful – just silly name-calling, mostly. In fact, it never seemed to affect her and she just ignored it all. She's always been very tough, my sister – determined to get on with her life without letting anyone or anything else bother her, and I've always looked up to her for that. I'm far too sensitive, by comparison. Even then, when we were at school, instead of rushing to protect her, I used to burst into tears every time someone started making fun of her. Silly, really.

Speaker 4
We might be twins but our characters are very different – I'm much more confident and outgoing, for one thing, and she's fairly quiet and shy. We don't share the same taste in music, we have different interests, and we also argue a lot, but then I think most brothers and sisters do, don't they? In our case it's because we want to be better than each other, at sports, at school and even at getting boyfriends. When people see us fighting they immediately think we don't get on with each other, but nothing could be further from the truth.

Speaker 5
She always liked dressing up and putting on loads of make-up. When we were kids she always wore the shortest mini-skirts and she smelt like a perfume factory. She used to make fun of me because I was so plain and unconcerned about my appearance, and she laughed openly at my clothes. It never bothered me though. I knew I couldn't compete with her looks so I just laughed back. I called her 'Alexis' after that woman in one of those 70s soap operas on the telly.

Unit 6 (Page 75)

🔘 1.29

FCE Part 2 – Descriptions

M = Marion   S = Steven   K = Karen

M: Oh well, that's easy. I know who I'm going to write about.

K: Already?

M: Yes, the mysterious Eilean.

S: Go on then, Marion. What happened?

M: Well, it was last summer. We were driving down to the coast to spend a week with my relatives. All my dad's family live down in Brighton, about a five-hour drive from here. Anyway, just as we were coming into the outskirts of the town all this steam started coming out of the engine. So we all got out of the car and mum and dad had a look under the bonnet, but all they could do was scratch their heads. They hadn't the faintest idea about cars.

K: So what did you do?

M: Well fortunately this other car stopped and the driver offered to help. And that's how I met Eilean, his daughter. She was ready to sort out the problem herself but her dad told her she'd get herself dirty so *he* did it. I suppose the first thing I noticed about her was her clothes. They were 'hippy-style'– all long and flowing with lots of bright, cheerful colours. And that's how *she* was really – bright and cheerful and we had a real laugh together there on the side of the motorway, and on the one or two other occasions we met as well. She was also incredibly tall, with long flowing hair that seemed to go down as far as her knees.

S: She sounds a bit like one of my ex-girlfriends, Marcia.

K: One of the thousands, no doubt.

S: Actually, come to think of it, I could write about *her*. We were both watching this street entertainer, a magician he was, and he asked for two volunteers to come out onto his 'stage', which was this low wall. So – I went out and so did Marcia, and that's how we met. I remember thinking how soft her features were and when I looked into her eyes I realized I'd fallen for her in a big way.

M: How romantic!

S: And then the magician asked us to focus on this rabbit he had in a box, but I just couldn't keep my eyes off Marcia, so I didn't have a clue what was going on and the magician got quite angry. That's when she smiled at me and I got so nervous I nearly fell off the stage! Brought together by magic, we were.

M: That's almost what Eilean said, only she believed in Destiny, and according to her that's what caused us to meet. She was a bit strange, but I'd still like to have kept in touch with her. I *have* written a few times, but the most recent letters have gone unanswered and she seems to have disappeared off the face of the Earth.

S: Probably that magician again! How about you, Karen?

K: Well, it looks as if I'm going to have to make something up. Nothing like either of your two stories has ever happened to me. But, I often go walking in the mountains so I'm going to write about a rescue when I was trapped in the snow with a broken leg.

M: Sounds good.

K: It gets better. The man who rescued me was a gorgeous, well-built hunk with piercing blue eyes and a beautifully dark complexion, let's say – a – Mediterranean type.

S: Oh dream on!

M: And his gentle manner and soft spoken voice comforted me in the freezing cold and almost made me forget my pain. The best bit though was when he picked me up in his arms and carried me down the mountain – that can be my last paragraph, leaving the reader wondering what happened next.

S: I've just thought of another story – the one of how Marcia and I split up with each other. We were at the theatre one night and one of the actors kept looking at her ...

Unit 7 (Page 83)

🔘 1.30

FCE Part 2 – Sentence completion

A = Announcer   M = Matthew

A: And next on 'Consumer Watch' I have with me Matthew Brereton, UK head of the Safebuy supermarket chain. He's here to give away a few secrets on the psychology of supermarkets, and how the big companies design their shops. Matthew.

M: Thanks Barbara. Well, the layout of most major supermarkets is roughly the same, and for more or less the same reasons. You'll notice that the entrance, for example, is usually situated to one side of the building. This is to ensure, of course, that shoppers walk down as many aisles as possible before they leave the store. Ah – if we had it in the middle, then they might visit only one half of the supermarket and as a result only buy half as much. The first thing you often see as you come through the entrance is the fruit and vegetable area. As well as being pleasant to the eye, er, this also gives customers the impression they are coming into an outdoor market. Fresh, colourful products are far more attractive than tins of convenience food so the customer is put in a good mood, from the start.

A: A good mood to buy things, you mean?

M: Exactly. And next to the fruit and vegetable area is the confectionery; umm, crisps, chocolates, sweets and so on. Parents often come shopping with their children and we need to ensure that they are kept happy and interested so that they don't disturb mum and dad from the business of spending money. Then at the back of the supermarket in the corner you'll probably find the fresh meat counter. This is partly to make sure that as little room as possible is taken away from the main display areas by the staff who are serving. But it's also there so as not to distract customers when we have deliveries. Er, they really don't want to see us bringing big carcasses of meat through the store, so, er, it's brought in through the back door. And very close to the fresh meat you can expect to see the pre-packed meat. Ah, people who are put off by the sight of blood and um – dead animals prefer to buy their meat in the form of convenience food to prevent them having to make the connection between the product and the animal. Er, they buy a lamb chop, but they don't think of a baby lamb in the field. The freezer goods are nearby. There's a limited amount of space so the smaller suppliers often find it difficult to get room for their products. Ah, that's why you only tend to see the well-known brands here.

A: And how about those areas at the end of the aisle? How do you decide what to put there?

M: Yes, these are key selling sites, and sales of goods at these points can be as much as five times higher than other areas. So we generally move goods to the end of aisle areas when we want to sell them quickly: goods which have not been selling well, and especially those which are nearing their sell-by date. Bread, too, needs to be sold quickly, but we put the bakery section in the far corner, as far away from the entrance as possible, next to other basic foodstuffs such as milk. This is so that customers have to walk past hundreds of products to reach it. Um, it's expensive to run a bakery but it increases sales of other products. The smell, too, is an important factor as it helps to create a warm, homely atmosphere in the store.

A: And the alcoholic drinks. They're often at the far end too, aren't they Matthew?

M: Yes, very near the exit. Er, by this time the shopper is beginning to enjoy the shopping experience, so he or she will buy more alcohol if it's here than if it's by the entrance. Er, the same is true for those products we put at the checkouts; er, more sweets and chocolates, usually. The kind of things people buy on impulse as they wait to pay – er, a reward they give themselves for doing the shopping.

A: Thank you very much, Matthew, for taking us through that shopping experience.

M: Thank you.

A: Next week, the department store, and we'll be talking to...

Unit 7 (Page 87)

🔘 1.31

FCE Part 4 – Multiple choice

I = Interviewer   R= Rebecca   G = Greg

I: What made you go and live in the countryside, Rebecca?

R: I suppose my priorities had changed with age. When I first went to London, I used to love the hustle and bustle of the place. But then I gradually became more aware of the planes roaring overhead, car horns beeping all the time, music blaring out at strange hours. I needed a break.

I: Greg, I can see you're smiling.

G: Yes. I remember when I first moved out with my family, we all found it a little too quiet. But we quickly got used to it, and now we prefer living with less noise. We also like the fact that you don't have to worry about the kids so much if they go off on their own.

R: Hmm, I'm not so sure. Some people drive like maniacs on those narrow roads. I feel I have to keep an even closer eye on my two kids than before. And there are lots of wide open spaces for them to get lost in, too.

G: But that's where the neighbours come in. Everyone seems to know everyone else's business in the village. That could be seen as an intrusion, but it's very handy if your kids go wandering off, or you're worried about burglars breaking into your house.

R: You're right there. In fact, we leave everything unlocked, and the neighbours sometimes just come into our house without even knocking on the door. We don't mind, though. It's like having a big extended family.

I: What about the amenities where you live?

G: The basics are within walking distance from us; the school, the shops, even a couple of tennis courts.

R: I wish I could say the same. We have to get the car out just to go and buy a loaf of bread. And you really do need to be able to drive to live where we do; the bus service is just too infrequent.

G: It's better than not having one at all. We're actually trying to get the local authorities to put on at least one bus a day, particularly for the older residents who don't have a car and who sometimes need to go into town.

R: Yes, and I'm actually wondering how my two are going to find it when they become teenagers. Well, they'll want to go into town, too. They'll probably complain of boredom and want us to go and live in the city again.

G: And who can blame them? I know at that age I would have been bored out of my mind! No cinemas, no decent shops, no cafés to sit in, no discos to go to ...

I: Do you think either of you will ever go and live in the city again?

G: Naturally, I'd prefer to stay in the village and work at home rather than do a nine-to-five job in an office. I have my computer, email and the phone and a wonderful working environment. However, anything can happen and we'd be prepared to move back to London if we felt it was to our advantage.

I: Rebecca?

R: I'll be going back to work just as soon as my youngest child starts school. Obviously I've thought about it a lot, and the fact that living where I do now will mean spending two hours driving to and from work every day. But I'd rather do that than give up my life in the country.

I: Well, thank you for both coming all that way to speak to us today. We'll have a break for music now and then it's competition time once again ...

Unit 8 (Page 99)

🔘 1.32–1.39

FCE Part 1 – Multiple choice

One

We really didn't expect this. We thought it'd be the typical economy type hotel. You know, nothing special, just a bed, a wardrobe and a shower in the room if you're lucky. Well, the en suite bathroom was a big surprise, I can tell you. It's twice the size of ours at home. And as for the view from the balcony, it's unbelievable. We really can't complain.

Two

... and I think that although my experience running a restaurant may not seem very relevant, it's still a people-orientated job. I am definitely a 'people person'. I like dealing with the public. So whether it's listening to customers and giving them advice on the best places to go, or talking on the phone to tour operators and trying to get the best deal, I think I'd be well suited to the job. I have good people skills and I think that's an important strength.

Three

TG = Tour Guide   W = Woman

TG: Are you sure you had it when you left the hotel?

W: Positive: I didn't want to bring it but my husband made me put it in my bag. He said you should never leave your money or your passport in your room. And then when we were having a drink and I went to pay, it had gone. Well, someone must have put their hand in when I wasn't looking.

TG: We'll have to report it straight away.

Four

We went there because we wanted to see the stained glass windows. They say they're among the finest in Europe and the colours are supposed to be incredible when the sun shines through them. Unfortunately we couldn't go in because we weren't properly dressed – they won't let you in if you're wearing short trousers. And the next morning when we went back it was Easter Sunday. So of course, we couldn't get to the part where the windows are because there was a special service.

Five
M = Man   B = Boy

M: Yes, your skin is quite badly burnt. How long were you out in the sun for?

B: About an hour, maybe. It was after lunch and I fell asleep on the beach.

M: Do you have any other symptoms – dizziness, a temperature?

B: No, it just really hurts.

M: Well, it doesn't sound like sunstroke. This cream should take away the sting, but if you start to feel sick or dizzy, get yourself to a doctor straight away.

B: Thanks. How much do I owe you?

M: I'll just check. One second.

Six
I shouldn't complain really. I mean, the whole economy of this town is based on tourism and if they stopped coming, then a lot of people would be out of work and on the dole. But I do wish they'd show a little more respect. There are a lot of them who have music blaring out of their cars during the day, and then at night you get big groups coming into the centre for the pubs and clubs. And they don't seem to care that we can't sleep with them making such a racket. Most of them drunk, I shouldn't wonder.

Seven
B = Boy   M = Mother

B: Where are we going?

M: Well, we picked up a leaflet for a nature park just outside the town. They've got all sorts of wild animals and you can drive through and see them in their natural habitat. It looks very good.

B: But you said we were going to go to the Aqua Park.

M: We can't go in this weather. And besides, your father and I want to do something different.

B: But that's not fair. You can't just change your mind like that.

M: Don't be selfish, Steven. It's our turn today.

Eight
No, the 14th … That's right. Saturday the 14th … Well, my plans have changed and I'm not going to Bristol any more. I couldn't get anywhere to stay there, so I had to find somewhere in the city of Bath … But I don't see why I have to pick it up two days before. Surely you could just give me the new one the day I travel, on the 14th … Yes, I appreciate that's the procedure, but it's very inconvenient.

Unit 9 (Page 108)

🔘 **1.40**

FCE Part 4 – Multiple choice

I = Interviewer   A = Alastair Agnew

I: We have in the studio today Alastair Agnew, Chairman of the Ghost Club in London. He's here to give us some advice on how to correctly identify ghosts. Alastair, a see-through figure in white that walks through walls. That's a fair enough description of a ghost, isn't it?

A: Well, only one out of three correct, I'm afraid Jean. Far from having the translucent appearance they do in the films, ghosts look solid, just like real people. The only thing that gives them away is the fact that, as you rightly say, they can walk through walls. And the only reason they do *that* is that when they were alive the wall may not have existed. Indeed, what's interesting is that in many cases you may only see them from the knees upwards, due to the fact that the ground level was lower in their day.

I: And how about the noises we usually associate with ghosts? The footsteps and the moaning sounds we all make when we imitate one …

A: … and the sound of laughter, crying and even the noise of music. Yes, these have all been heard when ghosts have been sighted. In fact, in a study carried out in England it was revealed that in 39 per cent of hauntings people claimed to have heard ghostly footsteps. One popular explanation for these sounds is the 'stone-tape theory'.

I: And what does that say?

A: That the brickwork or stones of a building can somehow absorb sounds and later play them back, rather like a tape recorder. And the same theory is used to explain some of the smells which are given off when ghosts are around. Smells such as decaying flesh, baking bread or animal odours are supposedly absorbed into the walls and then later released. So a building that was once used as a church, for example, may give off the smell of incense.

I: And as Chairman of the Ghost Club you would not agree with that explanation, would you?

A: It may account for some of the phenomena, but it certainly does not prove that ghosts do not exist. Sceptics have yet to put forward a theory to explain why, for example, some people have their hair stroked or sometimes feel a sharp poke in the side of their body when no one else is around.

I: And are there any places where ghosts are more likely to occur than others?

A: If your house is on or near a crossroads, you may well be haunted. That's because these used to be burial places for suicides and many criminals who were hanged nearby. The number of car crashes at crossroads is also presumed to raise the spirit count. And even if you don't live on a crossroads, if you wait at one for a bus, there's a good chance a spirit will follow you and give you a bit of a surprise.

I: And finally Alastair, are we all able to see ghosts?

A: Certainly, yes, though some people are more likely to attract paranormal attention than others. Similarly, some household pets are also good indicators that there's a spirit in the vicinity. Dogs, for example, may stubbornly refuse to enter one part of a room or start growling without explanation if they sense a ghost. Cats may hiss and spit, while a budgie or a hamster will look on wondering what all the fuss is about.

I: Thank you Alastair. So then, if you or your dog think you might have spotted a ghost, the Ghost Club would love to hear from you. We'll be giving out their address at the end of the programme. Now it's over to Jeremy …

Listening scripts

Unit 9 (Page 109)

🔊 1.41

Language Focus – Question tags

2

That's a fair enough description of a ghost, isn't it?
And as chairman of the Ghost Club you would not agree with that explanation, would you?

3

1   You don't believe him, do you?
2   You won't let me down, will you?
3   You went away for the weekend, didn't you?
4   He's not playing very well, is he?
5   He's already passed First Certificate, hasn't he?
6   I'm right about that, aren't I?
7   You can play chess, can't you?
8   Let's phone Paul, shall we?

Unit 10 (Page 123)

🔊 1.42

FCE Part 2 – Sentence completion

P = Presenter   O = Police Officer

P: And now it's time for our regular 'Crimewatch' slot and here with us today is Police Officer Richard Woodcock from the Crime Prevention Unit of the Metropolitan Police. Richard, perhaps you could begin by telling us what characterizes a typical burglary.

O: Well, burglary is one of the crimes most people worry about, not so much because of the loss of property, but more because of the sense of invasion it causes – the idea that someone has gone through all your personal belongings. Many residential burglaries occur because of common misconceptions. For example, while people typically worry about night-time thefts, nearly 50 per cent of residential break-ins happen during the day, when homes are vacant because owners are out working. What's more, robbing a house takes less time than many people think. Most burglars get in and out in less than ten minutes.

P: And how does the police go about combating the problem?

O: Police forces all over the country have targeted burglary. Operation Bumblebee, for example, was a major crime-prevention campaign run by the Metropolitan Police and aimed at beating the burglars. The scheme has included raids on criminals who are known to sell stolen goods. At the end of Operation Bumblebee's first year burglaries fell by 13 per cent, a figure which has to be considered a success.

P: Mm. And what would you say are the most important measures our listeners can take to protect their own homes?

O: Most householders are aware of the risk of being burgled and the majority have already installed locks on doors and windows. What many of these same people don't do, however, is use them! So rule number one is lock up before you go out. And whatever you do, don't leave spare keys under the doormat, thinking that no one is going to find them. It's the most obvious place for a burglar to look and an open invitation to walk in unchallenged. If you have another set of keys leave them with a trusted neighbour or friend. A home alarm system is another must, and a good deterrent to any would-be burglars, but make sure you have it put in by an installer who works to the British standard. Your local crime prevention officer can give you advice on how to choose an installer. And I mentioned locks earlier, but don't forget about the garage door as well. This can provide easy access for burglars, allowing them to gain access not only to your car, but directly into your home if there's an adjoining door.

P: Thank you, Richard. Now, many listeners have phoned in asking about Neighbourhood Watch Schemes and how to set them up. What information can you give them?

O: Well, the best thing about these schemes is that they bring the community together and provide everyone with the chance to fight local crime. Your neighbours look out for you, your family, your home and your street, and you do the same for them. If you see anyone acting suspiciously near a neighbour's house, you contact the police. It especially enables people to check on vulnerable members of the community, such as the elderly or disabled. The schemes have come a long way since the early view some people held of nosy neighbours interfering in other people's business. There are now more than 155,000 Neighbourhood Watch schemes in the country, with more than ten million residents directly benefiting from them. It's the largest voluntary organization in the country and one of the most effective for beating crime.

P: And where should listeners go to ask about starting one?

O: The local police station will tell you all about it or you can phone the National Neighbourhood Watch Association on – and I have the number here – 020 72 72 3348.

P: Thank you Richard. We'll give that number again at the end of the programme ...

Unit 10 (Page 131)

🔊 1.43–1.47

FCE Part 3 – Multiple matching

Speaker 1

My mum gave me nearly £100 in cash to pay for a trip to France with my school. When I went to give the money to the French teacher, I couldn't find it anywhere. I knew my mum would be angry with me for losing it – so I told her I'd been mugged by two boys on the way to school. So she phoned the school, who called the police and when they came to the school to interview me the next day, they realized I was lying, because I kept giving different descriptions of my attackers. I've never been told off by so many people – my mum, the teachers, the police. Later that day I realized I needn't have lied after all – I found the money in the bottom of my jacket pocket.

Speaker 2

We were just going shopping, not far away, just to the shopping centre in town. And anyway, I was supposed to check that all the windows were closed upstairs in the house – before we left, like. Well, I forgot, didn't I, and when dad asked me if I'd remembered to 'check the windows were closed' I couldn't be bothered to get out of the car and go back to do it. So I said I had. Well, we were only going to be out for a short while, so I thought we didn't need to worry. That morning we were burgled – we lost £3,000 worth of stuff, including my whole music system. I had to own up – I mean it was obvious they got in through the window, wasn't it? And there was no sign of forced entry.

Speaker 3

We weren't allowed to have parties in our house when I was a teenager, my mum and dad wouldn't let us. They didn't really approve of our friends – they didn't want them smoking in the house and spilling drinks and stuff on the new carpet. So when they went away for the weekend to celebrate their wedding anniversary, me and my brother decided to have a celebration of our own, with some friends, of course. We would have got away with it – if they hadn't phoned up in the middle of the party. They heard all the music and all our friends and everything. They never let us do anything after that.

Speaker 4

I once wrote a note to my teacher, you know, a fake one in my mum's handwriting, so I could get out of doing sport. My mum found out and went mad. I'd written a couple of practice letters before doing a final copy, you know, to practise her writing, and the next day she found them in the bin. I should have burned them or torn them up into pieces. I can still hear her now: 'You've let us down, my boy. We've brought you up to be honest and you've let us down.' She was really upset. I didn't have to do sport, though.

Speaker 5

All the time I was growing up I don't think I ever told one lie to my parents. There were things I got up to, you know, things I wasn't supposed to do that I did, like most people. I mean I wasn't an angel, by any means. I smoked the odd cigarette with friends, got into trouble at school for not being polite to teachers, that kind of thing. But if I wanted to do something like go to an all-night party I knew how to get round my dad so he'd let me go. You know, I'd wash his car or offer to do the gardening or something like that. But telling lies? No, I didn't need to do that.

Unit 11 (Page 137)

 2.1

FCE Part 2 – Sentence completion

I = Interviewer   P = Paul Murphy

I: So Paul, how did you get involved with the International Rescue Corps?

P: One of the founder members of the organization lived near me in the East of England. He helped set up the IRC way back in 1981 after the Italian earthquake. He was a friend of mine but also a fellow firefighter. I joined because I've got a skill to offer, and I thought it would be exciting to travel all over the world rescuing people.

I: And how many missions have you been on?

P: Eight abroad – seven earthquakes and a hurricane – and about 10 in the UK. Er, in this country we're often called upon to find missing people, especially in bad weather. Er, if a disaster strikes a foreign country, er, we sometimes make offers of help to the government there via the British Embassy, but more often than not the country goes to the United Nations and er, asks for rescue teams like ours.

I: And what can IRC offer that other agencies can't?

P: Er, as well as being able to offer our services free of charge, er, we carry our own specialist equipment for finding and saving people who are trapped in collapsed buildings. That includes fibre optic probes, er, where we can put a camera into the smallest of holes to see what's happening, microphones to pick up voices or vibrations and er, thermal imaging to detect heat.

I: Who pays for you to go?

P: Now, IRC is a charity, and none of our members receives any kind of payment. They're volunteers, so they also have to ask for time off work to go abroad.

I: What's the worst weather you've worked in, Paul?

P: Armenia was freezing cold but Nicaragua was bad because of the heat and mosquitoes, which never stopped biting. And the rain was horrendous, too. When we got there the hurricane had been reclassified as a tropical storm, but we had to suffer torrential rain all the time we were there.

I: What's the most amazing survival story you have come across?

P: I suppose it has to be the time we went to Japan after the Kobe earthquake. Er, one woman had been trapped for over 40 hours when we discovered she was there, and it took us another four hours to get her out. The remarkable thing about that is that normally, once people have been trapped for 24 hours after an earthquake, not many come out alive. The thing which saved her was a wardrobe, which had fallen on top of her and protected her from the falling debris. She was partly inside it. And I remember the first thing she said when we finally got her out was that she was bored! Not the kind of emotion you'd expect from an earthquake victim, is it?

I: Certainly not! And what advice would you give to people if they get caught in an earthquake?

P: As soon as you feel the slightest shake, get out of the building and into the open air. That's often easier said than done, of course, especially if you're on the tenth floor when it happens. Um, if it's not possible to get out, then you should take cover in the safest area of the building to stop other things falling on you. But really it's up to the governments of countries in earthquake zones to take the initiative and construct safer buildings. In this way damage is minimized and er, lives are saved.

I: Thank you, Paul, and the best of luck on your future missions.

Unit 11 (Page 143)

 2.2–2.9

FCE Part 1 – Multiple choice

One

I really can't understand why they put it all the way out there. They maintained that if they'd built it in the heart of the city there would have been problems getting out to fires in the rural areas. Too far and too much traffic, they said. But that's exactly why it would have made more sense to build it in the centre instead of on the edge. You know, it takes a fire engine nearly 20 minutes to get from that suburb to the other side of the city.

Two

If I was a member of the Council I'd make sure something was done about the mess on the streets. It's an absolute disgrace. Local people need more help to keep them clean, and that help has to come from the authorities. There aren't enough litter bins, for one thing, so the pavements outside my premises are covered with paper, drink cans and cigarette butts. Before I open up in the morning I have to spend about 10 minutes sweeping it all up. I wouldn't sell anything if I didn't.

Three

You have to remember that some species of plants were facing extinction in the area. People would come out to the countryside for a picnic, see all these beautiful flowers and pick them, without realizing the effect this was having. If we hadn't made this a conservation area and limited the number of people coming in, then we'd have no flowers at all, and people would be really upset. As it is, we can congratulate ourselves on the action we took and look forward to a brighter future for this patch of countryside.

Four

W1 = Woman 1   W2 = Woman 2

W1: So what was it like?
W2: Marvellous. Just what we were looking for.
W1: And what was that?
W2: Well, if we'd gone to one of the other islands, we'd have had to put up with busy roads and crowded beaches.
W1: So weren't there many tourists where you went?
W2: Oh plenty. More than we expected really. But it didn't seem to matter, because with the vehicle restrictions there was almost a total lack of exhaust fumes, no congestion and very little noise. And because the island's so small, you could walk everywhere anyway.

Five

M = Man   W = Woman

M: I think we should all get together and decide what we're going to do. I can't put up with it any more.
W: Neither can we. The noise of that boy's music makes the whole house shake. My husband says it's just like being in an earthquake, only worse.
M: Of course it's the parents' fault, but it's no good talking to them. They're no better than he is.
W: And his teachers can't control him, either. Apparently, he's as rude to them as he is to all of us.
M: So, let's have a meeting of all the residents in the street and we'll decide how to deal with him.

Six

Violent storms swept across the south coast today, causing widespread damage to property. Torrential rain and gale-force winds lashed seaside towns and several people had to be evacuated from their flooded homes by rescue services. One man in Bognor narrowly escaped death as the car he was driving was crushed by a falling tree, which had been struck by lightning.

Seven

W = Woman   M = Man

W: What's the problem, John?
M: Well, we lost a lot of our plants last night.
W: It wasn't our cat, was it?
M: No, the wind. Pulled up all the roses, it did. Blew down a few bushes, too.
W: I'm sorry to hear that.
M: Oh, not to worry. I'd be grateful if you'd give me a hand to clear up the mess, though.
W: I'd be pleased to.

Eight

Something's got to be done. These massive petrol tankers should just not be allowed to sail so close to our shores. The oil slick has already killed thousands of birds and the beaches are a disaster area. Demonstrating is all very well, but it's not going to clean up the mess, is it? We can't leave it in the hands of the politicians, so we've just got to get down to the coast and get our hands dirty with the rest of the volunteers. You coming?

Unit 12 (Page 147)

⊙ 2.10–2.14

FCE Part 3 – Multiple matching

Speaker 1
I tried crash diets, such as one where you just eat cabbage soup, and another where you drink nothing but lemonade with some salt and pepper for about seven days without any food. They worked temporarily, but after a while I put the weight back on. Then I was introduced to these diet pills and my weight went down to 65 kilos. But I wasn't earning a great deal of money and I simply couldn't afford to keep it up. That's when I decided to save my money and join a gym.

Speaker 2
I used to eat a lot of junk food. It was quick, inexpensive and it satisfied my hunger immediately. The problem was, I ate very little fresh food, and this had a serious effect on my health. I became overweight and suffered all sorts of illnesses. The doctor strongly advised me to rethink my attitude to food. If not, he said, the consequences could be very serious. Well, you can't ignore advice like that, can you? So I started to eat more healthily. And now if I get hungry between meals, I have a little cheese or some nuts, just to fill the hole.

Speaker 3
I'm under no real pressure to lose weight, but I take care over what I eat, simply because it makes me feel better. When I want to treat myself I have a piece of cake or a few biscuits. I read a lot about dieting, and most nutritionists seem to agree that as long as you eat sweet things after a meal, then there's no problem. So, for example, I only ever eat chocolates after lunch or dinner. And never too many of course – just one or two.

Speaker 4
I like eating and I'm not at all interested in dieting. But I do go to see a nutritionist, who helps me maintain a sensible, balanced diet: plenty of fresh fruit and vegetables, meat and fish, carbohydrates such as rice and pasta, several glasses of water a day – and no snacks between meals. She told me to give up cheese, but I ignored her. I enjoy good food and I don't want to deprive myself of the things I love.

Speaker 5
A large number of people follow diets, but very few of them are happier as a result. We are constantly under attack from advertizing and the media, who tell us that 'thin is beautiful'. I used to believe this and think that I wouldn't find a boyfriend unless I was really skinny, that I had to weigh under 60 kilos for boys to like me. But of course, now I realize that there's more to it than that. Just being yourself is what counts and I don't pay much attention to what others think or say.

Ready for Listening (Page 158)

⊙ 2.15–2.21

Part 1 – Multiple choice

Two
These two sides are very well matched. You'll remember they both met in the semi-finals last year, when the game ended in a draw. This year we've had some heavy showers in the

last few days and one or two of the players are finding the playing conditions on the pitch more than a little difficult. But it's a throw-in now. Briggs takes it and passes to Duckham. Duckham tries a shot ... and it goes just wide of the post.

Three

I thought at first it was some kind of virus, but now I'm wondering if it might be something more serious ... No, it's annoying. I simply can't do any work on it at the moment ... Yes, I phoned them, but they said they'd need to have it for three days before they could give me an answer ... Well, I was wondering if you wouldn't mind having a look at it for me ... Could you come round after work? ... No, that's great; the sooner the better as far as I'm concerned, as long as your boss doesn't mind.

Four

M = Man   W = Woman

M: Lots of room for the legs, that's nice.
W: Mm, and so comfortable. It's like my favourite armchair. I could go to sleep here and now.
M: Yes, we should've had a coffee after the meal to keep us awake.
W: We'd never have got a ticket to see this if we had.
M: That's true. The queue was enormous.
W: Anyway, wake me up when it starts, won't you?

Five

You can't fault the food, really. Even my husband was impressed and he's always the first to complain if it's not cooked properly. No, I just felt a little uncomfortable; silver cutlery, antique furniture and everyone dressed as if it was a wedding, including the waiters. And the way they spoke to us! It was 'Sir' and 'Madam' every sentence. I suppose I'm just not used to it, that's all.

Six

W = Woman   M = Man

W: Just look at that. It's incredible.
M: What do you mean?
W: Well, there must be about 20 different types of butter in this section. Low-fat, high-fat, Irish, Dutch, Australian – you name it, they've got it.
M: Confusing, isn't it?
W: No, that's not the point. I'm sure a lot of people will be disappointed there aren't 20 types of carrots and 60 different varieties of cheese. I just don't see why we need them all. And when you think of the transport costs and the fuel needed to import all this stuff and the effect this has on the environment. It makes my blood boil.

Seven

The play finishes at about 11 ... Well, I had at first thought of coming back on the train straight afterwards, but the last one's at 11.05, so I probably wouldn't make it ... Are you sure you don't mind? ... I could always stay in a hotel. There are plenty of cheap ones in that part of town ... OK, well, if you're going to put me up for the night, then you'll have to let me take you out for a meal ... No, I insist.

Eight

We all know juvenile crime's on the increase. The police do all they can with very limited resources and then it's up to people like ourselves to sort the problem out. In this school alone we have more than 20 youngsters with a criminal record and we get virtually no support from the parents. Social services come in occasionally to give us advice on how to deal with them, but once they've gone and we close the classroom door, we're very much on our own.

Ready for Listening (Pages 159–160)

👁 2.22

FCE Part 2 – Sentence completion

Argentina is a country known internationally for the tango, gaucho cowboys and premium quality beef. To many people, therefore, it comes as some surprise to discover that in certain parts of Patagonia, in the south of the country, one of the 'musts' for any tourist is a visit to a Welsh tea house, a place where you can sip tea and enjoy delicious cakes, baked according to traditional Welsh recipes. Perhaps even more surprising, though, is the fact that some of the locals can actually be heard speaking in Welsh. Exactly how many native Welsh speakers there are in the region is not known, but most estimates put the figure at several hundred, a relatively high number, given that there are just under 600,000 speakers of the language in Wales itself.

But how did these Welsh speakers come to be there? The first wave of settlers arrived from Wales in 1865. Unhappy with conditions at home, they were looking for an isolated area to set up a colony, a place where their language and identity would be preserved intact and not assimilated into the dominant culture, as had already happened in the United States. The 153 colonists who landed on the east coast of Argentina included carpenters, tailors and miners, but no real doctors and just one or two farmers. This was rather worrying, since the Chubut valley where they settled was virtually a desert, and what they needed most of all were agricultural skills.

Against all the odds, though, they survived, overcoming droughts, floods and a succession of crop failures. They were also quick to establish friendly relations with the local Indians, who helped the Welsh through the hard times and taught them some of their ways, how to ride and how to hunt. Twenty years after their arrival, some of the settlers moved up into a green fertile region of the Andes mountains, an area which they named Cwm Hyfryd, meaning 'beautiful valley'. Indeed, quite a number of places in Patagonia still bear Welsh names: Bryn Gwyn which means 'white hill', Trevelin, meaning 'milltown' and Trelew or 'Lewistown', named after Lewis Jones, one of the founders.

The Welsh have left their mark in other ways, too. Their windmills and chapels can be found throughout the region and there are a number of cultural activities, such as poetry readings, male voice choirs and the annual Welsh song and dance festival, a smaller version of the International Eisteddfod held in Wales each year. All of this helps to keep the language and traditions alive in a small corner of the world, 8,000 miles from the homeland. And so too does the fact that every year, as part of a programme administered by the National Assembly for Wales, groups of teachers come to Patagonia to teach the language to the growing number of people who are interested in learning it.

And then, of course, there are the Welsh teas. For my afternoon treat, I visit *Nain Ceri*, reputed to be one of the best tea houses in Gaiman, where the streets and houses are adorned with Welsh flags, a reminder to visitors that they are in the self-proclaimed Patagonian-Welsh capital of Chubut. Inside, *Nain Ceri* is decorated with prints and paintings of Wales and the music playing is that of a traditional all-male choir. I sit next to the fireplace and my mouth begins to water as I look at the various cakes on offer. I am about to order the cream-topped apple pie to accompany my tea, when I catch sight of

229

an irresistible-looking chocolate cake and choose that instead. I am not disappointed – it is absolutely delicious. Afterwards, I chat at length to the owner, Ceri Morgan – in Spanish, as she speaks no English and I speak no Welsh. She tells me a little more about the history of …

Ready for Listening (Page 160)

👁 **2.23–2.27**

FCE Part 3 – Multiple matching

Speaker 1

I've been writing for as long as I can remember, and it's something I want to continue to do for a living when I've finished university. I say 'continue' because I've already had one collection of short stories published and I've just started another. I write mostly late at night and at weekends, always after I've finished my course work. I'm doing a maths degree, which has little to do with writing, but I believe in keeping my options open, just in case my creativity runs out.

Speaker 2

For some strange reason I want to be a tattoo artist; you know, paint people's bodies. I'm doing a course in graphic design at art college, which I've been told will be useful. The brother of a friend of mine has a studio and he lets me go and watch him work when I'm not studying at the college. It's the only way to learn, as there are no official courses and no specific qualifications for tattoo artists. At least, not as far as I know.

Speaker 3

As soon as I leave school I'm going to join the Army. I tried to do it when I was 10 but they told me to go back when I was older – so I will! You can learn a trade and do almost any job you want to, and they let you study while you're working. I'd like to work as a physical training instructor, and then maybe later try and get an engineering qualification or something like that. My granddad's an ex-soldier and he always told such good stories that I knew that was what I wanted to do. My parents just think I'm crazy.

Speaker 4

I hope one day to be a speech therapist. I'll have to get a degree in speech therapy first, and to do that I'll need to get good grades next year in my 'A' levels. It's a job which involves helping people who have difficulty communicating, and I've always known I wanted to work in one of the 'caring professions'. My uncle's a speech therapist, but I learnt all about it from a TV documentary I saw a few years ago. And that's when I thought; 'I want to do that'. Then last year I did some voluntary work while I was studying for my GCSEs, and I was hooked.

Speaker 5

I haven't made up my mind yet, but I'd quite like to go into teaching. Naturally I've had lots of advice from teachers at school about how to go about it and how hard I'll have to work for my exams. But to be honest my decision is based not so much on my academic abilities but rather on the fact that I just feel I'd be right for the job. The teachers I look up to at school are all dynamic, outgoing people and that's precisely how I like to see myself.

Ready for Listening (Page 161)

👁 **2.28**

FCE Part 4 – Multiple choice

P: Do you consider yourself to be tall, medium or short? At one metre 84 I've always thought of myself as being a little on the tall side, particularly when I stand next to the people I work with here in the Round Britain studio. Rather curiously, most of them are below the national average height of one metre 78 for men and one 62 for women. But when I popped in yesterday to the annual conference of the TPC – that's the Tall Person's Club of Great Britain and Ireland – I felt decidedly small. I asked one of the organizers, Jenny Parfitt, to tell me about the conference.

J: Well, this is the main event in the club's very busy social calendar. Throughout the year we put on a whole number of activities for members in their local area, like barbecues, theatre excursions, walks and so on. And this conference is the highlight of that year. It's a three-day event that gives tall people from all over the country the chance to meet in the comfort of a hotel, where they can chat, eat, dance and go sightseeing with others who are also above average height.

P: But there's also a serious side to it as well, I gather.

J: That's right, it's not all partying! We discuss a lot of important issues, too. One of the aims of the TPC is to promote the interests of tall people, to change current attitudes. We live in a heightist world, where tall people are discriminated against. Beds in hotels are usually too short for us, and we often have to sleep with our feet hanging off the end. Travelling by bus, train or plane is a major problem too – there's very little leg room and it can feel very cramped. The main difficulty, though, is finding shops that sell long enough trousers or big enough shoes. That can be a real headache.

P: I imagine too that the attitudes of other people can be a problem.

J: Yes, people do tend to stare at us when we walk into the room, treat us like circus freaks. And some actually laugh out loud, as if something funny has just happened. I think if I weren't so used to it now, I might take offence – I know many fellow TPC members do. But to be honest, I find it a little bit annoying. You get tired of it all, particularly when the fifteenth person in a day says something like 'What's the weather like up there?' And they think it's so funny.

P: Yes, not very original, is it? Does the club offer help to tall people who come across attitudes like these?

J: Yes, we regularly give advice to victims of insults and bullying at school or in the workplace. But perhaps the greatest benefit of the club is the opportunity to see that as a tall person you are not alone. When people come to their first meeting and walk into a room full of tall people, they start standing up straighter. They lose their shyness and very soon begin to feel less awkward, more comfortable about their height. It's a remarkable transformation.

P: You've mentioned some of the negative aspects of being taller than average. But surely there must be some advantages, too?

J: Oh yes, there are plenty of them. Erm, for example, you can always see over everyone's head if you're watching something in a crowd or an audience, and if you're in a supermarket you can get things off the top shelf that most other people have a job to reach. And then also you automatically become first choice for sports like basketball, volleyball or rowing. I've never been very good at volleyball, but I always got picked for the university team when I was a student.

P: Now, one thing of course we've failed to mention, Jenny, is your height. How tall are you?

J: One metre 88. And actually, I'm one of the smaller members at this conference. The tallest woman here is exactly two metres and the tallest man two metres 30, that's an incredible 7 foot six inches.

P: Goodness me!

J: Yes, impressive, isn't it? Incidentally, though, you don't need to be above a certain height to qualify as a member of the Tall Person's Club. Unlike some clubs in the USA, which can be difficult to join because of their restrictions, we are very inclusive over here. We believe that people know for themselves whether they are tall or not and it's up to them to decide if they should join.

P: Jenny, it's been fascinating talking to you …

Unit 13 (Page 168)

 2.29

FCE Part 2 – Sentence completion

A = Announcer   G = Grace

A: Grace, how long have you had problems with your eyes?

G: Well, I was actually born completely blind and my sight didn't develop until I was about a year old. Ever since that age I've only ever been able to see out of one eye. I kind of got used to that, and I thought it was quite normal. Then one day when I was about eight I was having a bit of a laugh with my mum. Just for a joke she covered up my left eye, the good one, and said, 'How many fingers?' and I said, 'I don't know.' 'What do you mean you don't know?' she said. She thought I was playing around, but when she realized I wasn't she took me straight down to the doctor. That's when I found out I have an incurable eye disease, which may or may not get worse, but definitely won't get any better.

A: And *has* it got worse?

G: Not really, no. It's been more or less the same ever since. Though I was having a check-up when I was a bit older and they discovered I had tunnel vision as well.

A: What exactly is that?

G: It means I only have central view. I don't have any lateral view, so I'm unable to see anything which isn't directly in front of me. Not like most people who can see slightly to the side when they look ahead. It sounds a bit weird, but to me it's normal.

A: So did you have to go to a special school when you were younger?

G: I was determined to go to a normal school because I was convinced that if I did it would teach me to cope better. I kind of suspected, and my parents warned me, that it wouldn't be easy. You know how cruel kids of 11 and 12 can be to each other. And sure enough they called me names and bullied me and I must have cried every day for a year. And I did get to the point when I wanted to leave, but my dad told me to carry on and see it through. He said it'd get better – and it did. A lot of those who'd called me names became good friends.

A: You eventually left school at 16 , didn't you?

G: That's right. I guess I got to the point where I felt like I knew that all I wanted to do was sing and play the guitar. My dad said I was too young and tried to put me off the idea. But then when he saw how determined I was, he told me I'd need to get a job if I wanted to save up enough money to record a demo. So I did get a job and very quickly managed to get enough money together to do the demo.

A: And that led to your first record deal.

G: And everything else that went with it – the contacts, the song writing, the touring. I love it all, especially going on tour, though you wouldn't believe the stresses and strains involved. Most people think it's a breeze, like dead easy and no worries. But the way I see it, you have a kind of responsibility when you're up there on stage. Being an entertainer is all about being larger than life and making people feel good.

A: So you've come a long way from your schooldays when the other kids made you cry!

G: Right. But in a way going through that experience at school helped me get over my shyness. So I don't worry any more what people think about my eyes. I'm far too busy worrying about what they think of my music!

A: Well, your first single was a number one hit in America, so you certainly don't seem to have anything to worry about there …

Unit 13 (Page 171)

2.30–2.37

FCE Part 1 – Multiple choice

One

Of course, I wasn't very happy about him losing his job. We had a few sleepless nights, I can tell you, what with the mortgage to pay and two hungry kids to feed. But no one was to blame for what happened, and thankfully it all worked out in the end. I'm just glad it's all over now. I don't know how we'd have managed to cope if he hadn't been taken on at the power station.

Two

W = Woman   M = Man

W: Dave's done well for himself, hasn't he?

M: Yes, well, it's hardly surprising, is it?

W: Why do you say that?

M: Well, it was the same thing at school. Fortune always smiled on him. He passed exams with the minimum of effort and now he's making money in the same way. He makes a few good decisions, invests in the right companies and bingo! Suddenly he's a millionaire. Still, it couldn't happen to a nicer guy. No one deserves it more than him.

Three

M = Man   W = Woman

M: Looking forward to going rock climbing, Sally?

W: Well, to tell you the truth, I haven't made my mind up about it. Everyone tells me it's great fun, especially when you realize that you're quite safe, with all the ropes and everything. But what if you get stuck and can't go on? That's what worries me. I can't see I'm going to enjoy myself, clinging to a rock waiting for someone to come and pull me off. Still, I won't know if I don't try, will I?

Four

Yes, well, we're very pleased you actually managed to phone us. At least you've done something right. You may have noticed, however, that it is now two o'clock in the morning … Yes, but you said you would be home by 12. If you can't keep promises then you shouldn't make them … No, we can't come and pick you up. You're old enough to be able to solve your own problems now.

Five

Oh come on, you said you'd help me out. I'll pay you back as soon as I get paid. It's just that it's our anniversary and I want to take her somewhere special to celebrate. … I can't ask Mum! You know how she is with money. She didn't lend you any that time you were broke, so I don't see why it'd be any different for me.

Six

W = Woman   M = Man

W: How on earth did you manage to get in such a mess?
M: It's toner from the photocopier. I was changing it and it went all over my clothes.
W: If your mother could see you now, she'd have a fit!
M: Have you got anything to clean it off with?
W: No, you'll have to go next door and get something from the shop. But don't take too long about it. I've got a few jobs I want you to do in the sales department.

Seven

I'd like to say how flattered I feel to have been invited to open this magnificent sports centre. And I am particularly proud of the fact that you voted unanimously for my name to be given to the centre. If I think back to all my sporting successes, the medals I have won and records I've broken, none of them ever gave me as much pleasure as this moment today. As a child growing up in this area, I never dreamed I would one day …

Eight

What I like about it is that you're doing things that nobody else has done before, discovering things about yourself as well as the world you live in. I've been to places I never knew existed until I got there, and I've travelled enormous distances without seeing another living soul. It's not whether it's the highest, the hottest or the coldest that matters to me, but being the first person to set foot there. That's why I do it.

Unit 14 (Page 179)

 2.38

FCE Part 4 – Multiple choice

P = male **Presenter**
S = Sally, a middle-aged pet shop owner

P: Ants, spiders, snakes and rats may not sound like ideal house companions, but as Sally Jefferson can confirm, they have become the pets of choice for an increasing number of pet-lovers in the Radio Carston area. Sally is the owner of Animal Crackers, a large pet shop in the centre of Carston. Sally, why the move away from cats and dogs?
S: Well, primarily, I think the trend reflects changing lifestyles. Cats and dogs need a lot of looking after, whereas insects and spiders, for example, are very low-maintenance – they more or less take care of themselves. And that's perfect for busy working couples who are out of the home most of the day and can't afford to spend a great deal of time on the more traditional kinds of pets. And, er, and then of course, there's the so-called educational pet, ants in particular.
P: Yes, I was surprised to hear that you sell a lot of them in your shop.
S: That's right, leaf-cutter ants mostly. You can create your own colony in an ant farm – that's a glass box like a big fish tank filled with clean sand or soil. You can watch them in their nest, digging tunnels and cutting leaves, all collaborating to achieve a common goal. It's a great lesson in the benefits of teamwork, especially for children. And for that reason a lot of parents come in and buy them.
P: And do the kids like them?
S: Yes, most do – after all, ants are fascinating creatures to watch close up. But of course, they're not furry or cuddly, and children can't interact with them in the same way that they can with a cat or a dog. If you pick them up or try to play with them, they can give you quite a nasty bite. So inevitably some children start to grow tired of them, pay less attention to them.
P: Right. And how about spiders? You were telling me before the programme that you sell tarantulas – can they be handled?
S: It's not advisable, but in this case it's more because of the risk involved to the tarantula than to the owner. They do bite, of course, and as we've seen in films, sometimes with fatal results. But a bite from the species we sell is rather like being stung by a bee. No, the main problem is that they are fragile creatures and if they run around when they're on your hand or arm, there's a danger they'll fall off and hurt themselves very badly. So best not to get them out of their cage too often.
P: No, indeed. Now let's move on to another type of pet that seems to be in fashion these days – snakes. Do they need a lot of care and attention?
S: That really depends on the species you buy – different species have different requirements. What's common to the corn snakes and ball pythons that we sell is that they can sometimes go for months without eating. So if you're going on holiday you don't have to worry about finding someone to feed them while you're away. However, it's important to realize that many snakes have a lifespan of more than 20 years – so you need to be aware that you are making a long-term commitment when you buy one.
P: And what sort of things do they eat?
S: Mice, mainly, and perhaps rats or even rabbits for some of the larger species. It's better to give them pre-killed animals, which can be bought frozen at reasonably little cost from pet stores. It's more humane for the mice and rats and so on, and also safer for the snakes. A rat can seriously wound a snake when it's acting in self-defence.
P: Interesting that you mention rats, because of course, they too are kept as pets nowadays, aren't they?
S: That's right. They make very good pets and they don't bite quite as readily as most people think. You need to bear in mind, though, that they like being with other rats, so they really need to be kept in pairs or even groups, and in a large cage, too. Technically, of course, they're nocturnal animals but they will adapt to their owners' schedules and are happy to come out and play when people are around during the day.
P: You don't feed them to the snakes, do you, Sally?
S: No, don't worry, we never do that …

Unit 15 (Page 186)

 2.39–2.43

FCE Part 3 – Multiple matching

Speaker 1
I never had time to go to the German classes my company arranged for us at work, so I used to put tapes on in the car on the way in every morning and just let the language wash

over me. I was completely immersed in it for the whole journey. Then I'd listen to the same section on the way home and that was enough to ensure I learnt what I'd heard in the morning. When I go to Germany on sales trips now I have very few problems understanding people. Business seems to be improving, too.

Speaker 2

I went to Spain twice when I was studying languages at university; once on holiday and the next year to work in a bar. The holiday was a disaster in terms of language learning. I spent most of the time with my English friends and hardly learnt a thing. When I went back there to work, though, I spoke Spanish all day and my speaking and understanding really improved. That experience working abroad helped me pass my final exams just as much as studying, I'm convinced. Oh, and I'm getting married this year to my Spanish girlfriend.

Speaker 3

I spent three years teaching English in Poland with my boyfriend back in the early 90s. It took us both quite a long time to learn any Polish in the beginning, partly because of laziness, but mostly because we were working long hours teaching and speaking English all day. Things got better, though, once we eventually got to know a few Polish people and we had more chance to speak the language. We both became much more integrated after that. We even saw a few films in Polish at the cinema.

Speaker 4

Here in Wales everyone can speak English, but more and more young people are learning Welsh, the real native language. My mum and dad both came to Wales from England, so I only ever spoke in English till I came to this school. But all lessons are in Welsh, see? Right from day one everything has been in Welsh and I've learnt really quickly. So now I've got the two languages. I speak in Welsh with my friends and I speak it at home, too, with my brother. It's great 'cause we can talk about things in front of my mum and dad and they've got no idea what either of us is saying – really useful sometimes!

Speaker 5

When I left university I desperately wanted to work abroad, but all three French-owned companies that I applied to turned me down at the interview stage. I'd only ever learnt grammar when I was at school so when I had to speak French in the interview I couldn't understand the questions and I'm sure the interviewers couldn't understand a word of what I was saying. So I signed up for a two-month course in Paris and when I came back I got the first job I applied for.

Ready for Speaking (Page 197)

 2.44

FCE Part 1 – Interview

I = Interviewer   P = Paolo   C = Christina

I: Good morning. My name is Allan Reeves and this is my colleague Teresa Riley. And your names are?
C: Christina.
P: My name is Paolo.
I: Can I have your marksheets, please? Thank you. First of all we'd like to know something about you. Where are you from, Paolo?
P: From a small town near Ravenna. In Italy.

I: And you Christina?
C: I'm from Corinth, in Greece. I have lived there all my life. I live there with my three sisters and my parents. I am in my last year at school. My mother works in a shop and my …
I: Thank you, Christina. What do you like about living in Corinth?
C: Ah well, yes. Erm, it is by the sea, so we can go swimming. Also there are parks, er, and lots of bars and things to do in the evening, so, er, it is very lively, especially in summer. In winter it is more quieter. But it is very interesting to live there. It is very ancient.
I: And what about you Paolo?
P: My town?
I: Yes.
P: It is a little boring. I mean, I don't really like living there. There's more to do in Ravenna.
I: OK, Christina, what subjects do you enjoy most at school?
C: Well, I like languages very much, but my favourite subject is mathematics. I always like it, since I was very young. It is something I can do, working with numbers and usually I get very good marks. I wish my English would be as good!
I: Paolo, do you work or are you a student?
P: I work in my uncle's computer business.
I: And how important is English for your work?
P: Well, yes, it's very important. I have to read a lot of things about computers in English, and sometimes I must talk to foreign customers.
I: Now, let's move on to what you do in your spare time. Paolo, what kind of sports are you interested in?
P: Er, I play football, tennis, and, er, I go swimming.
I: And how often do you play football?
P: Once a week. Yes, every Saturday. I play in a team. It's good fun.
I: And Christina, do you have any hobbies?
C: Well, not really hobbies, but in my free time I like to go to the cinema, going out with my friends and things like that.
I: Which sort of films do you like to watch?
C: Oh, I like action films. I like films where many things happen. I don't like romantic films or historical films. I think they are a little bored.
I: Now, thinking about the future, Christina. What do you hope to do in the next few years?
C: Well, I want to go to the university and study business studies first. Then after that, if it is possible I'll work in a big company, as an accountant or something like that. Maybe, in the future I can use my English and find a job in another country. That would be very exciting.
I: And what kind of job do you hope to be doing in ten years' time, Paolo?
P: Well, ten years is a long time, so I'm not sure what will happen. First, I want to help my uncle expanding his business and then maybe in the future, I could set up my own business.

Ready for Speaking (Page 198)

 2.45–46

FCE Part 2 – Talking about photographs

I = Interviewer   C = Christina   P = Paolo

I: In this part of the test, I'm going to give each of you two photographs. I'd like you to talk about your photographs on your own for about a minute, and also to answer a short question about your partner's photographs.

Christina, it's your turn first. Here are your photographs. They show grandfathers with their grandchildren. I'd like you to compare the photographs, and say how important grandparents can be in situations like these. All right?

C: Yes, er, in the first picture the girl is playing the piano with her grandfather whereas in the other one the man is teaching his granddaughter to ride a bicycle. In both pictures everybody is smiling and seems to be enjoying themselves. Er, what else? Yes, in the first picture they are indoors whereas in this one they are outside and the girl is wearing a special hat for protect her head if she falls over. I can't make out how old is the man in this picture, but I think he is younger that the other grandfather. Er, let me see, well, I think grandparents can help a lot, especially nowadays, because parents are very busy and often they don't have the time to be with their children. Grandparents can look after the grandchildren, during the school holidays, er, cook for them and make sure they are not in danger. They can even play with them, like in these pictures. Children can learn many things from their grandparents, maybe not things like use the computer, but more traditional activities, such as riding a bike or making things, er ..

I: Thank you, Paolo, has an older relative taught you to do something?

P: Yes, my uncle taught me to play golf.

I: Thank you.

I: Now, Paolo, here are your photographs. They show people in an emergency situation. I'd like you to compare the photographs, and say how serious you think each of the situations looks. All right?

P: OK. In this picture I can see a television journalist interviewing a policeman. They must be in America because the policeman's uniform is the typical one you see in films and on TV. Also the writing is in English. It's not obvious what has happened but maybe there's been an accident or there might have been a crime, even. Perhaps a murder or something, I don't know. Er, in this picture it looks as if they are in an ambulance, because the woman's wearing a thing on her face for air, for oxygen, and the man's writing down the details about the woman. Er, it's difficult to say which is more serious, we don't really know what's happened. In the first picture the television camera is there, and nobody is allowed to cross the, the, line, so it must be quite important. It's not just an ordinary crime or accident. In the second one, the woman looks quite relaxed, well, not relaxed, maybe, but she isn't panicking, so I think this situation isn't very serious.

I: Thank you. Christina, do you think you could be a policewoman?

C: Oh, no. I think it is a very difficult job. It's maybe good to meet lots of people and work outside, but it's too dangerous – I wouldn't like to do it, no.

I: Thank you.

Ready for Speaking (Page 199)

🔊 2.47

FCE Part 3 – Collaborative task

I = Interviewer   C = Christina   P = Paolo

I: Now I'd like you to talk about something together for about three minutes. I'd like you to imagine that the History Museum in your town would like to attract more visitors. Here are some ideas for improving the museum.

First, talk to each other about the proposals saying how they might appeal to different people. Then decide which two would be the most successful in attracting new visitors. All right?

C: Which one shall we start with?

P: Er, let's talk about the interactive computer programme first. In my opinion it will appeal to a lot of people, because computers are so important in our lives today. Most people know how to use a computer now, don't they?

C: Well, no everyone, no, I don't agree. And anyway, I don't think the people go to the museums to use a computer. They can do that at home or at work. A medieval fair would be something very different, though. That would be interesting for people of all ages. It could be good fun, don't you think?

P: Yes, that's true. The visitors could take part in different activities and eat medieval food. And if the organizers dressed up in costumes, that would make history very colourful and realistic. It sounds like a great idea.

C: So that could be one of the two things we choose. Now, what do you think about the concerts? Visitors to the museum would like to listen music. People who work could come in their lunch break and have a relaxing moment.

P: Yes, but I really don't think it would attract many people who work, particularly if the museum is in a city – everyone is busy all day. Retired people would probably appreciate it and have more time to enjoy it, but that wouldn't increase the number of visitors very much, would it?

C: No, I suppose you're right.

P: Personally, I think we need to have activities which appeal to children, because if children want to come, their parents will have to come too.

C: Yes, I agree. So, let's have a look for something. Well, children could enjoy coin-making, but it wouldn't make parents say, "we really must take our children to the museum"!

P: You're right. It's a bit dull.

C: But how about the cave painting? That sounds really enjoyable for children. If they have to paint like prehistoric man, then I imagine they will have to use their hands, and make a mess. And children love doing that. Don't you agree?

P: Yes, I do. They would enjoy themselves very much. But let's look at the others before we decide. Er, the exhibition of kitchens is nothing special. I mean, you can see things like that in lots of places, can't you?

C: Yes, it isn't the most fascinating idea. I don't know who would want to see that. Maybe some adults, but not many. And the Megascreen, well, that's like the computers. Nobody will go to a museum to see a film. What do you think, Paolo?

P: I completely disagree. To my mind that's the kind of thing that will make it different to other museums and would appeal to all types of different people. And the screen would be very big, so it's not the same that watching it on television or at the cinema.

C: Well, I'm really keen on films, but I rather go to a real cinema. I prefer the atmosphere there. And historical films are old and a bit boring, especially for children, so not many people would go.

P: Well, I think that should be one of the two things we choose, personally. I think it would bring people who don't normally go to museums or even who have never been.

C: OK, well we agree on the medieval fair, but not on the Megascreen. I think the cave painting is a better idea.

What do you think of the fashion shows?

P: Oh no. I don't know anyone who is interested in fashion shows.

C: Really?

I: Thank you.

Ready for Speaking (Page 199)

🔘 2.48

FCE Part 4 – Further discussion

I = Interviewer   C = Christina   P = Paolo

I: Christina, what do you think makes a good museum?

C: I don't know really. I suppose that, I think that, in general the museums are a little bored. You only look at objects which are in, in, erm, how do you say? Erm, well, like boxes, in glass boxes or cupboards, so there is nothing to do. I think if you could touch the things in an exhibition, that would make it more interesting, a more enjoyable experience.

I: Uh huh. Paolo?

P: I think ideas like the medieval fair are good because they help you to have a better idea of life in the past. The last year I went to a museum where people in costumes explained how different things were used. Even they cooked with some old saucepans and things. Perhaps they weren't real, but it doesn't matter. The important is that you can imagine how people lived before.

I: How could the teaching of history in schools be improved?

C: I'm not quite sure, but, well, er, at school we just sit and listen the teachers, listen to the teachers, and write what they say. In Greece there are so many ancient monuments so perhaps we could visit more and not just read and write about them all the time.

I: What do you think, Paolo?

P: Er, when I was at school we just listened to the teachers. I think history was the worst subject for many people. I think we need better teachers who are good at making a subject more interesting for pupils. I don't know, but I think it depends on the teacher.

I: What was the most important moment in the history of the twentieth century?

C: Er, I haven't thought about it before, really, but, er, perhaps it was, yes, I think it was when the first man landed on the Moon. I have seen pictures of this, and I think it should, it must have been something quite incredible at the time. Now, going into space is quite normal, but that moment was very different. What do you think, Paolo?

P: Well, I think the landing on the Moon was important, but travel in space would not be possible if we did not have computers. The invention of the computer, for me, was the most important moment. It changed the way we live …

C: You only say that because you like computers!

P: No, but almost everything we do needs computers nowadays. Aeroplanes, industries, banks, companies – they all need to have computers. And if the computers break down, there are always many problems for these things. We cannot survive without computers.

C: Maybe, but I think there are more important things that happened in the last century. Things with people and not machines. For example, when people started to think about the environment more. The planet is in a bad condition, and if organizations like Greenpeace didn't exist, it would be worse. Don't you agree?

P: Yes, you're right, but even organizations like Greenpeace need computers to do their work!

I: Paolo, what items from our lives today will be in the history museums of the future?

P: That's a difficult question. Possibly, some things we have in the house, some domestic ap, er, domestic applications? No, well, it doesn't matter, domestic machines we use for cooking or other jobs, things like the cooker, the vacuum cleaner or the iron. I think some of these things will be replaced for robots which do not need people to use them.

C: Do you really think we will have robots?

P: Yes, we already have them now. In only a few years, I think we will be able to use them in the home for doing simple things.

C: Well, I think one thing in the museums of the future will be the money. I think the credit cards will be the only thing we use. Already now, some people never pay for things with cash. In only a few years I think they will stop making the money.

I: Thank you. That is the end of the test.

Answer Key

Unit 1 Lifestyle

Vocabulary 1: Clothes Page 2

1
People from left to right
1 waistcoat, bow tie (shirt, shoes, trousers)
2 scarf, blazer (shirt/blouse, shoes, skirt, tie, tights)
3 trainers, dungarees (hat, jacket, T-shirt)
4 bracelet, cardigan, high-heeled shoes (dress, necklace, tights, watch)
5 jumper (jeans, shoes)
6 trainers, tracksuit bottoms (baseball cap, T-shirt)
Note: *dinner jacket* does not appear in this picture

2
Suggested answers
1 formal, plain, tasteful, smart
2 unfashionable, smart
3 casual, unfashionable, shabby, colourful (jacket), waterproof (jacket)
4 formal, colourful, tasteful, smart (shoes), tight-fitting (dress)
5 baggy (jumper), casual, colourful (jumper), plain
6 baggy (T-shirt/tracksuit bottoms), casual, colourful (baseball cap), plain (T-shirt), trendy (trainers/ tracksuit bottoms)

3
A 1 go with/match **2** match **3** suit **4** fit
B 1 get dressed **2** put on **3** wearing

Reading: Gapped text Page 3

How to go about it
a they, them, theirs   **b** D

Reading task
1 D **2** B **3** H **4** F **5** A **6** C **7** E
G is not used because:
● in many cases the pronoun *she* does not fit the grammatical context surrounding the gaps.
● it does not make meaningful sense in any of the contexts.

Language focus 1: Habitual behaviour Page 5

B Frequency adverbs

2
a main verbs immediately before (or before the subject – see Grammar reference page 206)
b after the verb *to be*
c after the auxiliary verb

Practice

1
1 Correct (*or* Hardly do I get clothes for my birthday or for Christmas.)
2 I sometimes have breakfast in my pyjamas. (*or* Sometimes I have breakfast in my pyjamas.)
3 I always fold my clothes up before I go to bed.
4 Correct
5 When I go shopping for clothes I can rarely find jeans which fit me perfectly.
6 Correct (*or* I occasionally wash my own clothes, but my mum or dad normally does it.)

C *Used to* and *would*
Practice
1 a **2** a **3** b **4** c **5** a **6** b **7** b **8** c **9** c

Vocabulary 2: *Get* Page 6

A Expressions with *get*
1 C **2** D **3** A **4** A **5** B **6** B **7** A **8** C

B Meanings of *get*

1
1 c **2** e **3** f **4** d **5** b **6** a **7** h (*or* a) **8** g

2
Sometimes we had to console them even when they did get the job they wanted.
a receive/obtain
Kate Moss had to get to Paris.
f arrive/reach
I flew with her to Brussels with the intention of getting the train from there.
e catch
Parents were usually encouraged to get involved with their daughters' careers.
c become

Listening: Multiple matching Page 7

1-2
Possible answers
A a wedding: guest, witness, priest, best man, church, registry office ...
B a birthday party: guest, host, at home, at a disco ...
C a job interview: candidate, interviewer, panel, in an office or other place of work
D a sporting event: spectator, competitor, star, opponent, in a stadium, at a sports centre
E a film premiere: a star, audience, director, producer, at a cinema
F an examination: candidate, invigilator, in an examination hall

3
There are many possible answers.

Listening task

1 A **2** F **3** D **4** C **5** B

Language focus 2: *Be used to, get used to* and *used to* Page 8

1

1a **2**b **3**a

2

Be used to + *-ing*/noun in the affirmative describes the state in which one no longer finds situations new or strange.
eg *I am used to the heat* means it is no problem for me now.
Get used to + *ing*/noun in the affirmative describes the process of reaching normality with a new or strange situation.
eg *I am getting used to the heat* means it is less of a problem for me now than before.

3

the gerund

Practice

2c

1 get used to having **2** used to cook
3 is/has got used to eating **4** used to write **5** get used to
6 be/have got used to driving **7** get used to driving

Writing: Informal letters Page 10

1

Mark wants to know how I am settling in to the new house. He wants to know if I can visit to help them in the summer.

2

Paragraph 2 to describe how he spends a typical day
Paragraph 3 to give news and invite you to visit
Paragraph 4 to finish and ask for a reply

3

1 e **2** a **3** no, because this expression is too formal **4** c **5** g
6 no, too formal **7** no, too formal **8** d **9** b **10** f

4

1 while **2** as **3** and, as well **4** but **5** so **6** but, while

5

1 giving news **2** asking for help **3** inviting **4** refusing an invitation **5** accepting an invitation **6** apologizing

6

Paragraph 1
Thank Mark for his letter. Make a friendly comment about his life on the farm.
Paragraph 2
Mention what you have/haven't got used to. Say whether you have made any friends. Say two or three things about your daily routine. Mention how long it takes to get to school/work.

Paragraph 3
Accept or refuse the invitation and give a reason.
Paragraph 4
Explain why you have to finish the letter. Refer to a possible future meeting/letter.

Sample answer

Dear Mark,
I'm writing to you to tell you that I'm not going to go to your farm in summer because of my new work. However, I'll try to see you as soon as possible.

As you know, I moved to a new house six months ago and since then I've met new people.

I think that living there is better than I thought and with regard to my new surroundings I must say that they are excellent. I usually get up at half past seven and I went to work. Then I have a breakfast with my friends and I go to improve my English spoken in the afternoon in a specific classe. In the evening, I'm used to going to the cinema because here it's cheaper.

After all, I think is good have a new experience in your life and this is an example to explain it. As far as I'm concerned, I don't know if I'll have to return to my city, but it doesn't matter so much in these moments.

I hope you write me as you did.
All the best
Luis
186 words

Examiner's comment
Content: Adequate coverage of points.
Accuracy: The errors do not obscure communication but they may distract the reader – *I'm used to going to the cinema* is not appropriate here, the use of *went* instead of *go* in the third paragraph, the omission of the subject in *I think is good* are some examples of inaccuracies.
Range: Vocabulary is generally appropriate except for *a breakfast, a specific classe*. Tenses are generally correct – *since then I've met new people*.
Organization and cohesion: An abrupt beginning but the letter is organized into paragraphs. Successful use of simple sequencing in the third paragraph – *then, in the afternoon/evening*.
Register and format: Awkward at times – *with regard to my new surroundings* (too formal for the context), and some confusion is evident in the use of *After all* and *As far as I'm concerned*.
Target reader: The overall effect would be reasonably positive: the information asked for has been provided and the tone, although inconsistent at times, would not cause problems.
Mark: good band 3

Review 1 Page 12

Use of English: Transformations

1 is slowly getting over **2** getting rid of **3** tend to buy
4 always borrowing my things without **5** we would often go **6** get used to sharing **7** got used to working
8 looking forward to seeing **9** 'd/had better phone

Vocabulary
A Clothes
1 *afternoon* 2 baggy 3 waterproof 4 tight-fitting
5 long-sleeved 6 waist

B Expressions crossword
Expressions for use in informal letters
Across 1 thanks 5 forward 8 way 9 love 12 taken
Down 2 know 7 better 11 hear

Expressions with *get*
Across 3 rid 4 on 10 touch 13 paid
Down 1 trouble 3 ready 6 dressed

C People
1 e 2 f 3 a 4 b 5 d 6 c

1 competitor, spectators 2 host, guests 3 bride, groom
4 audience, performers 5 doctor, patient
6 candidates, invigilator

Unit 2 High energy

Vocabulary 1: Music Page 14

2
a Photograph 1: flute, trumpet, sousaphone (a type of
tuba)
Photograph 2: violin, viola, cello, double bass, harp,
flute, clarinet
b 1 lead 2 a song 3 musician 4 on 5 play 6 live* 7 in
8 instrument
*pronunciation /laɪv/

Listening 1: Sentence completion Page 15

3
1 the seventies 2 three 3 talented musicians
4 mixing tracks 5 ten thousand 6 weekend 7 on a journey
8 (a form of) meditation 9 computer programmes
10 a younger audience

Language focus 1: Indirect ways of asking questions Page 16

2
a word order – no inversion of subject/verb
auxiliary verbs – in the present simple and the past
simple *do/does/did* are not used.
Notice that some indirect questions do not need a
question mark.
b Questions like this are commonly known as 'Yes/No'
questions. They need *if* or *whether* in the indirect form.
I'd like to know *if/whether a gig requires much preparation.*

Practice
Possible answers
1 Could you explain why dance music is so popular?
2 Would you mind telling us what a clubber has to pay
to see you perform?
3 I'd be interested to know when you did your first gig.
4 Could you tell us if/whether you plan to work with any
famous groups?

5 I was wondering if you could tell me what you like
most about DJ-ing.
6 We'd like to know how you became a DJ.
7 Could you tell us if/whether anything has ever gone
wrong at a gig?

Writing 1: Letters: Asking for information Page 16

2
formal register is appropriate
1 would like 2 I would be grateful for 3 I would
4 some queries 5 indicate
6 I would be pleased to receive 7 I look
8 receiving your reply

3
a Yes
b ... *last week's edition of 'International Musician' ...*
... *interested in having violin lessons ...*
... *If you have a brochure with photographs ...*
c (included in the price?) ... *whether the cost of excursions
is included?*
(ask!) ... *I would like to know the price of a one-month
course ...*

Sample answer

Dear Sir/Madam
I am writing about your advertisement on the
Saturday's edition of 'El Pais'. I am interested in the
Rock Festival which will take place in Oxford in two
weeks time. I would like to receive further information
about some details of the festival.

Firstly, I would appreciate if you could indicate me
the timetables of the transport you provide between
Heathrow and Oxford. This information would be
quite important for us, since we have to take the plane
back to Madrid on Sunday at 9.15pm and we do not
want to miss it.

Furthermore we can not come on Friday and we would
know wether we can have a reduction if we only assist
to the festival for two days. Finally, we would like to
stay all in the same room, so we would be grateful if
you could tell us if a room for three is available.

We look forward to receiving your reply
Yours faithfully
Elena García
159 words

Examiner's comment
Content: All major points covered, with good
manipulation and development of information in the
input material (eg second paragraph).
Accuracy: There are a number of inaccuracies but they
generally do not impede understanding – *two weeks (')
time, I would appreciate (it) if you could indicate (to) me,
we would (like to) know w(h)ether, assist to (attend) the
festival.*
Range: Good range of grammar and appropriate range
of vocabulary – *I would like to receive further information
about, we would be grateful if you could tell us if a room
for three is available.*

Organization and cohesion: The letter is clearly organized with suitable paragraphs and the linking devices are used accurately: *Firstly, Furthermore, Finally, since we have to, so we would be grateful.* The opening and closing are appropriate, except for *on the Saturday's.*
Style and format: Entirely appropriate to the task.
Target reader: Would have a clear idea about the writer's questions.
Mark: band 4

Reading: Multiple matching Page 18

2
A Street luge 3 **B** Ice-climbing 2 **C** BASE-jumping 4
D Zorbing 1

3
1 B 2 D 3 A 4 C 5 D 6 A 7 B **8/9** A, D in any order
10 C **11** B **12** C **13** D **14** A **15** C

Language focus 2: Gerunds and infinitives A Page 20

1
a Zorbing **b** Base-jumping **c** Base-jumping

2
a 3 b 1 c 2

3
a infinitive **b** gerund **c** gerund

4
b *began*
(*Begin* can be followed by the infinitive *to jump* with no change in meaning.)

Practice

1
1 going, to meet **2** smiling, to hit **3** (to) improve, taking
4 to take, studying **5** to let, asking

2
detest, hate, can't stand, don't like, don't mind, quite like, really enjoy, love, absolutely adore

3
interested **in**
fond **of**
good/bad **at**
bored **with**
excited **about**

Listening 2: Multiple choice Page 21

2
1 B 2 C 3 C 4 A 5 C 6 A 7 B

Word formation: Affixes Page 22

1
8	instruct	instructor
9	eco**no**mic	eco**no**mist
10	**moun**tain	mountain**eer**
11	elec**tric**	elec**tri**cian
12	entertain	entertainer
13	assist	assistant
14	**in**terview	interview**ee**/interviewer

(The sections in **bold** type indicate a change in the word stress.)

2
1 *un* **2** in **3** il **4** im **5** im **6** ir **7** dis

3
under	too little/not enough
over	too much/excessive
pre	before
post	after
hyper	very big
micro	very small
mis	wrongly
re	again
ex-	former
-ess	woman

Language focus 3: Gerunds and infinitives B Page 22

1
a 1 **b** 2

2
1a

I remember studying this piece of grammar last year.
(First I studied it and later I remembered the action. = remember doing an earlier action)

b

I must remember to study my notes on gerunds and infinitives tonight.
(First I need to remember and then I need to study. = remember to do a later action)

2 a First action – we regret
Second action – announce
b First action – I caught the train
Second action – I regretted it
3 a First action – I stopped what I was doing (eg walking, driving)
Second action – I bought a newspaper (infinitive of purpose)
b First action – buying newspapers

Second action – stop: I do not buy newspapers any more.
4 a This describes an experiment, doing something to see if it will solve the problem (s/he had lessons)
b This means that s/he made an effort (s/he did not have lessons)
5 a meant = entailed/involved
b meant = intended/planned

Vocabulary 2: Sports Page 23

1

do	go	play
athletics	skiing	volleyball
gymnastics	cycling	tennis
	swimming	basketball
		football

2

You play volleyball, basketball and tennis on a court.
You go skiing on ski slopes.
You go cycling or do athletics on a track.
You do gymnastics in a gym.
You play football on a pitch.
You go swimming in a pool.

3

volleyball player, tennis player, basketball player, skier, cyclist, swimmer, gymnast, footballer

4

1 take part, take place **2** win, beat **3** play, practise
4 spectators, audience

Writing 2: Articles Page 23

How to go about it

2

Paragraph 1 c Paragraph 2 a
Paragraph 3 d Paragraph 4 b

3

It is written for readers of *International Sports Weekly* magazine.

4

The style is informal.
a Contractions: *doesn't, you've, you'll, I'm, you're, don't, they're*
b Informal linkers: *So, And, Also*
c Direct questions: *Have you ever seen a smile on the face of a long distance runner? So what is the attraction of running?*
d Phrasal verbs: *give up, take up, put off*

5

1 c 2 a 3 b

Examiner's comment
Content: Adequate coverage of points 1 and 3 but point 2 (why do you like it?) not really dealt with. The question incites a personal response but the information given is mostly rather general again.
Accuracy: Reasonable. One missing verb (*I extremely fond of* – a slip?) one spelling mistake (*usuful*) one false agreement (*professionals teams*). The problem is awkwardness rather than pure inaccuracy (positive error). Final sentence doesn't communicate.
Range: Doesn't have all the vocabulary (*occupy with them, many particularities, big football courts*) though makes good attempts (*fond of, anything else apart from football, go into training, because of the injuries*). Some variety of structures, some complex sentences.
Organization and cohesion: Four paragraphs including an introduction and conclusion. Conventional paragraph links (*Firstly, Secondly*). Some sentence links (*although, if, because of*).
Style and format: Consistently neutral. Acceptable article format.
Target reader: Message not entirely clear; certainly some enthusiasm conveyed to the reader, but why does the writer like football so much? Some awkwardness of expressions may distract target reader, and the final sentence is obscure.
Mark: borderline band 2/3

Review 2 Page 24
Word formation

1

1 undersleep **2** overlittle **3** oversing **4** missucceed
5 dislove **6** doctoress

2

1 undercharged **2** overgrown **3** overslept

4 misspelt/misspelled **5** disappearance **6** waitress
Use of English: Word formation
1 impossible **2** Competitors **3** disappearing **4** divers
5 uncommon **6** underwater **7** discourage **8** unlikely
9 misjudged **10** director

Gerunds and infinitives

1

1 to write **2** getting **3** tapping **4** to have **5** talking
6 to study **7** to open **8** putting

2

1 finish (takes the gerund, the others take the infinitive)
2 begin (all of them can be used with the gerund or
the infinitive, but *begin* is the only one for which the
meaning remains the same)
3 feel like (takes the gerund, the others take the infinitive)
4 tend to (takes the infinitive, the others take the gerund)
5 can't afford (takes the infinitive, the others take the
gerund)

Vocabulary: Music

1 on the radio **2** play a tune **3** in the charts
4 session musicians **5** in tune **6** mime a song **7** on tour
8 play a track

Unit 3 A change for the better?

Vocabulary: Machines and devices Page 26

2

electric carving knife – gadget or appliance, depending on
the speaker's viewpoint: if it is considered indispensable
then it could be called an appliance. If not, a gadget.
(adjectives – handy, labour-saving, etc)
electric pencil sharpener – gadget
(adjectives – handy, unusual, complicated, etc)
automatic curtains – gadget
(adjectives – clever, unusual, complicated, etc)

Reading: Multiple choice Page 26

1

1 c

2

2 B line 12 'The things that are supposed to speed up and
simplify our lives more often than not have the opposite
effect...'
3 C line 19 'they had come to expect machines to do
almost everything for them.'
4 C in paragraph 5 the author is exaggerating for comic
effect
5 D line 26 'and the whole thing (the knife is in his
hands, not the turkey) flew out of his hands'
6 A line 35 'People are so addicted to convenience that
they have become trapped in a vicious circle...'
7 B
8 D line 44 'We didn't go anywhere near them after the
first week.'

Language focus 1: Comparisons Page 29

1 quicker (line 8) **2** speedier, more convenient (line 10)
3 more, than (line 13) **4** as, as (line 23)
5 less than (line 31) **6** with (line 32)
7 more, harder (lines 36-7) **8** easier (line 40)

A Comparative and superlative adjectives

1 *quick-er, quick-est* one-syllable words eg older, louder,
taller
speedi-er, speedi-est two-syllable words ending in *–y*
eg noisy, happy, silly
more convenient, the most convenient words with two or
more syllables eg modern, confident, comfortable
2 cleaner, the cleanest
hotter, the hottest
stranger, the strangest
more clever (cleverer), the most clever (the cleverest)
better, the best
worse, the worst
farther, the farthest *or* further, the furthest
3 big differences *far, a lot, significantly*
small differences *a bit, slightly*

Practice

1

1 *c* **2** a **3** e **4** b **5** f **6** d

3

1 *d* **2** c **3** a **4** b **5** f **6** e

4

1 was far worse than
2 as sad as she
3 the least enjoyable
4 you work now, the less
5 quite as much experience as

Word formation: Suffixes *-ful* and *-less* Page 30

1

Root	Positive	Negative
success (n)	successful	unsuccessful
skill (n)	skilful (Am*: skillful)	unskilled
home (n)	—	homeless
cheer (n/v)	cheerful	**cheerless
delight (n/v)	delightful	—
thought (n)	thoughtful	thoughtless
harm (n/v)	harmful	harmless
pain (n/v)	painful	painless
end (n/v)	—	endless
power (n)	powerful	powerless
care (n/v)	careful	careless
price (n/v)	pricey (informal)	priceless

*In the exam candidates must consistently use *either*
British *or* American spelling.
** *cheerless* used mainly to describe the weather or a
room

Note the following:
endless possible opposite – *finite*
delightful possible opposite – *awful*
the adjective 'homely' (simple and pleasant in a way that makes you feel comfortable and at home) also exists.

2

tasty – used to describe food with a strong and pleasant flavour
tasteful – used to describe clothes, decoration, etc which is attractive and shows good taste.
1 helpful = useful
2 helplessly = unable to do anything
3 unhelpful = not willing/not wanting to help

3

1 adv	skilfully
2 adj	unsuccessful
3 noun	carelessness
4 adj	thoughtful
5 adj	uneventful
6 adj	harmful
7 adj	painless
8 noun	cheerfulness
9 adj	pointless
10 noun	homelessness

Listening 1: Multiple matching Page 31

2

1 D **2** A **3** E **4** B **5** C

Noticing language

1

1 as soon as = immediately/once
2 as long as = if/provided/providing/on condition that
3 as well as = in addition to/besides
4 as far as I'm concerned = in my opinion

2

1 long **2** soon **3** many **4** well **5** far **6** much

Speaking 1: Collaborative task Page 32

a past simple, *used to*, *would*
b present simple, adverbs of frequency, *tend to*
c to describe events which occurred at some time between the past and the present
d *used to*, *get used to*, *would* and comparatives

Language focus 2: Articles Page 33

1

a Many parents do not question the educational value of home computers although they themselves may not understand them.
b The Government is in favour of having more computers in schools in order to compete better with other countries.
c They believe that home computers cannot replace real teachers.

2

1 the	**2** a	**3** a	**4** the	**5** –
6 –	**7** –	**8** –	**9** the	**10** The
11 the	**12** The	**13** -	**14** the	**15** the
16 –	**17** a (or *the* if he is the only lecturer)			
18 –	**19** –	**20** –		

3

Question	Grammar reference section
The definite article	
12	A1
10	A2
1,4	A4
11, 14	A7
9, 15	A5a
The indefinite article	
0, 3	B1
17	B3
2	B4
No article	
5, 20	C1a
7, 13, 16	C1b
6, 19	C1c
8	C2
18	C3

Listening 2: Multiple choice Page 34

2

1 B **2** C **3** A **4** A **5** C **6** B **7** C

Writing: Essays Page 35

2

Paragraph 1 a general introduction
Paragraph 2 positive aspects/advantages of mobile phones
Paragraph 3 negative aspects/disadvantages of mobile phones
Paragraph 4 conclusion/summary of opinions

3

Expressing contrasts
On the one hand/On the other hand, Some people feel that, Others argue that
Adding information
In addition (to this), What is more, Another disadvantage is, Besides this, Furthermore
Concluding
To sum up, On balance

4

they, them, models, the mobile phone, (drivers who use) one, (what for many people is a) useful device, (for others is) a nuisance

5

Examiner's comment
Content: Good realization of the task. An appropriately balanced approach to the question.
Accuracy: Some awkwardness/inaccuracies – *which is in all kinds of jobs, learn to handle with them, has brought the chance to get, have been replace(d) by* but these do not cause misunderstandings or obscure communication.
Range: Generally the candidate shows good control of both vocabulary and grammar – *a great deal of, very little, thanks to the huge variety of, deal with information, such as doing sports …*
Organization and cohesion: Clear organization helped by good use of linking devices – *On the positive side, Moreover, Finally, On the other hand,* etc.
Style and format: Consistent, appropriate to the task.
Target reader: The reader would have a clear understanding of the writer's opinion based on a balanced evaluation of the advantages and disadvantages of computers.
Mark: band 4

Review 3 Page 36
Vocabulary: Word partnerships

1

1 food 2 knife 3 oven 4 machine 5 sharpener 6 steamer 7 control 8 device 9 appliance 10 toothbrush

2

Student's own answers.

Comparisons

1

1 *d* 2 e 3 a 4 b 5 h 6 c 7 f 8 g

2-4
Student's own answers.

Articles

2

3 in **the** home 4 spend ~~the~~ more 5 killed **the** art 6 write ~~the~~ emails 7 **the** less 8 **the** mobile phone 9 put in **a** 10 on **the** train 11 watched **a** young couple 12 not just **the** young 13 **a** high percentage 14 into ~~the~~ your phone 15 I'm **the** one 16 to **the** mountains

Use of English: Word formation
The writer is clearly an older person, possibly middle-aged or older.
1 painless 2 thoughtful 3 ungrateful 4 cheerfully 5 disadvantages 6 embarrassment 7 careless 8 effortlessly 9 wonderfully 10 fortunate

Ready for Reading

Part 1: Multiple choice Page 38

4
1
A Not stated. The writer says that 'The majority of mountain rescue statistics are made up from summer walkers suffering heart attacks' but this does not mean that heat is the main cause of heart attacks in general.
B Correct answer – 'The answer is to keep up your water intake' and 'keep taking regular swigs from your water bottle'.
C Not stated.
D Not stated. The writer implies merely that if you are not fit you will suffer the effects of heat even more.
2
A Not stated
B No – it replaces the body salts lost through sweating, but it doesn't prevent their loss.
C No – it is a treatment for diarrhoea, not a prevention.
D Correct answer – 'Dioralyte will do the job just as well.'
3
A illogical
B Correct answer
C when the hat dries off, so will the head
D 'water' does not dry off: when a hat (or anything else) dries off, the water disappears
4
A No – 'cool water … reduces swelling and helps … comfort'.
B Your boots become tight because of the heat.
C Correct answer – 'Extra sweating makes the skin softer and increases the chance of blisters forming, in the same way as when water leaks into your boots and gets to your feet.'

D Not stated – 'Cool water from a stream reduces swelling' may distract students. In addition, boots may be waterproof and not leak.

5

A Not stated – 'The answer, if this does develop, is to try and stay cool' is a distractor.

B The writer says walkers should ideally wear 'lightweight and loose-fitting' clothing. Being light is not the reason the author gives for wearing loose-fitting clothing.

C Correct answer – 'Tight clothing ... may even lead to the formation of an irritating rash known as 'prickly heat' on your skin.'

D Not stated

6

A Correct answer – 'It's understandable to want to remove any extraneous clothing when it's extremely hot ...'

7

A Correct answer – '... deceptive. It might not feel so hot, so you probably won't notice the damage being done.'

B Not stated – '... a good strong sun cream should therefore be applied' is a distractor.

C 'breeze' is not a strong wind – 'an apparently harmless breeze'

D Not stated – 'harmless' and 'damage' are distractors.

8

A Mountains are mentioned but the text is not exclusively for mountain walkers. See paragraph 3: 'Better still then if you can plunge into a river or the sea fully-clothed.'

B Not stated – the first sentence says, 'and if you're not very fit ...' but this is not the main aim of the article.

C Correct answer

D There is no indication that the people who go walking in summer do not also go walking at other times of the year.

Vocabulary in italics (paragraphs 5, 6 and 8)
swell (verb) to become bigger
blister (noun) a swelling on the surface of the skin, which contains a clear liquid
leak (verb) (in this case) the water gets into your boots
rash (noun) lots of red spots on your skin
breeze (noun) a light wind
deceptive (adj) from the verb 'deceive' – something which tricks you, which makes you believe something which is not true

Part 2: Gapped text Page 40

1 G **2** E **3** C **4** F **5** D **6** A B not used

Part 3: Multiple matching Page 40

1/2 B, D in any order **3** F **4/5** A, B in any order **6** C
7/8/9 B, E, F in any order **10/11** A, C in any order
12 F **13** A **14** D **15** F

Unit 4 A good story

Vocabulary 1: Films Page 42

1
Night at the Museum – comedy
Pride and Prejudice – historical drama/romance
Spider Man – science fiction/action film
Pirates of the Caribbean – action film/comedy/historical drama/romance

2
A 1 terrific **2** terrifying **3** terrible
B 1 review **2** critic **3** criticism

4
1 set **2** cast **3** stars **4** role **5** perform **6** plot
7 main characters **8** special effects

Language focus 1: *So and such* Page 43

Both words intensify the adjective or (adjective +) noun that follow.
so + adjective (or adverb)
such + (article) + (adjective) noun

Practice
1 were so good (that) **2** was such bad weather
3 was such a boring **4** were so many

Word formation: Adjectives ending in *-ing* and *-ed* Page 44

1
Examples of adjectives/adverbs in Review

To describe how we feel about something or someone
The plot is <u>complicated</u>.
...you will not feel <u>disappointed</u>.

To describe the thing or person that produces the feeling
... one of the most <u>entertaining</u> science fiction films I have seen.
The plot ... is ... at times <u>confusing</u>.
the special effects are <u>stunning</u>

Adverbs formed from present participle adjectives
<u>surprisingly</u> competent
<u>convincingly</u> choreographed

2

/d/	/t/	/ɪd/
surprised	embarrassed	excited
annoyed	astonished	frustrated
tired	impressed	disappointed
amused	relaxed	disgusted
bored		fascinated
frightened		
terrified		

3

impress impressive (adj)

4

Suggested answers

1 tiring 2 amused 3 annoying 4 disappointingly
5 fascinating 6 disgusting 7 Astonishingly

Writing Page 44

How to go about it box: 1 c 2 a 3 d 4 b

Sample answer

The last film I've seen on DVD was 'The Holiday' and it was alright. It is supposed it is a romantic comedy with Cameron Diaz, Kate Winslet, Jude Law and Jack Black and it is nice to watch but it is not a type of film that it makes you to laugh a lot.

The film is about two women very different. They are Iris, who is playing by Kate Winslet and Amanda (Cameron Diaz) and they decide to change houses for a holiday. Iris's house is a small one in England and Amanda's is enormous in Hollywood. Amanda falls in love to Iris's brother, who is widower, and Iris falls in love to Amanda's neighbour, who is componist. Kate Winslet is a bit disappointed in the role of Iris because she is normally very good actress. I like very much the photography and the music.

I would recommend the film to people who they are tired and they do not want to watch a complicate film. It is also very good for a rainy afternoon on Sunday of winter.

by David Benoa
180 words

Examiner's comments

Content: Reasonable realization of the task though rather a large section of the review is devoted to a simplistic summary of the plot.

Accuracy: A large number of distracting errors eg *it is supposed it is a romantic comedy, two women very different, who is playing by Kate Winslet* and use of relative clauses. *Disappointed* is used incorrectly *(disappointing)*, and it is not clear what is meant by *componist (composer?)*.

Range: Very limited range of structures and vocabulary, particularly when expressing opinions eg *very good* (twice) and *nice to watch.*

Organization and cohesion: Adequate paragraphing. Some sentences poorly organized eg second sentence of first paragraph.

Style and format: Appropriate to the task.

Target reader: Reader may have some difficulty following the review due to the number of errors.

Mark: band 2

Preparing for Listening: Focus on distractors Page 46

1
1 c 2 d 3 a 4 e 5 b

2
1 B 2 B 3 A 4 B 5 B

Listening: Multiple choice Page 46

1 C 2 B 3 C 4 A 5 B 6 A 7 B 8 C

Vocabulary 2: *Take* Page 47

A Phrasal verbs with *take*

1 to hire or rent

2
Possible titles – *Karate changed my life* or *How I became a karate fanatic*

3

a take after	resemble
b take up	start doing
c took to	start to like
d *taken me on	employ
e take over from	replace
f takes up	occupy

*note position of pronoun

B Expressions with *take*

1
1 take 2 'd/would take 3 taking/having taken 4 to take
5 took 6 had taken/had been taking 7 takes
8 are taking/have taken

2
1 take (me) to (school) 2 take (them) back to the (shop)
3 taking (his) advice 4 take (any of) the blame
5 take (more) interest in (the children) 6 taken pity on (it)
7 takes (a great deal of) courage 8 taking so long to (do this exercise)

3
1 D 2 A 3 C 4 B

4
to take pride in something C (3) to be taken to hospital
A (2) to take a joke B (4) to take the infinitive D (1)

Reading: Gapped text Page 48

3
1 H **2** C **3** B **4** E **5** A **6** G **7** D F not used

Language focus 2: Past tenses Page 49

1
1 past continuous **2** past perfect **3** past continuous + past simple **4** past simple (x3) **5** past perfect continuous

2
1 d **2** b **3** e **4** a **5** c

3
1 a He felt ill *during* the exam. (past continuous)
b He felt ill *after* the exam. (past perfect)
2 a I heard about it *while* I was listening to the radio. (past continuous)
b I heard about it, and *as a result* I listened to the radio. (past simple)
3 a I no longer live in Oxford. (past simple)
b I had been living in Oxford for six years *when* ... (past perfect cont. – the speaker may or may not live in Oxford now)
4 *While* can be used in place of *when* in **1a** and **2a**. It emphasizes that the two things happened at the same time, but does not change the meaning. *As soon as* can be used in place of *when* in **1b** and **2b**. It emphasizes that the action in the main clause happened immediately after the action in the clause introduced by *as soon as*.

Practice
1
1 A **2** C **3** B **4** C **5** B **6** C

2
Bus blush
1 was travelling **2** were having **3** saw **4** was sitting **5** ran **6** sat **7** had never seen **8** smiled **9** didn't stop **10** (had) got
Mobile control
11 had been going on **12** agreed **13** took **14** went **15** had phoned **16** (had) got **17** had taken **18** arrived **19** kept **20** had had

Writing: Short stories Page 50

2
B is the better entry because:
- it ends with the required words exactly
- it is organized into clearly defined paragraphs
- it is not repetitive (unlike A)
- it uses a variety of past tenses appropriately.

3
Content:
B Yes, see point 1 above. The length is fine.
A No, the story does not end correctly.
Range:
B Tenses: Yes, past perfect simple and continuous, past simple and past continuous.

B Vocabulary: Yes, *thrilled, sparkling, blanket of snow, set off on foot, freezing, exhausted, could hardly make out,* etc.
A Tenses: Not really, the writer uses only the past simple and past continuous.
A Vocabulary: No, the vocabulary is repetitive: *went, went, went, went ... they didn't have them, they didn't have them,* etc.

Organization and cohesion:
B Yes, use of tenses helps organize events.
B Linking devices are: *when, although, however, by the time, unfortunately, so, after, just as.*
A The events are organized chronologically so the telling of the story is not particularly interesting.
A Linking devices are more limited: *So* and *At last*

Style and format:
B Yes
A This story is rather informal – use of contractions and exclamation mark.
Target Reader:
B Yes, the reader would probably want to know what happened in the end. For all of these reasons, this entry would have a chance of winning the competition.
A No

4

> **Sample answer**
>
> The Incredible Girlfriend
> This is a story which may be very insignificant for the reader, but for me was one of the most surprising moments in my life.
>
> It happened two years ago, when my friend Antonio phoned me to make a date. He wanted to introduced me his girlfriend. At the first moment, I was very surprised; I had never seen him with a woman. He has always been very timid with girls. He used to say that he was not successful among women because he was short and ugly.
>
> The day of the date arrived and I was waiting for my friend sitting at the closest table to the entrance of the pub. I was very impatient to know my friend's girlfriend. My impatience changed into amazement when I saw my friend entering the pub with one of the most beautiful girls I had ever seen. I became petrified when I realised that she was one of most famous top models in Spain. I had never been so surprised in all my life.
> By José Vicente Acín Barea
> 171 words

Examiner's comment
Content: The task is achieved in that the writer has written a story ending with the words given.
Accuracy: Good control of a variety of narrative tenses shown in the second and third paragraphs. Some minor inaccuracies, eg *He wanted (to) introduce(d) me (to) his girlfriend. At the first moment* instead of *At first*, the word order of *closest table.*

Range: The writer uses some ambitious language – *I was impatient to know, My impatience changed into amazement when ...*

Organization and cohesion: Clear progression through the story indicated by tense use and time references – *It happened two years ago, The day of the date arrived.*

Style and format: Natural language use. Friendly tone.

Target reader: Very positive. The reader can easily follow the storyline.

Mark: good band 4

Review 4 Page 52

Use of English: Transformations

1 soon as the meeting had **2** the time we got to
3 once he had/was **4** leave until he (had) put
5 took to him **6** not to take him on **7** takes pride in
8 take much interest in **9** was so disappointed
10 was such a tiring

Correcting mistakes

1 *had, during* **2** part, As for ~~as~~ **3** that, of
4 when he ~~had~~ came, was **5** took ~~to~~ your advice, a

Vocabulary: The cinema

R	T	U	S	C	E	N	E	N	B
A	O	P	H	O	R	R	O	R	C
C	C	L	O	M	D	I	R	E	H
T	A	R	E	N	C	R	A	H	A
R	W	E	I	A	U	B	N	A	R
E	A	V	M	T	C	L	T	G	A
S	T	I	E	X	I	S	O	H	C
S	N	E	Y	F	A	C	R	F	T
A	C	W	M	C	P	L	O	T	E
S	B	T	H	R	I	L	L	E	R

Use of English: Word formation

1 increasingly **2** disappointing **3** amazingly
4 Interestingly **5** tired **6** motivated **7** impressed
8 surprised **9** astonishing **10** fascinating

Unit 5 Doing your Duty

Reading: Multiple matching Page 54

2

Advantages of home education
those mentioned in text
- no need to travel to school
- child receives more attention from teacher/parent
- child can learn at own pace
- more fun in certain subjects
- possibility of flexible timetable

Others
more comfortable learning environment

Disadvantages of learning at home
- child is isolated from other children
- child does not learn to work/play with others
- may suffer from overexposure to parents (and vice versa!)
- too many distractions at home (eg TV, toys, music, etc)
- parent may not be as knowledgeable/well qualified as teachers

Disadvantages of learning at school
those mentioned in text
- have to travel to get to school
- can get bored
- slower learners can hold back stronger students
- child may be bullied
- timetables can be too rigid

Others
- quality of teaching not the same in all schools
- the school may be poorly resourced

Advantages of learning at school
- school has better resources
- a variety of different teachers, each specialized in a particular subject
- child learns to work and play with others
- child learns discipline
- school is a preparation for the world of work

3

1 B **2** D **3** A **4** B **5** C **6** D **7** A **8/9** B, C in any order **10** D
11 A **12/13** B, C in any order **14** C **15** D

Vocabulary 1: Recording prepositions
Page 56

Adjective + preposition

Although she rapidly became bored *with* everything ...
Home schooling is increasingly popular among parents fed up *with* bullying, etc.
Further examples: *critical of, necessary for, ahead of*

Verb + preposition

Cassie approves *of* this flexible regime.
Rhiannon ... switches *to* maths.
Further examples: *opt for, withdraw from, work with*

Noun + preposition

... responsibility *for* ensuring that alternative arrangements are satisfactory does lie with local authorities.
Rhiannon may carry on with a subject she enjoys or is having problems *with*.
Further examples: *keep a check on, reason for, lack of, end of, package of*

Preposition + Noun

On average, home-schoolers are two years ahead of their schooled counterparts.

Now I can learn *at* my own pace.

Further examples: *on health grounds, at home, at work, at school*

Language focus: Obligation, necessity and permission Page 56

1

1 g – can ... listen

2 f – is not allowed to do g – can't watch
 h – mustn't distract

3 a – have to catch b – had to stay

4 c – do not have to follow d – do not need to tell
 e – need not be

2

a a teacher (to students)

b one student to another

● *Must* expresses the authority of the speaker, ie the obligation comes from the teacher and it is the teacher who is imposing the obligation (the speaker's internal obligation).

● *have to* is used to show that the authority does not come from the speaker but from someone else ie the teacher (the speaker's external obligation).

3

1 I don't have to/don't need to tidy **2** Do you have to ?/...
Must you ... ? **3** Last week I had to go ...
4 Were you allowed to watch ... **5** Now I have to start
6 we don't have to wear a tie **7** you need to prepare
8 You really should go/You really must go

4

a 1 made to sound **2** allowed to ('let' is not possible in the passive)

b 1 allowed **2** let **3** makes/made

5

a

1 don't have to **2** have to **3** don't have to **4** need to/have to
5 must **6** mustn't **7** have to **8** need to/have to

b *Be supposed to* = should do because it is a rule or because it is expected.

Had better = should do because it is a good idea.

6

1 wouldn't/didn't let me watch **2** was made to
3 can never do **4** aren't we allowed to
5 parents should smack **6** don't need to hand
7 had better tell **8** are supposed to do

Word formation: Nouns and adjectives
Page 58

1

1

Verb	Noun	Adjective
ignore	ignorance	ignorant
signify	significance	significant
appear	appearance	apparent
please	pleasure	pleasant
confide	*confidence*	*confident*
differ	difference	different
obey	obedience	obedient
depend	dependence	dependent*

Note: *dependant* is a noun; your *dependants* are the people you support financially, usually your children.

2 Opposite adjectives

intolerant, impatient, insignificant, disobedient, unpleasant, independent

Indifferent can also be formed, but this is not the opposite of *different*.

Adverbs are formed by adding -*ly* to the adjective, eg *impatiently, obediently*.

Use of English 1: Word formation Page 58

1 pleasantly (adv) **2** significantly (adv) **3** disobedient (adj)
4 pleasure (n) **5** importance (n) **6** appearance (n)
7 confidence (n) **8** resistance (n) **9** Apparently (adv)
10 independence (n)

Listening 1: True/False Page 59

2

1 F **2** T **3** F **4** F **5** T **6** T **7** F

Speaking 2: Collaborative task Page 59

The expressions heard in the recording are:
Where shall we begin? Let's talk about ... first.
So, that could be one of our three.
Shall we move on?
Let's have a look at the next one.
What have we decided (so far)?
We both seem to agree on ...

Vocabulary 2: The world of work Page 60

1

a 1 *be out of a job* **2** look for a job **3** apply for a job
4 go for an interview for a job **5** get a job

b 1 made redundant **2** resigned **3** sacked

2

a *study* a career is **not** possible

b *earn* a competition is **not** possible

3

to work shifts – work for a set period (eg 12am to 8am) before workers replace you for the next set period (eg 8am to 4pm)

to work long hours – work for many hours each day

to work overtime – work supplementary hours for which you are paid extra

to work flexitime – work with a flexible timetable: within limits you decide when you start and when you finish, as long as you work the required total number of hours each month

to work full-time – when you are contracted to work the entire time appropriate to that job, eg 35 hours per week (a full-time job)

to work part-time – when you are contracted to work fewer hours than the entire time appropriate eg 21 hours per week (a part-time job)

4

waitress, hairdresser, surgeon, dustman, hotel receptionist

Listening 2: Sentence completion Page 60

Don't forget! box

- You *don't need* to write more than three words for each answer.
- You *should* write a word or phrase that you actually hear.
- You *don't need* to rephrase.
- Minor spelling errors *can* be made, but the words you write *need* to be recognizable so you *should* check your spelling.
- You *can* expect to hear the answers in the same order as the questions.

1 academic qualifications **2** minimum height
3 back and legs **4** four **5** four days off **6** wear full uniform
7 fire engines **8** the evening **9** several hours
10 very satisfying

Use of English 2: Multiple-choice cloze Page 61

Despite the stress, he is proud of his new career and achievements.

1 D **2** B **3** A **4** C **5** A **6** C **7** B **8** C **9** B **10** A **11** A **12** C

Writing: Letters: An application Page 62

2

The applicant satisfies the requirements for the job and seems very suitable. He addresses all the points in the advertisement (and the exam question) and 'sells himself' very well. The effect on the target reader (ie camp organizer or personnel officer) would be very positive.

3

a I would like to apply for the job of Camp Helper
b I like working with children very much and I would enjoy the challenge of organizing activities for them on one of your camps and I am therefore very keen to improve my language skills in an English-speaking country before I go to university.

c I like working with children and I feel I have the necessary patience and energy to make a positive and enthusiastic contribution to your camps
d For the past seven years I have attended summer camps in my country with the scouts and last year I helped to run a number of events, including an orienteering competition and a kite-making workshop.
e In October I will be starting a degree course in English.
f Sports – basketball, tennis, Outdoor pursuits – orienteering, Other – guitar
g I have just finished school
h I hope you will consider my application favourably. I am available for interview at any time and look forward to hearing from you soon.

5

1 The register of the letter is not consistently formal, and the degree of informality of some of the language would have a negative effect on the target reader. The tone of the direct questions sounds rather rude.

2 Revised letter with suggested paragraphing.
Paragraph 1: Reason for writing
Paragraph 2: Relevant skills
Paragraph 3: Relevant experience
Paragraph 4: Reason for applying and questions about the work
Closing comments

Dear Sir or Madam,
c) I am writing to express an interest in the job I saw advertised in the publication 'Summer jobs in the UK'.
h) I am 25 years old and I (have) recently completed a short course on garden design. My level of English is intermediate and **f) I have a good knowledge of gardening**. I am particularly interested in the cultivation of roses and the use of trees in landscape design.
a) As you will see from my curriculum vitae d) I have a great deal of experience. j) This includes a temporary position on a campsite similar to those mentioned in your advertisement.
g) I enclose a reference from my previous employer. I like being part of a team and **i) I would enjoy the experience of working abroad.** I would be interested to know how many hours I would be expected to work each day. Could you also tell me how long the contract would be for? **e) I will be available to work from** the beginning of June.

b) I look forward to receiving your reply.
Yours faithfully

6

Examiner's comment

Content: No reference is made to 'working hours' but all other points covered. In a Part 2 task such as this, failure to cover all points in the question is not penalized quite so heavily as missing out elements in a Part 1 task. However, other factors in the candidate's writing must be dealt with reasonably well for the candidate not to lose marks.

Accuracy: Generally accurate. Minor spelling mistakes, eg – *phychology* (slip?), *acostumed*, as well as in more complex language attempts, eg *I am acostumed to work* instead of *accustomed to working* and in the 4ᵗʰ paragraph *I would* (to) *like you to provide me* (with) *more details*.

Range: Quite a good range of vocabulary and structures relevant to the task – *qualifications and relevant experience*, *I enclose a reference*, and correct word order in the indirect questions (4ᵗʰ paragraph).

Organization and cohesion: Generally appropriate with the exception of the position of *Besides*.

Style and format: Appropriate, although should avoid the use of contractions in this kind of writing.

Target reader: The reader would understand why the writer thinks she is suitable for the job.

Mark: borderline band 3/4

Review 5 Page 64

Use of English: Open cloze: Prepositions

How does talking to babies and young children benefit them? *It increases their intelligence.*

What is one of the main obstacles to a child's progress, according to the text? *television*

1 about/on **2** with **3** without **4** in **5** on **6** on **7** of **8** of/about **9** for **10** with **11** of **12** on

---

Word formation

1 differ (v)
different (adj), differently (adv), difference (n), indifferent (adj), indifferently (adv), indifference (n), differentiate (v)

2 appear (v)
apparent (adj), apparently (adv), appearance (n), disappear (v), disappearance (n)

3 frequent (adj)
frequently (adv), infrequent (adj), infrequently (adv), frequency (n), infrequency (n)

4 please (v)
pleased (adj), pleasingly (adv), pleasantly (adv), displease (v), displeasing (adj), displeasure (n), pleasing (adj), pleasant (adj), pleasure (n), displeased (adj), displeasingly (adv), pleasurable (adj)

5 tolerate (v)
tolerant (adj), intolerant (adj), tolerable (adj), intolerable (adj), tolerance (n), toleration (n), tolerantly (adv), intolerantly (adv), tolerably (adv), intolerably (adv), intolerance (n)

Vocabulary: The world of work

1 get **2** sack **3** career **4** sense **5** company **6** apply **7** shift **8** devote **9** skills **10** running **11** wage **12** earn a living

Use of English: Modal verbs

1 C **2** B **3** B **4** C **5** A **6** B **7** A **8** C

Unit 6 Relative relationships

Reading: Multiple matching Page 66

1 A **2** B **3** E **4** A **5/6** A, C in any order **7** D **8** B **9/10** A, E in any order **11** C **12** D **13/14** C, A in any order **15** B

Language focus 1: *Too* and *enough*

Page 68

2

a adjectives and adverbs **b** nouns **c** before **d** after

3

The structure of the sentence after *too* and *enough* is (+ *for* + object) + infinitive with *to*.

Practice

2

1 too quietly for me to **2** not tall enough to **3** are not enough eggs to **4** is too much sugar **5** there were too many

Vocabulary 1: Phrasal verbs Page 68

A Romance

1

1 c **2** e **3** a **4** b **5** f **6** d

2

1 to fall out with somebody **2** to split up with somebody
3 to be going out with somebody
4 to get on with somebody **5** to fall for somebody
6 to get over somebody

B Family

1

1 to raise a child **2** to become an adult
3 to do things you know you shouldn't
4 to reprimand somebody **5** to respect somebody
6 to disappoint somebody

2

1 to bring somebody up **2** to grow up
3 to get up to something **4** to tell somebody off
5 to look up to somebody **6** to let somebody down

Listening 1: Multiple matching Page 70

2

1 D **2** F **3** E **4** C **5** A

3

Possible answers
Speaker 3: the girl on the left of the first photo
Speaker 4: one of the girls in the second photo
Speaker 5: the woman on the right in the third photo

Language focus 2: Defining relative clauses Page 71

1

in the first sentence – *that*
in the second sentence – *which*
They cannot be omitted because they are the subject of
the verb in the relative clause.

2

She'd come back with **blackberries** (that/which) **she**'d
picked and tales of **wild rabbits** (that/which) **she**'d *seen*.

Note: In these sentences, the subject of the verbs *in italics*
is **she**; the underlined relative pronouns are the object of the
verbs in italics in the relative clauses. They can be omitted.

3

The first sentence is more formal. The relative pronoun
can be omitted in the second sentence.

4

a where **b** why **c** when **d** whose

Practice
1 where/in which (formal) **2** that/which **3** whose
4 that/which/ – **5** who/that **6** that/which **7** that/which/ –
8 when/ –

Reading Page 71

Parents and children. They go dancing.
a You have something in common with your parent, you
can talk about it.
b It brings back memories of his own youth. He probably
understands his son better.

Vocabulary 2: *Have* Page 72

A Expressions with *have*

1

to have: some fun, a relationship with someone, something
in common, a(n) (unique) insight into something

3

1 a scarf/a book **2** a scarf **3** a tooth (causative *have*)
4 hair (causative *have*) **5** something private **6** a headache

B Causative *have*

1

1 a She wants to dye her hair red (by herself).
b She wants to have her hair dyed red (by someone else).

2 a He took a photo of his daughter (himself).
b He had a photo taken of his daughter (by someone else).
'To use this structure we need the appropriate form of the
verb *to have* + the object + the past participle of the main
verb.'
Grammar reference for more information.

2

1 *to have, shaved* **2** having, taken **3** to have, pierced
4 had, filled **5** having, cut **6** has had, broken

Language focus 3: Non-defining relative clauses Page 73

2

The correct alternatives are:
a *who* or *which* cannot be replaced by *that*
b the relative pronoun cannot be omitted
c commas are used
Practice
1 We spent the weekend in York, where my mother was
   born.
2 My best friend, who always said she wanted to stay
   single, has just got married.
3 My oldest sister, whose husband is Greek, lives in
   Thessaloniki.
4 We're having our holiday in September, when
   everywhere is a lot less crowded.
5 His daughter borrowed the car, which he wasn't very
   happy about.

Open cloze: Relative clauses Page 73

1 which **2** that/which **3** who **4** that/which/ – **5** whose
6 where **7** when/ – **8** which/that

Vocabulary 3: Describing people Page 74

A Personality

1

Positive: sociable, reliable, sincere, cheerful, polite, tolerant, patient, decisive, mature, sensible, adventurous, practical, sensitive
Negative: bad-tempered, lazy, selfish, moody, mean

2

un-: unsociable, unadventurous, unselfish/selfless, unreliable
in-: intolerant, insincere, indecisive, insensitive
im-: impatient, impolite/rude, impractical, immature
different word: mean/generous, cheerful/miserable, sensible/silly or foolish, bad-tempered/sweet-tempered or calm, lazy/hard-working, selfish/selfless, moody/even-tempered

B Appearance

1

1 *bald 2 pierced 3 thinning 4 well-built
* We can say *he is bald* but not *he has bald hair.*

2

a
All the adjectives describe weighing too much.
Fat has negative connotations in many parts of the world.
Plump is more positive and can mean either weighing a little too much or can be used as a 'polite' way of describing someone who is fat.
Overweight is descriptive and of the three, is the most neutral.

b
Thin means having little fat on the body; it is descriptive and neutral.
Slim means being attractively thin and has positive connotations.
Skinny means being unattractively thin and has negative connotations.

Writing: Descriptions Page 75

2

1 ✓ 2 ✗ 3 ✗ 4 ✓ 5 ✗ 6 ✓ 7 ✗

3

Marion wrote it.
There are three factual differences:
- In the recording the breakdown occurred near the destination.
- In the recording Eilean's hair was long and flowing.
- In the recording Marion says they are no longer in touch with each other.

4

The correct spellings are in brackets.
holliday (holiday), mecanics (mechanics), extremly (extremely), noticeing (noticing), wich (which), colourfull (colourful), cheerfull (cheerful) chating (chatting), misteriously (mysteriously), moterway (motorway)

5

Organization
Paragraph 1 The background to the meeting
Paragraph 2 The meeting in unusual circumstances
Paragraph 3 What has happened since then

a paragraphs 1 and 3
b paragraph 2

Narrative elements
a past continuous (*my parents and I were driving*), past simple (*our car broke down*), past perfect simple (*we had been on the road*), present perfect simple (*We've kept in touch*)
b *broke down, pour from, pulled over, stretch her legs, spiky green, bright, cheerful*
c *while, after, when, but, who, which*

Descriptive elements
All of these aspects are mentioned except 'interests'
That and her colourful 'hippy' clothes were as bright and cheerful as she was ...
... was her spiky green hair, which seemed to grow out of her head like grass ...
I couldn't help noticing ... and *Perhaps her most striking feature was ...*

Other ways of expressing a strong impression are:
The first thing I noticed about her was ...
The first thing that struck me about her was ...
What struck me first about her was ...
What I most liked/admired about her was ...

Sample answer

Last week I went to the bank to ask a loan to buy a new car. I had an appointment with the branch's director. She was a woman very smartly-dressed, she had a shoulder-length hair, almond-shaped eyes and a smooth complexion.

While we were talking in her office we heard a very hard noise and someone shouting. Suddenly a man carrying a gun in his hand got into the office's director saying that that was a robbery. Then we had to get out of the office and lie down on the floor with the other people that was in the bank.

There was three armed robbers, two of them were keeping an eye on the hostages while the other was trying to get the money from the cashier's desk. In that moment, the cashier pushed the alarm and a very loud noise begun to sound. The robbers didn't know what to do and then the director hit one of them in the head with an extinguisher. When the other was turning to see what was happening she also hit his head. The third one runned away and it was impossible to catch him.
Since that day I fall in love with her (the director). I admire her bravery and her calm in that situation. By the way, I'm still trying to get the loan.

By Juan Carlos Lopez Gil
224 words

Use of English: Transformations
1 no difficulty (in) making 2 has nothing to do with
3 a strong influence on 4 have (got) the strength
5 are having the roof repaired 6 had his tonsils taken out
7 to have it done by

Ready for Use of English

What do you know about the Use of English Paper? Page 78

1 **False** All except Part 4 (Key word transformations) for which the eight questions are unrelated.

2 **True** Students should read for gist first. Looking first at the title and predicting the content of the text will help their overall understanding.

3 **False** There is one mark for each correct answer except in Part 4 (Key word transformations): in this part, two marks are given for a completely correct answer, one mark if it is partly correct.

4 **False** Parts 1 & 2 each contain twelve gaps, but Part 3 (Word formation) contains ten.

5 **True**

6 **True** Unfortunately, some students do this in the exam. If they write the answer to the example where the answer to the first question should go, all their answers will be in the wrong space.

7 **False** If students are unsure of an answer, they should eliminate any alternatives they consider to be clearly wrong and then, if they still cannot decide on the correct answer, make a sensible guess.

8 **False** Only one word. Note that contractions (eg *can't, won't, I've*) and hyphenated words (eg *one-way*) count as two words.

9 **True** No half marks are given in this paper (although one mark out of a possible two can be given in Part 4 – see 3 above)

10 **True**

Part 1: Multiple choice cloze Page 78

What to expect in the exam
1 A 2 C 3a D 3b C 4 B 5 D

Multiple-choice cloze task
1 B 2 A 3 B 4 D 5 D 6 A 7 C 8 C 9 D 10 B 11 B 12 C

Part 2: Open cloze Page 80

2

Type of word	Number and example		
Articles	1 an	4 the	
Prepositions	3 for	10 to	
Auxiliary verbs	11 was		
Personal pronouns	2 it		
Possessive adjectives	5 their	9 his	
Relative pronouns	6 who	8 that	
Intensifiers	7 so	12 such	

Examiner's comment
Content: Both parts of the question covered, with description of the person given through her actions, as well as her appearance and personality.
Accuracy: Frequent errors, none of which obscures meaning. The existence of so many errors distracts the reader – missing prepositions (for), word order, (*a*) *shoulder-length hair* in the first paragraph, spelling mistakes *shout(t)ing … keep(p)ing,* patchy control of past simple verb forms *begun, runned* and subject verb agreement problems.
Range: Suitable structural range and good vocabulary – *were keeping an eye on the hostages, cashier's desk, an extinguisher.*
Organization and cohesion: Clear. Use of a variety of time references.
Style and format: Appropriate to the task.
Target reader: The writer fulfils the task with a reasonably well told story but is penalized because of the number of errors.
Mark: band 3

Review 6 Page 76

Relative clauses
1 Jennifer Aniston, who is perhaps best known for her role as Rachel in 'Friends', has also appeared in several major films.
Non-defining (the name itself defines the person)
2 What's the name of the village where you got married?
Defining – *where* **cannot be omitted**
3 He hasn't given me back the book that I lent him.
Defining – *that* **can be omitted**
4 She told me that Vasilis had failed his driving test, which didn't surprise me at all.
Non-defining ('which' refers to the whole clause)
5 That song always reminds me of the time when I was working in Brazil.
Defining – *when* **can be omitted.**
6 He's the only person in this class whose first name begins with 'Z'.
Defining – *whose* **cannot be omitted.**
7 Emma received a phone call from the Managing Director, who had been impressed by her sales performance.
Non-defining (there is, we assume, only one Managing Director)
8 Few written records have survived so it is a period of history about which we know very little.
Defining – *which* **cannot be omitted as it follows a preposition. The sentence could be changed to:**
Few written records have survived so it is a period of history **which** *we know very little* **about.**
In this case, *which* **could be omitted.**

Vocabulary
A Phrasal verbs
1 let down 2 told off 3 brought up 4 looked up 5 get on 6 fell for 7 falling out 8 got over

B Describing people
Across 1 unsociable **3** greenish **6** generous **8** ear **9** in
10 selfish **11** skinny **12** bad **14** pale

3

1 who/that **2** which/that **3** does **4** it **5** his **6** The **7** been
8 on **9** was **10** for **11** such **12** for

Part 3: Word formation Page 81

1

1 humorous **2** employees **3** tighten **4** increasingly
5 uncomfortable **6** heat **7** saucepan **8** extraordinary

2

1 adjective; spelling change required (the second 'u' in
'humour' is dropped) **2** noun in the plural **3** verb **4** adverb
5 negative adjective **6** noun; spelling change required
7 compound noun **8** adjective

4

1 magicians **2** interested **3** ability **4** independent
5 energetic **6** physically **7** strength **8** easily **9** careless
10 disastrous

Unit 7 Value for money

Vocabulary 1: Shopping Page 82

1

1 out-of-town **2** corner **3** brands **4** own-brand
5 convenience **6** range **7** foodstuffs **8** value **9** aisles
10 trolley **11** checkout **12** till **13** cashier **14** receipt

Listening 1: Sentence completion Page 83

1 as many aisles   **6** (the) well-known brands
2 an outdoor market   **7** five times higher/greater/more
3 children   **8** bakery/bread
4 fresh meat   **9** shopping experience
5 the animal/animals   **10** buy on impulse

Reading: Gapped text Page 83

What type of people are shopaholics?
Mostly women; increasingly men. People with low
self-esteem.
What do they buy?
Women tend to buy items such as clothes, shoes,
make-up and jewellery. Men tend to buy power tools and
car accessories.
What effect does it have on them?
At first they feel happy, but they get into debt and feel
very unhappy afterwards.

1 E **2** B **3** G **4** D **5** H **6** A **7** F   C not used

Language focus 1: The present perfect
Page 85

**A The present perfect simple
Practice**

1

1 e **2** a **3** b,f **4** c,d

2

**To describe something that started in the past and
continues until the present:**
'I've been doing it *since I was 12* when my father would
give me his credit card,' she said.

Until now, few psychiatrists have regarded the problem
as worthy of serious medical attention.

People have *always* used shopping as a way of cheering
themselves up.

Since the announcement of his test programme, Koran's
office has been inundated with hundreds of calls from
shopping addicts clamouring to become his guinea pigs.

Silicon Valley ... has seen some of the fastest wealth
creation in America's history.

**To give news of recent past events which have some
relevance to the present:**
Professor Lorrin Koran of Stanford University in
California believes he has found a cure for shopaholics.

3a

Present perfect	Past simple
yet	last summer
so far today	in September
in the last few days	two weeks ago
for the last two years	before I came here
over the last week	on my 10th birthday
already	when I was younger
this month	
since I got up	

**B The present perfect continuous
Practice**

1

1 a incompleteness – the book is not finished
   b completed action – the book is finished
2 a temporary nature – he is not staying with her on a
     permanent basis
   b long-term – she has lived there for a long time and
     will probably continue to live there
3 a repetition – on a regular basis
   b one occasion – they are not here now
4 a duration – the speaker considers all day to be
     important
   b focus on completed action – the finished product
     rather than the duration is important to the speaker
     (and listener!) here

2

1 've/have just heard **2** have you been **3** proposed **4** kept
5 were **6** have (you) made **7** 've/have been saving
8 've/have both been working **9** 've/have already saved
10 have (you) been doing

Vocabulary 2: *Come* Page 86

A *to come as*
1 D *pleased* is not possible
Note: *pleasant* would be acceptable
2 C *permanent* is not possible

B *to come to*
1-2
Possible answers
1 *came to power* – see example
2 *come to any harm* – kidnappers talking to their hostage's mother or father
3 *come to a decision* – Trade Union representatives speaking to management
4 *coming to an end* – people who wanted to watch the film again without paying
5 *came to the conclusion* – girl speaking about a potential boyfriend
6 *came to nothing* – people at work discussing why their company did not win a big contract *or* bank robbers discussing why the robbery ended in failure

C Phrasal verbs with *come*

1
1 found by chance 2 visit me/come to my house
3 was mentioned *or* discussed 4 getting 5 think of

2
come down with a mysterious illness
come across my old school reports
came up in the exam
come round to my flat
come up with a solution to the problem

Language focus 2: Contrasting ideas
Page 87

Although the weather was bad, she enjoyed the trip.
She enjoyed the trip although the weather was bad.
The weather was bad. However, she enjoyed the trip.*
The weather was bad. She enjoyed the trip, however*
Despite the bad weather/Despite the fact that the weather was bad, she enjoyed the trip.
Despite the weather being bad, she enjoyed the trip.

*Notice the use of the comma in the two examples with *however*.

Practice
1 Although 2 in spite 3 despite 4 However 5 but
6 whereas

Listening 2: Multiple choice Page 87

2
1 B 2 C 3 A 4 C 5 A 6 B 7 C

Language focus 3: Expressing preferences Page 88

Practice
1 rather watch than take 2 buying books to borrowing
3 to phone him rather than 4 not go out

Vocabulary 3: Towns and villages Page 88

1
1 *e,f* 2 a,e 3 d 4 a,c,d 5 a,d 6 b 7 c 8 b

2
Positive: lively, bustling, pleasant, picturesque, prosperous, quaint
Negative: dull, run-down, shabby, depressing

Writing: Emails Page 90

2 Yes: friendly and informal

3
Paragraph 2: *Describing the positive and negative aspects of the house*
Paragraph 3: *Describing the positive and negative aspects of the flat*
Paragraph 4: *Stating a preference and giving reasons.*

4
a

Input material	Email
properties	*places*
residential area	*neighbourhood*
overlooking the .. river	*by the river*
within walking distance of the city centre	*you can walk to the centre*
in the heart of historic York	*central*
with shops and all amenities nearby	*really close to everything*

b
I looked on the map
so we wouldn't have to get up early for class
that could be a bit noisy for me
the walk to school would be good for us

5
a *great, alright, really, a bit, let me know, all the best*
b *I've, there's, it's, wouldn't, it's, I'd, it's*
c *exclamation mark in final paragraph*

Sample answer

Hi Ricardo
I'm really interested about going on a shopping trip and I've found two alternatives.

The first one is to Boulogne in France for just £21. That would be interesting as it would give both us a chance to practise our French and also we can buy things like wine and cheese in the hypermarket – delicious! Unfortunately, though, the coach leaves at 6 in the morning and I know you hate getting up early.
The other one is to Oxford Street in London and costs just £7 return. The clothes they sell there are fantastic and I really need to buy some new ones.

However, I think if you don't mind to pay a bit more, the one to Boulogne will be better because it takes three hours to get to London. That's a total of 6 hours in the coach, which I would find extremely tedious.

Let me know what you think
Best wishes
Jan (Ruber)

154 words

Examiner's comments

Content: All points covered and the writer builds on the information given eg *I know you hate getting up early, I really need to buy some new ones.*

Accuracy: Generally accurate and errors do not impede understanding eg *interested about going, give both us a chance, if you don't mind to pay.*

Range: A good range of structure and vocabulary eg *it would give both us a chance to practise, which I would find extremely tedious.*

Organization and cohesion: Good paragraphing and use of cohesive devices (*The first one, The other one, Unfortunately, though, However, That would be interesting as it would etc*).

Style and format: Appropriately informal email.

Target reader: Would be informed of the nature of the two options.

Mark: borderline band 4/5

Review 7 Page 92

Vocabulary: Shopping
1 *walking* 2 range 3 value 4 corner 5 meat 6 out-of-town 7 convenience 8 own-brand 9 brand 10 goods

Use of English: Open cloze
1 of 2 the 3 than 4 to 5 One 6 came 7 despite 8 was 9 for 10 rather/sooner 11 as 12 to

Use of English: Transformations
A The present perfect
1 1 c and e 2 b and d 3 a and f

2
1 last time I spoke to
2 first time I have/'ve eaten
3 has/'s been playing tennis since
4 ages since he (last) saw/has seen
5 haven't/have not been swimming for
6 biggest supermarket I have/'ve (ever)

B Language of contrast
1 being able to speak fluent
2 the fact (that) his behaviour
3 she performed well, she lost
4 in spite of/despite the/an increase

Unit 8 Time Travel

Reading 1: Gapped text Page 94

3
1 C 2 G 3 A 4 F 5 H 6 B 7 D E not used

Vocabulary 1: Phrasal verbs
1 think about and plan 2 compensate for 3 tolerate
4 provide with everything that will be needed
5 go towards

Language focus: The future Page 96
A Making predictions
a 1 b 2,3 and 4 c 5 and 6

	Negative forms
will definitely	*definitely won't/will not*
are likely to	*are not/aren't likely to*
will probably	*probably won't*
may well*	
might	*might not*
could	*could not* (but note that the negative form changes the meaning to 'certainty' or 'logical impossibility')

* *may well not* exists but *may well* is normally only used in the positive
B Other futures
1 a 2 d 3 e 4 c 5 i 6 h 7 f 8 b 9 g

C Time linkers
1 before 2 By the time 3 until 4 when/as soon as

Practice

1
A 1 is going to rain
   2 we're going
   3 we'll have to

B 4 takes off
   5 I'll get up
   6 we'll be driving

C 7 I'm seeing
   8 will last
   9 are only going to sign
  10 will have/be finished

D 11 shall we meet
  12 don't open
  13 will/'ll get
  14 will/'ll probably see

Vocabulary 2: Travel Page 97

1

1 flight **2** journey **3** trip **4** travel **5** voyage **6** cruise

3

1 holiday **2** campsite **3** stayed **4** relax **5** funny **6** excursion
7 crowded **8** package

Listening: Multiple choice Page 99

1 A **2** B **3** C **4** A **5** B **6** C **7** B **8** C

Reading 2: Multiple choice Page 100

2

1 B **2** B **3** A **4** B **5** D

Word formation: *-en* suffix Page 102

1

Adjective	Noun	Verb
broad	*breadth* /e/	*broaden*
wide	*width* /ɪ/	*widen* /aɪ/
deep	depth	deepen
high	height	heighten
long	length	lengthen
short	shortness	shorten
strong	strength	strengthen
weak	weakness	weaken
deaf	deafness	deafen

2

1 lengthen **2** weakened **3** widening **4** strength **5** deafening
6 height

Writing: Essays Page 102

2

The writer agrees with the statement.

3

The writer gives three main reasons introduced by *Firstly*,
Secondly and *Another benefit is*. Further supporting ideas
are introduced by *Consequently*, *It seems to me* and *As a
result*. The purpose of the first and last paragraphs is to
state the writer's opinion, ie to agree with the statement.

4

1 Introduce the writer's opinion	2 Indicate the order of points
Personally, I think	Firstly
It seems to me that	Secondly
I strongly believe	Another benefit is
In my opinion	*Another drawback/*
To my mind,	*disadvantage is*
	Lastly
	First of all

3 Show the result or consequence of something	4 Bring the essay to an end
Consequently ... / ... lead to ... /... owes a great deal to ...	To conclude
As a result	*To sum up*
Therefore result(s) in ... thus	*In conclusion*

Review 8 Page 104

Use of English: Transformations

1

1 c **2** a **3** f **4** b **5** e **6** d

2

1 are you planning to spend/planning on spending
2 on the point of saying **3** is likely to rise
4 probably won't/will not **5** will probably (all) have died/
may well (all) have died

Use of English: Word formation

1 unpleasant **2** widened **3** deafening **4** sleepless
5 Unable **6** politely **7** successful **8** worsened **9** shorten
10 broadens

Use of English: Multiple-choice cloze

1 C **2** B **3** A **4** B **5** D **6** C **7** A **8** C **9** B **10** A **11** C **12** B

Writing: Articles Page 105

> **Sample answer**
>
> Natal
> Where to go and put your feet up in winter's days
> without worring about catching a cold? Natal, in the
> North-east of Brazil, has the same warm temperatures
> during all over the year.
>
> Natal is one of the emergent places for a new kind of
> tourists interest – beaches throughout there are included
> in the route of called 'Ecological Tourism'. Travel agents
> orient you how to enjoy your holiday without damaging
> the environment. You can stay in hotels, in Youth
> Hostels as well as in the local people's house: Natal
> inhabitants are very kind and hospitable.
>
> Besides relaxing in different beaches each day, you can
> go to the city centre to enjoy 'frevo', a kind of dance in
> the street, conducted by a carnival band. But if you are
> a sort of shopaholic, there are a lot of craft markets in
> addition to conventional markets and shopping mals.
>
> Moreover, if you have some extra time and want to
> know about their culture you can see the sight of the
> town, constructed by Portuguese, Dutch and English
> conquerors. Afterwards you still can eat fishes only
> just caught and grilled on the seashore. You should go
> and see!
>
> By Nicola Veret
> 195 words

Examiner's comment
Content: Good realization of the task set. All points
covered and different interests catered for.
Accuracy: The first two paragraphs contain numerous
mistakes but these do not impede understanding
although they may distract the reader – *in winter's days,
worring, during all over the year, tourists interest,* etc.
Otherwise, it is generally accurately expressed.
Range: Appropriate with some examples of natural
language use – *if you are a sort of shopaholic, craft
markets, without damaging the environment, grilled on the
seashore ...*
Organization and cohesion: Good use of appropriate
linking devices in the third and fourth paragraphs

Style and format: Informative and friendly, appropriate to the audience.
Target Reader: Would be suitably informed.
Mark: band 4

Unit 9 Fact or fiction?

Reading 1: Multiple choice Page 106

3
1 C 2 A 3 C 4 D 5 C 6 B 7 A 8 B

Language focus 1: Modal verbs of speculation Page 108

1a a and c **1b** b **2** *have* + past participle **3** could, may
4 No

Practice

2
1 b 2 d 3 e 4 a 5 f 6 c

3
a present, continuous infinitive without *to*
b present, infinitive without *to*
c past, *have* + past participle
d past, *have* + past participle (continuous)
e past, *have* + past participle
f present, infinitive without *to*

Listening: Multiple choice Page 108
1 C 2 A 3 C 4 B 5 C 6 A 7 B

Language focus 2: Question tags
Page 109

1
The subject and the auxiliary verbs are repeated and the order is reversed. If they are affirmative in the sentence they change to negative in the tag. Notice that the demonstrative pronoun *that* in the first sentence becomes *it* in the tag.

2
a sentence 1 is a real question
b in sentence 2 the speaker expects agreement
The difference is in the intonation:
rising intonation
(➚) = real question
falling intonation
(➘) = asking for confirmation

3-4
1 You don't believe him, do you? ➚

2 You won't let me down, will you? ➚

3 You went away for the weekend, didn't you? ➚

4 He's not playing very well, is he? ➘

5 He's already passed First Certificate, hasn't he? ➘

6 I'm right about that, aren't I? ➘

7 You can play chess, can't you? ➚

8 Let's phone Paul, shall we?

Note: these intonation patterns are the more typical patterns in a given situation. Other patterns are possible when one is expressing surprise, and with imperatives, etc.

Vocabulary: *Give* Page 110
A Phrasal verbs with *give*

1
1 b 2 a 3 c

2
1 revealing *or* betraying 2 stop a habit 3 distribute
4 submit/hand to the teacher, return
5 yielded/agreed (usually after a long argument)

B Expressions with *give*

1
Part A
1 d 2 c 3 e 4 a 5 b
Part B
1 e 2 d 3 f 4 a 5 b 6 c

2-3
a 3 give great pleasure, 4 give someone a nasty shock
b 5 give an impressive performance, 6 give a lengthy speech
c 1 give your best regards, 2 give full details

Use of English: Open cloze Page 111

1 been **2** whose **3** but/though/although **4** over **5** make
6 Without **7** in **8** lot/number **9** sort/kind/type **10** the
11 be **12** their

Reading 2: Gapped text Page 112

2
1 F 2 H 3 D 4 A 5 E 6 G 7 C B not used.

Word formation: Adjectives Page 113

1
foggy (adj) *fog* (noun)
numerous (adj) number (noun)
contro**ver**sial (adj) con**tro**versy (noun) *or* **con**troversy
impressive (adj) impress (verb)

2
1 ambiti<u>ous</u>, religi<u>ous</u>, infecti<u>ous</u>, cauti<u>ous</u> (remove -*on* and add -*ous*)
2 occupation<u>al</u>, profession<u>al</u>, emotion<u>al</u>, sensation<u>al</u> (add -*al*)
3 cloud<u>y</u>, wind<u>y</u>, rain<u>y</u>, ic<u>y</u>* (add -*y*) *no *e* in the adjective
4 deci<u>sive</u>, inclu<u>sive</u>, explo<u>sive</u>, offen<u>sive</u> (remove -*de/d* and add -*sive*)
5 biolog<u>ical</u>, geograph<u>ical</u>, econom<u>ical</u>*, histor<u>ical</u>* (remove -*y* and add -*ical*)
6 dange<u>rous</u>, disast<u>rous</u>, humo<u>rous</u>, poison<u>ous</u> (add -*ous*)
note further changes:
disaster – disastrous, humour – humorous

7 compar*ative*, imagin*ative*, compet*itive*, sens*itive**
(remove final *e* and add -*ative/itive*)

8 anx*ious*, var*ious*, cur*ious*, gener*ous* (remove -*ety/-ity*
and add or incorporate -*ous*)

9 bene*fic*ial, influen*tial*, residen*tial*, finan*cial* (remove
final *ce* and add -*cial/-tial*) note further change:
benefit – beneficial

10 health*y*, wealth*y*, funn*y*, luck*y* (add -*y*) note the
doubled consonant: fun – funny

*note the difference in meaning between the following
pairs of adjectives:
economic: of or relating to an economy eg a purely
economic decision, the government's economic policy
economical: not wasteful, cheap to run or operate eg an
economical car/washing machine
historic: famous or important in history eg an historic
event/monument
historical: belonging to or typical of the study of history
eg a historical document/film
sensitive: describes a person who shows understanding
of people's needs, problems or feelings; sensitive about
something: easily worried or offended when someone
talks about it
sensible: describes an action or decision which is based
on reason rather than emotions; a person who behaves in
this way
funny (adj): amusing
fun (n): something is fun, it is enjoyable; to have fun
means to have a good time

Speaking 1: Collaborative task Page 114

1
1 couldn't it? **2** will it? **3** don't they? **4** would they?
5 wouldn't it? **6** shall we?
2 Positive: colourful, impressive, enjoyable, exciting,
inexpensive, entertaining, spectacular, lively, thrilling,
cheerful, bright
Negative: dull, costly, impractical, uninspiring

Writing 1: Informal letters Page 115

2
You attended an event last weekend to celebrate a
traditional festival in your country. Write a letter to your
English-speaking penfriend, describing the event. Briefly
explain the origins of the festival to your penfriend, then
describe what happened and say whether you enjoyed
yourself.

4
Yes, the writer has answered all parts of the question.
a The origins of the festival are explained in paragraph 1.
b He describes what happened in paragraphs 2 and 3.
c He says whether he enjoyed himself in paragraph 3:
excellent food, delicious, the mulled wine kept everyone
smiling.*
* *'mulled wine' is hot wine with spices, popular in very
cold weather.*

5
Phrasal verbs
give off: produce and send into the air
put on: organize an event
make up for: compensate for
Adjectives
impressive, welcome, chilly, disappointing, costly,
excellent, delicious
Linking words
so, and, As you can imagine, Unfortunately, but, Anyway,
Well
Relative clauses
... 1605, when Guy Fawkes ..., ... heat, which is very
welcome ..., ... Fawkes, which is burnt on top ...
Useful expressions for informal letters
Sorry it's taken me so long to write, but ...
Well, that's all from me.
Let me know what you've been doing recently.
All the best,

Sample answer
....

Dear Maria Luisa
Sorry it's taken me so long to write but you know I'm
very bad at writting letters.

I wrote after enjoying one of the numerous fiestas there
are in Spain. It's name is Las Fallas and takes place
in Valencia. Las Folios begins on 21 of March and
commemorates the fiestas that ancient people did. They
used to burn piles of wood and danced around these fires.

Nowadays instead of piles of wood, valencianos
burn sculptures called ninots, these ninots ridiculize
politicians and local customs. Los Folios takes a week
and has a bonfire every day.

I spent a wonderful week, although I think I drank
more than enough some days, but everything I did was
worth going to Valencia.

Well, I send you my email, since I think it'll be more
confortable and quicker to talk.
All the best
Kisses
Arturo Mendoza Fernández
143 words

Examiner's comment
Content: The candidate describes the whole week
rather than one weekend as specified in the question.
He also describes what generally happens and does not
focus much on his own experience of the festival. The
realization of this Part 2 task is therefore just satisfactory.
Accuracy: Few mistakes, generally minor: spelling
– *writting, I spent a wonderful week* as opposed to *had a
wonderful week, kisses* rather than *best wishes* or similar
etc.
Range: Good range of appropriate vocabulary – *takes
place in, piles of wood, danced around, bonfire.*
Organization and cohesion: Adequate.
Style and format: Consistently friendly.
Target reader: The target reader would have had some
idea of the origins of the festival but would not get a clear
idea of how the writer spent his time.
Mark: band 3

Review 9 Page 116

Word formation

1 thirsty, guilty, stormy, sleepy, cloudy, lengthy, hilly

2

Noun	Adjective
1 finance	financial
2 commerce	commercial
3 psychology	psychological
4 politics	political
5 anxiety	anxious
6 variety	various
7 influence	influential
8 residence	residential
9 mystery	mysterious
10 advantage	advantageous

4 Pronunciation changes shown in **bold**

compare	comp**a**rative
defend	defensive
compete	comp**e**titive
describe	descr**i**ptive
receive	rec**e**ptive
represent	representative
produce	prod**u**ctive

Use of English: Word formation

1 noisily	**6** suspicious
2 traditional	**7** amazing
3 colourful/colorful(AE)	**8** imprisoned
4 Surprisingly	**9** Shortly
5 Evidently	**10** mysterious

Use of English: Transformations

1 might not be playing
2 must have been pleased to
3 can't/couldn't have phoned
4 might have stolen your purse
5 may have given
6 give away a secret/give a secret away, would
7 'd/had better give/hand
8 gave a nervous laugh

Ready for Writing

Formal or informal? Page 119

1

1 d informal **2** e formal **3** a informal **4** c formal **5** b formal

2

Extracts Pages 118 & 119

The writing in **bold** indicates the unit or units in which this writing type has so far been seen.

1 b Informal letter or email (Replying to a letter) – informal **Units 1** (informal letters) **and 9**
Linker: *Anyway*
Phrasal verb: *put you up* (for the night)
Contraction: *you're*
Punctuation: dash
Other language: *if you want* (would like); *let us know* (inform)

2 d Essay – neutral/formal **Units 3 and 8**
Linkers: *therefore, However*
No phrasal verbs or contractions. Note also *Some people feel that* and *others argue that* as typical language for introducing different views.

3 c Article – fairly informal **Units 2 and 8** (describing a place)
Questions: direct, addressing the readers to engage them from the start. Note use of contraction *it's* suggesting a less formal style.

4 a Formal letter or email (requesting information) – formal **Unit 2**
No contractions or phrasal verbs and the questions are indirect; *I would be grateful if you could tell me*, is a typical way of introducing a polite request.

5 g Short story – neutral/informal **Units 4 and 9**
Note typical narrative elements:
Time linker: *As soon as*
Tenses: past perfect and past simple
Phrasal verb: *head for*
Adverb: *desperately*
Contraction: *wasn't*

6 f Review – neutral **Unit 4**
Vocabulary of the theatre: *musical, cast, stage*
Opinion: *But my favourite moment of all was*

7 e Report – formal **Unit 7**
Linkers: *To sum up, although*
No contractions or phrasal verbs
Other language: *of the highest quality* (very good/ excellent), *offers a greater selection of dishes* (has more dishes), *provides its customers with* (gives its customers)

8 h Description – neutral/informal **Unit 6** (Descriptive short story)
Contraction: *he's*
Phrasal verb: *look up to*
Linker: *Despite*
Language of description: *cheerful, his piercing blue eyes … light up when he smiles*

9 i Background reading text – semi formal/ neutral (possibly an essay or a review) **Unit 14**
No contractions or phrasal verbs
Linker: *To begin with*
Other language: references to set text

Note: Words or expressions in brackets indicate a contrasting register.

Answering questions Page 119

Part 1: Emails

2

Email A

Content

a All the points are included, although the writer does not develop them by adding points of his/her own.
b The opening is not relevant to the body of the email. 3 sentences (over 40 words) are spent talking about the friend's relationship with Marco. This looks like a piece of pre-learnt material, reproduced here in order to include some phrasal verbs (*fall out* and *make it up*) and an idiomatic expression (*you were made for each other*). Examiners would not be impressed.

Organization and cohesion

a The paragraphing is clear and logical.

b Linking words have been used, sometimes appropriately (eg *Anyway, this summer…*), sometimes not (eg the formal *Furthermore*).

c The opening is inappropriate (*Dear friend*) and the continuation irrelevant (see Content). The ending is appropriate, despite the errors (*I must to go now* and *think in*), although it is spoiled further by inconsistent register (*do not hesitate to contact me*) and the final *Kisses*.

Range and accuracy

a The writer shows reasonable control of indirect questions (*I would be grateful if you could **to** tell me which fruit **it** is picked in July*) though the register is inappropriately formal. Other language and structures are used reasonably well with similar non-impeding errors (see last paragraph).

Other errors: *I am thinking in going, you have worked in the same place last year, wether*

b *I would be grateful if you could (to) tell me* is used twice, as is *Anyway*.

c The sentence beginning *I know you have worked.* is copied (incorrectly) from the rubric.

Style and format

a See above for comments on register, which is inconsistent.

b It is clearly set out as an email. (Note incorrect use of colon after *Dear friend:*)

Target reader

The reader would be reasonably well informed, although the intention behind the question *I would be grateful if you could tell me wether you earned enough money?* is not entirely clear. The formal questions would not sound very friendly.

Mark: 3.1

Email B
Content

a All the points are included.

b The content, including the opening paragraph, is relevant to the question. The writer builds on the notes with relevant additions:

July, which fruit? - *when my exams have finished.*
days off? - *I really want to go sightseeing in London*
travel the next - *I'm thinking of setting off on a month's tour of England*
any more advice? - *such as suggestions on how to get there and what clothes to take.*
Note that the length of the email is slightly over 150 words (155). This is not serious but it serves to show students that adding points of their own should not be done at the expense of other criteria, namely writing within the word limit and covering all the points.

Organization and cohesion

a The email is written in one paragraph. This would be penalized.

b Good use of (informal) linking words: *but, when, so, then, after, anyway.* Ideas logically organized.

c Opening and ending both appropriate.

Range and accuracy

a Good variety of structures to express plans, intentions and preferences:
I hope to, I (really) want to, I'd like to, I'm planning on, I'm thinking of
Appropriate use of informal expressions for emails:
That's all for now, Hope to hear from you soon, All the best
Other vocabulary:
go sightseeing, setting off on a month's tour, Let me know

b No unnecessary repetition. Notice techniques for avoiding it:
like you did last year (went fruit picking)
in that month (July)
do you think I'd have enough (money) to do that (go on a month's tour of England)?

c No evidence of 'lifting' (copying whole phrases) from the rubric.

Style and format

a Register appropriately and consistently informal.

b Clearly an email, though paragraphing would make it clearer.

Target reader

The reader would be fully informed and clear about what the writer wants to know.

Mark: 5.2

3
Don't forget!

- The target reader is an employee of Family Adventure Holidays.
- Use formal style.
- Questions will be indirect.

Sample answer

Dear Sir
When I was watching the news I saw your advertisement, and I found it enjoyable. I thought I could take my family there but before taking that decision I wanted to ask some questions.

Firstly, I wanted to ask you about the activities. I wanted to know if apart from those you put in the advertisement, is it possible to go sailing because everyone who had done sailing told me that it is great fun. I also noticed something in the activities that said parents are encouraged to participate with their children, and does this mean all the time? And finally I saw that the holidays were from Saturday to Saturday but I would like to arrive there on Friday, and my question is, how much will cost an extra night?

I am waiting for your response
Yours sincerely
Javier Buendía
142 words

Examiner's comment

Content: The writer has not followed the rubric exactly in that the question states 'you have found the following advertisement' and the writer states *I was watching the news and I saw your advertisement.* Other points are covered except the proposed date of arrival. Normally in Part 1 questions, failure to cover key points in the question results in a maximum mark of 2.3 only. In this letter the date is important but not essential as the writer is asking for information not actually booking the holiday. In most other respects this is a convincing letter with few errors.

Accuracy: Generally minimal errors – *who had done* instead of the use of the present perfect, omission of the subject in *that (it) is great fun,* and word order in *how much will cost an extra night?* (although in other examples the writer forms indirect questions correctly).

Range: Although there is some awkwardness of expression – *I am waiting for your response* – there are examples of good handling of vocabulary and grammar: *apart from those, I also noticed something in the activities that said.*

Organization and cohesion: Well organized, although the middle paragraph could be divided into two paragraphs.

Style and format: Consistently appropriate.

Target reader: Would be informed as to the queries the writer has, except the date of arrival.

Mark: band 3

Part 2 Page 121

How to go about it

1 Your college magazine has invited you to write an article about a member of your family, who helped you in some way. Describe the person and explain what they did that was helpful to you.

Style: could range from informal to formal. As with all writing tasks it must be consistent throughout.

2 You have had a class discussion on the following statement:
It should be illegal for parents to smack their children.

Your teacher has asked you to write an essay giving your views on the statement.

Style: neutral/formal essay

3 You recently visited a place which you had not been to for a long time. Your cousin, who now lives abroad, also knew this place very well. Write a letter to your cousin, describing the changes and your feelings about them. Do not write any postal addresses.

Style: informal

4 You have a part-time job in a games centre, where people can go to play computer games. The owner would like to buy some new software and he has asked you to write a report, suggesting two games for the centre. You should briefly describe each game and explain why you think the customers would enjoy both games.

Style: could range from informal (relationship with owner could be very friendly) to formal

5 Your school's English language magazine has invited readers to write a review of a holiday they spent recently in a seaside resort. You should include information on your accommodation and what there is to do in the resort, and say whether you would recommend the holiday to other people.

Style: could range from formal to informal

6 You have decided to enter a short story competition. The competition rules say that the must begin or end with the following words:
They were sad to leave, but they had no choice.

Style: neutral or informal narrative

Unit 10 Nothing but the truth

Vocabulary 1: Crime and punishment
Page 122

A Crimes and criminals

1-2
1 murderer – murder **2** smuggler – smuggling
3 arsonist – arson **4** pickpocket – pickpocketing
5 blackmailer – blackmail **6** shoplifter – shoplifting
7 kidnapper – kidnap(ping) **8** hijacker – hijack(ing)
9 vandal – vandalism **10** mugger – mugging

2
4 pickpocketing **6** shoplifting **10** mugging

3
a burgle **b** steal **c** rob

B Punishment

1
d to order someone to pay a £200 fine (a penalty of £200 for breaking the law)
b To order someone to do 200 hours of community service (instead of going to prison, an offender has to work for the benefit of the community, eg picking up litter, cleaning walls of graffiti, etc)
e To give someone a two-year prison sentence (to send someone to prison for two years)
a to sentence someone to life imprisonment (in Britain, the maximum prison sentence)
c to sentence someone to death (to order that an offender be executed)

Listening 1: Sentence completion Page 123

2
1 during the day **2** less than ten **3** sell stolen goods
4 13/thirteen per cent/% **5** under the doormat
6 home alarm system **7** garage door **8** fight local crime
9 elderly *and* disabled **10** ten million

Vocabulary 2: Phrasal verbs Page 124

2

1 *own up to doing something* to confess to something which you are to blame for

2 *make something up* to invent (a story)

3 *take somebody in* to trick or deceive someone

4 *let somebody off* to give someone a lighter punishment than they expected, or not punish them at all

5 *get away with something* to avoid being caught or punished for something wrong you have done

6 *find something out* to discover or hear about something

7 *show off* to try to impress people by telling or showing them what you are capable of

8 *look into something* to investigate

Writing 1 Page 125

1 How to go about it
Style
The target readers are other students at your school or language school.
The style could be either formal/neutral because of the topic, or informal to suit the target readers.

Reading: Multiple choice Page 126

3
1 D **2** C **3** C **4** A **5** B **6** D **7** C **8** A

Language focus 1: Passives page 127

1

a Sometimes they bug telephones with parents' consent, though usually they follow the children and film any wrongdoings.

b They see it as an invasion of privacy, caused by a lack of communcation between parents and children.

2

1 are **2** be **3** has **4** were **5** have **6** be **7** to be **8** is **9** to be **10** are **11** is **12** was **13** been **14** being **15** being

3

Present simple	(1) are hired
	(8) is not done
	(10) are followed
	(11) is captured
Present continuous	(0) are being used
Present perfect	(3) has been caused
Past simple	(4) were kept
	(12) was interviewed
Past perfect	(13) had been caught
Future simple	(6) will be published
Infinitive	(7) to be bugged
	(9) to be (done)
Gerund	(14) being subjected
	(15) being filmed

The passive is formed with the appropriate form of the verb be + past participle

Practice
is believed (that) they sole/have stolen £3 million

Transformations
1 must not be taken **2** is known to have broken
3 is not thought to be **4** will be made to
5 must have been tapped **6** has not been contacted by

Further practice: Passives
1 letting/he let **2** *was found **3** will send/sends
4 have been fined **5** put **6** are fined **7** caught
8 do not clean (*will not clean* = refusal) **9** was told
10 was invited **11** being followed/having been followed
12 being ordered
*note: not *has been found*. In newspaper reports like this the present perfect tends to be used to introduce the story, and the past simple to give further details.

Writing 2: Articles Page 129

1
1 Personally **2** Astonishingly **3** Sadly
4 Unfortunately/ Sadly **5** Curiously **6** Worryingly
7 Interestingly **8** Happily

4

a *A load of rubbish* [this expression can also be used to express disagreement or criticize something]

b *I'm sure the people of Brenton don't drop crisp packets and drink cans on the floor in their own home.*

c *So why do so many think it's acceptable to do so on the streets of our town?*
But surely they, more than anyone, want a town they can be proud of, don't they?

d *Incredibly, Clearly, Unfortunately, surely*

e *So, And, But* [Normally, these are used as conjunctions to link two ideas in the same sentence. Here they are used informally at the beginning of a sentence to link the ideas which follow with those in the previous sentence.]

f *But surely they, more than anyone, want a town they can be proud of, don't they?*

5
Paragraph 1
A criticism of some of Brenton's residents and their tendency to drop litter.

Paragraph 2
The serious nature of the problem in Brenton, and the impression left on tourists.

Paragraph 3
Suggested solutions.

Paragraph 4
A criticism of the council and a reason why they should take action.

Listening 2: Multiple matching Page 131

2
1 C **2** A **3** F **4** E **5** D

Language focus 2: Past necessity Page 131

Speaker 1**b** Speaker 5**a**

Practice

1 needn't have written
2 didn't need to set
3 didn't need to go
4 needn't have bothered
5 needn't have worried

Review 10 Page 132

The passive

1 has been robbed **2** were arrested **3** be made
4 being burgled **5** are (being) smuggled
6 will be given/is going to be given
7 are currently being looked **8** had never been told

Vocabulary
Phrasal verbs

1

A 1 *c* 2 a 3 e 4 b 5 f 6 d
B 1 c 2 f 3 a 4 b 5 d 6 e

Use of English: Multiple-choice cloze
1 D 2 A 3 B 4 C 5 D 6 C 7 A 8 B 9 A 10 C 11 C 12 D

Unit 11 What on Earth's going on?

Vocabulary 1: Weather Page 134

1

1 storm 2 rain 3 wind 4 sunshine 5 sea 6 clouds
7 showers

Reading: Multiple matching Page 134

2

1 C 2 A 3 D 4/5 A,B 6 C 7 B 8 A 9/10 A,C 11 B 12 A 13 D
14 C 15 B

Language focus 1: Conditionals
Page 136

A Real or imaginary?

In this sentence the speaker is referring to a situation in
the *past*. The situation she describes is imaginary because
we know that the guide *shouted* at them to get out of the
way, and that the consequences *were not* tragic.

B Context
1-2

Zero conditional   text C
present simple, present simple, present simple
First conditional   text A
will + infinitive without *to*, present simple
Second conditional   text D
past simple, *would* + infinitive without *to*
Third conditional   text C
past perfect, *would* + infinitive without *to*
Mixed conditional   text B
past perfect, *would* + infinitive without *to*

C Meaning

1

a third conditional **b** second conditional
c first conditional **d** mixed conditional **e** zero conditional

2

Both sentences refer to the future.
In the first sentence (first conditional) the speaker sees it
as a real possibility that there will be another tornado. In
the second sentence (second conditional) the speaker sees
it as unlikely.

3

1 **a** certainty **b** possibility
2 **a** certainty **b** possibility

4

a *as long as*, *provided*, *providing*, *on condition* can all
replace *if* in the sentence.
b unless

Practice

1

1 If you'd asked me, ... **2** ... if I find out **3** What will you
do if she doesn't come ...? or What would you do if she
didn't come ...? **4** If I drink **5** I'll never go *or*
If they lost ... I'd ...

Conditionals: Expressing regret Page 137

Suggested answers

1 If I hadn't gone skiing, I wouldn't have broken my arm.
2 If I hadn't committed a foul, the referee wouldn't have
sent (be sending) me off.
3 If I hadn't been using my mobile phone, I wouldn't
have crashed into a tree.
4 If I hadn't gone out of the room, the cat wouldn't have
eaten the fish.
5 If I'd worked harder, I would have got a better grade.

Note: In each of the above sentences, *might* can substitute
would in order to express possibility rather than
certainty. The negative auxiliaries *hadn't* and *wouldn't* are
usually stressed but in the affirmative they are usually
unstressed.

Listening 1: Sentence completion Page 137

2

1 firefighter 2 find missing people 3 United Nations
4 specialist equipment 5 volunteers 6 mosquitoes *and*
(the) (torrential) rain 7 four hours 8 wardrobe 9 bored
10 safer buildings

Vocabulary 2: *Put* Page 138

A Phrasal verbs with *put*

1

1 C discourage
1 A 2 B 3 D

2

A The missing word is *on*.

1 C **2** B **3** A

B The missing word is *up*.

1 C **2** A **3** B

B Expressions with *put*

1

Text A

1 *night* **2** touch **3** smoking **4** risk **5** cigarette

Text B

6 pressure **7** effort

Text C

8 feet **9** book

Text D

10 money **11** blame **12** position

2

1 *put her up for the night at my house* let her stay at my house for one night

2 *put her in touch with my friend* give her my friend's address or telephone number so she can make contact

3 *put up with anyone smoking* tolerate smoking

4 *put his health at risk* endanger his health

5 *put out her cigarette* extinguish her cigarette

6 *put pressure on me to study* strongly persuaded me or forced me to study

7 *put more time and effort into it* dedicate enough time and effort to

8 *put my feet up* rest my feet on something or just relax in general

9 *can't put the book down* keep reading because it is so good

10 *putting some money aside* saving some money

11 *put the blame on me* blame me

12 *put yourself in my position* see the situation from my point of view

Reading Page 140

She is protesting against a construction company's plans to build luxury houses on an area of woodland.
She and others are camping on the proposed site and they have built underground tunnels.
Her mother worries about her and does not really agree with her methods but she supports her.

Language focus 2: *So, neither* and *nor*

Page 141

1

Neither and *so* are used when something is true for all people referred to in the sentence.
Neither is used with reference to grammatical negatives and *so* with reference to affirmatives:
The auxiliary used in the short reply is the same auxiliary that is needed to form the question or negative.

2a

1 c **2** e **3** f **4** g **5** a **6** h **7** b **8** d

Use of English: Open cloze Page 141

1 This/The **2** is **3** to **4** order **5** if **6** part
7 although/though/but **8** which/that **9** such **10** However
11 has **12** without

Speaking: Collaborative task Page 142

1

Recycling	**Keeping cities clean**	**River and sea pollution**
recycled paper	*dog mess*	*toxic effluent*
bottle bank	dropping litter	oil slick
plastic containers	cigarette butts	dumping waste

Traffic pollution	**Climate change**	**Animal welfare**
carbon monoxide	*rising sea levels*	*facing extinction*
unleaded petrol	global warming	nature reserve
exhaust fumes	(the) greenhouse effect	endangered species

Listening 2: Multiple choice Page 143

1 C **2** A **3** C **4** B **5** C **6** B **7** A **8** A

Review 11 Page 144

Vocabulary

A Weather

1

1 light *rain/wind/showers* **2** heavy *rain/storm/showers*
3 strong *wind*

2

1 gentle *breeze* **2** angry looking clouds **3** rough sea
4 torrential rain **5** scattered showers **6** brilliant sunshine
7 overcast sky **8** tidal wave **9** violent storm
10 gale-force wind

B Put

1 down **2** out **3** up **4** on **5** in **6** off

Conditional sentences

1 stays, 'll probably **2** had known, could have prepared
3 wouldn't do, paid **4** had taken, wouldn't be
5 do, 'll make **6** would have done, hadn't helped
7 am, always watch **8** would go, had

Use of English: Transformations

1 if it wasn't/was not/weren't/were not so/too
2 if I hadn't/had not spoken **3** I would not have written
4 not help you unless you **5** I had/'d remembered to take
6 give up smoking you put **7** to put up with
8 is being put at **9** provided it is **10** as long as you give

Unit 12 Looking after yourself

Language focus 1: Countable and uncountable nouns A Page 146

1

milk, health, spaghetti **U** chocolate **U, C** meal **C**
(**U** = animal feed) chicken **U/C** (for a whole one)
pepper **C** (vegetable)/**U** (spice) diet, chip **C** cake **U/C**

2

1 a piece of cheese, toast, cake, chocolate
2 cheese, toast, cake **3** spaghetti* (also *plateful*)
4 sugar, salt **5** salt **6** chocolate **7** jam **8** milk
*notice that 'spaghetti' takes a singular verb in English

Listening: Multiple matching Page 147

2

1 B **2** E **3** A **4** F **5** C D not used

Language focus 2: Countable and uncountable nouns B Page 147

Speaker 1
a some **b** any/much **c** deal
Speaker 2
d lot **e** little **f** little **g** some/several
Speaker 3
h piece **i** few **j** no/little **k** many
Speaker 4
l plenty **m** several/many **n** no/few
Speaker 5
o number **p** few **q** much/any

Reading: Multiple matching Page 148

1 A **2** D **3** C **4** B **5** A **6** E **7** C **8** D **9** B **10** A **11** C **12** E
13/14/15 A, D, E in any order

Language focus 3: Reported speech
Page 149

1 The verb tense 'steps back' from the present simple (direct speech) in this example. *Under what circumstances would the following reported speech version be possible?* If the statement being reported is still true.

2
Reported speech
b She said she *had seen* him twice *that* day.
c He told me she *had been* living *there* for years.
d He said he *had spoken* to her *the previous* week.
e He told me he *had been* working *the day* before.
f They said they *had asked* her several times.

3

Direct speech	Reported speech
a present continuous	→ past continuous
b present perfect simple	→ past perfect simple
c present perfect continuous	→ past perfect continuous
d past simple	→ past perfect simple
e past continuous	→ past perfect continuous
f past perfect simple	→ past perfect simple

4

Direct speech	Reported speech
will	→ *would*
would	→ *would*
can	→ *could*
could	→ *could*
should	→ *should*
must	→ *had to*
may	→ *might*
might	→ *might*
ought to	→ *ought to*

5

two days ago: → two days before/earlier/ previously
next month: → the following/next month
tonight: → that night/evening
this morning: → that morning
now: → then

Language focus 4: Reporting verbs
Page 150

2

advise	**offer**
(verb + object + infinitive)	(verb + infinitive)
order	refuse
urge	threaten
persuade	*promise
warn	
tell	
remind	
ask	
encourage	
recommend (and same patterns as suggest)	

* can also take an object, eg *He promised me that he would ...*

3

1 refused to clean her room **2** reminded him to take his sandwiches **3** threatened to call the police if I didn't turn my music down **4** warned/advised her not to take the car out (as/because/since the roads were very icy)
5 ordered/told him to get out of his/her office immediately
6 urged/encouraged/persuaded me to report the theft to the police

4

Suggest is not possible with the pattern in the first sentence.

Use of English 1: Multiple-choice cloze
Page 151

3

1 B **2** D **3** A **4** C **5** A **6** D **7** D **8** B **9** D **10** A **11** A **12** C

Writing 1: Reports Page 152

2

1 C **2** F **3** E **4** A **5** B D not used

3

The restaurant manager is the target reader. The style is semi-formal/formal.

4

a *Many of those under sixteen, Most parents, a large number of teenagers, 80% of those interviewed, over 90% of those under twelve, Several younger parents*

b *those under sixteen... felt that, Most parents expected to see, 80%... said they, 90%... wanted chips with everything, a large number... thought that*

c *recommend + should –I would recommend that the restaurant should ...*
suggest + gerund –I also suggest extending the menu ...

5
a *The aim of this report is to ... , The report is based on a survey of...*
b *on the other hand ... , whereas ...*
c *Understandably, Not surprisingly*

8

Sample answer
This is a report about the main dishes in my area, especially for young people. The report is based on a survey of 100 people aged between 12 and 20 who live in Asturias and is referred about regional dishes.
The most popular and important dishes are always based on natural food. Although a large number of young people – almost 80% – declare they like fast food in some situations, everybody prefers absolutely their own regional food based on vegetables, beans, meat, pork and, on the other hand, seafruits.
The people of our survey, either boys or girls, give the best qualification to the 'fabada', the most known dish of the Asturias kitchen; it is made with a especial beans – 'fabes' – and pork products such as ham, bacon, blood pudding. Another variations with 'fabes' are too expensive for young people, as for instance, partridges or shellfishes.
The most popular pudding is rice pudding, very famous in Asturias. Young people like it very much.
In the end, there is a lot of natural food dishes for young people in Asturias, though some of them are expensive, especially with seafruits. Of course, if you like fast food you'll get a burger as in any part of the world.
By Emilio Jiménez Aparicio
206 words

Examiner's comment
Content: Good realization of the task. Rather longer than necessary but it is well expressed and relevant and so is not penalized.
Accuracy: Some minor inaccuracies – *is referred about* rather than *refers to* or *is about, prefers absolutely*, etc as well as more obtrusive errors which could cause confusion – *seafruits, the best qualification.*
Range: Good range of appropriate expressions for this type of task – *the report is based on, a large number of young people declare, pork products such as ...* The writer also shows good knowledge of food vocabulary.
Organization and cohesion: The report is clearly divided into appropriate sections.
Style and format: Consistently neutral.
Target reader: Would be suitably informed about the culinary possibilities in the region to be visited.
Mark: band 4

Language focus 5: Reported questions
Page 153

1
1 What facilities should a family restaurant have?
2 Do you think it is important to have a non-smoking area?

2
● Word order - changes from verb + subject to subject + verb when we report.
● Auxiliary verbs *do, does, did* – disappear
● Verb tenses – 'step back' a tense unless the question is reported in the same time period
● Yes/No questions – use *if/whether*

3
1 what type of food they expected to see on the menu.
2 how important the price of the food was.
3 if/whether they always ate the same things when they went to a restaurant.
4 what other things they would like a restaurant to offer.

Vocabulary: Health matters Page 154

1
A **1** heart attack **2** stomach ache **3** blood pressure
4 ear infection
B **1** black eye **2** sore throat **3** runny nose **4** sprained ankle

3
1 bandage **2** a plaster **3** prescription **4** plaster **5** injection

Word formation: Noun suffixes Page 154

1
treat – treatment, prescribe – prescription,
weak – weakness, severe – severity

2–3

Verbs	Nouns
a'muse	a'musement
de'cide	de'cision
ap'pear	ap'pearance
enter'tain	enter'tainment
ex'plain	**explan'ation**
per'form	per'formance
i'magine	**imagin'ation**
de'velop	de'velopment
Adjectives	**Nouns**
im'portant	im'portance
fit	fitness
sin'cere	sin'cerity
'happy	'happiness
se'cure	se'curity
'evident	'evidence
'careless	'carelessness
o'riginal	**origin'ality**

Use of English 2: Word formation Page 155

1 competition **2** ability **3** stiffness **4** operation **5** majority
6 complications **7** activity/activities **8** improvement
9 movements **10** tiredness

Writing 2: Letters: Giving information
Page 155

1

> **Sample answer**
>
> Dear Trevor
>
> I'm glad you stopped thinking that I was crazy when I decided to go to a health spa last year.
>
> The first thing I have to tell you is that it is the best place to go if you want to relax after you exams. It was very quiet place and I remember going for a walk in the evening because there was a really nice landscape. However, if you prefer not to go out, there was an outdoor thermal pool which temperature was wonderful!
>
> As for food, it was well-cooked and there were lots of vegetable dishes to choose, but a bit small portions.
>
> I don't think you will get bored because there were lots of enjoyable things to do. As well as discos, there was karaoke, which was great fun, and bingo.
>
> I hope you have a good time and I'm sure you will cheer up.
>
> Lots of love
> Coral Berriochoa Hausmann
> 151 words

Content: All content points have been covered.
Accuracy: Generally accurate. Errors do not obscure meaning, eg *after you(r) exams, it was (a) very quiet place, pool which (whose) temperature*. Examples of accurate language use in often difficult areas are *stopped thinking, remember going, prefer not to go out*.
Range: A reasonably good range of structure and vocabulary for the task. Examples of good vocabulary are *well-cooked, get bored, enjoyable, great fun, cheer up*.
Organization and cohesion: The introduction and conclusion are well expressed. The letter is well organized with suitable paragraphs and the writer uses linking expressions, eg *As for food, However, As well as discos*
Style and format: The tone is friendly and natural.
Target reader: This would have a very positive effect on the reader, whose questions are answered.
Mark: Band 5

Review 12 Page 156

Use of English: Open cloze
1 few 2 when 3 to 4 had 5 no 6 her 7 where 8 as 9 so
10 off 11 in 12 not

Use of English: Transformations
1 Roy if he had bought 2 was such a rapid improvement
3 advised Matt not to go 4 knowledge of English amazes
5 her if she was able 6 offered to give Dawn
7 would not be (very) many
8 suggested eating out the next/following

Vocabulary: Health matters
1 a black eye 2 a sore throat 3 a sprained ankle/wrist
4 a runny nose 5 an eye/ear infection 6 a nose bleed
7 a heart attack 8 a stomach ache

Use of English: Word formation
1 ability 2 relationship 3 patience 4 argument
5 performance 6 sadness 7 explanation

Collocation revision: Units 1-12
1 clothes 2 musician 3 device 4 film 5 job/work 6 hair
7 town/neighbourhood/area 8 trip 9 give 10 sentence
11 wind(s) 12 food

Ready for Listening

Part 1: Multiple choice Page 158
Predicting
Similarities and differences:
A dress also covers part of the top half of the body like a blouse.
A blouse has **sleeves**, and a dress may do too.
A dress and a blouse may have **collars**, whereas a skirt wouldn't.
A blouse is more likely to have several **buttons** whereas the other two may have just one.
Dresses and skirts can be **short** or **long**, reaching as far as the knees, the ankles, etc.
Answer: A a blouse

Key words and expressions
It'll go really well with a skirt I bought last week.
The sleeves are a bit short, but if I wear a jacket over it ...
Distractors
Cheaper than getting a dress ...
It'll go really well with a skirt I bought last week.
Listening
2 C 3 A 4 A 5 C 6 B 7 B 8 C

Part 2: Sentence completion Page 159

1
1 False. All parts of the listening paper are heard twice.
2 True 3 True 4 False. The maximum number of words you need to write is normally three. 5 False. It is not necessary to rephrase the words you hear. 6 False. You do usually hear the answers in the same order as the questions. 7 False. If you are having difficulty with a question, move quickly onto the next. You may miss later answers if you spend too long on one answer. 8 True. Spelling errors are accepted, but if the word is so badly spelt it is unrecognizable, then it may be marked wrong.

Listening
1 tea house 2 several hundred 3 isolated 4 farmers
5 (local) Indians 6 beautiful valley 7 song and dance
8 (groups of) teachers 9 (Welsh) flags 10 chocolate cake

Part 3: Multiple matching Page 160

2

Suggested answers

E is very different from **A** because it talks about personal qualities rather than academic qualifications.

B This is the only sentence which clearly suggests the person is already doing the job.

C & D Both these sentences mention the fact that the person has been told by someone about work or a specific job.

E see example. Both **E** and **C** express an opinion: *I disagree with ...* and *I think I have ...*

F see example. Note the following difference between **A**, **B** and **F**:

A We do not know if the person is studying or not for that qualification.

B The person is studying though we do not know if it is relevant to the work they are doing.

F The person is studying now and the subject is relevant either to what they are doing and/or what they are going to do.

Suggested underlinings of key words

Note also the different tenses in A (future), B (present simple), D (past simple) and F (present continuous). Grammatical features such as this may also be relevant.

A I will need a specific qualification to do this job.
B I combine work with studying.
C I disagree with the careers advice I have been given.
D I heard about this job from someone in my family.
E I think I have the necessary personal qualities.
F I am studying a relevant subject.

Words related to *qualification*
degree, 'A' Levels, diploma, certificate

3

Listening
1 B 2 F 3 D 4 A 5 E C not used

Part 4: Multiple choice Page 161

3
C Underline the whole of the first sentence.

4

A: Most of the people he works with are below average height. At one metre 84, he is above the average height of one metre 78 for British men.

B: We are told that he is taller than most, if not all, of the people in his studio, but we we do not know if he is taller than most people in his profession.

Multiple choice

5
2 B   3 A   4 A   5 B   6 B   7 C

6
2
A We are only told that tall people come from all over the country to stay in a hotel.
C Not mentioned.
3
B & C are both mentioned as problems but not the biggest.
4
B People who make comments like 'What's the weather like up there?' think they are funny. Jenny does not.
C Jenny says that many fellow TPC members take offence, but she is used to it now.
5
A They stand up straighter as they grow in confidence. No one encourages them to do so.
C Not mentioned.
6
A Not mentioned. Jenny says 'I've never been very good at volleyball, but I always got picked for the university team when I was a student.'
C Not mentioned. The word 'job' is mentioned when she says 'you can get things off the top shelf that most other people have a job to reach.'
7
A Not mentioned. Jenny merely compares the GB and Ireland club with those in America.
B No. People decide for themselves if they should join.

Unit 13 Against the odds

Vocabulary 1: Money Page 162

2
1 stock market 2 rate of interest 3 account 4 currency
5 rate of exchange

3
1 for, for 2 on, on 3 in, in 4 to, to

Reading 1: Multiple choice Page 163
1 C 2 B 3 C 4 A 5 D 6 C 7 D 8 B

Language focus 1: Ability Page 165

1
a travel b reaching c to retire d to get e setting

2
- *can* is not possible in **c** because it does not have an infinitive form.
- *could* is not possible in **d** because this sentence refers to a specific occasion not a general ability in the past.
- *could* is not possible in **e** because it does not have a participle form.
- We can use the negative form *couldn't* to refer to specific occasions in the past.

3

1 was capable of swimming **2** finally managed to give up
3 was unable to finish **4** succeeded in finding out
5 be able to find **6** didn't manage to buy

4

1 could **3** couldn't **6** couldn't

Vocabulary 2: *Make* and *do* Page 166

A *Make* or *do*

1

1 made **2** made **3** do (make is also possible with *deals*)
4 doing **5** made **6** make

2

1 damage **2** an effort **3** someone a favour **4** the beds
5 an experiment **6** an exercise **7** progress **8** a job

1 MAKE a plan, an appointment, an arrangement
arranging or planning to do things
2 DO homework, a course, a degree *all related to study*
3 MAKE up your mind, a decision, a choice *decisions*
4 DO the housework, the washing-up, the ironing
housework
5 MAKE a speech, a phone call, a complaint
communication
6 MAKE a film, a cake, a cup of tea *creation*
7 DO badly in an exam, well at school, your best *all refer
to how successful or unsuccessful a person is*
8 MAKE a mistake, a mess, a lot of noise *to cause
something with a negative result*

MAKE	DO
a profit	business
money	the ironing
a loss	damage
a plan	an experimen
an appointment	homework
an arrangement	an exercise
an effort	a course
up your mind	badly in an exam
a decision	a degree
a choice	well at school
the beds	someone a favour
a speech	your best
a phone call	the housework
a complaint	a job
a film	the washing-up
a cake	
a cup of tea	
progress	
a mistake	
a mess	
a lot of noise	

B Phrasal verbs with *make* and *do*

1

1 fasten it **2** become friends again **3** invent it
4 renovated and decorated it **5** hear properly
6 pretended/feigned **7** need **8** couldn't manage/survive

Writing: Formal letters Page 167

1

- The target reader is the Director of St George's House.

- The effect would not be positive. As well as making
several requests concerning the school and the class
(Manchester, the class size, idiomatic expressions), the
applicant gives rather frivolous reasons for wanting
to go to England: meeting a relative, going clubbing,
using it as a base for travelling. This does not sound
like a serious letter from someone asking for money
and the application would probably not be successful.

3

Examples of other reasons:

- A course in the UK would help you pass FCE.

- Your writing and grammar are fine but you
would like to improve your fluency in speaking.

- You are going to study English at university next year.

- You are interested in meeting speakers of English
from other countries.

- You will be working for two years overseas for a
charity and English is a requirement.

Examples of further details relating to the other three
reasons in the Coursebook:

- A period of study in the UK would improve your
chances of obtaining a job in your own country.

  *You would like to work in the travel industry but your
  job applications are repeatedly rejected because of your
  level of spoken English.*

- A recent illness has caused you to fall behind in your
studies.

  *You were absent from school for three months after
  a car accident and this has affected your chances of
  passing First Certificate.*

- You are interested in learning about British culture
and the British way of life.

  *You believe that knowledge of the culture would increase
  your enjoyment of the subject and provide an important
  context for your study of the language.*

Listening 1: Sentence completion Page 168

2
1 one or a/one year old
2 left
3 (any) better
4 tunnel
5 normal
6 called names
7 became good friends
8 get a job
9 going on tour/touring
10 shyness

Word formation: Miscellaneous nouns Page 168

1
choice, loss, complaint, speech

2
1 Sales **2** signature **3** laughter **4** behaviour **5** arrival
6 beings **7** *proof **8** saying
*uncountable, *proofs* is not possible in this context

Reading 2: Gapped text Page 169

2
1 E **2** H **3** G **4** A **5** F **6** C **7** B   **D** not used

Language focus 2: Verbs followed by prepositions Page 170

1
1 for **2** for **3** against

2
1 *for*, d **2** for, a **3** for, f **4** from, b **5** from, c **6** on, g **7** on, e

Vocabulary 3: Ways of looking Page 170

1
a *see* = (the ability) to use your eyes, one of the five senses
b *look at* = pay attention to or examine someone or something with the eyes.
c *watch* = (usually) to pay attention to someone or something that is moving

2
1 look at **2** see **3** watching (the image moves) **4** seen
5 Watch

3
1 d **2** e **3** b **4** a **5** c

4
1 peered **2** glanced **3** gazed **4** stared **5** glimpse

Listening 2: Multiple choice Page 171
1 C **2** A **3** C **4** B **5** C **6** B **7** B **8** A

Review 13 Page 172
Use of English: Word formation
1 saying **2** Advertising **3** signature **4** laughter **5** speeches
6 poverty **7** wealthiest **8** growth **9** success **10** choices

Use of English: Transformations
1 blamed Helen for starting/having started
2 apologized for being **3** warned us against/about
4 prevented him (from) coming **5** insisted on seeing
6 did not/didn't succeed in finding
7 didn't/did not manage to get
8 make a complaint

Vocabulary
A *Make* and *do*
1 do **2** do **3** make **4** made **5** making **6** do **7** make **8** do

B Ways of looking
1 c **2** d **3** e **4** a **5** b

Unit 14 As pretty as a picture

Vocabulary 1: The Arts Page 174

1
1 classical **2** opera **3** stone **4** gallery **5** painting **6** novel

2
music musician, composer, conductor, orchestra, pianist, violinist, etc
literature novelist, writer, author, publisher
art artist, painter, art collector
opera opera singer, tenor, soprano, cast
ballet ballet dancer, ballerina, choreographer
sculpture sculptor

Reading 1: Gapped text Page 174
2
1 C **2** G **3** D **4** A **5** H **6** E **7** B   **F** not used

Language focus: Hypothetical situations Page 176
A Wishes
2
a the past simple **b** *would* + base form
c the past perfect

3
a I wish I ~~would~~ **could** give up smoking.
I wish I would is not normally said.
b *I wish she could come to my party on Saturday.*
The speaker <u>knows</u> that she cannot come.
I hope she can come to my party on Saturday.
The speaker <u>does not know</u> if she can come or not.

Practice

1
1 could **2** didn't **3** hadn't bought **4** would **5** you'd listened

2
1 were **2** would stop **3** had gone **4** had **5** would make

B *It's time* and *would rather*
1 I'd rather you *didn't* bring a mobile phone to school.
2 It's time you *went* to bed now.

Word formation: Adjective suffixes *-ible* and *-able* Page 177

1 un**predictable 2** reason**ably 3** im**possibility**
4 in**credibly**, comfort**ably 5** valu**ables**, respons**ibility**
6 un**bearably 7** in**accessible 8** consider**ably**

Vocabulary 2: Animals Page 178

1
1 a bat **2** a bee **3** a mouse **4** a fox **5** a mule **6** an owl
7 a peacock

2
1 fly **2** horse **3** fish **4** cat, dog **5** bear **6** frog

3
a bird **b** fish **c** cat **d** horse

Listening: Multiple choice Page 179

2
1 C **2** A **3** B **4** B **5** A **6** C **7** B

Writing 1: Set books Page 180

2
Question 7

3

Has the writer answered both parts of the question satisfactorily?
The writer has answered both parts satisfactorily. The description of the place is brief (no more is given in the book itself) and the reader is fully informed of its importance in the story.

What is the purpose of each of the paragraphs?
1 A brief description of the farmhouse and the animals' initial reaction to it.
2 How the farmhouse comes to show the inequality between the pigs and the other animals.
3 How the leader in the farmhouse separates himself from his subjects.
4 The final scene in the farmhouse and its importance to one of the themes of the book.
Which words are used to link ideas?
Paragraph 1: After, at the beginning, and
Paragraph 2: However, while, As (in Jones's time), whereas
Paragraph 3: Furthermore, In this way
Paragraph 4: At the end, then, (Note also the use of 'It is ... that' to create emphasis.)

Has the writer quoted directly from the text?
Yes – 'the unbelievable luxury'. The quotation is short and relevant.

Reading 2: Multiple matching Page 181

2
1 D **2/3** C, E in any order **4** A **5** B **6/7** A, F in any order
8 C **9/10** D, E in any order **11** F **12** B
13/14 A, F in any order **15** C

Vocabulary 4: Phrasal verbs Page 183

1
stop (the habit of watching television)
accept

2
1 d **2** e **3** h **4** b, f **5** i **6** c **7** a **8** g

Review 14 Page 184
Use of English: Word formation
1 peacefully **2** remarkable **3** originally **4** including
5 responsibility **6** retirement **7** appearance **8** proof
9 seasonal **10** unreliable

Vocabulary
A The Arts
1 portrait **2** sculptures **3** novel **4** open-air **5** priceless
6 playwright **7** composer **8** exhibition

B Animals
1 a lion

C Phrasal verbs
1 clear up/throw away **2** take over **3** eats up **4** get on with **5** got through

Use of English: Transformations: Hypothetical situations
1 wish I lived **2** wish I hadn't told
3 rather you didn't wear **4** time we went
5 wish I could go **6** only you had brought
7 wish you wouldn't speak **8** wish I knew/could know

Unit 15 Mind your language

Listening: Multiple matching Page 186

1
aferdersiniz – Turkish
disculpe – Spanish/Castilian
entschuldigen Sie – German
mi scusi – Italian
permisi – Indonesian
ursäkta mig – Swedish
elnézést – Hungarian
excusez-moi – French

2
1 C **2** E **3** F **4** B **5** A D not used

Vocabulary 1: Page 186

A Phrasal verbs with *turn*

2

1 g 2 c 3 e 4 a 5 f 6 b 7 d

3

a turn into something **b** turn something up **c** turn out that **d** turn up **e** turn off something **f** turn back **g** turn something off

B Compound adjectives

1

1 English-speaking 2 five-minute 3 Italian-born 4 1,000-word 5 American-educated 6 one-hour 7 Irish-made 8 11-year-old

2

1 a five-pound (bank) note 2 a twelve-hour shift 3 a ten-man team 4 a three-course meal 5 a two-week holiday

3

Possible answers
We have six 50-minute lessons a day.
It was a 10-day holiday in Majorca. We had a two-hour flight from London.
It's a twenty-minute car journey/a five-kilometre bus ride/ a 15-minute walk
a fifteen-unit/a 217-page book

Reading 1: Multiple choice Page 188

2

1 C 2 D 3 A 4 C 5 D 6 B 7 B 8 A

Vocabulary 2: Abbreviations Page 189

1

Professor
United Kingdom

2

The original Latin terms are in brackets.
1 eg for example (exempli gratia)
etc and so on (et cetera)
2 ie that is (id est)
3 NB please note (nota bene)
www World Wide Web
4 PS postscript
ASAP as soon as possible
5 PTO please turn over

3

British Broadcasting Corporation
United Nations
compact disc
Member of Parliament
Federal Bureau of Investigation
European Union

Language focus: Expressing purpose

Page 190

A *In order to, so as to* and *so that*

2

so that + present simple/*can/will* = future
so that + *could/would* = past

Practice
Possible answers
1 she can call us if she needs help.
2 to get a good seat near the front/not to miss it/to see the team arrive.
3 as to increase my chances of getting a job/ that I can concentrate on my other studies/ I can prove my level of English/my parents will be happy.
4 as not to have to do sport/I wouldn't have to take the exam/I could stay at home and watch television.
5 to find information about cheap flights.
6 to avoid waking anyone up.
7 I can go out afterwards/I don't forget what we studied in class/I can enjoy the rest of the evening.

B *In case*
Possible answers
1 the other one runs out of ink/you need to use a different colour.
2 it broke down again/there was heavy traffic on the roads.
3 you are burgled/there's a fire/you break something valuable.
4 I have to do overtime.
5 I saw something good for my dad's birthday present.
6 we lock ourselves out/they need to borrow anything/ there's a fire.

Reading 2: Gapped text Page 191

2

1 H 2 A 3 G 4 D 5 F 6 B 7 E C not used

Vocabulary 3 Page 193

A American English

2

1 *b* 2 a 3 g 4 d 5 f 6 e 7 c

3

1 underground (*or* tube) 2 petrol station (*or* filling station) 3 motorway 4 holiday 5 railway 6 car park 7 return ticket

4

1 She took the *rubbish* out to the *dustbin* in the *garden*. *Yard* might be possible in British English, depending on what is referred to).
2 The *lorry* driver slowed down and pulled into the *petrol* station on the *motorway*.
3 'I can't find my *trousers* anywhere, *Mum*!' 'Try looking in the *wardrobe, darling.*'

4 No *biscuits* or *sweets* for me thanks, I'm *on a diet*.

5 It was early *autumn*. The *pavements* in the *neighbourhood* were covered with leaves of different shapes and *colours* and the summer *holiday* was just a distant memory.

B Education

1

1 nursery school - for young children aged between 2 and 5
primary school - for children aged between 5 and 11

2 a state school - one which is controlled and funded by the government or a local authority
a public school - a private school; pupils' parents pay fees for their child to attend

3 a grammar school - a secondary school for children (aged 11-18) with a high academic ability
a comprehensive school - a secondary school for children of all abilities; the majority of secondary schools in Britain are comprehensive schools

4 a degree - a course of study at a college or university; the qualification you are given when you pass the course, eg *I'm doing a degree in chemistry.*
I got a degree in French.
a career - an occupation or profession

5 a teacher - in a school, for example
a professor - the most senior teacher in a university department

6 a qualification - an exam you have passed, eg First Certificate in English; the degree, or certificate which you are awarded for this, eg *What qualifications do you need for the job?*
a title - the name of a book, film, etc; *Mr, Mrs, Ms, Lady, Lord* are all titles.

Review 15 Page 194

Use of English: Multiple-choice cloze
1 C 2 B 3 A 4 D 5 D 6 A 7 C 8 C 9 B 10 D 11 B 12 A

Vocabulary
A Abbreviations
1 eg 2 etc 3 ie 4 NB 5 www 6 PS 7 ASAP 8 PTO

B Compound adjectives
1 clock 2 shift 3 baby girl 4 meal 5 composition 6 lesson 7 holiday 8 note

C American English
1 pants 2 trashcan/garbage can 3 closet 4 yard 5 freeway 6 truck 7 parking lot 8 sidewalk

Use of English Transformations
1 in order not to get 2 so as not to miss
3 in case it doesn't/does not 4 so that she would not
5 turned down an/the offer
6 did Mike (eventually) turn up

Ready for Speaking

Introduction Page 196

1
Part 1 b Part 2 d Part 3 a Part 4 c

2
Part 1
a No. Certainly, students should avoid trying to give over-complicated answers which cause them to become confused and so make unnecessary mistakes. However, very short one-word answers are usually inadequate and do not give the examiners a sufficient sample of language to assess. Students should therefore answer questions with appropriate detail.

b No. Long, pre-prepared answers are usually obvious to the interlocutor and will be interrupted. As well as sounding unnatural they are often inappropriate to the question asked and do not therefore form part of effective interactive communication, one of the criteria for assessment in the speaking exam. Students may practise for this part of the test, but they should not try to prepare and learn long answers.

c Yes. Students will be nervous at the beginning but this part of the test is designed to relax them by asking questions on areas which are familiar to them.

Part 2
a No. Students are not required to describe the photographs in detail. They should therefore listen carefully to and follow the instructions given to them by the interlocutor.

b Yes, as long as the student has tried to address both parts of the question. It is better to fill the minute and be interrupted than to run out of things to say before the allotted time finishes.

c Clearly the student should focus on the instructions that the interlocutor gives, though exam nerves often cause students to miss part of the instructions and it is perfectly acceptable for students to ask for them to be repeated. However, this should not be necessary as the second part of the interlocutor's instructions is printed in the form of a question alongside the photographs.

Part 3
a Good that the student had a lot to say. However, it seems that he/she may not have been respecting the rules of turn-taking, an aspect of interactive communication, mentioned above. If students are paired with quiet, more reticent candidates, they should invite them to take part in the discussion by asking questions such as 'What do you think?' or 'What would you do?' Attempts to dominate the conversation will be penalized.

b No. As with Part 2, students should aim to fill the time allotted and not reach their decision too soon. Students are penalized if they run out of things to say. The aim is not to find a solution in the shortest time possible: rather, students should be aiming to provide enough relevant and appropriate contributions for the examiners to assess their English accurately.

c Yes. This student and his/her partner has clearly made full use of the time available. Students do not necessarily have to complete the task, as long as it is clear that they are at least trying to reach a decision. See Unit 5 for Useful language, which will be useful later in this unit when practising Part 3.

Part 4

a Yes. Candidates should certainly be speaking more than the examiner! The implication here also seems to be that the candidates have been responding to each others' comments, something which is actively encouraged by examiners in Part 4 and which is part of interactive communication.

b No. It is not only what you say but how you say it which is important throughout the exam. 'Nonsense, you must be mad' sounds rude and is not the best way to disagree with someone in a discussion such as this. Alternative expressions of agreeing and disagreeing are given on page 123 in Unit 10.

c No. Students should respond to questions appropriately and not try to divert the discussion to their favourite topic of conversation.

Part 1: Interview

3

2 Christina has obviously come with a prepared speech. The interlocutor asks her about her home town, and having answered the question, she begins to talk about her family. The interlocutor will interrupt if a student does this in the exam.

3 He should develop his answers more, particularly in relation to his home town and his interest in football.

Part 2: Talking about photographs Page 198

Christina compares the photographs very well, using language such as *both pictures* and *whereas*. Paolo does not compare them.

Part 3: Collaborative task Page 199

interesting eg fascinating, enjoyable, good fun, appealing
boring eg dull, uninteresting, monotonous, tedious
good eg ideal, excellent, marvellous, wonderful, suitable

1 They both agree on the medieval fair. Christina's second choice is cave-painting whereas Paolo's is the Megascreen.

2 Christina summarizes their decision at the end, but they more or less decided on the medieval fair in the first half of the conversation as they discussed it.

3 Christina asks Paolo questions to encourage him to speak.

Which one shall we start with?
It could be fun, don't you think?
Now, what do you think about the concerts?
And children love doing that, don't you agree?
How about the cave painting?
What do you think, Paolo?
What do you think of the fashion shows?

Note that Paolo uses tag questions to invite Christina's opinion: *don't they? would it? Can't you?*

Part 4: Further discussion Page 199

1 When answering the first two questions they do not interact at all, failing to respond to what each other says. Rather than a discussion, there is a series of short monologues. Students should be referred to the interaction patterns at the beginning of this unit. They interact much better in the second half of Part 4.

2 In the second half Christina helps the interaction by asking questions to involve Paolo: *What do you think Paolo? Don't you agree?* and *Do you really think we will have robots?* and Paolo responds accordingly.

Macmillan Education
Between Towns Road, Oxford OX4 3PP
A division of Macmillan Publishers Limited
Companies and representatives throughout the world

ISBN 978-0-230-02760-2 (+key edition)
ISBN 978-0-230-02761-9 (-key edition)

Text © Roy Norris 2008
Design and illustration © Macmillan Publishers Limited 2008

First published 2008

Original design by Andrew Jones.
Page make up by eMC Design, www.emcdesign.org.uk
Illustrated by Anne Cakebread, Richard Duszczak, Stephen Elford, Tim Kahane, Bob Lea, Laszlo Veres
Cover design by Barbara Mercer
Cover photograph by Getty Images / Riser / David Epperson

The author would like to thank his wife, Azucena, for her invaluable help and constant support. The author also wishes to thank his colleagues at International House, Madrid, for their encouragement and inspiration, as well as the many teachers and students who helped with piloting, especially Gail Butler, Steven McGuire, Andrew Graydon, Joanna Herbert, Anne Horkan, Kuldip Kaur, Stephen Nicolls, Karen Reeves, Paul Scannell, Katie Smart, Hilary Thomson, Alice Tierney and Alistair Wood. Special thanks also to Helen Holwill, Amanda Anderson and Julie Reeves for their excellent editorial work and Sarah Curtis for her faith in the project.

The publishers would like to thank all those who participated in the development of the project, with special thanks to Sophia Ashton, Helen Barmakellis, Liam Bellamy, Margarita E. Garraman de Monzani, Vasilis Karalis, Jean Lister, Nick Milner, Jackie Newman, David Pearce, Joanna Porebska, Lynn Smith, George Vasilakis, Peter Williamson, Malcolm Wren and Grzegorz Œpiewak.

The author and publisher are grateful for permission to reprint the following copyright material:
Extract adapted from 'Handle with care' by Jess Hallett, copyright © The Times 1999, first published in Style Magazine 28.11.99, reprinted by permission of the publisher.
Extract adapted from 'Rodean girl sinks to depths men can't' by Alex O'Connell, copyright © The Times 1999, first published in The Times 24.09.99, reprinted by permission of the publisher.
Extract adapted from 'Notes From A Big Country' by Bill Bryson (Doubleday, 1998) reprinted by permission of Random House Group Limited.
Extract adapted from 'Home is where the school is' by Alan Road first published in Reader's Digest April 1999, reprinted by permission of the publisher.
Extract adapted from 'A more commercial tune' by Sara Edgehill, copyright © The Independent 1995, first published in The Independent 06.11.95, reprinted by permission of the publisher.
Extract adapted from 'Gift of your Gab' first published in The Daily Mail, reprinted by permission of Solo Syndication Limited.
Extract adapted from 'Rock of the ages' by Jennifer Rodger, copyright © The Times 1999, first published in Style Magazine 28.11.99, reprinted by permission of the publisher.
Extract adapted from 'It narrows the mind and distends the stomach, so lets travel less' by John Rentoul, copyright © The Independent 1998, first published in the Independent 12.01.98, reprinted by permission of the publisher.
Extract adapted from 'Short breaks for every month of the year' first published in Woman's Weekly 10.08.99, copyright © IPC, reprinted by permission of the publisher.
Extract adapted from 'How to tell a Ghost Story' by Fiona McClymont, copyright © The Independent 1999, first published in The Independent 22.10.99, reprinted by permission of the publisher.
Extract adapted from 'Man fined £800 for not clearing up his dog's mess' by Helen Johnstone, copyright © The Times 1999, first published in The Times 03.12.99, reprinted by permission of the publisher.
Extract adapted from 'Dad would be proud of what I do' by Daisy Price, copyright © The Independent 1999, first published in The Independent 06.12.99, reprinted by permission of the publisher.
Extract adapted from 'Karaoke rolls those excess stones – but a drink or two will put them back' by Michael Fitzpatrick, copyright © Telegraph Group Limited 1999, first published in The Telegraph 05.08.99, reprinted by permission of the publisher.
Extract adapted from 'Why Hallowe'en is hateful' by James Delingpole, copyright © Telegraph Group Limited 1996, first published in The Telegraph 26.10.96, reprinted by permission of the publisher.
Extract adapted from 'Better buy them a book' by Robert Matthews, copyright © Telegraph Group Limited 1997, first published in The Telegraph 05.01.97, reprinted by permission of the publisher.
Extract adapted from 'Internet ends 38 year search' by Nigel Bunyan, copyright © Telegraph Group Limited 2000, first published in The Telegraph 11.02.00, reprinted by permission of the publisher.
Extract from 'World Famous Strange but True' by Colin Damon & Rowan Wilson (Magpie Books Ltd. 1994), reprinted by permission of Constable & Robinson Ltd. London.
Extract from 'International rescuer' interview by Caroline Rees, first published in FHM Magazine February 2000, reprinted by permission of the publisher.
Extract adapted from 'Roast Ghost' from 'Bizarre Tales' taken from New Scientist 12.03.94, reprinted by permission of the publisher.
Extract adapted from 'Scooter importer aims to have city buzzing with his success' by Henrietta Lake, copyright © The Times 1999, first published in The Times 18.12.99, reprinted by permission of the publisher.
Extract adapted from ' He's my river hero' by Theresa Bruce first published in Woman's Own 22.02.00, copyright © IPC, reprinted by permission of the publisher.
Extract adapted from 'Oldest goldfish Tish has his chips at 43' by Paul Stokes, copyright © Telegraph Group Limited 1999, first published in The Telegraph 07.08.99, reprinted by permission of the publisher.
Extract adapted from 'American High' by Victoria Stanley, copyright © Telegraph Group Limited 2000, first published in The Telegraph 11.03.00, reprinted by permission of the publisher.
Extract adapted from 'Location groupies force sale of the UK's second most famous door' by Kate Watson-Smith, copyright © The Independent 1999, first published in The Independent 16.09.99, reprinted by permission of the publisher.
Extract adapted from 'When the heat is on' by Clive Tully, first publishing in Country Walking July 1996, reprinted by permission of the publisher.
Extract adapted from 'Set your sites high and go surfing' by Emma Haughton, copyright © The Independent 2000, first published in The Independent 16.03.00, reprinted by permission of the publisher.
Extract adapted from 'It's the real thing' by Kate Hilpern, copyright © The independent 2003, first published in The Independent 23.06.03, reprinted by permission of the publisher.
Extract from 'Learning the real local lingo can be child's play' by Sarah Monaghan, copyright © Telegraph Group Limited 2006, first published in The Telegraph 14.06.06, reprinted by permission of the publisher.
Extract from 'Love parties but dread dancing' by Peta Bee copyright © Peta Bee/Sunday Times 1999, first published in Sunday Times 31.10.99, reprinted by permission of the publisher.
Adapted extracts from 'You can't be sisters' first published in Woman's Realm 30.11.99, copyright © IPC, reprinted by permission of the publisher.

These materials may contain links for third party websites. We have no control over, and are not responsible for, the contents of such third party websites. Please use care when accessing them.

The author and publishers would like to thank the following for permission to reproduce their photographs:
Alamy p31 (l, c), 34(r), 38, 45(br), 48, 54(l), 60(t), 61, 70(l0, cr), 74(l, r), 87(r), 101, 112, 115, 122(r), 130, 134(l, bl), 141, 150(4), 160, 161;
All Sport p21;
Corbis pp3, 14(r), 18(2), 31(tr), 32(bl), 45(tl), Corbis / Sygma 43, 54(r), 60(bc, b), 66, 82, 100, 134(tr), 162(r), 186, 198(l), 201(b);
Eye Ubiquitous pp18(1), 74(c, cml), 80(b);
Getty Images pp9, 14(lt, lb), 15, 18(3), 27, 31(br), 32(top all, bc, br,bcr), 34(l), 45(bl), 60(tc, c), 70(r, cl), 80(ct), 87(l), 103, 108, 115, 122(l), 123,134(lt,br), 139, 140, 164, 174, 198 (r), 201(t);
Photodisc pp74 (cmr), 89(t), 98, 113, 150(1, 3), 169, 179(br), 191;
Photolibrary Group pp18 (4), 62, 80(cb), 90, 131, 148, 150(2), 162(l), 179(tr, tl, bl), 188;
Ronald Grant Archive p42.

All commissioned photography Haddon Davies / Macmillan Publishers Limited

Although we have tried to trace and contact copyright holders before publication, in some cases this has not been possible. If contacted, we will be pleased to rectify any errors or omissions at the earliest opportunity.

Printed and bound in Thailand.